Ethical Standards and Practice in International Relations

F. Sigmund Topor
Keio University, Japan

A volume in the Advances in
Business Strategy and Competitive
Advantage (ABSCA) Book Series

Published in the United States of America by
IGI Global
Information Science Reference (an imprint of IGI Global)
701 E. Chocolate Avenue
Hershey PA, USA 17033
Tel: 717-533-8845
Fax: 717-533-8661
E-mail: cust@igi-global.com
Web site: http://www.igi-global.com

Library of Congress Cataloging-in-Publication Data

Names: Topor, Francis Sigmund, 1957- editor.
Title: Ethical standards and practice in international relations / F. Sigmund
   Topor, editor.
Description: Hershey, PA : Information Science Reference, 2018.
Identifiers: LCCN 2017008485| ISBN 9781522526506 (hardcover) | ISBN
   9781522526513 (ebook)
Subjects: LCSH: Ethics--Cross-cultural studies. | Cross-cultural
   studies--Moral and ethical aspects. | International relations--Moral and
   ethical aspects.
Classification: LCC BJ1031 .E756 2018 | DDC 172/.4--dc23 LC record available at https://lccn.loc.
gov/2017008485

This book is published in the IGI Global book series Advances in Business Strategy and
Competitive Advantage (ABSCA) (ISSN: 2327-3429; eISSN: 2327-3437)

British Cataloguing in Publication Data
A Cataloguing in Publication record for this book is available from the British Library.

All work contributed to this book is new, previously-unpublished material.
The views expressed in this book are those of the authors, but not necessarily of the publisher.

For electronic access to this publication, please contact: eresources@igi-global.com.

Advances in Business Strategy and Competitive Advantage (ABSCA) Book Series

ISSN:2327-3429
EISSN:2327-3437

Editor-in-Chief: Patricia Ordóñez de Pablos, Universidad de Oviedo, Spain

MISSION

Business entities are constantly seeking new ways through which to gain advantage over their competitors and strengthen their position within the business environment. With competition at an all-time high due to technological advancements allowing for competition on a global scale, firms continue to seek new ways through which to improve and strengthen their business processes, procedures, and profitability.

The **Advances in Business Strategy and Competitive Advantage (ABSCA) Book Series** is a timely series responding to the high demand for state-of-the-art research on how business strategies are created, implemented and re-designed to meet the demands of globalized competitive markets. With a focus on local and global challenges, business opportunities and the needs of society, the **ABSCA** encourages scientific discourse on doing business and managing information technologies for the creation of sustainable competitive advantage.

COVERAGE

- Foreign Investment Decision Process
- Value Creation
- Innovation Strategy
- Balanced Scorecard
- Business Models
- International Business Strategy
- Differentiation Strategy
- Value Chain
- Strategic alliances
- Small and Medium Enterprises

IGI Global is currently accepting manuscripts for publication within this series. To submit a proposal for a volume in this series, please contact our Acquisition Editors at Acquisitions@igi-global.com or visit: http://www.igi-global.com/publish/.

Titles in this Series

For a list of additional titles in this series, please visit:
https://www.igi-global.com/book-series/advances-business-strategy-competitive-advantage/73672

Global Practices in Knowledge Management for Societal and Organizational Development
Neeta Baporikar (Namibia University of Science and Technology, Namibia & University of Pune, India)
Business Science Reference • ©2018 • 475pp • H/C (ISBN: 9781522530091) • US $240.00

Exploring the Global Competitiveness of Agri-Food Sectors and Serbia's...
Svetlana Ignjatijević (University of Business Academy in Novi Sad, Serbia) and Drago Cvijanović (University of Kragujevac, Serbia)
Business Science Reference • ©2018 • 193pp • H/C (ISBN: 9781522527626) • US $165.00

Evolving Entrepreneurial Strategies for Self-Sustainability in Vulnerable...
Luis Javier Sanchez-Barrios (Universidad del Norte, Colombia) and Liyis Gomez-Nunez (Universidad del Norte, Colombia)
Business Science Reference • ©2018 • 378pp • H/C (ISBN: 9781522528609) • US $225.00

Influence of Public Policy on Small Social Enterprises...
Chi Maher (St. Mary's University, Twickenham, London, UK)
Business Science Reference • ©2018 • 154pp • H/C (ISBN: 9781522527701) • US $155.00

Nascent Entrepreneurship and Successful New Venture Creation
António Carrizo Moreira (University of Aveiro, Portugal) José Guilherme Leitão Dantas (Politechnic Institute of Leiria, Portugal) and Fernando Manuel Valente (Politechnic Institute of Setubal, Portugal)
Business Science Reference • ©2018 • 415pp • H/C (ISBN: 9781522529361) • US $235.00

Business Models for Renewable Energy Initiatives Emerging Research and Opportunities
Adrian Tantau (Bucharest University of Economic Studies, Romania) and Robert Staiger (E3xpert, Germany)
Business Science Reference • ©2018 • 194pp • H/C (ISBN: 9781522526889) • US $165.00

For an enitre list of titles in this series, please visit:
https://www.igi-global.com/book-series/advances-business-strategy-competitive-advantage/73672

701 East Chocolate Avenue, Hershey, PA 17033, USA
Tel: 717-533-8845 x100 • Fax: 717-533-8661
E-Mail: cust@igi-global.com • www.igi-global.com

List of Reviewers

Rick Ansoff, *Alliant International University, USA*
Barrie Bennett, *University of Toronto, Canada*
Robert J. Bulik, *LPI Global Consultants, USA*
Latoya C. Conner, *Columbia University, USA*
Natalie H. Coulter, *York University, Canada*
George Dei, *University of Toronto, Canada*
Reva Joshee, *University of Toronto, Canada*
Gillian Judson, *Simon Fraser University, Canada*
Alena Lagumdzija, *Karolinska Hospital, Sweden*
Siu-Yau Lee, *Hong Kong Institute of Education, China*
Carolyn Mamchur, *Simon Fraser University, Canada*
Eric R. Parks, *Capella University, USA*
John Portelli, *University of Toronto, Canada*
Phillip M. Randall, *Capella University, USA*
Michiko M. Sudo, *Juntendo University, Japan*
Tamara Swenson, *Osaka Jogakuin University, Japan*
Yukio Tono, *Tokyo University of Foreign Studies, Japan*
Earl Woodruff, *University of Toronto, Canada*

Table of Contents

Detailed Table of Contents

Chapter 1
The Influence of CSR on B2B Relationships: Leveraging Ethical Behaviors
to Create Value..1
> *Susan Saurage-Altenloh, Saurage Research Inc., USA*
> *Phillip M. Randall, Capella University, USA*

The chapter addresses how ethical actions deliver value through sustainable competitive advantage. Corporate social responsibility (CSR) has a proven role in developing audience trust that increases brand equity among target audiences and stakeholders, thus ensuring that the brand sustains its competitive advantage through improved profitability and reputation in the market. Not only do businesses have a social responsibility to the markets from which they earn revenues, but buyers expect ethical businesses to have an established CSR program in place. Businesses that engage in CSR activities within the process of corporate brand management experience stronger reputation that drives loyalty and sales, resulting in a competitive, sustainable market advantage.

Chapter 2
The Relationship Between Leadership Ethics and Organizational Success:
Ethics and Organizational Success 22
> *Enoch T. Osei, Bowie State University, USA*
> *Velmarie K. Swing, Oklahoma Wesleyan University, USA*

Over the last few decades, business fraud and examples of scandalous management behaviors have sparked a lot of attention among several interested stakeholders. These increasing scandals have necessitated the question on the necessary steps required to prevent their frequent occurrence. The lack of commitment to strong ethical standards by management has been underpinned as the cause of ethical misconducts in organizations. The fiscal crisis of 2007-2009 witnessed many leadership misconducts and abuse of leadership responsibility. The fiscal crisis revealed the loss of about $11 trillion in household wealth, 26 million Americans losing their jobs, and 4.5 million Americans who could not afford their mortgages. These events and statistics show the prevalent lack of ethical leadership in organizations. While leadership ethics is a concern for all stakeholders within business organizations in the United States, only a few segments of the industry are taking steps to incorporate ethical awareness within their organizations.

Chapter 3

This chapter examines the unusually swift downturn in Russo-Bulgarian relations between 1879 and 1883. In 1879, relations between the two countries were unusually good, founded on a basis of mutual sympathy, geopolitical necessity, and strong administrative ties. By 1883, however, a series of lapses in Russian diplomatic practice damaged Russo-Bulgarian relations to the point that all of Bulgaria's political elite was united in opposition to the Russians, and by 1886 diplomatic relations were severed altogether. This chapter examines three incidents in particular – the Titles Controversy of late 1879/early 1880, the Coup of 1881, and the tenure of Generals L. N. Sobolev and A. V. Kaul'bars in 1882-1883. Ultimately, this chapter demonstrates how flawed diplomatic practice may result in undesirable foreign policy outcomes.

Chapter 4

Observable harm has been inflicted upon business by unethical decisions and misconduct. Much of this phenomenon can be traced to impoverished ethical attitudes. Among the various reasons for this problem is that of a manager's culture, which has a distinct influence on attitudes and behaviors. The purpose of this chapter was to determine, through empirical data, whether differences rooted in culture significantly contribute to differences in ethical attitudes. Management scholar Geert Hofstede's classification of cultural elements for understanding and explaining aspects of national culture was correlated with the ethical attitudes of business managers in the two national cultures of the United States and Mexico. Results indicated a significant positive relationship between national culture and ethical attitudes and the dultural dimensions of uncertainty avoidance, masculinity, and long-term orientation. A significant difference in ethical attitudes between managers from the United States and Mexico was also found.

Chapter 5

This chapter provides a review not only of classic literature on healthcare business and ethics, but also an introduction to the legal changes in the Greek healthcare system with ethical values on focus. A study examining in both a quantitative and qualitative way what the Greek healthcare experts think and feel about ethics and healthcare services presents the factors that shape attitudes towards ethical values from the viewpoint of the healthcare professionals. For this reason, 34 semi-structured interviews, accompanied by the administration of perceived cohesion scale, generalized immediacy scale, job affect scale, state anxiety inventory, Maslach burnout inventory, and the attitude towards business ethics questionnaire revealed that healthcare professionals do have knowledge of ethical values and moral responsibility, but no clear connections with specific emotional aspects were found. The chapter concludes with future directions on how business ethics can be further examined and applied.

Chapter 6

Punitive attitudes in criminal justice staff towards felony drug offenders, as related to level of social dominance orientation, right wing authoritarianism, protestant work ethic orientation, and openness to change were examined. These traits were hypothesized to be factors contributing to continued acceptance of a paradigm emphasizing use penalties and punishment to address substance abuse. The study utilized 28 law enforcement officers, 14 corrections officers, and 58 non-criminal justice individuals. Data was collected using Altemeyer abbreviated RWA scale, SDO-6 scale, Miles and Garrett protestant work ethic scale, attitudes to organizational change, officer's attitude survey, and researcher designed survey. Results indicated both moderating and mediating effects between variables, except in the case of openness to change. To reduce unwanted behaviors, focus needs to be on assisting criminal justice staff with challenges in a more psychologically healthy manner.

After the Korean War, it became acceptable and expected that American families would adopt Korean children into their homes, symbolizing American prosperity and security. As significant a role as social work played in this process, there currently exists no research that examines the activities of the profession and the origins of Korean adoption. This chapter discusses the maternalist nature of adoption efforts during the 1950s by one international social welfare agency after the Korean War: the American Branch of International Social Service (ISS-USA). Predicated on maternalist ideologies that shaped the social work profession during the Progressive Era, in what the author calls Cold War maternalism, the gendered notions of motherhood were expanded to genderless notions of parenthood. Anticommunist sentiments thrust adoptive parenthood into the political spotlight on an international level, thus serving the best interests of adoptive parents and the nation long before serving those of the children.

This chapter aims to prominently position the African philosophical notion of the self within the clinical trials context (and the larger bioethics project). As opposed to autonomy-based principlism, this other-regarding or communalist perspective is proposed as the preferred alternative model. The intent is to draw further attention to the inadequacy of the principlist approach particularly in multicultural settings. It also engenders a rethink, stimulates interest, and re-assesses the failed assumptions of universal ethical principles. As a novel attempt that runs against much of the prevailing (Euro-American) intellectual mood, this approach strives to introduce the African view point by making explicit the import of the self in a re-contextualized (nay, globalized) arena. Viewed as such, research ethics is guided to go beyond autonomy-based considerations for the individual with absolute right to self-determination; to embrace more holistic-based approach, recognizing that the individual is embedded in his/her family, community, and the environment.

A basic element that separates primates from us Homo sapiens is language, which serves as a socializing catalyst for interpersonal and intercultural communication. Linguistic rules can be regarded as the ethics of communication. Without such rules, encoding and decoding of communication between a speaker/writer and a listener/reader would be impossible. Etiquette and the social emotion of shame, which have dissimilar connotations in Confucian heritage cultures of the East and Socratic or Judeo-Christian cultures of the West, are examples of moral qualities having different attributes and applications for diverse peoples. Whereas distinctive societies, cultures, and civilizations define morality based on their particular history and culture, including religion, humans everywhere are the same. Thus, drawing on Jean-Jacques Rousseau's 1762 Social Contract, the current reality of globalization requires a cultural contract that harmonizes the morals and ethics of Eastern and Western civilizations.

Chapter 10

F. Sigmund Topor, Keio University, Japan
June C. Hysell, Rowan Cabarrus Community College, USA

This chapter investigates ethical dilemmas associated with early childhood education in Confucian heritage countries. It draws on literature in philosophy, psychology, sociology, and anthropology in concluding that sociocultural differences between Eastern and Western civilizations amount to an ethical dilemma, which threatens to prevent a basic epistemology as well as a pedagogy for the education of children in the context of globalization and the information technology revolution. As evidenced by inventions, innovations, developments, and other technological and scientific breakthroughs, Western learners enroll in science and technology courses. It seems as though Eastern learners are duty-bound to fulfill a national or cultural objective, which calls for studies in the science and engineering disciplines at the expense of subjects in the arts, independent of individual desire or competency.

Preface

ETHICS AND MORALITY

Morality refers to the inclination to act or behave in a particular manner – right or wrong, towards another individual. For developmentalists, the determination of moral rectitude is a function of an individuals' sense of cooperative reciprocity and what they perceive as being just or right. In Tokyo, for example, it is typically unethical; hence immoral, for a younger person to sit in the section on a passenger train that is designated for the elderly or women who are conceived. However, the same restrictions do not apply in other sections of a commuter train. And refusing to yield one's seat to an elderly person or a pregnant woman would not be unethical, although a person with a higher moral character would tend to observe the same mannerism as the ethics prescribe in the designated sitting areas on the commuter train. In other words, an individuals' sense of justice determines his/her judgment of what is morally right or wrong.

The growing convergence of cultures qua globalization cannot have succeeded without a unifying code of communication, a global *lingua franca* – the English language. Not only does a standard global code ensures understanding, harmony, fairness, and equality, but anyone who decries vigilante solutions would agree that a basic code of ethics is an indispensable constituent of predictability that facilitates international and intercultural relationships and provides as well as sustain peace and harmony among the peoples of the world.

The term ethics refers to a moral code that restricts human behavior in specific professions, organizations or societies. Most, if not all, penal codes across civilizations and cultures are derivatives of religious or spiritual belief systems. One of the earliest penal codes, referred to as *The Code of Hammurabi,* was instituted in Ancient Mesopotamia by King Hammurabi (1792–1750 BCE). The Code of *Hammurabi* was a precursor to the *lex talionis,* Judeo-Christian moral and ethical principles of reciprocity, which is the foundation of the Western legal concept of proportionality, exemplified by the dictum: "an eye for an eye and a tooth for a tooth" (*Exodus* 21: 23–25; *Leviticus* 24:17–20) is an example of reciprocal justice for wrongdoers.

ETHICS AND RELIGION

Religion, as a major component of culture, exerts strong influence on the beliefs and attitudes of a people. In his 1996 article entitled: "Religion as Political Resource: Culture or Ideology?", published in the *Journal for the Scientific Study of Religion,* vol. 35, no. 4, 1996, pp. 368–378, Rhys H. Williams acknowledged the role of religion in political life.

Informed by such violent events in the history of the Roman Catholic Church, i.e., the Spanish Inquisition (1478 - 1834), and the Protestant Reformation of the 16th century, Andrew Sullivan, on October 7, 2001, wrote in the New York Times newspaper about the devastating effects of religious wars conducted under the Roman Catholic Church, which is, for all intents and purposes, the embodiment of Western civilization. Sullivan explained that for nearly three centuries, fire was used to torture, persecute, and murder those who were deemed unfaithful and to force the weak to convert to Christianity. Religious atrocities were not confined to Christianity or the West civilization. The association of violence with religion has beleaguered all of humanity for centuries. Holy wars, militant martyrdom, and human sacrificial rites exemplify the dark side of religion. And, as Juergensmeyer, Kitts, and Jerryson acknowledged in *The Oxford Handbook of Religion and Violence*, published by Oxford University Press, 2013, religious violence continues to mystify scholars and members of the general public.

Ample accounts of religious killing by political leaders in Ancient China have been a subject of abundant scholarship. There is also something to be said about the confusion over the classification of Confucianism as a religion or a philosophy. Ancient Chinese leadership strove to emulate, if not usurp the power and influence of religious or spiritual leaders who earned the allegiance of congregants. Given the power of those charismatic religious leaders in commanding the allegiance of a people in desperate search for answers to shattering natural phenomena such as illness and death, ecclesiastical rites or ceremonial rituals were obvious imitations for political leaders who were keen on political legitimacy and obsessed with the total allegiance of the masses.

Intermingling political and religious matters had been a Chinese tradition before the inception of Confucius and his teaching. Nevertheless, a workable meaning or definition of the phenomenon known as religion remains fleeting. In the interim, unrelenting scholarly debate persists among anthropologists, ethologists, philosophers, psychologists, sociologists, theologians, and others. Unsettled disputes include the function of Confucianism regarding it religiosity or philosophical ideological treaties in Confucius heritage cultures and societies. Differences between Eastern and Western civilizations are more pronounced than the similarities of religious atrocities that have so far been explored and explained. Moral and ethical differences between Eastern and Western civilizations require a unifying standard of ethics.

CONTAMINANTS OF INTERNATIONAL RELATIONSHIPS

Diverse Cultural Epistemologies

Judeo-Christian morals and ethics, which is the foundation of Western culture, require children to honor their parents (Ephesians 6:2; Exodus 20:12, Matthew 15:4), while at the same time advocating respect for autonomy, beneficence, justice, and equality. According to D F-C Tsai, Assistant Professor in the Department of Social Medicine and Department of Family Medicine of the National Taiwan University College of Medicine, Confucian heritage cultures generally require the participation of individuals in research routines while disallowing them access to the necessary information pertinent to the research. Professor Tsai's (2005) article is entitled: "The bioethical principles and Confucius' moral philosophy," published in the Journal of Medical Ethics, volume 31, Number 3, pages 159-163.

In these countries, i.e., China, Japan, Korea, and others, research subjects typically consent to research and other matters without being informed. Western countries, by and large, respect individual agency and autonomy. Conversely, the guiding principles involving research in Confucian ethics stress self-sacrifice, and particularism as codified in filial piety, which denotes hierarchical inequality.

Linguistic hurdles typify a communicative disorder that amplifies a void that functions as a contaminant in relationships involving intercultural, international research, and communication. This condition is avoidable only if prevailing differential epistemic or doxastic customs are replaced with a standardized code of ethics and epistemology. Standardized codes already exist in areas such as Information Technology and the natural sciences such as biology and physics. However, business and international relations do not enjoy similar basic codes that the sciences including medicine and health care enjoy and from which both Eastern and Western cultures benefit. That researchers from Japan, a Confucian heritage culture, shy away from Nobel prices in the humanities says little about competence and speaks volumes about the apathy for non-science subjects; for example, literature, music and philosophy. The humanities are less financially rewarding than those in science and technology.

MEDICAL TOURISM AND GLOBAL ETHICS

In healthcare, for example, the transfer and proliferation of medical services from local communities to global or transnational operators occurs across geopolitical, social, ideological, and linguistic boundaries. The movement of people in fulfillment of their medical aspirations demonstrates not only the usefulness international and intercultural accord but also the obvious utility of a single code of morality and ethics.

The phenomenon of medical tourism involves ethics encompassing diverse moral and civil laws and regulations. The business of travelling from industrialized economies to less developed ones by people in search of affordable or even cheaper medical treatment is commonly known as medical tourism. Increases in the number of medical tourists are accompanied by increases in the need for a standardized code of ethics in order to accommodate the multinational and multicultural patients. Most medical tourists are from Western industrialized countries, including the United States, Canada, and Europe. None-reciprocal visa requirements demonstrate inequality, which is characteristic of Confucianism as established in the Confucian ethics of filial piety. Visa requirements constitute unequal access for those from countries without reciprocal visa waver agreements and are therefore required to obtain vasa to their desired destinations as medial tourists.

Although some Confucian Heritage countries, including China and Japan have taken steps to stop people from refusing to donate vital organs on religious, spiritual, and cultural grounds, the literature on informed consent, autonomy, and appreciation of individual rights, indicates that Confucian heritage societies have yet to match those of Western societies.

OVERVIEW OF THE CONTENTS

Ethical Standards and Practice in International Relations contains ten chapters covering ethics and international or intercultural relations. All chapters were written by scholars from multidisciplinary backgrounds.

Chapter 1 deals with leveraging ethical behavior to create value. The authors argue that corporate social responsibility, the positive predisposition, and communication of ethical behavior embraced by organizations serve to strengthen their market position by conveying the root composition of their value proposition. The authors, Dr. Susan Saurage-Altenloh and Dr. Phillip M. Randall maintain that a clear means to grow their market share and increase the associated bottom line is for corporations to learn and understand the rules that govern the ethical behavior of their market partners and customers. Chapter 2 discusses the relationship between leadership ethics and organizational success. Ethics and Organizational Success explore the ethical behavior of the leadership misconduct that occurs within the financial services sector. The chapter evaluates how leadership ethics relate to organizational success in the financial services sector of the U. S. economy. The authors, Dr. Enoch Osei, and Dr. Velmarie Swing contribute to studies on ethical leadership and the Leader-Member Exchange theory by exploring the key ethical leadership variables required by corporate supervisors in achieving organizational success.

Chapter 3, Dr. Mikhail Sergeyevich Rekun investigates the remarkably swift downturn in Russo-Bulgarian relations and the circumstances that led Tsar Alexander III to recall all Russian officers from Bulgaria. The chapter explains how flawed diplomatic practices may result in undesirable foreign policy outcomes; it examines the Russo-Serbian alliance and the events that played a pivotal role in plunging Europe into the First World War. In Chapter 4, Dr. Mark Anderson discusses the requirement for current and accurate information by scholars and practitioners to study improved ways of conducting business in the growing and dynamic area of international trade. Considering the current climate of globalization, intercultural knowledge is a needed by managers in order to improve international trade through better understanding.

In Chapter 5, Dr. Vaitsa Giannouli conducts a detailed exploration of hierarchical moral values as part of the cultural environment of people, regardless of social, historical, spiritual, cultural and/or economic context. The examination of values inherently includes all relevant thoughts and actions in order to overcome the difficulties and barriers of the exterior world. For Dr. Giannouli, the relevance of these values depends on the cultural environment and may present differences both in terms of understanding the concepts of value differences and the weight that individuals assign to each value. In Chapter 6, Dr. Karin Celosse focuses on interactions between personality traits of law enforcement, corrections officers, and attitudes toward felony drug offenders. Dr. Celosse investings the punitive attitudes in criminal justice professionals towards felony drug offenders as related to the level of Social Dominance Orientation, Right Wing Authoritarianism, Protestant Work Ethic orientation, and openness to change. These traits were hypothesized to be factors contributing to continued acceptance of a paradigm emphasizing the use of penalties and punishment to address substance abuse.

In Chapter 7, Dr. Shawyn Lee examines how Korean orphans were inculcated with American and Christian morals and values both before they came to the U.S., and certainly after placement in their families. Dr. Lee uses historical research methods situated within a maternalist framework to provide a critical analysis of social work child-rescue efforts in postwar South Korea during the 1950s, as embodied the American Branch of International Social Service (ISS-USA). The chapter also analyzes how this social work organization established and institutionalized intercountry adoption practices in the aftermath of the Korean War. Chapter 8 centers on the African philosophical notion and a communalist perspective of the self within the clinical trials context and the larger bioethics project. The author, Dr. Ike Valentine Iyioke engenders a rethink and re-assessment of the failed assumptions of universal ethical principles. Recognizing that the individual is embedded in his/her family, community and the environment, the chapter challenges to embrace more holistic-based approach by moving beyond autonomy-based considerations for the individual with absolute right to self-determination.

In Chapter 9, Dr. F. Sigmund Topor argues for the establishment of an ethics code of global proportions that can guide international and intercultural research. Etiquette and the social emotion of shame, which have dissimilar connotations in Confucian Heritage cultures of the East and Socratic or Judeo-Christian cultures of the West, are examples of moral qualities having different attributes and applications for diverse peoples. Whereas distinctive societies, cultures, and civilizations define morality based on their particular history and culture. Nevertheless, ethics is required, if not integrated, in nearly all areas of human interaction involving contact, communication, or other collaborative activities. In Chapter 10, Dr. F. Sigmund Topor and Dr. June C. Hysell explore and discuss ethical dilemmas associated with early childhood education. The authors examine literature in philosophy, psychology, sociology, and anthropology in concluding that sociocultural differences between Eastern and Western civilizations amount to an ethical dilemma that threatens to prevent a basic epistemology as well as pedagogy for the education of children in the context of globalization and the Information Technology revolution.

F. Sigmund Topor
Keio University, Japan

Acknowledgment

This book cannot have been published without the generosity of many people who provided support, including comments, suggestions, editing, listening me and suggesting solutions to my problems. I would like to express my gratitude to the many researchers and co-authors, teachers, mentors, colleagues, my proofreader, and friends whose ideas, suggestions, and critical assessments inspired me to finish this book.

I also wish to thank IGI Global for its continuous interest in publishing academic books and for giving me the opportunity to publish this book.

F. Sigmund Topor

Chapter 1
The Influence of CSR on B2B Relationships:
Leveraging Ethical Behaviors to Create Value

Susan Saurage-Altenloh
Saurage Research Inc., USA

Phillip M. Randall
Capella University, USA

ABSTRACT

The chapter addresses how ethical actions deliver value through sustainable competitive advantage. Corporate social responsibility (CSR) has a proven role in developing audience trust that increases brand equity among target audiences and stakeholders, thus ensuring that the brand sustains its competitive advantage through improved profitability and reputation in the market. Not only do businesses have a social responsibility to the markets from which they earn revenues, but buyers expect ethical businesses to have an established CSR program in place. Businesses that engage in CSR activities within the process of corporate brand management experience stronger reputation that drives loyalty and sales, resulting in a competitive, sustainable market advantage.

INTRODUCTION

Organizations integrate ethical behavior and social responsibility in their internal operations and external communications programs to strengthen their market position and financial success in a credible manner. Establishing and communicating ethical

DOI: 10.4018/978-1-5225-2650-6.ch001

behaviors and initiatives effectively advances relationships with other organizations as well as the communities in which they conduct business. This chapter addresses the way value and CSR relate to ethical behavior; the role of ethics as it impacts trust, loyalty, brand equity, and reputation; and the efficacy of CSR in creating sustainable advantage that drives brand equity and brand value in the B2B environment.

BACKGROUND

For decades, organizations have integrated corporate social responsibility (CSR) as a business strategy to engage multiple stakeholders in a favorable manner. Corporate social responsibility has a proven role in developing audience trust that increases brand equity among target audiences, thus ensuring that the brand sustains its competitive advantage through improved profitability and reputation in the market. Research also has confirmed the value of CSR as influencing financial performance, also termed brand performance. Not only does business have a social responsibility to the community from which it secures revenues, but buyers expect ethical businesses to have an established CSR program in place. Businesses that engage in CSR activities within the process of corporate brand management experience stronger reputation that drives loyalty and sales, resulting in a competitive, sustainable market advantage.

CORPORATE ETHICAL BEHAVIOR

Ethical behavior as an organizational endeavor may be defined and exacted in multiple ways. In their exploration of ethics in international business situations, Amine, Chakor, and Alaoui (2012) indicated that integrating ethical dimensions into overall organizational values represented a company's commitment to an ethical approach. At the same time, Amine et al. determined that a firm's leadership established the relevant ethical values that ultimately were institutionalized by way of incorporation into the decision structure. Jose and Thibodeaux (1999) declared that the formal, explicit incorporation of ethics into organizational culture, leadership, and communication revealed a deep commitment to ethical behavior. Peloza and Shang (2011) recognized ethical behavior as taking the form of socially responsible business practices, philanthropy, and product-related aspects such as biodegradability or quality. Many cohorts within an organization can exhibit, benefit from, or influence ethical behavior, including company leadership (Ponnu & Tennakoon, 2009; Pučėtaitė & Lämsä, 2008), employees (Valentine & Barnett, 2003), corporate marketers (Murphy, Laczniak, & Wood, 2007), and even corporate reputational character (Valenzuela, Mulki, & Jaramillo, 2010).

2

Ethical behavior is an expectation by key stakeholders, which may include company shareholders, internal workforce, current and potential customers, suppliers and partners, regulatory agencies, and financial markets. Failure to meet these expectations of ethical behavior can harm the firm's reputation with catastrophic results to shareholder value.

Ethical Behavior and Value

The absence of ethical behavior and the presence of unethical activities may devalue the reputation of an organization, according to Choi and Moon (2016). Indeed, Ho (2013) recognized unethical behavior in the Hong Kong construction industry based on increased incidence of ethical malpractice, or industry corruption, resulting from the deterioration of ethical standards within the industry. Unethical moral claims—environmental disasters, support of despotic governments, abuse of human rights—that deviated from institutionalized norms were seen as challenging corporate legitimacy, a form of moral standards (Schrempf-Stirling, Palazzo, & Phillips, 2016). Matten and Moon (2008) made the case for corporate moral agency, recognizing that each unique organizational entity was morally responsible for actions it might control. Shum and Yam (2011) determined that company decisions about social responsibility required trade-offs such as maximizing profitability or improving a product or workplace, indicating that investing in ethical improvements reduced short-term profits while the unethical decision to forego better consumer products or safer workplaces yielded higher shareholder profits. In its global study with more than a thousand executives in 21 countries, Weber Shandwick (2016) affirmed that ethical behavior informs reputation, which drives more than half of a company's market value. The relationship between ethical behavior and corporate financial performance represents an irrefutable, perhaps compulsory, path for corporate managers to navigate with their relevant stakeholder groups.

Ethical Behavior and CSR

In the early 1970s, company leaders recognized that corporate social responsibility, or CSR, was the standard of cultivated global society, that U.S. businesses already had begun a trend to social commitment, and that organizations not choosing the socially responsible path might incur denunciation by their target stakeholders. Davis (1973) articulated some of the many benefits of social responsibility as including long-run profit maximization, improved public image and reputation, increased business viability, reduced regulatory environment, sociocultural norms that influenced business leaders to include CSR among their many goals, responsiveness to stockholder interests, employing business' problem-solving abilities where other institutions had failed, access to business resources and expertise, businesses innovating to profit from social problems, and the value of addressing issues sooner rather than later.

The formal definition of CSR developed to concentrate on company performance and business ethics (Carroll & Shabana, 2010). For instance, Vaaland, Heide, and Grønhaug (2008) reframed the idea of CSR as the process of governing stakeholder interest in environmental, ethical, and social phenomena in a manner that benefits the corporation. Vaaland et al. (2008) recognized the concept of CSR as consisting of both responsible and immoral acts while including ethical dimensions reflecting business conduct, environmental impact, and interference with human and social rights. In a more complex comparison, socially responsible actions were recognized as determining a company's ethical identity even as its aspirational values and strategic objectives informed the firm's CSR activities (Hildebrand, Sen, & Bhattacharya, 2011). In essence, a firm's CSR activities reflect both its aspirations and its actual behavior, resulting in an ethical identity encompassing both traits and values of the corporation.

It was critical to make the business case for CSR initiatives by translating the social responsibility investment and commitment into a recognizable return in value. Brand performance, measured intrinsically through awareness, reputation, and customer loyalty as well as financially in terms of market strength, sales growth, profit margin, and share of market (Luu, 2012) represented corporate value. In research, brand performance relied on strong brand equity that encouraged higher customer revenues and improved the bottom line (Chirani, Taleghani, & Moghadam, 2012; Lai, Chiu, Yang, & Pai, 2010). Berrone, Surroca, and Tribó (2007) found that organizations strongly identified with ethical behavior evidenced positive financial performance. Cognizant of their need to provide select stakeholders with proof of the financial return on investment in marketing and related social initiatives, corporate marketers and leaders began to codify their ethical behaviors and integrate CSR activities into marketing and corporate strategies.

Over the last five decades, the premise of ethical behavior in the form of social responsibility has worked its way into the functional and reputational structure of organizations. Early efforts to clarify the link between socially responsible, ethical behaviors and corporate financial performance revealed higher costs for companies embarking on a program of corporate citizenship (McGuire, Sundgren, & Schneeweis, 1988). Helmig, Spraul, and Ingenhoff (2016) determined that socially responsible behaviors favorably impacted market performance (market share, customer attraction, and customer retention) while encouraging stakeholder-managerial relationships. Creel (2012) characterized the normal operations of business as including socially responsible activities that related to environmental and social issues, thus generating positive reputation and financial benefits.

Socially responsible behavior influences corporate value by connecting numerous stakeholder groups. Van Beurden and Gössling (2008) explored the relationship between CSR and corporate financial performance to reveal a positive relationship between the two. Taghian, D'Souza, and Polonsky (2015) determined that a stakeholder-defined CSR strategy advanced a favorable corporate reputation that, in turn, favorably impacted business performance. Luo and Bhattacharya (2006) found that organizations investing in CSR initiatives drove financial success through the positive impact of customer satisfaction. Zhu, Sun, and Leung (2014) determined that social responsibility fostered improved firm reputation and firm performance, influenced by ethical leadership.

The relationship between ethical behavior and corporate value often includes layers of relational complexity. Saeidi, Sofian, Saeidi, Saeidi, and Saaeidi (2015) indicated that the intricacy of the CSR-financial performance relationship necessitated the presence of mediating variables to effectively link the effects of ethical social behavior to improved financial performance. Wang and Qian (2011) demonstrated that corporate philanthropy improved stakeholder responses as well as political resources, resulting in stronger corporate financial performance. Additionally, companies that engaged in ethical behavior improved value through enriched corporate financial performance (Gherghina & Simionescu, 2015) and positive correlations with organizational performance (Sledge, 2015). Understanding the close relationship of ethical behavior and corporate social responsibility helps explain the favorable impact of CSR on financial performance. The demonstrated return on investment in relevant ethical behaviors has fostered a standard of CSR integration into corporate budgets and strategies.

ROLE OF ETHICAL BEHAVIOR IN BUSINESS

Organizations that invest in corporate social responsibility to improve the quality of a community, population, or stakeholder group expect a return on their investment in the form of improved brand equity, expanded brand performance, moral agency, and greater consideration in the competitive environment. To meet those expectations, corporate decision makers must understand how ethical behavior, social trust, CSR, loyalty, reputation, brand equity, value, and brand financial performance interrelate.

Ethical Behavior and Social Trust

It is broadly known that successful organizational and business relationships and cooperatives require a base trust that is formulated and built on an ethical foundation. Clearly, this foundation is informed by a set of acceptable and agreed to social norms. Because the world has grown smaller through the advent of the internet and rapid development of new technologies, coupled with the associated product and services, effective B2B cooperation has grown increasingly complex and, unquestionably, more desirable. In fact, economic life has become grossly dependent on what Francis Fukuyama (1995) referred to as social trust. At both the individual and organizational level, it meant, "the unspoken, unwritten bond between fellow citizens that facilitates transactions, empowers individual creativity, and justifies collective action" (Fukuyama, 1995, p. 6).

Notably, social trust and ethics are, indeed, reciprocal. High social trust engenders ethics (Thornton, 2013). Fukuyama (1995) stated that "trust is the expectation that arises within a community of regular, honest, and cooperative behavior based on commonly shared norms, on the part of other members of that community" (p. 26). In this discussion, the communities addressed more specifically are the business as well as the economic community at large. Thus, it is fully understood that said community consists of individuals as well as organizations.

While those individuals are members of the organizations and businesses, there is no less a demand for shared norms and behaviors considered necessary or expected for an effective, trusting community. These combinations result in the consequence of social capital. At the liberty of assuming this collected expectation of trust can be explained, "social capital is the capability that arises from the prevalence of trust in a society or in certain parts of it. It requires adherence to moral norms of a community and the acquisition of virtues like loyalty, honesty, and dependability" (Fukuyama, 1995, pp. 26-27).

Given the complexity of economic life, decisions made with incomplete information often lead to economically and socially inefficient outcomes. Examples from very different fields include the global financial crisis, environmental damage, and new health problems around the globe. When this occurs, one may well look to government regulation. However, social trust can be offered as a shortcut or interim solution. In other words, where social trust exists, organizations and businesses can rely on a commonly agreed to and understood set of social norms and ethical foundation.

To further this discussion and provide an exclamation point, it is useful to explore some diametrically different scenarios about ethical and unethical behavior in the global community where the common set of social norms has been supported and not supported. In the case of the unethical, arguably one of the most extreme cases of unethical behavior and broken social trust thrust upon humans was the activities of King Leopold II of Belgium in the late 1800s and early 1900s in his effort to create his own private colony. Reportedly, King Leopold II killed more than 10 million innocent Congolese and mutilated thousands more, giving birth to today's instability.

Unfortunately, even today, it continues to be both reminiscent and reflective of his unethical behavior ("Congo: White King," 2003).

As the story is told, it presents an unparalleled extravagance and violation of social trust. Although time has served to sanitize and blunt the egregious edge of King Leopold II's unethical behavior, modern society and the conditions of social trust can only gasp at the astonishing misdeeds that occurred in a region of Africa which is now known as the Democratic Republic of the Congo.

Looking inside of the BBC's account of this historic atrocity, one noted brutal activity carried out by King Leopold II's agents was the chopping off of hands. This was executed by his agents when they were required to show that they did not waste precious bullets in hunting monkeys; they were mandated to bring the hand of the person killed to evidence their alleged adherence to the cost saving tactic and to ensure that those Congolese who failed to gather the proper amount of rubber plants were duly punished. This activity is only one of many shocking human travesties and clear breaches of ethics and social trust carried out by King Leopold II and his agents in the Congo Free State.

In contrast, ethical behavior can be described as acting in a manner that agrees with what society considers to be *good morals* and that which facilitates social trust, and may well create the adhesive for society's social bonding. We know that ethical behaviors are important in that they provide direction for one's actions. In addition to social trust, as previously mentioned, ethical behavior includes integrity, fairness, honesty, and dignity.

An example of ethical behavior and social trust in the world, more specially in business and the community at large, is the company Alphabet Inc.'s Google, which regularly makes good on its motto, "Don't be evil" (Alphabet Investor Relations, 2017). As a member of the global community, Google has set forth an environmental strategy anchored in the ethos of sustainability. At their locations around the world, they have reportedly decreased their own carbon footprint by using energy efficient buildings and public transportation. Consequently, Google has been carbon neutral since 2007. In 2017, the company reached 100% renewable energy for their operations, including its data centers and offices. Most notably, they have invested $2.5 billion in renewable energy projects, and freely shared technology "to give everyone everywhere the tools and opportunities they need to play their own part in protecting the planet" ("Solving for sustainability," 2017, para. 3).

As an employer, Google has been instrumental in setting the high mark for the business community in how to provide and administer employee benefits as an exemplar beacon for managing human capital. To name a few, Google provides free health care and treatment from onsite doctors, free legal advice with discounted legal services, a fully stocked snack pantry and onsite cafeteria (staffed by world-class chefs, no less), and a free onsite nursery ("How we care for Googlers," 2017).

Google's influence in the communities in which it is located may be illustrated best by the dozens of collaborative partnerships it has forged with local school districts, government entities, and service organizations. Given its remarkable record of social awareness and positive approach to human capital, Google may well be the preeminent example of ethics in the corporate world today.

Moreover, the abovementioned examples of ethical and unethical behavior and the support and nonsupport of social trust have been shared to shed light on what it looks like to the community when these behaviors are demonstrated. While the examples were offered to emphasize their difference at the community level, the examples also provide a lens into what is desired and not desired from community partners in terms of ethical and unethical behavior and social trust. Hopefully, the stark contrast presented by the selected examples makes clear the difference in ethical and unethical behavior and social trust as well as the reciprocity so evident as a need.

The ethical foundation and social trust that looms so critical for successful communities, including the global business community, cannot be understated. Rather, it amounts to a clarion for the continued pursuit knowing that, as a global community, we are not finished and require continued learning and relearning of that which is essential to the overall sustainability of the community.

CSR and Trust

Ethical behaviors and social trust define the significant role of CSR in the marketing and branding model. According to Vallaster, Lindgreen, and Maon (2012), the corporate brand served as the visual, behavioral expression of a firm's business model and engaged internal and external stakeholder groups in aligning processes and systems with the brand. Kitchin (2003) found that a brand's social responsibility was linked to both the social promise it made and the trust it established with its stakeholders. A corporate brand became unavoidably linked to its core identity (Vallaster et al., 2012), making it incumbent on each brand to elevate its identity through appropriate CSR activities. As a result, brand strategy crafted the identity of an organization and included its social commitments, its trustworthiness, and its audience communications as part of that identity.

Elements such as reputational brand value, potential employee appeal, innovation profile, revenues (sales and margins), and costs (risks) promoted and influenced business model change (Dickson & Chang, 2015) to build a case for CSR and its associated ethical behavior in developing trust among stakeholders. In similar fashion, Lopatta, Buchholz, and Kaspereit (2016) argued that CSR initiatives expanded corporate trustworthiness, resulting in lower monitoring costs while increasing firm value. From a different perspective, Brammer, Jackson, and Matten (2012) recognized that demonstrating virtue as a viable market might powerfully influence corporate managers to choose more responsible behavior. Du and Vieira (2012) concluded that framing CSR efforts as a long-term strategic approach rather than as peripheral public relations delivered social legitimacy and trustworthiness to large global organizations while encouraging positive stakeholder response. Elving, Golob, Podnar, Ellerup-Nielsen, and Thomson (2015) expanded on this idea to characterize two options for framing the concept of ethical responsibility: CSR as a business case to institutionalize the concept or CSR as a form of business discourse to achieve shared understanding by multiple constituent groups. Worthington, Ram, Boyal, and Shah (2007) indicated that CSR based on a firm's strategic intent benefited the organization and society at a greater level than coerced or altruistic CSR.

Since the initial definition of CSR, the number of companies choosing to invest in socially responsible practices to enhance their image, encourage their employees, and connect with their customers has significantly advanced (Creel, 2012). In an effort to engage target audiences, organizations have communicated publicly and regularly about their CSR commitment to win recognition for their good behavior (Eberle, Berens, & Li, 2013). This earned recognition is known as brand equity.

CSR and Brand Equity

Brand equity is the value incurred by a known brand in the form of revenues that rise in parallel with increased brand recognition, integrity, and character. The benefits of brand equity were described by Keller and Lehmann (2006) as the value amassed through brand influence on customer, financial, or product markets. Christodoulides and de Chernatony (2010) agreed that understanding and building brand equity delivered desirable barriers to competition and produced brand wealth. CSR as an investment in socially responsible citizenship amplified an organization's performance (Wang et al., 2015; Wang, Hsu, & Chang, 2012) while socially irresponsible behaviors resulted in reduced rewards and greater punishment by buyers (Fournier & Avery, 2011; Sweetin, Knowles, Summey, & McQueen, 2013).

While brand equity, also known as brand value, was normally measured in financial terms, brand image was represented by brand reputation, brand regard, and brand trust (Christodoulides & de Chernatony, 2010). These measures of brand equity—the essence of which ranged well beyond the value of the product or service—were based on characteristics with no innate value (Keller & Lehmann, 2006). Buyers proved their brand loyalty through repeat purchases that reflected their trust (Srinivasan, Park, & Chang, 2005). Lai et al. (2010) recognized that buyer decisions were influenced by intangible attributes such as image, reputation, and trust.

Brand equity was linked to brand performance within the CSR framework (Davcik, da Silva, & Hair, 2015; Lai et al., 2010). Further, brand performance was recognized as the outcome of brand equity by Chirani et al. (2012) through increased awareness, quality, and loyalty that strengthened customer preference for the brand. In similar fashion, Lai et al. (2010) recognized the positive influence of CSR initiatives on brand equity and brand performance. Khan and Manwani (2013) reported that CSR activities encouraged buyer purchasing and premium pricing that resulted in improved brand performance.

In a favorable manner, companies that invested in ethical behaviors expanded their corporate brand equity, thus securing a sustainable competitive advantage in the market (Creel, 2012; Eberle et al., 2013; Lai et al., 2010), expanded their familiarity among consumers in a positive manner (Du, Bhattacharya, & Sen, 2007), and favorably influenced brand preference (Liu, Wong, Shi, Chu, & Brock, 2014). Additionally, evidence revealed that CSR significantly influenced competitiveness on a global scale (Boulouta & Pitelis, 2013). In the absence of CSR commitment, companies imperiled their brand, reputation, and profitability; CSR transitioned from a potential competitive advantage into a strategic fundamental (Story & Neves, 2014) and business proscription (Helmig et al., 2016).

Corporate citizenship, through its influence on brand equity and reputation, was an integral element in securing and maintaining a competitive advantage through brand performance in the B2B environment (Lai et al., 2010; Wang, Chen, Yu, & Hsiao, 2015). Further, it is evident that increased brand performance advances the supplier-buyer relationship in the B2B environment, reducing customer acquisition and retention costs as a result. As companies have integrated CSR into their organizational and brand structures, commitment to CSR initiatives has exerted greater influence and increased value across the various dimensions of brand management. Aguinis and Glavas (2012) affirmed that CSR, by retaining shareholder value and maintaining corporate financial success, assisted businesses in circumventing regulatory strangleholds while influencing long-term organizational viability. Mattera and Baena (2015) determined that proper management of ethical initiatives created value in the form of presence, relevance, and voluntarism. Additionally, Vaaland et al. (2008) reported that CSR linked unique business brands to society through their ethical behavior, impact of operations on the environment, and influence of activities on human and social rights. In summary, socially responsible initiatives serve as ethical behaviors that garner improved levels of brand equity.

Brand Equity and Competitive Advantage

At the turn of the century, organizations continued to structure programs to integrate CSR into their marketing and management processes as a way of balancing stakeholder and shareholder expectations (Maignan, Ferrell, & Ferrell, 2005). Corporate brand managers relied on measures of brand equity, brand personality, and brand value to determine the effectiveness of CSR initiatives in developing brand trust (Ghosh,

Ghosh, & Das, 2013). Brand equity mediated the relationship between CSR and perceived value (Staudt, Shao, Dubinsky, & Wilson, 2014) in an effort to secure sustainable competitive advantage. Large organizations invested heavily in CSR (Luo & Bhattacharya, 2006) to present a favorable appearance of promoting corporate reputation and strategically differentiating the brand from competitors (Hsu, 2012). Financial performance and ethical behavior favorably impacted perceptions of CSR, resulting in profiles of corporate reputation and trust, both of which influenced loyalty (Stanaland, Lewin, & Murphy, 2011). Organizational commitment to effectively integrating CSR into the corporate structure transitioned from the vision of a unique few to a business standard.

CSR must be clearly communicated to the target market in order to be known and effective. Organizations that choose not to engage in CSR may hope to avoid stakeholders' negative attributions of exaggerated outcomes or they may be concerned about misalignment with corporate mission (Shim & Yang, 2016). However, organizations that engage in CSR initiatives post more favorable financial performance than those refraining from socially responsible activities (Mikołajek-Gocejna, 2016). Large U.S. firms employing CSR practices showed significantly higher returns on assets and revenues over a ten-year period than large U.S. firms that refrained from investing in CSR (Sledge, 2015). CSR practices motivate and assure employees to stronger performance that generates greater financial success (Story & Neves, 2014). Clearly, the investment in CSR works with the resulting brand performance and brand equity to create sustainable competitive advantage for businesses investing in ethical behaviors and the outward-facing communications of these activities.

CSR AND SUSTAINABLE COMPETITIVE ADVANTAGE

Numerous studies of individual customers, international markets, and B2B segments have revealed that CSR commitment drives favorable customer perceptions and increases supplier brand equity. Further, brand equity has been shown to positively impact brand performance. The role of CSR in the marketing and branding model is linked to the trust it establishes with its stakeholders (Kitchin, 2003), improved competitive advantage and corporate reputation (Melo & Garrido-Morgado, 2012), improved brand equity (Torres et al., 2012; Hur et al., 2014), and the organization's core identity with internal and external audiences (Vallaster et al., 2012). Corporate values illustrated by way of CSR behaviors create favorable brand equity that influences premium pricing, brand preference, and, ultimately, a stronger bottom line in the form of higher revenues and value.

Saurage-Altenloh (2017) assessed the influence of supplier CSR on brand performance expectations along with the indirect consequences of brand equity among U.S. corporate buyers. The research quantified the benefits of supplier CSR as a sustainable value that benefits the corporate brand and numerous company stakeholders through its impact on corporate buyer brand performance expectations, via brand equity, confirming that supplier CSR initiatives benefit both suppliers and buyers in the U.S. The research attached a metric to the value of CSR's leverage of brand equity and brand performance with its target market of corporate buyers, thereby explaining value creation from expectations of ethical behaviors in the B2B environment.

Lai et al. (2010) determined that, in the B2B environment, Taiwanese supplier CSR created brand value and brand equity. The study focused on three aspects: (1) the effects of CSR and corporate reputation on industrial brand equity; (2) the effects of CSR, corporate reputation, and brand equity on brand performance; and (3) the mediating effects of corporate reputation and industrial brand equity on the relationship between CSR and brand performance. Lai et al. found that supplier CSR generated positive effects on industrial brand equity and brand performance. Results verified that corporate reputation and industrial brand equity mediated the relationship between ethical behaviors, in the form of CSR, and brand performance.

Across cultures, socially responsible and ethical behaviors have affected performance, and therefore value, in various ways (Scholtens & Kang, 2013), including redemption of socially irresponsible actions as a route to recovered trade relationships (Cai, Jo, & Pan, 2012), greater profits during Spain's economic crisis for banks committed to CSR (Escobar Pérez & Mar Miras Rodríguez, 2013), government involvement and support of Asian enterprises engaging in CSR programs (Moon & Shen, 2010), and improved CSR-related standards for Chinese workers' health, safety, and wages (Wang & Juslin, 2009). In their empirical study, Zhang and He (2014) determined that value co-creation among stakeholders worked to elevate industrial customer perceptions of brand value that led to higher brand performance. These are but a few of the examples confirming that investment in CSR initiatives (comprised of ethical behaviors) increases a company's brand equity and influences brand performance and shareholder value.

SOLUTIONS AND RECOMMENDATION

Businesses that integrate ethical standards into their operations through a company-wide commitment to corporate social responsibility improve their relationship with stakeholders. The process of engaging internal and external audiences in ethical, socially-cognizant activities generates awareness, acknowledgement, improved brand value, social trust, and sustainable competitive advantage in the B2B environment. Organizations that engage in CSR to influence buyers require a return on their investment in the form of improved, sustainable brand consideration in the competitive environment. Businesses have a social responsibility to their stakeholders, including buyers and market partners, while B2B purchasers expect ethical organizations to have structured CSR initiatives integrated into their marketing efforts. As a result, organizations that strategically engage in externally-evident ethical behaviors are rewarded for their social commitments while companies refraining from social engagement tarnish their brand equity and negatively impact shareholder value. There is a growing body of evidence that CSR influences B2B buyer expectations of brand performance, which increases B2B customer loyalty, resulting in a competitive, sustainable market advantage for corporations that invest in CSR. As more firms address production, regulation, and speed to market issues through globalization to improve financial performance, the value of committing to socially responsible initiatives that are ethically anchored continues to expand as a critical component of corporate reputation and success.

FUTURE RESEARCH DIRECTIONS

The value of corporate investment in the marketing and communications of CSR initiatives to educate and influence business-to-business customers has been established. Organizations that communicate their corporate social commitment to B2B decision makers favorably influence purchase interest and likelihood and, therefore, their brand value. Incontrovertible evidence that business buyers expect brand performance to improve as a result of doing business with companies that invest in social initiatives informed by ethical behaviors continues to build within and across countries and cultures. Therefore, it is critical to explore how buyer expectations differ around the globe. With this accelerated comprehension, corporate marketers are more able to invest effectively in new markets using a strategy that resonates uniquely with the target market and its ethical behavior predisposition.

CONCLUSION

In reflection, the positive predisposition and communication of ethical behavior and social responsibility embraced by organizations serves to strengthen their market position by conveying the root composition of their value proposition. Further, it solidifies their relationship with other businesses and organizations that share like value propositions that serve to nurture and enhance the prospects of B2B activities for mutual benefit of the organizations as well as the communities in which they conduct business. Clearly, a clarion for organizations and businesses around the globe as a means to grow their market share and increase the associated bottom line is to learn and understand the rules that govern the ethical behavior of their market partners and customers.

REFERENCES

Aguinis, H., & Glavas, A. (2012). What we know and don't know about corporate social responsibility: A review and research agenda. *Journal of Management, 38*(4), 932–968. doi:10.1177/0149206311436079

Alphabet Investor Relations. (2017, August 7). *Google code of conduct.* Retrieved September 22, 2017, from https://abc.xyz/investor/other/google-code-of-conduct.html

Bate, P. (Director). (2003). *Congo: White king, red rubber, black death* [Documentary series episode]. British Broadcasting Corporation. Retrieved September 22, 2017, from https://topdocumentaryfilms.com/congo-white-king-red-rubber-black-death/

Berrone, P., Surroca, J., & Tribó, J. A. (2007). Corporate ethical identity as a determinant of firm performance: A test of the mediating role of stakeholder satisfaction. *Journal of Business Ethics, 76*(1), 35–53. doi:10.1007/s10551-006-9276-1

Boulouta, I., & Pitelis, C. N. (2014). Who needs CSR? The impact of corporate social responsibility on national competitiveness. *Journal of Business Ethics, 119*(3), 349–364. doi:10.1007/s10551-013-1633-2

Brammer, S., Jackson, G., & Matten, D. (2012). Corporate social responsibility and institutional theory: New perspectives on private governance. *Socio-economic Review, 10*(1), 3–28. doi:10.1093/ser/mwr030

Cai, Y., Jo, H., & Pan, C. (2012). Doing well while doing bad? CSR in controversial industry sectors. *Journal of Business Ethics, 108*(4), 467–480. doi:10.1007/s10551-011-1103-7

Carroll, A. B., & Shabana, K. M. (2010). The business case for corporate social responsibility: A review of concepts, research and practice. *International Journal of Management Reviews, 12*(1), 85–105. doi:10.1111/j.1468-2370.2009.00275.x

Chirani, E., Taleghani, M., & Moghadam, N. E. (2012). Brand performance and brand equity. *Interdisciplinary Journal of Contemporary Research in Business*, *3*, 1033–1036. Retrieved from http://www.journal-archieves14.webs.com/jan12.pdf

Choi, H., & Moon, D. (2016). Perceptions of corporate social responsibility in the capital market. *Journal of Applied Business Research*, *32*(5), 1507–1518. doi:10.19030/jabr.v32i5.9777

Christodoulides, G., & Chernatony, L. D. (2010). Consumer-based brand equity conceptualisation and measurement: A literature review. *International Journal of Market Research*, *52*(1), 43–66. doi:10.2501/S1470785310201053

Creel, T. (2012). How corporate social responsibility influences brand equity. *Management Accounting Quarterly*, *13*(4), 20–24. Retrieved from https://www.imanet.org/insights-and-trends/management-accounting-quarterly/maq-index/2012/summer-2012?ssopc=1

Davcik, N. S., Vinhas da Silva, R., & Hair, J. F. (2015). Towards a unified theory of brand equity: Conceptualizations, taxonomy and avenues for future research. *Journal of Product and Brand Management*, *24*(1), 3–17. doi:10.1108/JPBM-06-2014-0639

Davis, K. (1973). The case for and against business assumption of social responsibilities. *Academy of Management Journal*, *16*(2), 312–322. doi:10.2307/255331

Dickson, M. A., & Chang, R. K. (2015). Apparel manufacturers and the business case for social sustainability: World class CSR and business model innovation. *Journal of Corporate Citizenship*, *2015*(57), 55–72. doi:10.9774/GLEAF.4700.2015.ma.00006

Du, S., Bhattacharya, C. B., & Sen, S. (2007). Reaping relational rewards from corporate social responsibility: The role of competitive positioning. *International Journal of Research in Marketing*, *24*(3), 224–241. doi:10.1016/j.ijresmar.2007.01.001

Du, S., & Vieira, E. T. (2012). Striving for legitimacy through corporate social responsibility: Insights from oil companies. *Journal of Business Ethics*, *11*(4), 413–427. doi:10.1007/s10551-012-1490-4

Eberle, D., Berens, G., & Li, T. (2013). The impact of interactive corporate social responsibility communication on corporate reputation. *Journal of Business Ethics*, *118*(4), 731–746. doi:10.1007/s10551-013-1957-y

Elving, W., Golob, U., Podnar, K., Ellerup-Nielsen, A., & Thomson, C. (2015). The bad, the ugly and the good: New challenges for CSR communication. *Corporate Communications*, *20*(2), 118–127. doi:10.1108/CCIJ-02-2015-0006

Escobar Pérez, B., & Mar Miras Rodríguez, M. (2013). Spanish savings banks' social commitment: Just pretty words? *Social Responsibility Journal, 9*(3), 427–440. doi:10.1108/SRJ-09-2011-0084

Fukuyama, F. (1995). Trust: The social virtues and the creation of prosperity. New York, NY: The Free Press (A Division of Simon & Schuster, Inc.).

Gherghina, S. C., & Simionescu, L. N. (2015). Does entrepreneurship and corporate social responsibility act as catalyst towards firm performance and brand value? *International Journal of Economics and Finance, 7*(4), 23–34. doi:10.5539/ijef.v7n4p23

Ghosh, D., Ghosh, P., & Das, B. (2013). Brand personality from corporate social responsibility: A critical review of the brand image through CSR. *Parikalpana: KIIT Journal of Management, 9*, 22-33. Retrieved from http://connection.ebscohost.com/c/ articles/93980833

Helmig, B., Spraul, K., & Ingenhoff, D. (2016). Under positive pressure: How stakeholder pressure affects corporate social responsibility implementation. *Business & Society, 55*(2), 151–187. doi:10.1177/0007650313477841

Hildebrand, D., Sen, S., & Bhattacharya, C. B. (2011). Corporate social responsibility: A corporate marketing perspective. *European Journal of Marketing, 45*(9/10), 1353–1364. doi:10.1108/03090561111151790

How we care for Googlers. (2017). Retrieved September 23, 2017, from https:// careers.google.com/how-we-care-for-googlers/

Hsu, K. (2012). The advertising effects of corporate social responsibility on corporate reputation and brand equity: Evidence from the life insurance industry in Taiwan. *Journal of Business Ethics, 109*(2), 189–201. doi:10.1007/s10551-011-1118-0

Jose, A., & Thibodeaux, M. S. (1999). Institutionalization of ethics: The perspective of managers. *Journal of Business Ethics, 22*(2), 133–143. doi:10.1023/A:1006027423495

Keller, K. L., & Lehmann, D. R. (2006). Brands and branding: Research findings and future priorities. *Marketing Science, 25*(6), 740–759. doi:10.1287/mksc.1050.0153

Khan, A. A., & Manwani, D. T. (2013). Sustainability & corporate brand equity through corporate social responsibility initiatives. *Asia Pacific Journal of Management & Entrepreneurship Research, 2*, 267-279. Retrieved from https://www.questia.com/ library/ journal/1P3-2974214771

Kitchin, T. (2003). Corporate social responsibility: A brand explanation. *Journal of Brand Management, 10*(4), 312–326. doi:10.1057/palgrave.bm.2540127

Lai, C., Chiu, C., Yang, C., & Pai, D. (2010). The effects of corporate social responsibility on brand performance: The mediating effect of industrial brand equity and corporate reputation. *Journal of Business Ethics, 95*(3), 457–469. doi:10.1007/s10551-010-0433-1

Liu, M., Wong, I., Shi, G., Chu, R., & Brock, J. (2014). The impact of corporate social responsibility (CSR) performance and perceived brand quality on customer-based brand preference. *Journal of Services Marketing, 28*, 181–194. doi:10.1108/JSM-09-2012-0171

Lopatta, K., Buchholz, F., & Kaspereit, T. (2015). Asymmetric information and corporate social responsibility. *Business & Society, 55*(3), 458–488. doi:10.1177/0007650315575488

Luo, X., & Bhattacharya, C. (2006). Corporate social responsibility, customer satisfaction, and market value. *Journal of Marketing, 70*(4), 1–18. doi:10.1509/jmkg.70.4.1

Luu, T. T. (2012). Behind brand performance. *Asia-Pacific Journal of Business Administration, 4*(1), 42–57. doi:10.1108/17574321211207962

Maignan, I., Ferrell, O. C., & Ferrell, L. (2005). A stakeholder model for implementing social responsibility in marketing. *European Journal of Marketing, 39*(9/10), 956–977. doi:10.1108/03090560510610662

Mattera, M., & Baena, V. (2015). The key to carving out a high corporate reputation based on innovation: Corporate social responsibility. *Social Responsibility Journal, 11*(2), 221–241. doi:10.1108/SRJ-03-2013-0035

McGuire, J. B., Sundgren, A., & Schneeweis, T. (1988). Corporate social responsibility and firm financial performance. *Academy of Management Journal, 31*(4), 854–872. doi:10.2307/256342

Melo, T., & Garrido-Morgado, A. (2012). Corporate reputation: A combination of social responsibility and industry. *Corporate Social Responsibility and Environmental Management, 19*(1), 11–31. doi:10.1002/csr.260

Mikołajek-Gocejna, M. (2016). The relationship between corporate social responsibility and corporate financial performance – Evidence from empirical studies. *Comparative Economic Research, 19*(4), 67–83. doi:10.1515/cer-2016-0030

Murphy, P. E., Laczniak, G. R., & Wood, G. (2007). An ethical basis for relationship marketing: A virtue ethics perspective. *European Journal of Marketing, 41*(1/2), 37–57. doi:10.1108/03090560710718102

Ponnu, C. H., & Tennakoon, G. (2009). The association between ethical leadership and employee outcomes – the Malaysian case. *Electronic Journal of Business Ethics and Organization Studies, 14*(1), 21-32. Retrieved from http://urn.fi/ URN:NBN:fi:jyu-201010052947

Pučėtaitė, R., & Lämsä, A. M. (2008). Developing organizational trust through advancement of employees' work ethic in a post-socialist context. *Journal of Business Ethics, 82*(2), 325–337. doi:10.1007/s10551-008-9922-x

Saeidi, S. P., Sofian, S., Saeidi, P., Saeidi, S. P., & Saaeidi, S. A. (2015). How does corporate social responsibility contribute to firm financial performance? The mediating role of competitive advantage, reputation, and customer satisfaction. *Journal of Business Research, 68*(2), 341–350. doi:10.1016/j.jbusres.2014.06.024

Saurage-Altenloh, S. M. (2017). *The measured influence of supplier CSR on brand performance expectations in B2B relationships.* Retrieved from ProQuest Dissertations. (Order No. 10262262)

Scholtens, B., & Kang, F. (2013). Corporate social responsibility and earnings management: Evidence from Asian economies. *Corporate Social Responsibility and Environmental Management, 20*(2), 95–112. doi:10.1002/csr.1286

Schrempf-Stirling, J., Palazzo, G., & Phillips, R. (2015). Historic corporate social responsibility. *Academy of Management Review.* doi:10.5465/amr.2014.0137

Shim, K., & Yang, S.-U. (2016). The effect of bad reputation: The occurrence of crisis, corporate social responsibility, and perceptions of hypocrisy and attitudes toward a company. *Public Relations Review, 42*(1), 68–78. doi:10.1016/j.pubrev.2015.11.009

Sledge, S. (2015). An examination of corporate social responsibility practices and firm performance in U.S. corporations. *Academy of Strategic Management Journal, 14*(2), 171-184. Retrieved from https://www.questia.com/library/journal/1P3-3934076471

Solving for sustainability. (2017) Retrieved September 22, 2017, from https:// environment.google/approach/

Srinivasan, V., Park, C. S., & Chang, D. R. (2005). An approach to the measurement, analysis, and prediction of brand equity and its sources. *Management Science, 51*(9), 1433–1448. doi:10.1287/mnsc.1050.0405

Stanaland, A. J. S., Lewin, M. O., & Murphy, P. E. (2011). Consumer perceptions of the antecedents and consequences of corporate social responsibility. *Journal of Business Ethics, 102*(1), 47–55. doi:10.1007/s10551-011-0904-z

Staudt, S., Shao, C. Y., Dubinsky, A. J., & Wilson, P. H. (2014). Corporate social responsibility, perceived customer value, and customer-based brand equity: A cross-national comparison. *Journal of Strategic Innovation and Sustainability*, *10*(1), 65–87. Retrieved from www.na-businesspress.com/JSIS/ADubinskyWeb10-1.pdf

Story, J., & Neves, P. (2014). When corporate social responsibility (CSR) increases performance: Exploring the role of intrinsic and extrinsic CSR attribution. *Business Ethics (Oxford, England)*, *24*(2), 111–124. doi:10.1111/beer.12084

Taghian, M., D'Souza, C., & Polonsky, M. (2015). A stakeholder approach to corporate social responsibility, reputation and business performance. *Social Responsibility Journal*, *11*(2), 340–363. doi:10.1108/SRJ-06-2012-0068

Thornton, L. F. (2013). *7 Lenses: Learning the principles and practices of ethical leadership*. Richmond, VA: Leading in Context, LLC.

Torres, A., Bijmolt, T. H. A., Tribó, J. A., & Verhoef, P. (2012). Generating global brand equity through corporate social responsibility to key stakeholders. *International Journal of Research in Marketing*, *29*(1), 13–24. doi:10.1016/j.ijresmar.2011.10.002

Vaaland, T. I., Heide, M., & Grønhaug, K. (2008). Corporate social responsibility: Investigating theory and research in the marketing context. *European Journal of Marketing*, *42*(9/10), 927–953. doi:10.1108/03090560810891082

Valentine, S., & Barnett, T. (2003). Ethics code awareness, perceived ethical values, and organizational commitment. *Journal of Personal Selling & Sales Management*, *23*, 359–367. Retrieved from http://www.jstor.org/stable/40471934

Valenzuela, L. M., Mulki, J. P., & Jaramillo, J. F. (2010). Impact of customer orientation, inducements and ethics on loyalty to the firm: Customers' Perspective. *Journal of Business Ethics*, *93*(2), 277–291. doi:10.1007/s10551-009-0220-z

Vallaster, C., Lindgreen, A., & Maon, F. (2012). Strategically leveraging corporate social responsibility: A corporate branding perspective. *California Management Review*, *54*(3), 34–60. doi:10.1525/cmr.2012.54.3.34

Van Beurden, P., & Gössling, T. (2008). The worth of values – A literature review on the relation between corporate social and financial performance. *Journal of Business Ethics*, *82*(2), 407–424. doi:10.1007/s10551-008-9894-x

Wang, D. H., Chen, P., Yu, T. H., & Hsiao, C. (2015). The effects of corporate social responsibility on brand equity and firm performance. *Journal of Business Research*, *68*(11), 2232–2236. doi:10.1016/j.jbusres.2015.06.003

Wang, H., & Qian, C. (2011). Corporate philanthropy and corporate financial performance: The roles of stakeholder response and political access. *Academy of Management Journal, 54*(6), 1159–1181. doi:10.5465/amj.2009.0548

Wang, L., & Juslin, H. (2009). The impact of Chinese culture on corporate social responsibility: The harmony approach. *Journal of Business Ethics, 88*(S3), 433–451. doi:10.1007/s10551-009-0306-7

Wang, Y., Hsu, L., & Chang, K. (2012). The relationship between corporate social responsibility and firm performance: An application of quantile regression. *Frontiers of Business Research in China, 6*, 218–244. doi:10.3868/s070-001-012-0011-3

Weber Shandwick. (2016). *The company behind the brand II: In goodness we trust.* Retrieved from http://www.webershandwick.com/uploads/news/files/company-behind-the-brand-in-goodness-we-trust.pdf

Worthington, I., Ram, M., Boyal, H., & Shah, M. (2007). Researching the drivers of socially responsible purchasing: A cross-national study of supplier diversity initiatives. *Journal of Business Ethics, 79*(3), 319–331. doi:10.1007/s10551-007-9400-x

Zhang, J., & He, Y. (2014). Key dimensions of brand value co-creation and its impacts upon customer perception and brand performance: An empirical research in the context of industrial service. *Nankai Business Review International, 5*(1), 43–69. doi:10.1108/NBRI-09-2013-0033

Zhu, Y., Sun, L., & Leung, A. S. M. (2014). Corporate social responsibility, firm reputation, and firm performance: The role of ethical leadership. *Asia Pacific Journal of Management, 31*(4), 925–947. doi:10.1007/s10490-013-9369-1

KEY TERMS AND DEFINITIONS

Brand Equity: The value of a known brand wherein greater brand recognition, integrity, and character equates to increased revenues.

Brand Performance: A form of corporate financial performance based on the contribution of a brand to corporate revenues.

Brand Reputation: How a brand is perceived by customers and the communities in which it operates.

Corporate Legitimacy: A perception that the activities and actions of a business are appropriate, genuine, and preferred.

Corporate Philanthropy: Investment of resources by an organization to enable a social benefit.

Corporate Social Responsibility (CSR): A corporate commitment to initiatives that extend social, environmental, and economic benefits to all stakeholder groups.

Ethical Behavior: Acting in a manner that upholds generally accepted good values imbued with moral principles such as honesty, fairness, dignity, and individual rights.

Social Trust: The bond among individuals that facilitates transactions, permits individual creativity, and legitimizes collective action.

Sustainable Competitive Advantage: The favorable long-term position of a business that results from securing unique attributes or abilities difficult for competitors to match or overcome.

Chapter 2
The Relationship Between Leadership Ethics and Organizational Success:
Ethics and Organizational Success

Enoch T. Osei
Bowie State University, USA

Velmarie K. Swing
Oklahoma Wesleyan University, USA

ABSTRACT

Over the last few decades, business fraud and examples of scandalous management behaviors have sparked a lot of attention among several interested stakeholders. These increasing scandals have necessitated the question on the necessary steps required to prevent their frequent occurrence. The lack of commitment to strong ethical standards by management has been underpinned as the cause of ethical misconducts in organizations. The fiscal crisis of 2007-2009 witnessed many leadership misconducts and abuse of leadership responsibility. The fiscal crisis revealed the loss of about $11 trillion in household wealth, 26 million Americans losing their jobs, and 4.5 million Americans who could not afford their mortgages. These events and statistics show the prevalent lack of ethical leadership in organizations. While leadership ethics is a concern for all stakeholders within business organizations in the United States, only a few segments of the industry are taking steps to incorporate ethical awareness within their organizations.

DOI: 10.4018/978-1-5225-2650-6.ch002

INTRODUCTION

Financial misconduct is extensive within corporate institutions in the United States (Zabihollah, 2002). Examples of questionable behaviors include using company assets for personal activities, asking work colleagues to clock in time cards while not at work locations, receiving bribes and kickbacks through contract awards, and deliberately presenting false accounting procedures to deceive investors (Kumar & Lee, 2014; Wilmoth & O'Brien, 2011). These types of misconduct have resulted in reputational damage, lawsuits, incarcerations, millions of dollars in settlements, and sometimes, the collapse of worthwhile organizations (Reuber & Fischer, 2010). The victims of fraudulent conduct are employee underlings, investors, and consumers. The frequency of these problems underscores the importance of examining the ethical behaviors of leadership and assessing how leadership ethics relate to organizational success within the financial services sector (Kroll, 2012; Stahl & Sully de Luque, 2014).

The financial services crisis of 2007–2009 and its aftershocks caused financial services organizations to suffer from an unprecedented decline in their reputations among the general public. The immediate effect of this crisis was the loss of more than $2 trillion in retirement savings and pension funds due to the steep decline of stock values in the U.S. market (Orszag, 2008). The long-term effect was massive unemployment in the United States, which reached 8.5% by the end of March 2009 (Bureau of Labor Statistics, 2010). Corporate scandals and abuse, such as the Enron scandal in the United States and Libor and Euribor in Europe, occurred within the financial services sector (Kraten, 2013). The financial services sector, even though highly regulated, is vulnerable to misconduct because of corporate executives' quest to enrich shareholders and senior executives while disregarding other stakeholders (McCuddy, 2012).

Although leadership ethics is a concern for all stakeholders within U.S. business organizations, only a few segments of the industry are taking steps to include ethical awareness within their organizations on the shortsighted argument that these measures reduce short-term profits (Ashforth, Gioia, Robinson, & Treviño, 2008). In many instances, corporate leaders are drivers of ethical or unethical conduct within their organizations (Leroy, Palanski, & Simmons, 2012). Ethical leadership is critical to organizational success because employees need to trust the integrity of their leaders and to model what their supervisors do (Sharif & Scandura, 2014). The Project Management Institute (2010) and Tanner, Brugger, Van Schie, and Lebherz (2010) identified responsibility, respect, fairness, and honesty as key ethical leadership values. According to Yueru, Weibo, Ribbens, and Juanmel (2013), corporate supervisors who demonstrate and act ethically are more likely to affect their employees in a positive way, thereby generating greater work and creativity. The leader-member exchange theory posits that successful managers are those who develop strong relationships with their subordinates (Graen & Cashman, 1975).

BACKGROUND

No matter where one looks, it appears that a disregard of the basic principles of right and wrong among organizational leaders has led people to a point where trust in organizations and the very systems that make society work are in critical danger. Business scandals in organizations such as Enron, Tyco, WorldCom, and Ahold have created many concerns for investors and other business stakeholders about the level of irresponsible behaviors in organizations (Marsh, 2013). Following the collapse of Enron, Tyco, and Worldcom, the U.S. Congress passed the Sarbanes-Oxley Act of 2002 to control the rate of fraudulent business practices, but this has not prevented corrupt practices and behaviors in organizations. Although legislation is necessary, many scholars and interested stakeholders are of the view that leadership needs to be the primary focus of ethical reform (Marsh, 2013). Several business failures have underscored the need to examine the role of business leaders and their ethical commitment to organizations. Leaders play an important role in supporting and implementing change, and employees require direction related to such changes as well as positive models to emulate (Sharif & Scandura, 2014).

Many organizational failures have been attributed to the lack of leadership integrity in organizations (Yukl, 2013). This statement underscores the importance of ethical leadership to organizational success. Yukl (2013) noted that leadership integrity is a key factor in ensuring leadership effectiveness. This implies that ethical leaders should be more effective than nonethical leaders. Even though great effort has been devoted to conceptualizing and measuring ethical leadership, more research is required to understand its complexity, and many fundamental questions are still unanswered (Frisch & Huppenbauer, 2014; Kalshoven, Den Hartgo, & De Hoogh, 2011; Tanner et al., 2010). The definition of ethical leaders refers to those who are required to behave appropriately, but what an appropriate behavior is remains unclear. Giessner and Quaquebeke (2011) found that defining appropriate conduct remains vague, and a concise definition is required to understand appropriate ethical conduct.

The purpose of this chapter is to provide empirical evidence on the relationship between leadership ethics and organizational success. The chapter offers a research-based study that provides a foundation for leaders to exhibit strong ethical conduct. Business leaders and other stakeholders can use the information from this study to understand the link among ethical leadership behaviors, employees' reactions to such behaviors, and organizational success. Although there is no lack of ethical leadership theories, what constitutes key ethical leadership behavior has not been clearly defined (Giessner & Quaquabeke, 2011). Many leadership theories, such as ethical leadership theory (Shweta & Srirang, 2013), transformational leadership theory (Gandolfi, 2012), and leader-member exchange theory, have attempted to provide an explanation of the leadership qualities required for organizations to be successful. In their study of ethical leadership, the Project Management Institute (2010) and Tanner et al. (2010) identified the ethical variables of respect, responsibility, fairness, and honesty as key ethical variables that can lead to project management effectiveness (Project Management Institute, 2010) and organizational success.

THEORETICAL FRAMEWORK FOR LEADERSHIP ETHICS

Various theoretical works on leadership ethics have been advanced over the years. Each theory attempts to provide an explanation of and clarity to a research problem. It would be an oversimplification to suggest that one theory is better than the other. Leader-member exchange theory and transformational leadership theory are critical when studying leadership ethics.

Leader-Member Exchange Theory

Leader-member exchange (LMX) is a theory grounded on the assumption that leaders develop relationships consisting of reciprocal exchange with their followers (Graen & Cashman, 1975). It is a relationship-based theory on social exchange and reciprocity where leaders develop an exchange with their subordinates, and the level of exchange influences the subordinates' sense of responsibility, decision influence, and access to resources and performance (Shweta & Srirang, 2013). Shweta and Siring (2013) found that the reciprocal exchange between managers and employees is usually grounded on assumptions concerning human nature and focuses on controlling behaviors.

Roles are crucial elements of LMX relationship theory and specify duties, communication patterns, hierarchical relationships, and informal norms and expectations (Shweta & Srirang, 2013). Roles assigned to employees define their expected relationship to their managers and their subordinates (Shweta & Srirang, 2013). According to Kulkarni and Ramamoorthy (2011), within an organizational situation, a hierarchical governance structure can be adjusted with stewardship behavior. They defined stewardship as the extent to which employees are motivated to "work in the best interest of the owners. LMX refers to how leaders act within their positions through many interactions with their subordinates in an organizational hierarchy. Low-level LMX exchanges are usually characterized by the following: minimum employee job performance, low level of employee trust and emotional support, low employee satisfaction and productivity and high employee turnover (Graen & Cashman, 1975). On the other hand, high-level LMX exchanges imply high levels of employee trust with collective leadership support and their acknowledgment of superior performance above the minimum required. High-quality LMX is usually related to the dual benefits of low employee turnover and high performance that lead to organizational effectiveness (Graen & Cashman, 1975). Figure 1 shows an overview of LMX theory. It broadly elucidates the behaviors of leaders and subordinates and the internal context that specifies the relationship for LMX theory (Kulkarni & Ramamoorthy, 2011).

Transformational Leadership Theory

James MacGregor Burns first introduced the idea of transformational leadership. Burns noted that this leadership style directs followers to a higher sense of morality and motivation through their leadership strengths and visions (Rigio, 2009). According to Yukl (2013), transformational leadership focuses on stimulating and improving organizations by engaging the moral values and ethical concerns of followers. The transformational leadership concept was later advanced by Bernard M. Bass and became the Bass transformational leadership theory (Bass, 1985). Bass (1985) noted that transformational leadership could be defined based on the impact it has on followers. Qualities such as trust, respect, and admiration were noted as key virtues of transformational leadership style. Whereas transformational leadership has been praised for its consideration of ethical standards in decision making, several scholars

Figure 1. Components of LMX theory
Source: Adapted from Kulkarni and Ramamoorthy (2011)

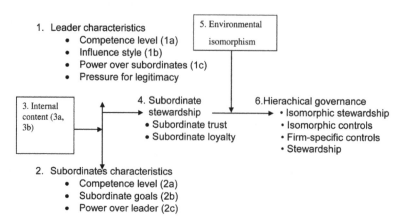

have questioned the inherent morality of this leadership style (Schuh, Zhang, & Tian, 2013). Bass and Steidlmeier (1999) noted that transformational leadership must not only be seen as being used in advancing common interests of the organization but also in the pursuit of immoral acts for the selfish gains of the leader.

According to Bass and Steidlmeier (1999), the behaviors observed in transformational leadership are neutral, and leaders can choose to adopt this leadership style for the pursuit of good or wrongful acts. Bass and Steidlmeier differentiated between two types of transformational leadership styles: a pseudo-transformational leadership style that is based on the leader and encourages dependence on the leader by employees and authentic transformational leadership where leaders find common constructs where their employees support them, and the employees in turn feel a sense of belonging. Whereas efforts have been made in distinguishing transformational leadership on a more balanced perspective, the reaction of followers to this leadership style has been overlooked (Schuh et al., 2013). How followers react to both the altruistic and the self-focused style of transformational leadership is unclear. The element of followers' reactions to leadership style is very important, as the success of any organization depends on employee performance (Podsakoff, Whiting, Podsakoff, & Blume, 2009). Schuh et al. (2013) noted in their research that behaviors of followers could change positively with an altruistic leadership behavior. Their research also found an increase in adverse reactions of followers' work output in a self-centered style of leadership. For example, when leaders are self- absorbed, do not listen to employee input, and make unilateral decisions without consulting employees, the organizational commitment of those employees is likely to reduce. The preceding statement suggests that followers' behavioral patterns are structured by the style of leadership employed by the leader.

The fundamental responsibility of leadership is motivating followers to attain higher objectives and to achieve greater outcomes (Grant, 2012). The transformational leadership style achieves this objective by engaging in inspirational behaviors such as advancing vision, exhibiting confidence and idealism, and emphasizing core values (Bass, 1985). Grant (2012) noted that there is a correlation between transformational leadership styles and followers' motivation in achieving performance.

The effectiveness of transformational leadership is achieved through the charisma of the leader. Gandolfi (2012) noted that transformational leadership was later named as an idealized influence that draws its main strength from inspirational motivation, intellectual stimulation, and consideration of the individual's reactions to the leader's behavioral actions. Idealized influence refers to the charismatic characteristics of the leader that are centered on beliefs, values, and a sense of mission in encouraging and motivating followers to perform beyond their limits (Gandolfi, 2012). Followers who identify themselves to their leaders are influenced by their leaders' behaviors and actions. This can result in respect and trust by the follower in identifying with the leader's objective in meeting the goals and objectives of the firm.

According to Gandolfi (2012), leaders who are inspirational motivators are able to enunciate values and goals that motivate followers to transcend their own self-interest. Followers inspired and motivated by their leaders are more likely to relate with them and are inclined to support them to meet mutually established goals. Leaders who are inspirational can actualize high levels of confidence and expectancy and lead their followers to achieve a high level of optimism and confidence (Keung, 2011). Intellectual stimulation relates to behaviors that advance the followers' interests in the realization of problems that enhance their abilities to analyze problems in a more holistic manner. Gandolfi noted that transformational leaders emphasize the importance of analyzing situations outside the box and create organizational cultures in which employees are motivated to challenge deep-rooted values, paradigms, and beliefs. Within transformational leadership, leaders foster a one-to-one relationship and create cohesion among followers. Transformational leaders are often regarded as mentors who coach followers to achieve optimal performance. Followers under transformational leadership receive personal attention, which boosts their confidence, motivation, and satisfaction at work (Lian & Tui, 2012). Supportive leadership under transformational leadership is concerned with followers' needs and directs attention to satisfying their welfare, which can result in a supportive work environment. According to Bass (1985), intellectual stimulation builds up employees' awareness of and interest in organizational problems, which allows them to think of problems in new dimensions. Followers achieve personal recognition when leaders appreciate their efforts and are rewarded for achieving outcomes that align with corporate goals and objectives.

ETHICAL LEADERSHIP IN PERSPECTIVE

The past 40 years have been dominated with bribery scandals, industry scandals, and accounting scandals in corporate America and across the globe (Steinbauer, Renn, Taylor, & Njoroge, 2014). Although governments have introduced more rules and regulations, unethical conduct and fraudulent practices are still common. In 2009, Bernard Madoff confessed to defrauding investors of billions of dollars in his Ponzi scheme arrangement. Similarly, R. Allen Stanford was sentenced to 110 years in prison for defrauding investors of billions of dollars with his own Ponzi scheme (Holzer, 2012). These and other fraudulent forms of conduct were caused by a single business leader whose activities harmed investors and those who worked with them. Brown and Treviño (2014) noted that ethical leadership theory accounts for how a leader's ethical conduct or behavior can influence his or her followers' ethical decisions and actions. Per ethical leadership theory, followers' ethical decisions are influenced by social exchange processes and the use of performance management in making employees accountable for their actions and conduct (Brown & Treviño, 2014). Mayer Aquino, Greenbaum, and Kuenzi (2012) found that ethical leadership affects followers' deviant behavior, and an ethical climate mediates the relationship between ethical leadership and followers' misconduct.

National surveys have shown that very few Americans trust the ethics and integrity of today's leaders in corporate institutions, government, and business entities (Jones, 2011). This statement confirms the perception that ethical leadership in organizations is at its weakest levels. According to Brown and Treviño (2014), to be perceived as an ethical leader, a leader must be both a moral person and a moral manager. The moral part of ethical leadership relates to the leader's honesty, integrity, trustworthiness, caring about people, openness to input, respect, and decision-making principles. Ethical leaders who act as moral managers use tools such as rewards, discipline, and decision making in communicating to employees the importance of ethics, standards setting, and accountability (Brown & Treviño, 2014). Research studies have found that ethical leadership is related to important positive employee behaviors and outcomes, including trust in a supervisor, interracial fairness, supervisor effectiveness, supervisor satisfaction, and the willingness to report problems to management (Walumbwa et al., 2011).

In his research into social identity theory to expatiate the relationship of ethical leadership on employee outcomes, Yang (2014) found that social identity theory explains the social phenomenon as it relates to people forming a sense of recognition and belonging to the organization, company, or a group of people to which they belong. Social identification can lead to shared beliefs that coincide with the organizational beliefs or identity that is prevalent within a group. Employees are likely to act with similar members within the organization and to varying degrees feel a sense of belonging to a social group. Brown and Mitchell (2015) noted that leaders' values can shape the culture of an organization, and leaders attract followers who have similar ethical values. A high-quality relationship between a leader and a follower is critical, since it can decide the fate of that subordinate and determine the ethical quality of the follower's behavior. In other words, employees with better relationships with their leaders have greater chances of job security, being promoted, and being mentored. Yukl (2013) noted that leaders' behaviors vary with different groups of employees and that those who are favored receive benefits such as wage increases, better work schedules, special benefits, and bigger office space.

LEADERSHIP SKILLS

It was once thought that successful leaders were born, not made (Kirkpatrick & Locke, 1996). The idea was that one had to come from some special breeds of families in order to lead, and those not fortunate to come from such breeds were followers (Germain, 2012). The general idea was that one's destiny was either to be born as a leader or as a follower, and no amount of learning or yearning could cause a change. A study conducted by Kirkpatrick and Locke (1996) found that there are six main factors that differentiate leaders from nonleaders: drive, desire to lead, honesty and integrity, self-confidence, cognitive ability, and knowledge of the business. Several different studies have noted that having certain personality traits are associated with leader effectiveness. According to Germain and Tejeda (2009), four main characteristics define effective leadership: intelligence, self-confidence, determination (drive), and sociability.

Germain (2012) noted that an effective leader is one who possesses the qualities of strong intellectual ability, perceptual ability, and reasoning ability. Intellectual ability denotes a leader who can solve complex problems and decide on issues effectively; these issues can include how to deal with ethical situations when confronted with an ethical dilemma. Germain and Tejeda (2009) noted that the link between leadership and expertise is made clear at this stage, as experts are problem solvers who can judge issues effectively. Leaders must therefore be able judge between a moral question of right and wrong. Self-confidence is another trait of leadership effectiveness. Self-confidence is defined as one's certainty of his or her competence and skills (Germain, 2012).

Leaders with self-confidence have a sense of self-esteem and self-assurance. Leaders who are not able to exhibit the trait of confidence are regarded as weak and lacking the requisite skills and competence. Leadership is about influencing others, and self-confidence serves to assure the leader that his or her influence is acceptable (Germain, 2012). Determinations relate to the individual's will to get the job the done and are components of the person's expert knowledge.

Levels of Leadership

Traits are leadership features that researchers have studied over long period of time. Zaccaro (2007) defined traits as an individual's integrated behavioral patterns that reflect a person's range of difference in fostering consistent leadership effectiveness across a variety of groups and organizational situations. Traits are one of the oldest-studied features of leadership. Superior personality traits have been noted as a factor that makes an effective leader (Ünsar & Karalar, 2013). One of the original traits theorists, Allport wrote that there are more than 4,000 adjectives in the English language that individuals can use to describe personality (Ünsar & Karalar, 2013). According to Allport, there are four types of traits: cardinal, central, secondary, and common (Ünsar & Karalar, 2013).

The cardinal trait of a leader challenges the leader to seek power and competition. A leader with such a trait always stays competitive and strives to win at all times (Ashcraft, 2011). According to Ashcraft (2011), people with such personalities often become so known for these traits that their names are frequently synonymous with these qualities. The origin and meaning of the terms *Freudian, Machiavellian, narcissistic, Don Juan,* and *Christlike* are examples of the cardinal trait. Allport suggested that cardinal traits are rare and tend to develop later in life. However, very few leaders have these cardinal traits (Ashcraft, 2011).

Central traits relate to the perception of people about others and how individuals are observed and described. According to Ünsar and Karalar (2013), central traits are mostly coherent with cardinal traits. These traits are the general characteristics that form the basic foundations of personality, and while not as dominating as cardinal traits, they are the major characteristics you might use to describe another person (Ünsar & Karalar, 2013). Terms such as *intelligent, honest, shy,* and *anxious* are considered central traits.

Secondary traits relate to preferences or desired traits that an individual strives to achieve. They usually vary from person to person. Allport noted that these traits sometimes relate to attitudes or preferences and often appear only in certain situations or under specific circumstances. Some examples include becoming anxious when speaking to a group or impatient while waiting in line (Ashcraft, 2011).

Finally, common traits refer to people's general behaviors that help them to identify one group from another. For example, a group could be said to nice, polite, humble, and disciplined. Allport argued that these traits are unique to individuals, and a person can understand another through the knowledge of these unique characteristics (Ashcraft, 2011).

Psychologists have grouped the various leadership traits into four main categories: psychological, intellectual, physical, and qualities of character (Ünsar & Karalar, 2013). The trait approach, which was formed from the notion of leadership, prescribes that successful and efficient leaders have leadership traits that are different from others. The traits of efficient leaders vary with their followers. The great person theory of leadership was based on the fact that leaders are different from others with average skills (Ünsar & Karalar, 2013). The five-factor model, or the big five personality, has five broad categories of human traits: neuroticism, extraversion, openness to experience, agreeableness, and conscientiousness (McCrae & Costa, 1997). Dyck and Neubert (2008) noted that extraversion, conscientiousness, and openness to experience are the general personality traits related to effective leadership. Understanding how personality traits affect people's behavior can be valuable assets for leaders (Daft, 2007).

A different way of categorizing leadership traits includes personality, motivation, and ability to learn (Nahavandi, 2003). Motivation and personality were discussed earlier; however, the ability to learn a new skill is critical, as it involves different stages of thinking. Nahavadi (2003) noted that the trait of an individual affects the way that person acquires a new skill. An individual's lack of intellect may prevent him or her from acquiring a new skill. The skills required to perform a task successfully also changes as a person attains a higher level of leadership. The level of leadership requires one to be visionary, conceptual, or technical. Visionary and conceptual skills require a lot of innovative reasoning and are more critical than technical skills (Hellriegel, Slocum, & Jackson, 2002).

According to Hellriegel et al. (2002), lower-level leadership usually supervises employees who require technical help. The skills necessary for this level of leadership are often technical in nature and within that leader's technical ability. The problems that leaders solve under this level are usually reoccurring and require the leader to have knowledge and understanding of the task level to solve problems as they arise. Even though interpersonal skills are needed under this level, technical knowledge is often applied.

Nahavandi (2003) noted that, as the leader's role expands into middle management, the problems become a bit more varied, and leaders require a more balanced skill set. While lower-level leaders work with employees on-site, middle-level leaders usually work outside the field and implement missions and objectives that have been set by the greater hierarchy of leadership. Leaders at this level have a good understanding of the technical limitation in addition to human limitations in accomplishing set targets. Technical knowledge and effective teamwork are used at this level to effectively set plans.

At the very top level of leadership, the situations are more complex and critical in nature. The company focus is planned and directed at this level and involves several varying components of the firm (Hellriegel et al., 2002). The course that leaders chart at this level involves new and unfamiliar boundaries for the firm. This explains why corporate executives have long-term visions and the ability to understand complex relationships among variables that are relevant to the organization's success (Yukl, 2013). Conceptual knowledge at this level is crucial because a simple misdirected step could lead the organization to bankruptcy. Interpersonal skills at this level are important, as the leader interacts with different management levels that implement the firm's targets and visions.

UNETHICAL BEHAVIORS AND ETHICAL LEADERSHIP

Over the last few decades, business fraud and examples of scandalous management behavior have sparked a lot of attention among several interested stakeholders. These increasing scandals have necessitated the question about the steps required to prevent their frequent occurrence. Politicians, economists, philosophers, jurists, and theologians have searched for solutions that could advance ethical leadership and prevent unethical behaviors in organizations (Frisch & Huppenbauer, 2014). Thus, regulations such as the Sarbanes-Oxley Act and voluntary commitment of different kinds of policies like codes of conduct, ethics programs, and corporate ethics officers have been introduced. The Sarbanes-Oxley Act was passed by Congress to control the rate of fraudulent conduct in organizations. However, the outcome of these measures has been insufficient in preventing corporate fraud and abuse. According to Webley and Werner (2008), codes of ethics alone do not insulate firms from ethical misconduct, and there are frequent instances of considerable differences between codes of conduct and actual ethical behaviors of employees. In recent times, the focus on ethical misconduct has been directed at corporate leaders and supervisors. The lack of commitment to strong ethical standards by management has been underpinned as the cause of ethical misconduct in organizations (Webley & Werner, 2008).

Even though much effort has been devoted to conceptualizing and measuring ethical leadership, a lot is required to understand its complexity, and several fundamental questions are still unclear (Frisch & Huppenbauer, 2014; Kalshoven et al., 2011; Tanner et al., 2010). The normal understanding of ethical leaders refers to those who are required to behave appropriately, but the question remains as to what can be regarded as appropriate behavior. Giessner and Quaquebeke (2011) noted that the definition of appropriate conduct remains vague and that a concise definition is warranted on what can be considered as appropriate ethical conduct. Scholars such as Kalshoven et al. (2011) and Tanner et al. (2010) found that ethical leadership has primarily focused on ethical leadership behavior toward employees. However, stakeholder theory emphasizes the need for ethical leaders to direct their attention toward interested stakeholder groups (Freeman, Harrison, Wicks, Parmar, & De Colle, 2010). Ethical leaders therefore have the authority to influence the behavioral patterns of employees within organizations.

Lok and Crawford (2004) found that leadership styles could affect the success or failure of organizations. Ethical leadership can be defined as the capacity to influence the ethical behaviors of followers. Many people will agree that good leadership must include the qualities of integrity and ethical conduct. Walumba et al. (2011) used social identity theory to explain the relationship between ethical leadership and employee outcomes, noting that this theory can capture the complex nature of studies on ethical leadership. Ethical leaders can influence employees in a positive manner, thereby increasing workplace productivity. The theory identifies behaviors that are compatible with the organizational culture or identities that are prevalent within assigned groups. Thus, employees are likely to behave in a similar way to other members of the group and to obtain a sense of satisfaction from their social identities. Giberson, Resick, and Dickson (2005) noted that leaders tend to surround themselves with employees with similar ethical values and standings.

There are several reasons to believe that ethical leadership can lead to the subjective well-being of employees within an organization (Yang, 2014). First, according to Brown and Mitchell (2015), employees who work with ethical leaders feel a sense of responsibility to return beneficial favors by increasing work output and behaving in an ethical manner. Second, organizations with strong ethical behavioral models support groups where employees feel a sense of belonging and can share moral dilemmas with those within the group (VanSandt & Neck, 2003). Third, the job satisfaction of employees can increase in an environment where employees feel a sense of support from ethical leaders. In their study of ethics in the nursing profession in Israel, Goldman and Tabak (2010) noted that there is a strong relationship between job satisfaction and those nurses who work in an ethical climate. Their study recommended ethics training for employees working as nurses in health-care institutions in Israel. According to Mayer et al. (2012), ethical leadership can impact active relationships in the workplace. An active relationship refers to a relationship between a leader and a subordinate, where the subordinate is able to interact with the leader and to seek direction when necessary. Toor and Ofori (2009) found that ethical leadership moderates the role between organizational culture and employee outcomes. Employees who work with ethical leaders are mostly satisfied with their jobs and more connected with the organization. When employees become satisfied with their jobs, they feel a sense of belonging and offer their best output at the workplace (Yang, 2014). The output of satisfied employees in an ethical environment is most likely to impact organizational success.

The Ethics of Respect

Respect is accepting the opinion of others and regarding those opinions without prejudice. Respect also embodies the understanding and honoring of other's customs, listening to other perspectives, attempting to resolve disagreements with others, behaving professionally, negotiating fairly, and avoiding abuse of authority (Project Management Institute, 2010). Respect involves fair negotiation and preventing abuse of leadership authority.

Regarding the relationship of corporate supervisors' ethics-related actions and organizational successes, Osei (2015) found that managers who exhibit the leadership traits of respect, responsibility, fairness, and honesty have strong relationships with organizational success, and those relationships can predict organizational success. The results of his study collaborate with other prior findings of respect as an important ethical value that leads to employee commitment and productivity (Kalshoven et al., 2011; Tanner et al., 2010). A prior study conducted by Feldman and Arnold (1983) found significant relationship between the leadership ethics of respect and organizational productivity. According to Kalshoven et al. (2011) ethical leadership behaviors, leaders who exhibit strong behaviors of respect can positively influence the commitment levels of employees. A study by Cortina, Magley, Williams, and Langhout (2001) on the ethical leadership behavior of respect showed that respect can have a significant effect on the psychological well-being of employees and that disrespectful behaviors can create greater psychological distress. Taylor (2010) noted that a disrespectful attitude by leaders toward employees affects their well-being and that employees' performance is impaired due to disrespectful attitudes. Adams et al. (2003) found that organizations that demonstrate mutual respect and exhibit solicitude and concern for others are likely to experience decreases in stress and burnout and attendant increases in performance. These prior studies confirm the link between leaders treating their employees with respect and their commitment toward improving performance.

The Ethics of Fairness

Fairness is being impartial, just, objective, or free of favoritism (Project Management Institute, 2010). The ethics of fairness ensures clarity in decision making and requires one to examine each circumstance to avoid being partial and subjective. It creates a platform for accessing information, discloses areas within the organization susceptible to conflict of interest, and prevents favoritism and discrimination (Project Management Institute, 2010)

A recent study by Osei (2015) revealed that the leadership trait of fairness has a significant relationship with organizational success and can predict organizational success. Prior studies on fairness have shown that the ethical value of respect is important to organizational performance and commitment (Bacha & Walker, 2013; Kalshoven et al., 2011; Tanner et al., 2010; Zhang, LePine, Buckman, & Wei, 2014). Bacha and Walker (2013) found fairness to benefit organizations, as employees who feel they are being treated fairly align with the mission and goals of their leaders. Their findings noted that leaders who exhibit the act of fairness motivate their employees and their ethical behavior, and this can serve as a catalyst for increased work output affecting organizational performance (Bacha & Walker, 2013). Research on leadership ethics has shown that fairness is related to greater satisfaction and acquiescence of decisions, decision validity, higher job satisfaction, commitment to organizations, and increased task performance (Zhang et al., 2014). Employees are concerned with fairness relative to the measure of whether their rewards compare to costs expended, expectations held, and similar rewards given to other employees for the same of amount of work performed (Zhang et al., 2014). Employees derive perceptions of fairness by noting whether they are treated with respect and sincerity and given honest and truthful explanations during their encounters with supervisors (Zhang et al., 2014). Leaders' use of fairness is measured per outcomes comparable to behaviors that are consistent, impartial, accurate, correctable, and ethical (Colquitt, 2012). Additionally, when leaders treat employees fairly, their work outcomes increase, which can affect performance (Colquitt2012).

The Ethics of Responsibility

The responsible behavior of corporate supervisors is defined as the acceptance of ownership for choices made by the supervisors (Project Management Institute, 2010). Responsibility also includes acting in the best interest of stakeholders, meeting commitments, admitting and correcting mistakes, protecting confidential information, understanding and obeying the law, and reporting unethical or unlawful behavior (Project Management Institute, 2010). A study performed by Osei (2015) revealed that the leadership trait of responsibility has a strong relationship with and can predict organizational success. Osei's research was consistent with similar studies, such as Jin, Drozdenko, and DeLoughy (2013) and Waldman and Galvin (2008). Bass (1990) noted that organizational success could be defined by the political and social strategies that organizations use to execute and engage employees in achieving optimal performance. Bass (1990) elaborated further by stating that success is measured by the scale of the organizational performance relative to its goals and missions. In their study of responsibility, Waldman and Galvin (2008) found that, despite a lack of agreement on what constituted responsible leadership, there was enormous evidence that perceptions, decisions, and actions of individual senior managers have an impact on social performance and long term-growth of organizations. Jin et al. (2013) also studied the ethical leadership value of responsibility and noted that leaders who demonstrate and use the ethical value of responsibility engage employees in exhibiting a strong work attitude, which can impact productivity.

Leadership responsibility does not take place in a vacuum; it is based on the immediate activity and organizational context, the institutional and cultural environment, and the supranational factors (Stahl & Sully de Luque, 2014). A broad body of studies in social psychology supports the idea that socially responsible behavior is based on contextual factors. Experimental work on obedience to authority noted that people obey out of fear or a desire to appear cooperative (Milgram, 1974). Zimbardo's (1972) prison experiment regarding the power of situation noted that people will readily conform to the social roles they are expected to play, especially if the roles are as strongly stereotyped as those of prison guards. These two experimental studies allude to a strong case of influencing behavior by responsible managers or supervisors in organizational settings in regard to employees' commitment and productivity. Transformational leadership in the form of CEO vision building and role modeling involves the desire of responsible managers to direct employees to higher standards of ethical behavior by inspiring them to transcend their own self-interest for the good of the organization (Stahl & Sully de Luque, 2014). Thus, responsible leadership affects employees' productivity and commitment toward their leaders.

The Ethics of Honesty

Honesty is being truthful in one's statements and actions. Honesty means that truth is maintained in all instances to avoid deceit and the telling of lies. The act of honesty requires that information provided is free from lies and commitment within organizations. It ensures that information given to third parties is accurate and not misleading (Project Management Institute, 2010). A recent study by Osei (2015) revealed that corporate supervisors' use of honesty had a strong positive correlation with organizational success. Contrary to expectation, honesty was not a significant predictor of organizational success. Osei's study corroborated similar findings that the ethical leadership use of honesty correlates with organizational outcomes but contradicted the same studies by revealing that the ethical value of leadership is not a significant predictor of organizational success (Brown, Treviño, & Harrison, 2005; Neubert, Wu, & Roberts, 2013).

Brown et al. (2005) found that ethical leadership is positively correlated with job performance, as traits such as honesty, trustworthiness, caring, and consideration are stronger values of ethical leadership. In their findings, they noted that ethical leaders were thought to be honest and trustworthy leaders. Their findings also revealed another aspect of ethical leadership that they labeled the moral manager dimension. They stated that this aspect of ethical leadership refers to leaders who exhibit honesty and who care for people and the broader society. Leaders who act honestly can achieve greater work output, thereby enhancing productivity (Tanner et al., 2010).

Research findings on ethical leadership have noted that honesty as an ethical leadership value predicts employee satisfaction with their supervisors, dedication, willingness to report problems to supervisors, and leader effectiveness (Dadhich & Bhal, 2008). Neubert et al. (2013) found that honest, ethical leaders influence employee job satisfaction and organizational improvement through ethical leadership development. They noted that leaders who are honest and trustworthy produce a virtuous cycle, which generates an ethical work climate and enables employees to prosper. While prior studies have underscored the measure of leadership honesty in predicting employee commitments and productivity, the results of Osei's (2015) study were inconsistent with these studies. However, Osei provided reasons why his research was inconsistent with other studies, noting that while the power generated by the sample size was adequate, additional participants could have changed the results. He also stated that survey respondents who participated in the study could simply be dishonest.

SOLUTIONS AND RECOMMENDATIONS

The results of this study have a practical implication. To start, there is the misconception that ethical leadership can only impact the moral behaviors of employees. This assertion does not find support in our current study. There is strong evidence noted in this chapter that leadership ethics is a predictor of organizational success. Given the predictive value of ethical leadership variables to organizational success, it is recommended that corporate leaders seek to understand the ethical environment of their organizations and to exploit key ethical variables and their impact on achieving success for their organizations. Specifically, leadership should leverage ethics in their mission, performance assessment, monitoring, and measurement in setting priorities that connect leadership ethics to decision making, operations, and strategic feasibility and promote leadership ethics as central to their organizational effectiveness and success. Ethical leadership is about influencing the ethical behaviors of followers, and the behaviors of leaders influence their followers. Leadership roles should provide direction on ethical standards by explicitly motivating and punishing certain behaviors.

It is recommended that employers encourage a formal assessment of the ethical values of their leaders and develop a feedback mechanism to increase corporate supervisors' self-awareness of key leadership values. Organizations should continue to delineate ongoing assessment and ethical leadership assessment through a feedback process. Human resource departments should place more significance on key values such as responsibility, respect, fairness, and honesty on the components of leadership assessment and development. Part of the challenge for many corporate supervisors is the lack of awareness relating to key leadership ethical values that drive effective leadership practices. Providing emerging leaders with an opportunity to use ethical values may lead to greater awareness of ethical dilemmas, and the activation of ethical decision making will influence organizational success. Organizational leaders responsible for hiring, training, and managing employees should take steps to ensure that corporate supervisors behave ethically to all stakeholders connected directly or indirectly to the organization. These steps must involve the implementation of a code of conduct that requires leaders to respect their employees, treat them fairly, take responsibility for their actions, and commit to acting honestly. Periodic training regarding the importance of ethical behavior could also be undertaken for corporate supervisors and employees.

FUTURE RESEARCH DIRECTIONS

The objective of this chapter was to conduct research on leadership ethics and organizational success. As such, it is important for an experimental study to be conducted on leadership ethics and organizational success. This is necessary to validate the analysis and recommendations derived in this study. To be specific, a quantitative meta-analysis design may be considered to contrast and combine results from the present and related studies to identify patterns among the study results and sources of disagreement among those results, causing interesting relationships to be revealed in the context of multiple studies.

Lastly, a qualitative study using a phenomenological inquiry is recommended to provide corporate leaders the opportunity to give further feedback regarding their ethical experiences and how they relate to organizational success. A phenomenological inquiry will give research participants an opportunity to express their actual behaviors and perspectives, which can be used to develop instruments that will be useful in measuring ethical leadership behaviors and organizational success.

CONCLUSION

Leaders have a strong influence on their employees and the organization. Ethical leadership in any organization is a complex topic that starts with a simple principle: If leaders and followers do the right thing, then unethical conduct can be avoided (Yukl, 2013). Doing what is right can only be achieved if leaders know what is right and are prepared to do what is right. Personal integrity is important for coexistence in organizations. The results of this chapter present evidence of how leadership ethics relate to organizational success.

Alternative methods for evaluating leadership ethics were explored. However, the Project Management Institute (2010) defined a professional code of conduct that included respect, responsibility, fairness, and honesty as key ethical values required for leadership effectiveness. Leadership traits and skills were discussed. Kirkpatrick and Locke (1996) noted that leadership was once taught as a matter of birth and that leaders were born, not made. Their study found that there are six main factors that differentiate leaders from nonleaders: drive, desire to lead, honesty and integrity, self-confidence, cognitive ability, and knowledge of the business.

Elements of integrity and ethical leadership theory were explored relative to business and leadership ethics. Brown and Treviño (2014) noted that ethical leadership theory accounts for how a leader's ethical conduct or behavior can influence his or her followers' ethical decisions and actions. According to ethical leadership theory, followers' ethical decisions are influenced by social exchange processes and the use of performance management in making employees accountable for their actions and conduct (Brown & Treviño, 2014).

The business failures of Enron, WorldCom, Tyco, Adelphia, and others should serve as examples of how leadership misconduct can have a negative effect on organizational success. The failures in all these companies were a result of unethical conduct by their leaders. Leadership misconduct that leads to business failure in organizations underpins the importance of leadership ethics and organizational success. This chapter presents evidence of how leadership ethics relate to organizational success. Employees model the behaviors of their supervisors, and supervisors who behave in an ethical manner can have an impact on the ethical behavior of their employees.

REFERENCES

Adams, V. H., Snyder, C. R., Rand, K. L., Kings, E. A., Sigmon, D. R., & Pulvers, K. M. (2003). Hope in the workplace. In R. A. Giacalone & C. L. Jurkiewicz (Eds.), *Handbook of workplace spirituality and organizational performance* (pp. 367–377). New York, NY: Sharpe.

Ashcraft, D. (2011). *Personality theories workbook* (5th ed.). Belmont, CA: Cengage.

Ashforth, B. E., Gioia, D. A., Robinson, S. L., & Treviño, L. K. (2008). Re-viewing organizational corruption. *Academy of Management Review, 33*(3), 670–684. doi:http://dx.org/10.5465/AMR.2008.32465714

Bacha, E., & Walker, S. (2013). The relationship between transformational leadership and followers' perceptions of fairness. *Journal of Business Ethics, 116*(3), 667–680. doi:10.1007/s10551-012-1507-z

Bass, B. M. (1985). *Leadership and performance beyond expectations.* New York, NY: The Free Press.

Bass, B. M. (1990). *Handbook of leadership, theory, research, and managerial applications.* New York, NY: The Free Press.

Bass, B. M., & Steidlmeier, P. (1999). Ethics, character, and authentic transformational leadership behavior. *The Leadership Quarterly, 10*(2), 181–217. doi:(99)00016-810.1016/S1048-9843

Brown, M. E., & Mitchell, M. S. (2015). Ethical and unethical leadership: Exploring new avenues for future research. *Business Ethics Quarterly, 20*(4), 583–616.

Brown, M. E., & Treviño, L. K. (2014). Do role models matter? An investigation of role modeling as an antecedent of perceived ethical leadership. *Journal of Business Ethics, 122*(4), 587–598. doi:10.1007/s10551-013-1769-0

Brown, M. E., Treviño, L. K., & Harrison, D. A. (2005). Ethical leadership: A social learning perspective for construct development and testing. *Organizational Behavior and Human Decision Processes, 97*(2), 117–134. doi:10.1016/j.obhdp.2005.03.002

Bureau of Labor Statistics. (2010). *Labor force statistics from the current population survey.* Retrieved from http://www.bls.gov/cps/

Colquitt, J. A. (2012). Organizational justice. In S. W. J. Kozlowski (Ed.), *The Oxford handbook of organizational psychology* (Vol. 1, pp. 526–547). New York, NY: Oxford University Press.

Cortina, L. M., Magley, V. J., Williams, J. H., & Langhout, R. D. (2001). Incivility in the workplace: Incidence and impact. *Journal of Occupational Health Psychology, 6*(1), 64–80. doi:10.1037/1076-8998.6.1.64 PMID:11199258

Dadhich, A., & Bhal, K. T. (2008). Ethical leader behaviour and leader-member exchange as predictors of subordinate behaviors. *Vikalpa: The Journal for Decision Makers, 33*(4), 15–25. doi:http:/dx.org/10.1177/0256090920080402

Daft, R. (2007). *The leadership experience* (4th ed.). Mason, OH: Thomson.

Dyck, B., & Neubert, M. (2008). *Management: Current practices and new directions.* Boston, MA: Houghton Mifflin Harcourt.

Feldman, D. C., & Alnold, H. J. (1983). *Managing individual and group behavior in organizations.* New York, NY: McGraw Hill.

Freeman, R. E., Harrison, J. S., Wicks, A. C., Parmar, B. L., & De Colle, S. (2010). *Stakeholder theory: The state of the art.* Cambridge, MA: Cambridge University Press. doi:10.1017/CBO9780511815768

Frisch, C., & Huppenbauer, M. (2014). New insights into ethical leadership: A qualitative investigation of the experiences of executive ethical leaders. *Journal of Business Ethics, 123*(1), 23–43. http:/dx.org/10.1007/s10551-013-1797-9

Gandolfi, F. (2012). A conceptual discussion of transformational leadership and intercultural competence. *Review of International Comparative Management, 13*(4), 522–534.

Germain, M. L. (2012). Traits and skills theories as the nexus between leadership and expertise: Reality or fallacy? *Performance Improvement, 51*(5), 32–39. doi:10.1002/pfi.21265

Germain, M. L., & Tejeda, M. J. (2009). *Development and preliminary validation of a psychometric measure of expertise.* New Orleans, LA: Society for Industrial and Organizational Psychology. doi:10.1037/e518422013-695

Giberson, T. R., Resick, C. J., & Dickson, M. W. (2005). Embedding leader characteristics: An examination of homogeneity of personality and values in organizations. *The Journal of Applied Psychology, 90*(5), 1002–1010. doi:10.1037/0021-9010.90.5.1002 PMID:16162072

Giessner, S., & Quaquebeke, N. (2011). Using a relational models perspective to understand normatively appropriate conduct in ethical leadership. *Journal of Business Ethics, 95*(S1), 43–55. doi:10.1007/s10551-011-0790-4

Goldman, A., & Tabak, N. (2010). Perception of ethical climate and its relationship to nurses' demographic characteristics and job satisfaction. *Nursing Ethics, 17*(2), 233–246. http:/dx.org/10.1177/0969733009352048

Graen, G. B., & Cashman, J. (1975). A role-making model of leadership in formal organizations: A developmental approach. In J. G. Hunt & L. L. Larson (Eds.), *Leadership frontiers* (pp. 143–165). Kent, OH: Kent State University Press.

Grant, A. M. (2012). Leading with meaning: Beneficiary contact, prosocial impact, and the performance effects of transformational leadership. *Academy of Management Journal, 55*(2), 458–476. doi:10.5465/amj.2010.0588

Hellriegel, D., Slocum, J. W., & Jackson, S. E. (2002). *Management: A competency-based approach* (9th ed.). Cincinnati, OH: South-Western.

Holzer, A. (2012, August 31). Stanford officials face civil charges. *Wall Street Journal, 259*(52), C3.

Jin, K. K., Drozdenko, R., & DeLoughy, S. (2013). The role of corporate value clusters in ethics, social responsibility, and performance: A study of financial professionals and implications for the financial meltdown. *Journal of Business Ethics, 112*(1), 15–24. doi:10.1007/s10551-012-1227-4

Jones, J. M. (2011, December 12). Record 64% rate honesty, ethics of members of congress low. *Politics*. Retrieved from http://www.gallup.com/poll/151460/Record-Rate-Honesty-Ethics-Members-Congress-Low.aspx

Kalshoven, K., Den Hartog, D. N., & De Hoogh, A. H. B. (2011). Ethical leadership at work questionnaire (ELW): Development and validation of a multidimensional measure. *The Leadership Quarterly, 22*(1), 51–69. doi:10.1016/j.leaqua.2010.12.007

Keung, E. K. (2011). *What factors of cultural intelligence predict transformational leadership: A study of international school leaders* (Doctoral dissertation). Liberty University, Lynchburg, VA.

Kirkpatrick, S. A., & Locke, E. A. (1996). Direct and indirect effects of three charismatic leadership components on performance and attitudes. *The Journal of Applied Psychology, 81*(1), 36–51. doi:10.1037/0021-9010.81.1.36

Kraten, M. (2013). Why Libor manipulation matters. *The CPA Journal, 83*(9), 6–10.

Kroll, K. (2012). Keeping the company safe: Preventing and detecting fraud. *Financial Executive, 28*(7), 20–23.

Kulkarni, S., & Ramamoorthy, N. (2011). Leader–member exchange, subordinate stewardship, and hierarchical governance. *International Journal of Human Resource Management, 22*(13), 2770–2793. doi:10.1080/09585192.2011.599954

Kumar, N., & Lee, C. C. (2014). Regulatory focus and workplace behavior. *Journal of General Management, 39*(4), 27–53. doi:10.1177/030630701403900403

Leroy, H., Palanski, M. E., & Simons, T. (2012). Authentic leadership and behavioral integrity as drivers of follower commitment and performance. *Journal of Business Ethics, 107*(3), 255–264. doi:10.1007/s10551-011-1036-1

Lian, L. K., & Tui, L. G. (2012). Leadership styles and organizational citizenship behavior: The mediating effect of subordinates' competence and downward influence tactics. *The Journal of Applied Business and Economics, 13*(2), 59–96.

Lok, P., & Crawford, J. (2004). The effect of organizational culture and leadership style on job satisfaction and organizational commitment: A cross-national comparison. *Journal of Management Development, 23*(4), 321–338. doi:10.1108/02621710410529785

Marsh, C. (2013). Business executives' perceptions of ethical leadership and its development. *Journal of Business Ethics, 114*(3), 565–582. doi:10.1007/s10551-012-1366-7

Mayer, D. M., Aquino, K., Greenbaum, R. L., & Kuenzi, M. (2012). Who displays ethical leadership, and why does it matter? An examination of antecedents and consequences of ethical leadership. *Academy of Management Journal, 55*(1), 151–171. doi:10.5465/amj.2008.0276

McCrae, R. R., & Costa, P. T. Jr. (1997). Personality trait structure as a human universal. *The American Psychologist, 52*(5), 509–516. doi:10.1037/0003-066X.52.5.509 PMID:9145021

McCuddy, M. K. (2012). The pursuit of profits in different industries: What is the impact of practice of business ethics? *Journal of the Academy of Business & Economics, 12*(5), 67–78.

Milgram, S. (1974). *Obedience to authority: An experimental view.* New York, NY: Harper & Row.

Nahavandi, A. (2003). *The art and science of leadership* (3rd ed.). Upper Saddle River, NJ: Prentice Hall.

Neubert, M. J., Wu, C., & Roberts, J. A. (2013). The influence of ethical leadership and regulatory focus on employee outcomes. *Business Ethics Quarterly, 23*(2), 269–296. doi:10.5840/beq201323217

Orszag, P. R. (2008). *The effects of recent turmoil in the financial markets on retirement security.* Retrieved from http://democrats-edworkforce.house.gov/imo/media/doc/2008-10-07-PeterOrszag.pdf

Osei, E. T. (2015). *The relationships between corporate supervisors' ethics-related actions and organizational success* (Doctoral dissertation). Available from ProQuest Dissertations and Theses database. (UMI No. 3684883)

Podsakoff, N. P., Whiting, S. W., Podsakoff, P. M., & Blume, B. D. (2009). Individual- and organizational-level consequences of organizational citizenship behaviors: A meta-analysis. *The Journal of Applied Psychology, 94*(1), 122–141. doi:10.1037/a0013079 PMID:19186900

Project Management Institute. (2010). *Code of ethics and professional conduct.* Retrieved from https://www.pmi.org/about/ethics/code

Reuber, A., & Fischer, E. (2010). Organizations behaving badly: When are discreditable actions likely to damage organizational reputation? *Journal of Business Ethics, 93*(1), 39–50. doi:10.1007/s10551-009-0180-3

Riggio, R. E. (2009). Are you a transformational leader? *Psychology Today*. Retrieved from https://www.psychologytoday.com/blog/cutting-edge-leadership/200903/are-you-transformational-leader

Schuh, S., Zhang, X., & Tian, P. (2013). For the good or the bad? Interactive effects of transformational moral and authoritarian leadership behaviors. *Journal of Business Ethics, 116*(3), 629–640. doi:10.1007/s10551-012-1486-0

Sharif, M. M., & Scandura, T. S. (2014). Do perceptions of ethical conduct matter during organizational change? Ethical leadership and employee involvement. *Journal of Business Ethics, 124*(2), 185–196. doi:10.1007/s10551-013-1869-x

Shweta, J., & Srirang, J. (2013). Leader-member exchange: A critique of theory & practice. *Journal of Management & Public Policy, 4*(2), 42–53.

Stahl, G. K., & Sully de Luque, M. (2014). Antecedents of responsible leader behavior: A research synthesis, conceptual framework and agenda for future research. *Academy of Management Perspectives, 28*(3), 235–254. doi:doi:10.5465/amp.2013.0126

Steinbauer, R., Renn, R., Taylor, R., & Njoroge, P. (2014). Ethical leadership and followers' moral judgment: The role of followers' perceived accountability and self-leadership. *Journal of Business Ethics, 120*(3), 381–392. doi:10.1007/s10551-013-1662-x

Tanner, C., Brugger, A., Van Schie, S., & Lebherz, C. (2010). Actions speak louder than words: The benefits of ethical behaviors of leaders. *The Journal of Psychology, 218*(4), 225–233.

Taylor, S. G. (2010). *Cold looks and hot tempers: Individual-level effects on incivility in the workplace* (Doctoral dissertation). Louisiana State University and Agricultural and Mechanical College, Baton Rouge, LA.

Toor, S. R., & Ofori, G. (2009). Ethical leadership: Examining the relationships with full range leadership model, employee outcomes, and organizational culture. *Journal of Business Ethics, 90*(4), 533–547. doi:10.1007/s10551-009-0059-3

Ünsar, A., & Karalar, S. (2013). The effect of personality traits on leadership behavior: A research of students of business administration. *Economic Review: Journal of Economics & Business, 11*(2), 45–56.

VanSandt, C. V., & Neck, C. P. (2003). Bridging ethics and self-leadership: Overcoming ethical discrepancies between employee and organizational standards. *Journal of Business Ethics, 43*(4), 363–38. doi:10.1023/A:1023009728390

Waldman, A., & Galvin, M. (2008). Alternative perspectives of responsible leadership. *Organizational Dynamics*, *37*(4), 327–341. doi:10.1016/j.orgdyn.2008.07.001

Walumbwa, F. O., Mayer, D. M., Wang, P., Wang, H., Workman, K., & Christensen, A. L. (2011). Linking ethical leadership to employee performance: The roles of leader–member exchange, self-efficacy, and organizational identification. *Organizational Behavior and Human Decision Processes*, *115*(2), 204–213. doi:10.1016/j.obhdp.2010.11.002

Webley, S., & Werner, A. (2008). Corporate codes of ethics: Necessary but not sufficient. *Business Ethics (Oxford, England)*, *17*(4), 405–415. doi:10.1111/j.1467-8608.2008.00543.x

Wilmoth, W., & O'Brien, W. (2011). White-collar crime with your company as the victim: Conducting a fraud investigation. *Energy & Mineral Law Institute*, *32*(1), 4–31.

Yang, C. (2014). Does ethical leadership lead to happy workers? A study on the impact of ethical leadership, subjective well-being, and life happiness in the Chinese culture. *Journal of Business Ethics*, *123*(3), 513–525. doi:10.1007/s10551-013-1852-6

Yueru, M., Weibo, C., Ribbens, B. A., & Juanmel, Z. (2013). Linking ethical leadership to employee creativity: Knowledge sharing and self-efficacy as mediators. *Social Behavior and Personality*, *41*(9), 1409–1420. doi:10.2224/sbp.2013.41.9.1409

Yukl, G. A. (2013). *Leadership in organizations* (8th ed.). Albany, NY: Pearson.

Zabihollah, R. (2003). Causes, consequences, and deterrence of financial statement fraud. *Critical Perspectives on Accounting*, *16*(3), 227–298. doi:10.1016/S1045-2354(03)00072-8

Zaccaro, S. J. (2007). Trait-based perspectives of leadership. *The American Psychologist*, *62*(1), 6–16. doi:10.1037/0003-066X.62.1.6 PMID:17209675

Zhang, Y., LePine, J. A., Buckman, B. R., & Wei, F. (2014). It's not fair . . . or is it? The role of justice and leadership in explaining work stressor–job performance relationships. *Academy of Management Journal*, *57*(3), 675–697. doi:10.5465/amj.2011.1110

Zimbardo, P. G. (1972). *The psychology of imprisonment: Privation, power and pathology*. Palo Alto, CA: Stanford University Press.

KEY TERMS AND DEFINITIONS

Corporate Codes of Conduct: Corporate codes of conduct refer to the practical accepted instrument that controls employee behavior in creating an established socially responsible organizational culture. Corporate codes of conduct are used to communicate responsible business ways of doing things and to establish an ethical organizational culture. The codes are used fundamentally to establish policies within the firm.

Ethics: Ethics is the process of engaging in a moral decision of right or wrong. Ethics are mostly descriptive and relate to the conduct of business organizations with stakeholders. It involves making a choice between alternatives of right or wrong. Decision making within an ethical framework requires acceptance by people in a group or society.

Fairness: Fairness is being impartial, just, objective, or free of favoritism. Fairness ensures clarity in decision making and requires one to examine each scenario to avoid being partial and subjective. It creates a platform for accessing information, discloses areas within the organization susceptible to conflict of interest, and prevents favoritism and discrimination.

Honesty: Honesty is being truthful in one's statements and actions. Honesty means that truth is maintained in all instances, devoid of deceit and the telling of lies. The act of honesty requires that information provided is free from lies and commitment within organizations. It ensures that information given to third parties is accurate and not misleading.

Organizational Culture: Organizational culture refers to the way people behave and do things within the organization. Organizational culture provides structuring within the organization in terms of what is acceptable and not acceptable and defines the organization's own set of rules, beliefs, and values. In many instances, the organizational culture refers to policies that are written or those that are not. The way an individual behaves within an organization is either formalized through the organizational codes of conduct or through accepted norms and values regarded within that organization as the way of doing things.

Organizational Values: Values are ideas and general standards that are derived within the organization and form the main principles of that organization. Organizational values direct and guide the individual to act in a responsible manner. They also direct the behavioral work patterns of the organization and form the core management practices over time. The organizational values of an entity reflect the individual and composite values of managers and employees that are encapsulated within the organization's code of conduct.

Respect: Respect is accepting the opinion of others and regarding those opinions without prejudice. Respect also embodies the understanding and honoring of other customs, listening to other perspectives, attempting to resolve disagreements with others, behaving professionally, negotiating fairly, and avoiding abuse of authority. Respect involves fair negotiation and preventing abuse of leadership authority.

Responsibility: Responsible behavior of corporate supervisors is defined as the acceptance of ownership for choices made by the supervisors. Responsibility also includes acting in the best interest of stakeholders, meeting commitments, admitting and correcting mistakes, protecting confidential information, understanding and obeying the law, and reporting unethical or unlawful behavior.

Chapter 3
A Swift Kick:
Russian Diplomatic Practice in Bulgaria, 1879–1883

Mikhail Sergeyevich Rekun
Independent Researcher, USA

ABSTRACT

This chapter examines the unusually swift downturn in Russo-Bulgarian relations between 1879 and 1883. In 1879, relations between the two countries were unusually good, founded on a basis of mutual sympathy, geopolitical necessity, and strong administrative ties. By 1883, however, a series of lapses in Russian diplomatic practice damaged Russo-Bulgarian relations to the point that all of Bulgaria's political elite was united in opposition to the Russians, and by 1886 diplomatic relations were severed altogether. This chapter examines three incidents in particular – the Titles Controversy of late 1879/early 1880, the Coup of 1881, and the tenure of Generals L. N. Sobolev and A. V. Kaul'bars in 1882-1883. Ultimately, this chapter demonstrates how flawed diplomatic practice may result in undesirable foreign policy outcomes.

INTRODUCTION

In early September of 1885, Prince Alexander von Battenberg, the German-born Prince (Knîāz) of Bulgaria, complained to a pair of Russian agents that there was no educated person in Bulgaria who had not been initially charmed by Russia, only to later receive "*des coups de pied dans le derrier*," or a kick in the rear (L'vov, 1886, pp. 100-101). This might be considered an odd comment for the Prince of Bulgaria

DOI: 10.4018/978-1-5225-2650-6.ch003

to make. After all, not quite a decade earlier, the Russian Empire had gone to war against the Ottoman Turks for the liberation of Bulgaria. It was to the Russian Empire that Bulgaria owed its independence. The Russian Tsar Alexander II was hailed as the *Tsar-Liberator*, with statues and boulevards named in his honor in the Bulgarian capital of Sofia. Battenberg himself was a minor German princeling elevated to the Bulgarian throne based on the strength of his close connections to the Russian Imperial Family; his aunt was the Empress Maria Alexandrovna, wife of Tsar Alexander II, born Marie of Hesse and by Rhine (Jelavich, 1958). In truth, by 1885, there was not a soul in Europe who would have been shocked by Battenberg's statements. Over the course of seven years, from 1879 to 1886, a series of Russian diplomatic and military agents had managed to dismantle Russia's relationship with Bulgaria.

Initial relations between the two countries were excellent. In 1878, twenty-three thousand Bulgarians signed a petition of thanksgiving addressed to Alexander II (Crampton, 2007). The Prince of Bulgaria was also the nephew of the Russian Tsar, and the Bulgarian Minister of War and the entire Bulgarian officer corps were Russian officers on detached duty from the Imperial Army (Crampton, 2007). Finally, Bulgaria relied upon Russian support to avoid being reconquered by the Ottoman Turks. There were therefore substantial emotional, administrative, and geopolitical reasons for relations between the two countries to be very strong.

Still, by 1886, relations had deteriorated to such a degree that St. Petersburg backed a coup against Battenberg. Russia considered occupying the country, and when that was deemed impractical, she chose to sever diplomatic relations—a state of affairs that lasted until 1894. The primary cause of this turn of events was the behavior of Russian military and diplomatic agents in Bulgaria, who managed to behave so obnoxiously that, in the words of the British Ambassador, they managed "to make the rival parties among the Bulgarians forget their animosities for the moment and united them against the [Russians]" (Victoria, 1926, pp. 444-445). The disintegration of Russo-Bulgarian relations occurred with a shocking swiftness, and it was a stunning defeat for Russian ambitions in the Balkans.

This chapter discusses three incidents to demonstrate how precisely the Russian agents in Bulgaria managed to severely damage Russo-Bulgarian relations. It is argued that lapses in diplomatic practices on behalf of the Russian Empire allowed them to cause such damage. The first event examined is the struggle between Prince Battenberg and General P.D. Parensov over the question of royal titles. The second is the royal coup organized by General Johann Casimir Ehrnrooth in 1881. The third and final example describes the tenures of Generals L. N. Sobolev and A. V. Kaul'bars as Bulgarian cabinet ministers from 1882 to 1883. Each of these events illustrate a particular flaw in Russian diplomatic practices that had significant ramifications for Russo-Bulgarian relations.

LITERATURE REVIEW AND METHODOLOGY

A Russian historian, Alfred J. Rieber, stated that "the historiography of Russian foreign policy has never enjoyed much of an intellectual vogue" (cited in Ragsdale & Ponomarev, 1993, p. 360). Rieber offered various reasons for this dearth of coverage, including simple preference for the drama of the Russian Revolution and the difficulty of gaining access to relevant sources, particularly during the Cold War. Still, over the years, many historians have done work on Russian diplomatic history, and of those a few have examined this period of Russo-Bulgarian relations.

Initially, research into the deterioration of Russo-Bulgarian relations was marked by memoirs and nationalistic histories. In the early 1920s, Count Egon Caesar Corti used the Battenberg private papers to write a pair of gossipy works: *Alexander von Battenberg* and *The Downfall of Three Dynasties.* Historians in Bulgaria and Russia also wrote on the subject; examples include Simeon Radev's *Founders of Contemporary Bulgaria* (1911) or S.D. Skazkin's *The End of the Austro-Russo-German Alliance* (1928). Today, these works are of limited analytical value, nonetheless, the documents Corti and his contemporaries collected will be valuable resources for scholars for generations.

Cyril Edwin Black was the first prominent Western historian to research Bulgaria's early independent history, writing *The Establishment of Constitutional Government in Bulgaria* at Princeton in 1943. Black's book was primarily a history of internal Bulgarian politics, but it also discussed Russian behavior. Black's work was followed by the Balkan nationalist historian Charles Jelavich's 1958 book, *Tsarist Russia and Balkan Nationalism.* Jelavich's work heavily emphasized the importance of Bulgarian nationalism in explaining the disintegration of Russo-Bulgarian diplomatic relations in the years after 1879. The trinity of Cold War Bulgarian scholars is completed by George Kennan and his 1979 book: *The Decline of Bismarck's European Order*, which includes a long section on Bulgaria's immediate post-war independence. Kennan's research primarily focused on the impacts of Russian court politics on the events. All three publications were remarkable for their insightful analyses, rigorous use of evidence, and well-articulated arguments. Unfortunately, all three authors had to deal with the same problem; they had limited access to the original Bulgarian and Russian material. They made do as best they could, using the writings of British, German, and Austrian diplomats in Bulgaria extensively. However, despite their best efforts, the diplomatic records in Russia and the personal diaries of important Bulgarian politicians remained locked away behind the Iron Curtain. Consequently, while all three scholars wrote about Russian behavior a great deal, they treated it as an external factor, a fact of political life that is acknowledged but not really explained.

This changed in 1992; however, the end of the Cold War signaled a sudden glut of research material at the exact same time, and thus official interest in Russian and Balkan history underwent a sharp downturn. The result was that the scholars who remained in the field had an embarrassment of scholarly riches, with the most attention being devoted to the history of the USSR, logically enough. Russo-Bulgarian relations in the post-independence field merited the occasional chapter, but no one has examined the subject in heavy detail. In the West, the leading historian of Bulgaria today is R. J. Crampton, now a Professor Emeritus at Oxford University. His final work on the subject, *Bulgaria*, was published in 2007 and takes advantage of a vast array of Bulgarian sources. Still, while he devoted some space to Russian influence in Bulgaria, Crampton was more interested in the effects of the dissolution rather than its causes. In Russia, A.V. Ignát'ev and V.M. Khevrolina's *Istoriiā vneshneĭ politiki Rossii (History of Russian Foreign Relations)*, published in 2011, also devotes a section to Russo-Bulgarian relations. They argued that while there were important diplomatic reasons for the breakdown of Russo-Bulgarian relations (including the lack of tact on the part of Russian agents), there was also an economic aspect. In brief, the two countries' economies were too similar and had nothing to gain from close relations, but the authors did not delve into the reasons that Russian agents behaved so poorly to begin with.

This is the gap in the scholarship that this author hopes to fill. To do so, this chapter draws upon considerable archival research. Methodologically, this is a fairly standard multiarchival research project. For this chapter, the most important archives used were the Central State Archives (TsDA) in Sofia, Bulgaria, and the Russian State Military-Historical Archive (RGVIA) and the Archive of the Foreign Policy of the Russian Empire (AVPRI), both in Moscow, Russia. Other useful archives were the State Archive of the Russia Federation (GARF) and the Russian State Library (RSL), both also in Moscow. The material used for this project consisted primarily of published memoirs, unpublished diaries (most notably of Konstantin Stoilov, a prominent Bulgarian politician from 1879 to 1883), diplomatic correspondence, and journalistic accounts (primarily the writings of Evgeniĭ L'vov, 1886).

BACKGROUND

In 1876, during the Great Eastern Crisis, which was a pan-Balkan conflagration of anti-Turkish war and revolution, the Bulgarian Revolutionary Central Committee launched an uprising against their Ottoman overlords. It was a fiasco. The rebels lacked organization, armaments, communication, and strategy, and they had drastically overestimated both their popular support among the Bulgarian people and the degree to which they would catch the Ottomans off-guard. From a military viewpoint, the April Uprising was a complete and utter failure (Crampton, 2007), but it guaranteed the creation of an independent Bulgaria. Stretched thin and pressed on multiple sides by uprisings and armies, the Ottomans dispatched irregular troops, or *bazhibazouks*, to suppress the uprising. These troops carried out a campaign of bloody vengeance upon the Bulgarian population, with the most famous incident being the Massacre at Batak, where *bashibazouks* slaughtered some five thousand people, many of whom were women and children seeking refuge in the village church (Crampton, 2007). These reprisals became known as the Bulgarian Atrocities, and they attracted worldwide attention, especially after an American journalist, Januarius MacGahan, visited Batak and published a haunting account of the destruction. MacGahan (1876) wrote in the *London Daily News* that:

…There were little curly heads there in that festering mass, crushed down by heavy stones; little feet not as long as your finger on which the flesh was dried hard, by the ardent heat before it had time to decompose; little baby hands stretched out as if for help; babes that had died wondering at the bright gleam of sabres and the red hands of the fierce-eyed men who wielded them; children who had died shrinking with fright and terror; young girls who had died weeping and sobbing and begging for mercy; mothers who died trying to shield their little ones with their own weak bodies, all lying there together, festering in one horrid mass. (pp. 5-6)

In short order, Bulgaria became a global sensation, and politicians and public figures around the world condemned the Ottomans. Nowhere was public opinion quite as agitated as it was in the Russian Empire, however. The Russian press published a stream of articles urging Russia to intervene. For example, Nikolaev Vestnik wrote that "In Bulgaria, more than 150 villages, places, churches, and monasteries have been turned into ruins… [this will continue] until Russia, the natural defenders of the Slavs, does not decide to energetically demand the improvement of their condition" (cited in Narochnitškiĭ, 1978, p. 114). Over the course of the following year, more articles, public petitions, and rallies heightened the war-fever to a crescendo, and in April, the Russo-Turkish War of 1877-78 began.

Though hard-fought, the war ended in a Russian victory, and Count N.P. Ignát'ev, one of Russia's best diplomats and a noted Panslav, dictated terms to the defeated Ottomans. The resulting Treaty of San Stefano allowed Bulgaria to gain independence as an enormous state, one stretching from the Black Sea to the Aegean and incorporating the historic areas of Thrace, Moesia, and Macedonia. Unfortunately, Ignát'ev had considered the reactions of the other Great Powers of Europe (Ragsdale & Ponomarev, 1993). The British, who had for generations used the Ottomans as a buffer state against Russian ambitions, and the Austro-Hungarians, who had no interest in a large Russian client state in the Balkans, managed to force a revision of the Treaty of San Stefano at the Congress of Berlin of 1878. There, Bulgaria was split into three parts: the effectively independent Principality of Bulgaria in the north, the autonomous Ottoman province of Eastern Rumelia in the south, and the regular Ottoman province of Macedonia in the southwest. Thus, Bulgaria was ushered into the brotherhood of nations (Jelavich, 1958).

This entire tale is important for a few key reasons. First, it establishes the depth of the solidarity between Russia and Bulgaria before 1879. The Bulgarians were being massacred by the Ottomans, and the Russian Empire spent blood and capital to liberate Bulgaria and to create the kind of state of which Bulgarian nationalists could only fantasize. It also establishes shared geopolitical ambitions. For the Russian Empire, control of the Dardanelles, the straits between the Black Sea and the Mediterranean, had been a key policy goal for almost a century. The aid of Bulgaria, a large and powerful client state right on Constantinople's doorstep, would bring that goal much closer to reality. Meanwhile, the Bulgarians were keenly aware that without a Great Power protector, they would have no defense against Ottoman efforts to bring them back into the fold, a turn of events that the Massacre at Batak and similar atrocities had made loathsome to them, or any hope of regaining the territory lost at the Congress of Berlin. Moreover, of the two possible protectors, Russia was far more convivial than Austria-Hungary.

In any case, while the Congress of Berlin divided Bulgaria into pieces, it was still widely recognized that the Russians would be the Principality's informal overlords. The Russian occupation forces were charged with administering the newly independent Principality and overseeing the vital task of writing a constitution. The new Bulgarian Prince would be selected by Tsar Alexander II, and even after the occupation forces left, the entire officer corps of the Bulgarian army, up to and including the Minister of War, would consist of Russian officers on detached duty. The Russian Consul-General, the agent of the Russian Ministry of Foreign Affairs, was to be an extremely influential figure in the fledgling state (Kuťsarov, 2008).

In 1879, a grand Constituent National Assembly in Tarnovo, Bulgaria, gathered to write a constitution. The Assembly was a highly representative body; the Bulgarian historian Stefan Balamezov observed in 1919 that "nobody has denied either then or since that it included absolutely all the prominent Bulgarians of the Principality" (cited in Black, 1943, p. 70). Yet, the Tarnovo Constitution, as it became known, was not a successful document. It created a powerful legislature, but it also entrusted the monarch with a great many executive powers. It also lacked much in the way of mechanisms for resolving disputes between the two. It was an unusually liberal document for its time and place, with universal male suffrage, unlimited freedom of movement, unlimited freedom of assembly, and a guaranteed freedom of the press. This would eventually lead to trouble.

RUSSO-BULGARIAN RELATIONS, 1879-1883

The Titles Controversy

By the late spring of 1879, Bulgaria was ready to begin its existence as an independent nation, or as a reasonable facsimile thereof at least. The Russian occupation forces were withdrawing, there was a new constitution, and the Bulgarian political scene was already splitting into two political parties. The Liberal Party led by Petko Karavelov, the younger brother of the revolutionary Lyuben Karavelov, was the dominant party in the legislature (Crampton, 1983). It was a party of the middle class and liberal values, and it supported a powerful legislature responsible to the people. The Conservatives, led by the triumvirate of Konstantin Stoilov, Dimit"r Grekov, and Grigor Nachovich, were the party of the old Bulgarian elites and favored a stronger executive branch (Black, 1943).

Prince Alexander von Battenberg, the new Prince of Bulgaria selected by the Tsar and confirmed by the Bulgarian National Assembly, now entered the scene. The second son of Prince Alexander of Hesse-Darmstadt, Battenberg was a young man of limited prospects, one of the swarm of German princelings left politically unemployed by the Unification of Germany a decade prior; however, he was handsome, charming, had served in the Russo-Turkish War with distinction on the Russian side, and had absolutely first-rate political connections. He was a German Prince and a lieutenant in the prestigious Prussian Gardes du Corps. His father was a general in the Austrian army. His aunt was the Empress of Russia. His brother was married to the granddaughter of Queen Victoria (Jelavich, 1958). Unfortunately, Battenberg, while charming and superficially intelligent due to his first-rate education, had a complete lack of political savvy. The German Ambassador to Russia, Hans Lothar von Schweinitz, put it delicately: "the Prince has many excellent qualities...but he is lacking in the gifts of statesmanship" (cited in Black, 1943, pp. 238-239). Battenberg was a military man by temperament, which combined with his youth (he was just twenty-two at the time of his arrival in Bulgaria) led to a great deal of trouble working with the Bulgarian politicians and Russian agents. Battenberg viewed himself as an autocrat, not as a constitutional monarch (Jelavich, 1958).

This swiftly embroiled him in a constitutional squabble with Major-General Pëtr Dmitrievich Parensov, Bulgaria's first Minister of War. Relatively young—thirty-six when he joined the Bulgarian government—Parensov had served in the Russo-Turkish War of 1877-78 and as part of the occupation force that helped craft the Bulgarian state, and he had considerable connections in the Russian government. He was on good terms with D.A. Miliutin, the powerful Russian Minister of War, and his wife was the niece of the Foreign Minister, N.K. Girs (Parensov, 1900). A generally competent and reasonable man, Parensov was not without his flaws. In his memoirs, written many years later, Parensov (1908b) wrote that:

Undoubtedly, I was at fault in a great many things. Major incidents, aside from [Parensov's taking offense at Battenberg over the titles issue, described later] I do not, I confess, recall; speaking of the tone of my actions, I freely admit that in them I was, likely, insufficiently restrained, there was (I admit) too many negative impressions and from that flowed a hot temper; there was not always enough thinking about my actions. (p. 264)

Other accounts, such as that of Adolf Koch (1887), Battenberg's chaplain, are essentially in agreement with Parensov's own memories. He could be hot-tempered and lacking in diplomatic tact. Parensov was also a self-admitted Panslav, which meant that he tended to be suspicious of the German Battenberg.

As one might expect, Battenberg and Parensov swiftly came to (political) blows. Battenberg fervently despised the Tarnovo Constitution, considered it "ridiculously liberal," and sought any means possible to change it (Corti, 1954, p. 256). The problem was that any legal changes in the constitution would require the support of the legislature, and the Liberals, who dominated that body, had no interest whatsoever in weakening their position and strengthening Battenberg's. Furthermore, any extralegal changes would have required the backing of the Russian Empire, who, after all, made up the officer corps of the army, and this was likewise not forthcoming. As Tsar Alexander II explained to his nephew, any effort on Russia's part to replace or remove the Tarnovo Constitution could be seen as Russia "exercising illegal intervention in the affairs of the Principality" and could prompt the action of the other Great Powers (cited in Corti, 1934, pp. 372-374). Thus, Parensov soon established himself as the guardian of the Tarnovo Constitution—becoming a hero of the Liberal Party in the process—to Battenberg's anger and the consternation of the conservative Russian general (Parensov, 1900). The two men eventually fought over a number of political and military matters, among them the Titles Controversy.

The Titles Controversy has the dubious distinction of being the earliest Russo-Bulgarian conflict as well as quite possibly the silliest. The facts of the matter are as follows. According to the Tarnovo Constitution, Battenberg, as Prince of Bulgaria, was to be addressed as "Светлост" ("Your Grace" in English or *Altesse Serénissime* in French); however, as Prince of Battenberg, the new monarch felt that his proper title should have been "Височество" ("Your Highness" or *Altesse*). No sooner had Battenberg arrived in the country, than he tried to do something about this. In July of 1879, at the formal dinner celebrating the inauguration of the first Bulgarian Cabinet, Battenberg gathered his ministers—all drawn from the Conservative Party—and ordered them to refer to him as Highness from then on. The ministers agreed and then went to find Parensov and asked him, as Minister of War, to do likewise; however, Parensov refused, stating that for him to do so would be to violate the Tarnovo Constitution. Parensov pointed out that while for the other ministers, the choice was essentially a private one, Parensov set policy for the Bulgarian army. Thus, the title the troops used for their monarch was a public matter. When pressed, Parensov threatened to resign rather than to agree (Parensov, 1900).

After the dinner, Parensov consulted with the Russian Consul-General, A.P. Davydov, and a compromise was reached. In Bulgarian, the army would continue to refer to Battenberg as "Your Grace," but in French, a useful lingua franca in which the German Prince, Russian officers, and Bulgarian soldiers often communicated in, they would simply use *Altesse*. This meant "Highness," but people already regularly dropped the *Serénissime* in casual conversation (Parensov, 1900). This settled the matter temporarily, but as in many compromises, it did not particularly please anyone. Battenberg complained about the situation regularly, and after one military review, he remarked to Parensov that "only the army calls me 'Your Grace,' at the same time as everyone else, 'Your Highness'" (Parensov, 1906, p. 281). The fact that the Liberal Party made a great deal of political hay out of the matter also failed to smooth tensions.

In September of 1879, Parensov visited St. Petersburg to give a report on political and military matters in Bulgaria, and along the way, he decided to determine the official Russian line on the matter. In a well-run foreign policy establishment, there would have been a single individual or committee charged with ultimately determining what the government's policy should be on any given matter. This was not the case in the Russian Empire in 1879.

Upon arriving in St. Petersburg, Parensov went to report to his immediate superior, the Russian Minister of War Count D.A. Miliutin. After bringing Miliutin up-to-date on the progress of the Bulgarian army, Parensov also mentioned the Titles Controversy. According to Parensov, Miliutin stated that the whole affair was a "stupidity. We were discussing the question of titles [when the Russian Empire was reviewing the Tarnovo Constitution], knowing perfectly well who would be the Prince. Please continue as you were" (Parensov, 1906, p. 521). Cheered, Parensov departed, and the following day went to visit his wife's uncle, the Foreign Minister N.K. Girs. Here, too, Parensov mentioned the Titles Controversy, though he neglected to say that he had already spoken to Miliutin. To the general's surprise, Girs told him, "Basically, my dear, if it makes him happy, why not go and call him 'Highness'?" (Parensov, 1906, pp. 521-522). Parensov left St. Petersburg no more enlightened than when he had arrived. Ultimately, the situation was not resolved until the following year when Tsar Alexander II decided to support Battenberg.

It is easy to be amused by the Titles Controversy; however, the way that the Russian Empire handled the matter illustrates serious flaws in the Russian diplomatic practices of the time. The fact that Girs and Miliutin were unable to put their heads together and set a single line of policy regarding what to call Battenberg shows a greater lack of organization and control in the internal structure of the Russian foreign policy apparatus. There was no one person put in charge of Russia's policy towards Bulgaria, which meant that what Russia's agents should do in any given situation was unclear.

The Coup of 1881

Even when the Russian Empire could agree on a single line of policy, it was not always able to force its agents in Bulgaria to follow. The Bulgarian Coup of 1881 serves as an ample demonstration of this.

By the spring of 1880, the Russian personnel in Bulgaria had been reshuffled. Davydov was replaced as Consul-General by Aleksĕ Mikhaĭlovich Kumani, while Parensov was recalled and Lieutenant-General Johann Casimir Ehrnrooth became the new Bulgarian Minister of War. Ehrnrooth, a veteran of numerous campaigns, and even more importantly, a confidante of the Tsar, was highly placed in the Russian military hierarchy (Stoilov, 1880). The problem for Russo-Bulgarian relations was that while Parensov had been a staunch defender of the Tarnovo Constitution, Ehrnrooth held the document in contempt. Later, Ehrnrooth (1886) would write that the Tarnovo Constitution "with its all-powerful legislature, with its parliamentary games, and so forth, was inappropriate for Bulgaria; so I thought in 1881, so I think today [in 1886]" (p. 478). Ehrnrooth was a man who preferred order, efficiency, and hierarchy, and he had little use for the give-and-take of parliamentary politics.

Over the course of 1880 and into 1881, Bulgaria's tempestuous political situation seemed to worsen. A series of Liberal Minister-Presidents only caused further controversy, with one of them, Dragan Tsankov, managing to become anathematized by the Bulgarian church (Crampton, 1983). Konstantin Stoilov, one of the leaders of the Conservative Party, recorded a meeting with Tsankov on October 6th, 1880, in his diary. Stoilov (1880) wrote:

Long talks with Tsankov on the situation. We don't live politically; we vegetate; chaos; the ministry has no ideas, no plan; hasn't got the strength to take on a single responsibility, especially in complicated times as might come next spring; this ministry's personnel can't take any action; are not trustworthy. (p. 84)

Battenberg was no more pleased than Tsankov. Two weeks later, Stoilov (1880) wrote that "His Highness is greatly overwrought. Again the Constitutional question" (p. 86). Ehrnrooth was likewise in agreement, telling Battenberg that "the Constitution is impossible" (cited in Stoilov, 1880). By the beginning of 1881, it was clear that Bulgaria was drifting towards a constitutional crisis.

However, the fundamental political dynamic in 1881 was the same as it had been two years earlier. To amend or alter the Tarnovo Constitution would have required the active participation of the Liberal Party, which had roughly 80% of the seats in the legislature. This, Tsankov's complaints notwithstanding, they would not do. The only other alternative was some manner of coup, which would require the support of the Russian Empire, and the Bulgarian army was still staffed entirely with Russian officers; however, the Russian Empire had no intention of backing a coup in Bulgaria because this would invite the interference of the other Great Powers.

This last point deserves to be reemphasized. It was the official position of the Russian government to oppose any coup or illegal measure that would result in the removal of the Tarnovo Constitution. Furthermore, this was widely known and clearly communicated to everyone in Bulgaria. Tsar Alexander II sent a letter to Battenberg laying out this position (Corti, 1934). Miĺutin echoed this in his telegrams and letters to Parensov (Parensov, 1908a). Stoilov (1879) wrote that Davydov told him that "Russia cannot and does not have the right to so interfere" in Bulgaria's constitutional problems (p. 60), and Battenberg's chaplain recorded Battenberg complaining at length about the Russian insistence on maintaining the Tarnovo Constitution (Koch, 1887). As late as early April of 1881, Girs instructed the new Consul-General, Mikhaíl Aleksándrovich Khitrovó, that "any attempt to change the state of affairs as they exist at present in Bulgaria through a constitutional reform should be made with extreme prudence and by legal means" (cited in Black, 1943, p. 192). The Russian insistence on maintaining the Tarnovo Constitution was as clear a policy as the Russian Empire had. Subsequent events should be examined with this point in mind.

On March 13th, 1881, the political scene was turned upside down when Tsar Alexander II was assassinated by the People's Will terrorist organization. An event with world-shaking implications for the future course of Russian history, the assassination also influenced Bulgarian history. There was an immediate right turn in Russian politics, as a backlash gathered not just against the People's Will but against any organization or ideology with the least bit of similarity to them—a category that included the Liberal Party of Bulgaria. Though the Liberals denounced the assassination and heaped praise on the Tsar-Liberator's memory, rumors swiftly spread (with a bit of Conservative help) that the Liberals were not quite as upset about the matter as they might have seemed (Black, 1943).

Upon hearing of the assassination, Battenberg immediately rushed to St. Petersburg to pay his respects to the fallen Tsar and to meet his cousin, the new Emperor of Russia, Tsar Alexander III. While there, and sensing that the mood had changed,

Battenberg secured a private audience with the new Tsar and Girs. No records exist of this conversation, but most sources agree that while Alexander III and Girs agreed with Battenberg that the Tarnovo Constitution was a deplorable document, they were unwilling to shift from their previous position (Black, 1943). Thwarted once more, Battenberg returned to Sofia late on April 16th, 1881.

He found Ehrnrooth in an uproar. The Minister of War had received information that the Liberal Party was planning to manipulate the results of the upcoming district council elections. Whether or not the Liberals were in fact planning to do so is impossible to determine, but the accusation was certainly plausible. More importantly, Ehrnrooth believed it (Stoilov, 1881). The day after meeting with Ehrnrooth, Battenberg conferred with Stoilov, who later recalled that:

His Majesty told me that the war minister was with him for four hours yesterday. They spoke for a long time and [Ehrnrooth] told the Prince that His Majesty cannot stay the way he has been hitherto now; he must immediately find a solution to the situation [of the Constitution]...His Majesty must, via a proclamation, declare he can't support this system anymore; must form his own government, to clear up the situation for the people, so everyone knows what is at stake i.e. that it is not about choosing between the Constitution and the Prince but between the Prince and chaos; the Great National Assembly, which should convene in about three months in Svishtov, must decide either for the Prince, and then he will govern for 7 or 5 years without a constitution... or if that doesn't pass, there is no point in [Ehrnrooth] staying... (Stoilov, 1881, pp. 43-44)

To put it bluntly, Ehrnrooth delivered Battenberg an ultimatum: either Battenberg would overthrow the Tarnovo Constitution, or Ehrnrooth would resign. Now, neither Battenberg nor Stoilov needed much convincing to launch this royal coup, but it should be noted that Ehrnrooth's was not a toothless threat. Ehrnrooth was one of Battenberg's closest political allies, and the British Ambassador noted that without Ehrnrooth, Battenberg "would not have been able to oppose the will of the [legislature]" (cited in Jelavich, 1958, p. 76). Ehrnrooth's resignation would severely weaken Battenberg's political position.

Yet, Ehrnrooth did more than simply violate his country's explicitly stated policy. He also kept St. Petersburg in the dark about it. In later years, Ehrnrooth (1886) would claim that he lacked the proper codes and ciphers to send a suitably secret message to the Russian government. Therefore, "worrying, before anything else, about keeping my intentions secret until the time to act came, I did not find it convenient to inform [St. Petersburg of my intentions] through the means of the diplomatic agency in Sofia, and I had in this my reasons" (Ehrnrooth, 1886, p. 477). An alternative explanation would be that Ehrnrooth was perfectly aware that if he told the Russian government about his plans, Girs or Miliutin would block the proposed coup. It was easier to ask for forgiveness once the government had been overthrown than to ask for permission ahead of time. Yet, this is almost a distinction without a difference. Either Ehrnrooth was unable to communicate with his government, or he decided it was in his best interests not to; either reveals severe flaws in the Russian diplomatic apparatus.

On May 9th, 1881, the coup was enacted. Battenberg dismissed the Liberal government and created a new ministry in which Ehrnrooth was Minister President, Minister for Foreign Affairs, and Minister of the Interior all at once. A set of constitutional changes was proposed, including a weaker legislature and reduced civil liberties, and a constitutional convention was called, with Battenberg and Ehrnrooth resorting to force to ensure the proper result. Liberals were attacked by mobs armed with clubs, and many of the leading Liberal politicians opted to flee the country (Crampton, 1983). The Russian state first learned of the coup from the newspapers, with Miliutin writing in his diary that "…a strange and utterly unexpected coup [has occurred] in Bulgaria. One could always expect from Battenberg some risky measure… but no one could have thought that such a decision would be forced upon him by our own Russian general, Ehrnrooth" (Miliutin, 1947, p. 66). Left with no good options, the Russian government accepted the *fait accompli* its own agent had crafted for it, and Tsar Alexander III acknowledged the change of government (Jelavich, 1958). Ehrnrooth was recalled, but the Russian state did not punish him for so grossly exceeding his instructions. Indeed, he later became the Minister-Secretary of State for Finnish Affairs.

Like the Titles Controversy, Ehrnrooth's ultimatum and the subsequent coup illustrate major flaws in Russian diplomatic capability. Yet, while Parensov's struggles in determining what to call Battenberg held an element of farce, the 1881 Coup was deadly serious. Ehrnrooth was essentially a rogue agent, a member of the Russian foreign policy apparatus who chose to violate a clearly stated position of the Russian state. It is difficult to imagine that Ehrnrooth did not know the gravity of his actions; no one, then or since, has accused Ehrnrooth of being a fool, and his decision not to inform St. Petersburg is certainly a telling one.

Furthermore, Ehrnrooth's actions would materially damage Russo-Bulgarian relations. Throughout this period, the Liberal Party was far and away the electorally dominant faction in Bulgarian politics. In the first elections of 1879, the Liberals won with a majority of 140 to 30 in the legislature, and these numbers did not significantly shift in the following years. Before the 1881 Coup, the Liberals had reasonably good relations with the Russian government—one may recall how they lionized Parensov during his struggles with Battenberg. But now, they had been attacked, forced from power, and put to flight, and this was something that the

Liberals would neither forgive nor forget. Ehrnrooth's coup permanently antagonized the largest electoral coalition in Bulgaria, and this would have dire consequences for the course of Russo-Bulgarian relations.

The Generals

So long as Russia maintained close alliance with Battenberg and the Conservatives, Russian influence in Bulgaria was secured; however, events have shown that the Russian government was unable to maintain that alliance.

Over the course of the following year, from mid-1881 to mid-1882, relations between Battenberg's faction and the Russian government continued to deteriorate. There were several controversies related to railroads, electoral commissions, and freedom of the press, but they are outside the scope of this chapter. Still, it was a self-evident truth that Battenberg and the Conservatives were unable to rule alone. They simply lacked the popular support, which meant that Battenberg needed the aid of either the Liberals or the Russians, and of the two, he far preferred the Russians. In the spring of 1882, Battenberg once more went to St. Petersburg to request new men in Bulgaria, and he received Lieutenant-General Leonid Nikolaevich Sobolev and Major-General Aleksandr Vasil'evich Kaul'bars. Sobolev was to be the Minister-President and Minister of the Interior, while Kaul'bars would be the Minister of War.

Both men had exemplary records. They were reasonably young (in their late thirties), career military officers, and graduates of Russia's Nicholas General Staff Academy. Sobolev had served in Central Asia prior to fighting in the Russo-Turkish War of 1877-78 and afterwards had been part of the occupation forces in charge of designing Bulgaria's civil administration. Kaul'bars had likewise served in Central Asia, but he was also a Siberian explorer and geographer of note. Like Sobolev, he had served in the Russo-Turkish War, and then he had been part of the commission that had drawn the boundaries that Bulgaria shared with its Balkan neighbors (Jelavich, 1958); however, unfortunately for Russo-Bulgarian relations, they were also both virulent Panslavs, probably the most aggressively Panslav individuals Russia sent to Bulgaria during Battenberg's reign. They were deeply suspicious of the West, and they despised Germany, which made it rather difficult for them to work with a German Prince. Sobolev (1886), the dominant figure in the partnership, later wrote that it was to Russia's great shame that "Russia, having freed the Bulgarians from the heavy Turkish knout, delivered them into slavery for a German Prince" (Sobolev, 1886, pp. 704-705). The Conservatives were likewise seen as being in Austrian pockets (Sobolev, 1886). Still, for the first six months of their tenure in Bulgaria, the Generals, as they came to be known, maintained reasonably amicable relations with Battenberg and a Conservative cabinet consisting of Konstantin Stoilov as Minister of Foreign Affairs & Religion, Dimit"r Grekov as Minister of Justice, and Grigor

Nachovich as Minister of Finance. Yet, over the course of the winter of 1882-1883, a series of conflicts broke out between the two groups.

The first was the issue of the Minister of Public Works. For several years, Bulgaria had been consumed by a complex debate over where to build railroads and who should pay for them. Though the full conflict is beyond the scope of this chapter, the key point is that there was a Conservative position and a Russian position. In late 1882, there was a proposal to establish a Ministry of Public Works to handle railroad matters; however, controversy arose over the question of who should lead the Ministry, and Sobolev advanced Prince Mikhail Ivanovich Khilkov, a Russian railroad magnate and supporter of the Russian position, as his candidate. The Conservatives balked and refused to appoint him, so Sobolev simply used his power as Minister-President to appoint Khilkov as the Assistant Minister of Public Works. Given that there was no *actual* Minister, this essentially put Khilkov in charge without having to be confirmed by the Conservatives. Needless to say, this enraged the Conservatives, and Battenberg was forced to step in and appoint Nachovich to the post to defuse the situation (Jelavich, 1958).

This was followed by the Dragoon Incident, where the Conservative ministers refused to approve funding for the maintenance of a controversial corps of dragoons (mounted infantry) that the Generals wanted to add to the Bulgarian army. In this case, Battenberg supported the Generals, and there was a stormy cabinet meeting on February 23rd, 1883. Battenberg ordered the Conservatives to approve the funds, and Nachovich and Grekov submitted their resignations. Sobolev, in his role as Minister-President, refused to accept the resignations, and a series of vicious recriminations followed. As Sobolev (1886) later recalled, he "told [the Conservatives] many bitter truths…that he has the full opportunity to take away their power and to turn them into the very same thing, that they had turned their political opponents" (pp. 715-716). Essentially, Sobolev told the heads of the Conservative party that he was willing and able to see their party smashed and its leadership cast into exile, just as the Liberals had been. Once again, Battenberg was able to smooth things over and persuaded Nachovich and Grekov to remain in the Cabinet (Jelavich, 1958).

It was a truce that would not last long, as the third and final major conflict between the Generals and the Conservatives began mere hours after the February 23rd cabinet meeting. This conflict requires a modicum of background explanation. The Metropolitan Meletiĭ was a popular Russophile preacher and the head of the church in Sofia; however, he had enemies in the hierarchy of the Bulgarian church, who chose this moment to act. On February 23rd, a letter was sent to Sofia, specifically to Konstantin Stoilov, who was the Minister of Foreign Affairs and Religion. Stoilov was directed by the church hierarchy to have Meletiĭ removed from his position and exiled to a monastery at Vratsa. Technically, Stoilov was supposed to carry out the letter's instructions without question, but as Meletiĭ was a popular man, Stoilov decided to be cautious. He first went to Battenberg and proposed a less onerous term of exile for Meletiĭ—that Meletiĭ be given a pension and exiled not to Vratsa but to the large and prestigious Rila Monastery. Battenberg agreed. Then, since Meletiĭ was also close to the Russians, Stoilov proceeded to secure Sobolev's acquiescence (Stoilov, 1883b).

This is where the accounts diverge. According to a memorandum Stoilov (1883b) wrote later, "His Excellency General Sobolev agreed completely with my views and during the entire conversation said absolutely nothing that would have caused one to think, that could have given me cause to suspect, that he was not entirely of my opinion" (p. 142); however, Sobolev (1886) wrote in his own memoirs a few years later that "wanting to think over this matter calmly, [I] proposed to Stoilov to wait and to inform the Metropolitan Meletiĭ beforehand, as was appropriate to the existing law, of the Exarch's decision" (p. 718). By this point, it is impossible to say what truly happened during that meeting, but it should be noted that both men were probably mentally and physically exhausted after the previous day's tense cabinet meeting, so one cannot rule out simple miscommunication.

In any case, Stoilov set about overseeing Meletiĭ's removal. According to Stoilov, Meletiĭ himself wished to leave Sofia as quickly as possible, and Stoilov gave him a military guard (Stoilov, 1883b); however, Sobolev took offense and interpreted this as a Conservative effort to embarrass Russia and called Stoilov's actions "the most outrageous uses of force upon the Metropolitan" (Sobolev, 1886, p. 718). Sobolev dispatched his own private secretary to intercept the Metropolitan—an act that greatly exceeding his authority—and then accused Stoilov of excessive force in the St. Petersburg *Nóvoe Vrémia* newspaper (Stoilov, 1883b).

This was the very last straw for both sides. On February 26th, Sobolev and Kaul'bars told Battenberg that they were no longer willing to work alongside Stoilov in the Bulgarian cabinet. Forced to choose, Battenberg sided with the Russians rather than risk a final break in Russo-Bulgarian relations, and on February 28th, 1883, Stoilov, Grekov, and Nachovich resigned from the Bulgarian cabinet (Jelavich, 1958). The Generals were now in absolute control of the Bulgarian government, but they had also antagonized the Conservatives to the breaking point. Nor, for that matter, was Battenberg particularly fond of them, and while Russia was still considered a key ally of Bulgaria, it was one thing to have Russian agents as part of the Bulgarian government and another thing entirely to have them be the *entirety* of the Bulgarian government.

Over the course of the spring and summer of 1883, the Generals continued to antagonize all key actors in Bulgaria. The Conservatives variously accused Sobolev and Kaul'bars of trying to bring back the Liberals, of trying to turn Bulgaria into effectively a Russian province, and most tellingly, of "threaten[ing] the existence of friendly relations between Russia and Bulgaria" (Sobolev, 1886, p. 736). Adolf

Koch (1887), Battenberg's personal chaplain, wrote that "the behavior of the two Generals towards the Bulgarians was both imperious and offensive. They might be heard saying on all occasions that the Bulgarians were all blockheads, who ought to be treated with the knout" (p. 134). Foreign observers likewise noticed that the Generals were antagonizing the Bulgarians to the breaking point. The Austrian ambassador to Sofia reported that "the two generals pay no attention to the limited susceptibilities of Bulgaria's national pride, nor are they adapting themselves to the form of government already established in the country. The regime which they seem to desire to set up in this country is a military dictatorship of two" (cited in Black, 1943, p. 230). The British ambassador wrote that the Generals were so obnoxious as "to make the rival parties among the Bulgarians forget their animosities for the moment and united them against the [Russians]" (cited in Victoria, 1926, pp. 444-445). Most interestingly, the Russian press and the Tsarist government were likewise aware that all was not well in Bulgaria. On March 31st, 1883, the prominent *Sankt-Peterbúrgskie Védomosti* reported that Sobolev's "arrogant attitude" and "ill-advised and peremptory measures" were damaging Russian influence in Bulgaria (cited in Jelavich, 1958, p. 120). Inside the Ministry of Foreign Affairs, one of Girs' closest advisors wrote that he was worried about the future of Russian influence in Bulgaria due to the Generals' actions (cited in Jelavich, 1958). There was a broad consensus in Bulgaria, in Russia, and in the rest of Europe that the tenures of Sobolev and Kaul'bars were a failure and were actively harmful to Russo-Bulgarian relations.

Yet, instead of removing them, Tsar Alexander III, who had by this point developed a genuine loathing for his cousin Battenberg, chose to exacerbate the situation. He sent a veteran diplomat, Aleksandr Semënovich Ionin, to force through another reworking of the Bulgarian constitution, one which would reduce Battenberg to essentially a figurehead monarch (Black, 1943). From there, matters proceeded to their inevitable conclusion. Battenberg and the Conservatives, fearing for their political lives, turned to the exiled Liberals, who still commanded considerable popular support. Tšankov, finding himself a kingmaker, demanded the return of the Tarnovo Constitution, telling Battenberg "alles oder gar nichts" ("all or nothing") when the latter tried to bargain with him (Corti, 1954, pp. 135-136). Left with no other alternatives, Battenberg agreed. On September 6th, 1883, Battenberg and Tšankov sprung their trap. Prepared by Tšankov, the legislature proposed the return of the Tarnovo Constitution, a motion that was passed with general acclaim. Sobolev and Kaul'bars, who were present at the time and realized what was going on, promptly left the room, followed by "shouts of triumph from the chamber" (Koch, 1887, p. 154). The following day, Battenberg restored the Constitution, and the Generals, after several hurried telegraphic exchanges with St. Petersburg, resigned and left Bulgaria. Konstantin Stoilov's (1883a) diary entry for September 7th reads in its entirety, "There is great joy. The Generals are expelled. The Constitution is restored" (p. 81). This was an absolutely stinging rebuke to Russia.

The affair of Sobolev and Kaul'bars demonstrates yet again the severe flaws in Russian diplomatic practices during this period. It was a commonly acknowledged fact that Sobolev and Kaul'bars had become toxic in Bulgaria. Logically, one might expect the Russian government to recall the two men and replace them with someone more willing to work with a country that was, after all, a close Russian ally and a vital client state. Instead, the Generals were allowed to remain until they had done immense damage to Russo-Bulgarian relations. By late 1883, because of the Generals, all of Bulgaria's political actors had come together in open defiance of Russia. Russo-Bulgarian relations could then be fairly described as an open crisis. There would be more troubles to come, including a Russian-backed coup against Battenberg in 1886, but September 7th, 1883, was the breaking point.

FUTURE RESEARCH DIRECTIONS

The events in Bulgaria serve as proof that, at least in this instance, Russian diplomatic practices were greatly flawed and thus led to negative results for Russian foreign policy, despite otherwise favorable circumstances. This suggests directions for future research.

First, one might consider whether Russo-Bulgarian relations during this period were typical of Russian foreign policy efforts, an extreme example of an otherwise standard situation, or an unrepresentative outlier. The author believes that the underlying factors leading to the downfall of Russo-Bulgarian relations (rogue agents, contradictory orders, etc.) would have manifested themselves in other areas of Russian foreign policy—even if not quite so dramatically. This is something that further research can confirm or deny by examining other Russian foreign policy efforts during the same time period. One particularly fruitful area of research would be the Russian efforts at the Congress of Berlin, which William Howard Brennan touched upon in his *The Russian Foreign Ministry and the Alliance with Germany, 1878-1884* (1973), but which has not been subsequently examined in equal detail. Another useful focus would be the Russo-Serbian relationship after 1886, when Serbia filled the void left by Bulgaria as Russia's primary Balkan ally. Further research along these lines would provide a richer understanding of the nature of Russian diplomatic practices during this time period.

A second research direction would be more internal. At present, no one has conducted a serious examination of Russian diplomatic practices or written a thorough history of the Russian Ministry of Foreign Affairs, as opposed to Russian foreign policy, on which a great deal has been written. An organizational history of this sort could be a considerably fruitful endeavor, particularly if it could link internal matters such as training or communications with outlying agents to particular moments in Russian foreign policy history. Up until fairly recently, such a history would have been impossible to write, but with the reopening of the Archive of the Foreign Relations of the Russian Empire (AVPRI), it is now possible.

A third and final avenue for research would be to determine to what extent Russian diplomatic practice was an outlier during this time period. Keith Hamilton and Richard Langhorne observed in their 1995 *The Practice of Diplomacy: Its Evolution, Theory, and Administration* that the 19th century was a time of considerable upheaval in the way diplomacy was conducted. While one can make a sound argument for the Russian Foreign Ministry being particularly behind the times (as was most of the Russian state), all other foreign ministries of the era were also working to keep up with the latest changes. A close examination of one or more countries' diplomatic relations—perhaps a history of the ways each of the Great Powers dealt with a single Balkan state diplomatically—may offer an interesting comparative history.

CONCLUSION

As this chapter demonstrates, there were a number of issues regarding the diplomatic practices of the Russian Empire in Bulgaria between 1879 and 1883. The case of Parensov demonstrates that no one individual was in charge of Russia's policy in the region and that key individuals gave contradictory orders. Ehrnrooth's case demonstrates that a rogue agent was able to completely overturn Russia's explicit and repeatedly stated policy to bring about an unsanctioned coup, and then he went unpunished. Finally, the case of Sobolev and Kaul'bars illustrates that Russian agents behaved in an obnoxious and tactless fashion and managed to antagonize local Bulgarian elites and that no one in St. Petersburg saw fit to recall them, even though it was public knowledge that they were damaging Russo-Bulgarian relations.

It should also be noted that the examples presented are simply some of the most prominent examples of the issues in Russian diplomatic practices and should by no means be considered an exhaustive list. For that matter, while the examples focus on the military men dispatched to Bulgaria, the Russian Consul-Generals proved to be as unskilled in advancing Russian interests as the military men. A. P. Davydov insulted a Liberal Minister-President by calling him an "unwashed, uncombed, country bumpkin" (Parensov, 1900, pp. 594-595). The Consul-General Mikhaíl Aleksándrovich Khitrovó (in Bulgaria from 1881 to 1882) managed to be so obnoxious that the Austrian representative in Bulgaria, Rüdiger Freiherr von Biegeleben, commented that the most skilled opponent of Russian influence in Bulgaria was Khitrovó himself (cited in Jelavich, 1958). The weaknesses of Russian diplomatic practices in late 19th century Bulgaria were deep and systemic and the result of profound disorganization and inefficiency in the Russian foreign policy apparatus.

These problems had enormous consequences. After the expulsion of Sobolev and Kaul'bars in 1883, Russo-Bulgarian relations continued to deteriorate. In 1885, the Principality of Bulgaria and Eastern Rumelia were united, and in response, Tsar Alexander III recalled all Russian officers stationed in the country—an act meant to punish Bulgaria but that mostly served to deprive Russia of its most useful tools for controlling events in the country. By 1886, a Bulgarian coup, initiated by local Bulgarian officers but supported by Russia, attempted to force Battenberg from power. It failed, and though Battenberg abdicated anyway, by the end of 1886 Russo-Bulgarian relations were severed entirely. They would not resume until 1894, when Nicholas II came to the throne of Russia. In turn, this meant that Russia lost what was to be its prized client state in the Balkans. In an effort to maintain its presence in the Balkans, Russia had to look further afield. Thus, the Russian Empire became a close supporter of Serbia.

The resulting Russo-Serbian alliance would be one of the most consequential in Balkan history. To begin with, it prevented any final rapprochement between Russia and Bulgaria – Bulgaria and Serbia were staunch competitors over the region of Macedonia, fighting more than one war over the subject, and in the end Russia came down on the Serbian side (Hall, 2011). The alliance would also play a pivotal role in plunging Europe into the First World War. During that war, Russia and Bulgaria fought on opposite sides, as they would again in the Second World War a generation later. The actions of Parensov, Ehrnrooth, Sobolev, and the others changed the course of Bulgarian history, and one might fairly say of Russian and world history as well.

Their actions become all the more interesting in light of recent events surrounding the Russian Federation. Since the rise of Putin in 2000, the Russian Federation has in many ways emulated its imperial predecessor in the realm of foreign policy, acting less like an ideological superpower, as the USSR had been, and more like a nationalist Great Power in the style of the Russian Empire. Girs and Miliutin would recognize a great deal in today's Russia. They would recognize Russian attitudes. Observers, including German Chancellor Angela Merkel, argue that "Putin believes… That it's a strong Russia of real men versus the decadent West that's too pampered, too spoiled, to stand up for their beliefs" – a belief shared with ardent Panslavs such as L. N. Sobolev (Packer, 2014). Girs and Miliutin would also recognize Russian tactics. Just as the Russian Empire tried to work around the Congress of Berlin, so does Putin's Rusia flout international law and diplomatic norms whenever it seems advantageous to do so (Kalb, 2015). Girs and Miliutin, finally, would recognize Russian goals. Putin, just like the Tsars before him, has sought to control his immediate geopolitical neighborhood – though in the straitened circumstances of post-1991 Russia, this means Ukraine rather than the Balkans (Kalb, 2015). The question, then, is whether or not Girs and Miliutin would recognize Russian diplomatic practice as well.

It will likely be decades before Russian archives are opened sufficiently to allow us to answer this question, but we can make some shrewd guesses in the meantime. Consider the matter of Ukraine. Prior to the removal of Ukrainian President Viktor Yanukovych in 2014's Euromaidan Revolution, the Russian government could have counted Ukraine as a loyal ally and client state. Now, some two years later, Ukraine is a country divided by civil war, with half the country violently resisting Russian influence and with Russia turned into something of an international pariah as a result. Under the circumstances, one is left to wonder how much of Russia's recent loss of influence in Ukraine might be the result of the same flaws in diplomatic practice that resulted in the loss of Bulgaria almost a century and a half previously. While it seems unlikely that any one Russian agent has the sort of influence that Johann Casimir Ehrnrooth had, the possibilities of rogue agents, of internal confusion, or of counter-productive agents cannot be ignored. As Brookings scholar Bobo Lo (2015) puts it, while "*implementation* is a much underestimated area of foreign policy… the reality [is] that without effective implementation there is no policy*making*" (p. 6). Ultimately, policymakers would be wise to consider that Russian foreign policy may not be as monolithic and as efficiently carried out as it might seem on the outside. A great deal may have changed in Russian politics and in diplomatic practices since the days of Battenberg, but just as much has stayed the same; thus, the lessons of Bulgaria remain as relevant as ever.

REFERENCES

Black, C. E. (1943). *The establishment of constitutional government in Bulgaria.* Princeton, NJ: Princeton University Press.

Brennan, W. H. (1973). *The Russian foreign ministry and the alliance with Germany, 1878-1884.* Ann Arbor, MI: University of Michigan Press.

Corti, E. C. (1934). *The downfall of three dynasties.* London, UK: Methuen.

Corti, E. C. (1954). *Alexander von Battenberg.* London, UK: Cassell.

Crampton, R. J. (1983). Bulgaria 1878-1918. Boulder, CO: East European Monographs.

Crampton, R. J. (2007). *Bulgaria.* Oxford, UK: Oxford University Press.

Ehrnrooth, J. C. G. (1886). K Noveishei istorii bolgarii. *Russkaia Starina, LII,* 475–483.

Hall, R. C. (2011). Bulgaria in the First World War. *Historian*, *73*(2), 300–315. doi:10.1111/j.1540-6563.2011.00293.x

Hamilton, K., & Langhorne, R. (2011). *The practice of diplomacy: Its evolution, theory, and administration* (2nd ed.). New York, NY: Routledge.

Jelavich, C. (1958). *Tsarist Russia and Balkan nationalism: Russian influence in the internal affairs of Bulgaria and Serbia, 1879-1886*. Berkeley, CA: University of California Press.

Kalb, M. (2015). *Imperial Gamble: Putin, Ukraine, and the New Cold War*. Washington, DC: Brookings Institution.

Kennan, G. F. (1979). *The decline of Bismarck's European order: Franco-Russian relations, 1875-1890*. Princeton, NJ: Princeton University Press.

Koch, A. (1887). *Prince Alexander of Battenberg; Reminiscences of his reign in Bulgaria, from authentic sources*. London, UK: Whitaker.

Kutsarov, P. (2003). *Vossoedinenie Bolgarii v 1885 Godu i Rossiĭskaia Imperiia* (Unpublished doctoral dissertation). Rossiĭskaia Akademiia Nauk, Institut Slavianovedeniia, Moscow.

L'vov, E. (1886). *Rumeliĭskiĭ perevorot*. Moscow.

Lo, B. (2015). *Russia and the New World Disorder*. London, UK: Brookings Institution.

MacGahan, J. A. (1876, August 22). The Turkish atrocities in Bulgaria: Horrible scenes at Batak. *The Daily News*, pp. 5–6. Retrieved from http://www.attackingthedevil. co.uk/related/macgahan.php

Miliutin, D. A. (1947). Dnevnik D. A. Miliutin. Moscow: Gosudarstvennaia biblioteka SSSR imeni V.I. Lenina, Otdel rukopiseĭ.

Narochnitskiĭ, A. L. (1978). *Rossiia i natsional'no-osvoboditel'naia bor'ba na Balkanakh, 1875-1878: Sbornik dokumentov*. Moscow: Nauka.

Packer, G. (2014, December 1). The Quiet German. *The New Yorker*. Retrieved from http://www.newyorker.com/magazine/2014/12/01/quiet-german

Parensov, P. D. (1900). V Bolgarii: vospominaniye ofitsera general'nago shtaba. Russkaia Starina, 101, 107-127, 359-381, 593-602.

Parensov, P. D. (1906). V Bolgarii: vospominaniye ofitsera general'nago shtaba. *Russkaia Starina, 125*, 62-74, 272-287, 509-527.

Parensov, P. D. (1908a). V Bolgarii: Vospominaniye ofitsera general'nago shtaba. *Russkaiā Starina*, *132*, 257–270.

Parensov, P. D. (1908b). V Bolgarii: vospominaniye ofitsera general'nago shtaba. *Russkaiā Starina*, *134*, 17-47, 257-282.

Queen Victoria of Great Britain. (1926). *The letters of Queen Victoria: A selection from Her Majesty's correspondence and journal between the years 1862 and 1878.* London: J. Murray.

Radev, S. (1911). *Stroitelite na săvremenna Bălgarija.* Sofia, Bulgaria: P. Glushkov.

Ragsdale, H., & Ponomarev, V. N. (1993). *Imperial Russian foreign policy.* Washington, DC: Woodrow Wilson Center.

Skazkin, S. D. (1928). *Konets͡avstro-russko-germanskogo soiūz͡a.* Moscow: Ranion.

Sobolev, L. N. (1886). K noveishei istorii bolgarii. *Russkaiā Starina*, *LI*, 703–752.

Stoilov, K. (1879). [Diary]. (Fond 600k, Opis 3, Delo 1), TSentralen d"rzhaven arkhiv Sofia, Bulgaria.

Stoilov, K. (1880). [Diary]. (Fond 600k, Opis 3, Delo 2), TSentralen d"rzhaven arkhiv Sofia, Bulgaria.

Stoilov, K. (1881). [Diary]. (Fond 600k, Opis 3, Delo 2), TSentralen d"rzhaven arkhiv Sofia, Bulgaria.

Stoilov, K. (1883). [Diary]. (Fond 600k, Opis 3, Delo 4), TSentralen d"rzhaven arkhiv Sofia, Bulgaria.

Stoilov, K. (1883). [Memorandum to Alexander von Battenberg]. (Fond 600k, Opis 3, Delo 383), TSentralen d"rzhaven arkhiv Sofia, Bulgaria.

KEY TERMS AND DEFINITIONS

Alexander von Battenberg: Prince of Bulgaria, 1879-1886. Of German heritage but related to the Russian court.

Coup of 1881: A royal coup by Ehrnrooth, Battenberg, and Stoilov, which overturned the Tarnovo Constitution.

Johann Casimir Ehrnrooth: Bulgarian Minister of War, 1880-1881, and a Russian Lieutenant-General.

Konstantin Stoilov: Leader of the Conservative Party in Bulgaria during the 1880s, and Foreign Minister in 1883.

L. N. Sobolev: Bulgarian Minister-President and Minister of Interior, 1882-1883, and a Russian Lieutenant-General.

P. D. Parensov: Bulgarian Minister of War, 1879-1880, and a Russian Major-General.

Tarnovo Constitution: The founding document of independent Bulgaria. Removed in the Coup of 1881, returned in 1883, lasted until 1947.

Chapter 4

Assessing the Correlation of Culture With Business Ethics of Company Managers in the United States and Mexico

Mark A. Anderson
Snow College, USA

ABSTRACT

Observable harm has been inflicted upon business by unethical decisions and misconduct. Much of this phenomenon can be traced to impoverished ethical attitudes. Among the various reasons for this problem is that of a manager's culture, which has a distinct influence on attitudes and behaviors. The purpose of this chapter was to determine, through empirical data, whether differences rooted in culture significantly contribute to differences in ethical attitudes. Management scholar Geert Hofstede's classification of cultural elements for understanding and explaining aspects of national culture was correlated with the ethical attitudes of business managers in the two national cultures of the United States and Mexico. Results indicated a significant positive relationship between national culture and ethical attitudes and the dultural dimensions of uncertainty avoidance, masculinity, and long-term orientation. A significant difference in ethical attitudes between managers from the United States and Mexico was also found.

INTRODUCTION

The globalization of commerce has an impact on an ever-widening circle of customers, suppliers, and employers, as well as other stakeholders in society. As the impact grows, so too, do the effects of individual choices made by managers and workers as their work affects larger numbers of people; actions have consequences.

DOI: 10.4018/978-1-5225-2650-6.ch004

Particularly important is the ethical component of decisions, where choices often have the potential of creating problems for large numbers of people. Some of these problems have grown to organization-threatening scales in recent years and continue to grow (Andreoli & Lefkowitz, 2009; Everhart, Martinez-Vazquez, & McNab, 2009; Rakas, 2011; Whitaker & Godwin, 2013). An international survey of 211 scholars in the field of business ethics found the decline of ethical behavior in society and organizations to be among the top issues facing the field of business in the future (Holland & Albrecht, 2013).

The present research was conducted to broaden the scholarship on the roots causes of unethical behavior and decisions by managers, and to bridge the gap between cultural influence and individual decisions, inductions, actions and inactions in management. In a global economy, with growing interactions among workers across the globe, managers ought to have a good understanding of cross-cultural issues. Managers need to know employees, as they can be influenced to engage in ethical behaviors (Doh, Husted, Matten & Santoro, 2010) and abstain from behavior that is unethical.

Considering the current climate of globalization, intercultural knowledge is a needed by managers in order to improve international trade through better understanding (Doh, Husted, Matten & Santoro, 2010; Franke & Nadler, 2008; Su, 2006). This knowledge would help to enhance corporate legitimacy, profitability, and competitive advantage in a multicultural marketplace, including North America (Ahmad & Ramayah, 2012; Zheng, Luo, & Wang, 2014). Benefits of such specialized knowledge include: improved collective organizational commitment and citizenship behaviors (Chun et al., 2013), improved legitimacy and financial performance (Harris 2007), positive linkage between a company's social responsibility and business performance (Buciuniene & Kazlauskaite, 2012), competitive advantage in international business (Takei, 2011), and corporate strategies that include moral values that are more successful in global business (Wieland, 2010).

Individual managers' decisions, indecisions, actions, and inactions have led to the diminution of wealth, deprivation of jobs, and ruination of businesses while simultaneously creating a distrust of business and its leaders (Beekun & Westerman, 2012; Rakas, 2011). Multiple influences shape attitudes and attitudes determine decisions (Holland & Albrecht, 2013). An example of such influences is culture (Doh, Husted, Matten, & Santoro,2010; Holland & Albrecht, 2013; Lian, Ferris, & Brown, 2011; Nielsen, 2010; Peterson & Søndergaard, 2011). Although it must be acknowledged that ethics and morality are culturally constructed and differentially defined in Confucius Heritage societies such as Japan, China, Korea, Taiwan, (Chung, Eichenseher, & Taniguchi, 2008; Shafer, Fukukawa, & Lee, 2007) and Western societies, including the United States, Germany, and other Western countries. Nevertheless, rather than the birthplace of where a manager was reared, impact and ramification of ethical breach depends more relevantly on the setting or location in which the act or failure to act occurs. Khera (2010) also reported that culture was among the root causes of the attitudes that have led to the kind of decisions that have harmed both business and society.

Understanding such choices and the attitudes that help shape them is crucial to influencing a positive work environment that would lead to favorable business outcomes and positive consequences in social and economic environments. Numerous factors influence such choices, however, for managers to better comprehend and guide their workers, scholars have called for more research (e. g., Holland & Albrecht, 2013; Li & Murphy, 2012; Lian, Ferris, & Brown, 2011; Peterson & Søndergaard, 2011; Schumacher & Wasieleski, 2013; Simha & Cullen, 2012).

BACKGROUND

Much research has been done on both (a) national culture and (b) ethical attitudes, to determine their influence on ethical attitudes. . Some scholars have argued that national culture is the most powerful influence on ethical attitudes (Westerman, Beekun, Stedham & Yamamura, 2010). Researchers have previously compared cultures from many parts of the world. Blodgett, Bakir and Rose (2008) stated that thousands of studies have been conducted using Hofstede's cultural dimensions alone. As noted in Ardichvili, Jondle, and Kowske (2010), very little research has been done in comparing ethical attitudes of U.S. managers with those of Mexican managers. In addition to cultural influences on ethical attitudes, spirituality and level of moral development has also been studied as antecedents to ethical attitudes (Beekun & Westerman, 2012). Andreoli and Lefkowitz (2009) found that compliance practices and the informal ethical climate have an effect on ethical attitudes, as well.

Other factors have proven to influence ethical attitudes in the workplace. Simha and Cullen (2012) found the following to be significant in influencing the ethical behaviors in an organization: external organizational context, community norms and values, organizational form, information technology perspective, nonprofit versus profit context, family versus nonfamily firms, strategic versus managerial orientation, effect of communication and empowerment, and leadership orientation.

MAIN FOCUS OF THE CHAPTER

The purpose of this quantitative correlational study was to examine the relationship between Hofstede's five cultural dimensions and the criterion variable of ethical attitude levels for the subjects studied. A secondary purpose was to assess whether there are significant differences between the national cultures of the United States and Mexico among business managers.

The aggregate of the utility, or the measure of usefulness of everything, is social utility. This concept indicates that individuals care enough about others to sacrifice much of their own benefit for the greater benefit of the others (Sheng & Sheng, 2004).

In an earlier study dealing with resolving U.S.-Mexico cultural differences, Stephens and Greer (1995) concluded that the differences offer a significant challenge to cross-border business. They concluded, however, that if managers made efforts to understand those cultural differences, the challenges would greatly decrease and the chances for success would be enhanced. Knowing more about another culture can help build effective relationships (Stedham & Beekun, 2013).

Scholars and practitioners require current and accurate information for studying improved ways of conducting business, particularly in the growing and dynamic area of international trade. Ethics is an area of growing scholarship in business decisions. Scholars focused on national cultures as they explore and discuss the importance of antecedents to ethical decision-making such as national culture (Holland & Albrecht, 2013; Li & Murphy, 2012; Lian, Ferris, & Brown, 2011; Peterson & Søndergaard, 2011; Schumacher & Wasieleski, 2013; Simha & Cullen, 2012).

Although numerous cross-cultural studies linking national culture and ethical attitudes have been done for many countries (e.g., Davis et al., 2013; Robertson, Olson, Gilley, & Bao, 2008), no previous studies have been conducted making a similar study on the trade partners of the United States and Mexico. Trade between these two countries has grown considerably in recent years, more than doubling in the years from 2000 to 2013, with an increase of 103.1% in exports from the US to Mexico during this period to \$226.1 billion and an increase of 106.3% in imports (U.S. Census Bureau).

Hofstede's cultural dimensions continue to be a valuable framework in which to study these differences (Beekun & Westerman, 2012). Both national culture and attitudes are measurable (Vitell, Paolillo, & Thomas, 2003). Figure 1 shows the flow of the influence of these concepts. Research for this study focused on the link between D_1, national culture and C, impoverished or unethical attitudes; this is the most measurable of the relationships.

Management scholar Geert Hofstede's well-known and validated classification of national cultural dimensions was used for understanding and explaining aspects of national culture and supports the study of the correlation with the ethical attitudes of business managers in the two divergent countries and national cultures of the United States and Mexico. Ethical differences both within and between countries cannot be understood without considering national culture (Stedham & Beekun, 2013).

Culture is defined as "the collective programming of the mind that distinguishes the members of one group or category of people from another" (Hofstede, 2001,

Figure 1. The flow of influence of harm caused by business

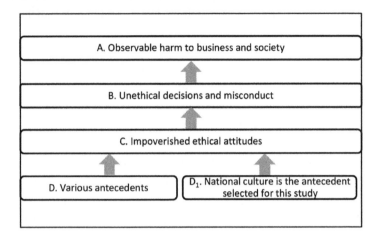

p. 9). The five dimensions of culture identified by Hofstede are power distance, uncertainty avoidance, individualism-collectivism, masculinity-femininity, and short-term/long-term orientation. The correlation between national cultures as characterized by Hofstede's five dimensions and the ethical attitudes of managers in companies in both the United States and in Mexico was investigated in this research. A well-validated measure of attitudes called PRESOR, or "perceptions of [the] relative importance of ethics and social responsibility" (Vitell, Paolillo, & Thomas, 2003, p. 64) was used to measure ethical attitudes. This instrument has been refined and validated since its inception in 1996. It has been used numerous times in scholarly research.

PREVIOUS RESEARCH

One of the advancements in business research on such attitudes has been the development of a valid and reliable survey instrument for assessing subjects' ethical attitudes. Singhapakdi, Vitell, Rallapalli, and Kraft (1996) Singhapakdi et al. (1996) developed the Ethics Position Questionnaire (EPQ), as an early instrument. Neumann and Reichel (1987) developed The Attitude Towards Business Ethics (ATBEQ) scale, another survey instrument that researchers have used in research. These have led to the PRESOR instrument utilized by this study. Vitell et al. (2003) identified ethics as a long term, top priority based on research using the ethical attitude level portion of the PRESOR.

Research linking the two variables of national culture and ethical attitudes includes a major study by the 2006 Global Leadership and Organizational Behavior

Effectiveness (GLOBE) project that examined cultures from 62 national cultures. The conclusion of this study was that culture has a fundamental influence on the values and ethics of individuals and that certain dimensions of culture essentially serve as predictors of ethical standards (Alas, 2006).

Utilizing a sample from 24 different countries, Scholtens and Dam, (2007) concluded that based on Hofstede's cultural dimension there are significant differences in business ethics among the cultures studied. Davis et al. (2013) found 161 articles from the period of 1990 to 2012 that dealt with Hofstede's uncertainty avoidance alone, establishing the validity of this construct for business research. Resick, Hanges, Dickson, and Mitchelson (2006) found a positive relationship between cultural differences and attributes of ethical leadership. Schepers (2006) found a strong correlation between culture and ethics, concluding that knowledge of cultural differences is helpful for managers to improve the ethical climate in their organizations. Additional research that supports the present study includes that conducted by El-Astal (2005), who concluded that there are significant differences in ethical judgments due to cultural background, as measured by nationality. Resick et al. (2006) found a similar positive relationship between cultural differences and attributes of ethical leadership. Strubler, Park, Agarwal, and Cayo (2012) believed that there is the possibility of developing an overarching model of cross-cultural ethics. In a world where international trade is growing, one's perception of the ethics of a potential trading partner from another culture is important in global trade (Gift et al., 2013).

The research for this study required the collection of quantifiable data from study subjects and was constructed as a correlational quantitative design, with an attempt to determine the strength of the correlation of the two variables of national culture and ethical attitudes. (Jacobs, 2011).

Based on data collected using the PRESOR instrument, hypothesis testing was conducted through multiple regression (Q1) and t-tests (Q2). First, the strength of the correlation between the variable of national culture and the variable of ethical attitudes was performed using multiple regression since the purpose of the study was to determine the strength of such correlations. This test was conducted among the five dimensions of culture and ethical attitude level. The second test, a t-test, was performed to attempt to determine the degree of cultural influence on ethical attitudes of different nationalities of both countries.

Significance of the Study

Normative ethical theory posits the notion that the interests of others and long-term consequences must be taken into account in making effective business decisions (Thorne, Ferrell, & Ferrell, 2011). These duties may be specified in a firm's code of ethics or not, but are a foundational decision-making skill of managers at all levels in recognizing ethical situations and responding in a positive way to them. Good ethical decisions lead to more successful business outcomes in the long run (Ahmad & Ramayah, 2012; Chun et al., 2013; Takei, 2011; Wieland, 2010). Further, an understanding of the antecedents that lead to more ethical decisions can help managers plan for and carry out better decisions in all areas of management decision making (Bremer, 2008; Everhart et al., 2009; Pearce, 2008; Scholtens & Dam, 2007).

Theoretically, this research was concerned with what factors and attitudes are present in the decisions made by managers in the workplace, decisions in the domain of business ethics. Further, it is a well-accepted concept in the field of ethics that individuals can improve their ethical decision-making abilities, in accordance with Lawrence Kohlberg's model of cognitive moral development (Kohlberg, 1984). Understanding the factors leading to decision-making can lead to growth in abilities to recognize ethical situations and the ability to make better such decisions (Thorne et al., 2011).

The significance of this research lies primarily in contributing more understanding as to how culture affects ethical attitudes among business managers, in the specific area of business ethics. Managers can develop practical policy decisions from its conclusion in determining what ethical training is needed and, particularly, how such policy should apply in a cross-cultural manner. Improved ethical attitudes may further result in enhanced profitability and business ability to respond to the ethical expectations of society. This includes working toward a more comprehensive international model of ethical decision-making and a better determination of the strength of the elements of culture in ethical decision-making (Schepers, 2006). A major current concern of business ethics scholars was that of globalization (Holland & Albrecht, 2013). Studying cross-cultural differences will help lead to an isolation of factors that contribute to unethical behaviors in the workplace (Beekun & Westerman, 2012).

Beyond this, the implications of such research for managerial practitioners include more understanding of cultural expectations in international business, reducing the legitimacy gap of societal expectations with company performance, and more understanding of cultural bias in ethical decision making (Schepers, 2006). Training and development of leaders and leader selection to protect against corrupt practices in business is another implication cited for such research (Pearce, Manz, & Sims (2008). Managers can then develop better understanding of the cultural influences and then target training to address issues uncovered (Holland & Albrecht, 2013).

Ethical differences between countries cannot be understood without considering national culture (Stedham & Beekun, 2013). In a world where trade is growing, one's perception of the ethics of a potential trading partner from another culture is important in global trade (Gift, Gift, & Zheng, 2013). Further advantages of enhanced knowledge in this area include improved collective organizational commitment and citizenship behaviors (Chun et al., 2013), improved legitimacy and financial performance (Harris 2007), positive linkage between a company's social responsibility and business performance (Buciuniene & Kazlauskaite, 2012), competitive advantage in international business (Takei, 2011), and corporate strategies that include moral values that are more successful in global business (Wieland, 2010). There is a need to discover the most significant of the five dimensions of culture that affect ethical attitudes and the nature of that relationship (Marta et al., 2008; Simha & Cullen, 2012).

Cross-border trade promises to grow further as a result of the North American Free Trade Agreement and other attempts to improve trade in the western hemisphere, such as the Central American Free Trade Agreement (CAFTA) ("What is CAFTA?" 2009). Other agreements with individual countries in South America such as the U.S.-Chile Free Trade Agreement (U.S.-Chile Free Trade Agreement, 2009) open the possibility for additional trade growth. Numerous U.S. corporations are engaged in business in Mexico and have management teams headed by U.S. citizens. They do not always know about the ethical environment they can expect to find in other countries. This research will help in clarifying these issues and results can be generalized to a degree to other international situations. The results of the research can help overcome the negative repercussions evident in Western culture because of the often-poor ethical decision-making in business cited.

Research Design

The particular sample for this study was management-level employees of companies with operations in the United States and Mexico. Employees at this level include any managers from the supervisory level to the highest management levels including professional employees who have no direct line supervisory responsibilities. Subjects were from all functional areas of management. This sample served as a focused study to understand the correlation of culture and ethical attitudes for managers in other businesses. A Power analysis determined that with purposive sampling the required number of respondents needed to be at least 138. The survey was made available on-line and an actual sample of useable responses of 198 was obtained.

Operational Definitions of Variables

The criterion (dependent) variable in the present study is ethical attitudes, as measured by the PRESOR variable. The predictor (independent) variables are Hofstede's five dimensions of national culture. Each of the five dimensions was measured on 7-point Likert scale with the following response options: strongly disagree, disagree, somewhat disagree, neither agree nor disagree, somewhat agree, agree, and strongly agree (Vitell et al., 2003).

The other variable studied is what Vitell et al. (2003) and previous authors have called PRESOR, or "perceptions of [the] relative importance of ethics and social responsibility" (p. 64). Based on a factor analysis of ethical attitudes, researchers determined that this composite variable is a suitable proxy for the full set of ethical attitudes being measured. These variables were also measured on 7-point Likert scale on the PRESOR questionnaire. The variables were operationalized as follows.

National Culture: Independent/Predictor Variable

Since national culture, as defined by Hofstede and as used in this research, is composed of five different dimensions, or components, each of the five were measured from three to five survey questions, each with a response range (on the Likert-type ordinal scale) from 1 to 7. A higher value for each corresponds to a greater agreement as to each of the facets of culture, reflecting a higher score on that component of culture. Negatively termed items were reverse coded. For the processing of the information, each of these were combined in an additive manner and then averaged to form the total second variable for each of the five dimensions of culture:

- **Power Distance:** Measures the inequality of power in society and gauges the acceptance of this inequality among members of society (Hofstede, 2001; Su, 2006). Operationally, it is defined as the degree to which members of society accept the inequality of power in society. A higher measure indicates greater acceptance of power inequality. In the current study, its presence and strength in national culture was measured by the judgment of survey respondents on a Likert-type ordinal scale of 1 to 7, where 1 is strongly disagree and 7 is strongly agree;
- **Uncertainty Avoidance:** Measures how people in society deal with future uncertainties. This is a measure of how comfortable they feel with uncertainty and ambiguity and how much they will do to reduce the uncertainties of life (Hofstede, 2001; Su, 2006). It is the degree, to which members of society feel uncomfortable with uncertainty, and are willing to take steps to reduce it. A higher measure shows more discomfort. It was also measured in the current study by the judgment of respondents on a Likert-type ordinal scale of 1 to 7, with 7 indicating a strong agreement with a high level of discomfort;
- **Individualism/Collectivism:** Measures how the individual relates to various groups in society. Individualistic cultures value achievement by the individual and often foster competition, while members of collectivist societies believe

that they benefit more from identifying with a group and the success of the group as a whole (Hofstede, 2001; Lalwani et al., 2009; Su, 2006). It is the degree to which members of society value individual achievement over group effort and accomplishment, with a higher measure demonstrating greater individualism. It was also measured by the judgment of respondents on a Likert-type ordinal scale of 1 to 7, with 7 indicating a strong agreement with individualism values;

- **Masculinity/Femininity:** Measures the distinction a culture places between gender roles. Masculine cultures view the roles as being very different from women, with women tending to be more modest and nurturing. In feminine cultures, there is less of a distinction between genders, and men and women take on roles similar to one another (Hofstede, 2001, Su, 2006). Masculinity/ Femininity is the degree to which members of society accept the differences in gender roles in society and a higher measure indicates greater acceptance of these differences. In the current study its presence and strength in national culture was measured by the judgment of survey respondents on a Likert-type ordinal scale of 1 to 7, where 1 is strongly disagree and 7 is strongly agree;
- **Long-term Orientation:** Measures the valuing of the future rewards, while *Short-term Orientation* values the benefits of the past and present. Members of high long-term orientation cultures will tend to pursue longer-term goals while short-term orientation cultures value the effects of shorter-range efforts (Hofstede, 2001). It is the degree to which members of society value long-term rewards over short-term ones, as measured by the judgment of respondents on a Likert-type ordinal scale of 1 to 7, with 7 indicating a strong agreement with long-term values. Findings in each of these areas will be discussed later.

Overall, national culture is operationally defined as the sum of the five components of culture as outlined above. For overall national culture, the scores for each of the five components were added. A higher score represents a greater degree of acceptance of the respondent's culture as defined by Hofstede and measured in the PRESOR instrument. This score represents the first variable in the current study.

Ethical Attitudes: Dependent/Outcome Variable

This is the second variable used in the research. The measurement of ethical attitudes was accomplished by seven questions on the PRESOR instrument that indicate a respondent's acceptance of each of the statements presented. Higher scores indicated a higher level of ethics, as posited in the definition of ethical attitudes in this research. The seven scores were combined in an additive manner and then averaged to achieve a total score. It was also measured as responses by survey respondents on a 7-point Likert scale, where 1 is strongly disagree (a low level of ethics) and 7 is strongly agree (a high level of ethics).

Data Collection and Analysis

The instrument was packaged with questions asking demographic data and the PRESOR itself with a seven-point Likert-type scale for responses to the questions with response categories of strongly agree, agree, somewhat agree neutral, somewhat disagree, disagree, and strongly disagree. Response categories for the reporting of demographic data were also appropriately designed for each of those categories. SurveyMonkey, an online survey software company was selected to facilitate the response for subjects. This was especially important due to the distance involved in gathering responses from Mexican subjects.

Since the questionnaire was administered to managers who speak either English or Spanish, the instrument was translated into Spanish, as outlined above. This enhanced the validity of the instrument, due to its need to be available in two languages. The required number of responses was gathered in a single day.

Recruitment of subjects proceeded as follows: Both U.S. and Mexican participants were identified by the SurveyMonkey Audience service as being qualified if they were (a) 18 years of age or older, and (b) being a supervisor or manager of a business in the United States or Mexico. SurveyMonkey is an online survey company that uses a pool of potential survey participants who have been recruited over time. This service matched the needs of this research with the profiles of their pool members whom they refer to as panelists in sufficient numbers to meet more than the required sample size. All panelists had access to the Internet and had previously joined the SurveyMonkey Audience program. Any incomplete response records were deleted.

In adopting the Vitell et al. (2003) instrument, which contains 21 questions that deal with culture and seven questions concerning ethical attitudes, this study used multiple regression analysis to determine the significance of the correlation of the two variables. To assess the second research question, whether there is a significant difference between the ethical attitudes of the Mexican and American managers, T-tests for each hypothesis comparing the two samples of U.S. and Mexican managers were done to determine the significance of the differences between the two groups.

Findings

In total, 209 surveys were completed. Of these, 102 were completed by managers in the United States and 107 were completed by managers in Mexico. The study sample was drawn from managers at a supervisory or higher level in the United States and Mexico.

Data Screening

Data were initially screened for invalid or outlying data points. Records that were found to have missing data were removed prior to data analysis. Eleven participants were removed in this way from the 209 total participants for missing data. Outliers were defined as data points outside the range of possible responses and none were found to exist in the data.

Description of the Sample

Survey results for 198 managers remained after preliminary screening. As Table 1 shows, over half of the respondents were female ($n = 105$, 53.0%), and just under half of them were male ($n = 93$, 47.0%). Most managers who responded to the survey were between the ages of 18 and 34 ($n = 67$, 33.8%), while nearly-equal representation was found among ages 35-49 ($n = 63$, 31.8%) and ages 50-64 ($n = 65$, 32.8%). The largest category of years of business experience was more than 10 ($n = 108$, 54.5%). The largest number of study participants were from the United States ($n = 102$, 51.5%), while a nearly equal number ($n = 96$, 48.5%) were from Mexico.

Descriptive Statistics

Subjects took the online PRESOR survey instrument to measure their national culture and their ethical attitudes toward misconduct. A score was calculated for each of the five dimensions of culture. The highest possible score for each of the five dimensions was 7, which is the total of the questions for that category averaged from the highest rating on the Likert scale of 7 (strongly agree). The lowest possible score was 1, which is the average of the five questions from the lowest rating of 1 (strongly disagree). Negatively worded items were reverse coded. The number of questions varied for each of the categories, from seven each for power distance and uncertainly avoidance, four each for masculinity and long-term orientation, and three for individualism. The different number of questions for each category (three, four, or seven) necessitated an averaging of each of the dimensions rather than an additive score to be able to make each dimension's score equivalent.

The dependent variable was measured in a similar manner. For the measurement of ethical attitudes (the dependent variable), the highest possible score was also 7, derived from an average of the seven questions for that category times the highest rating on the Likert scale of 7 (strongly agree). The lowest possible score was 1, which is the average of the lowest rating of 1 (strongly disagree).

Table 2 shows descriptive statistics for the variables in this study, the dimensions of culture and attitudes toward ethical misconduct, or PRESOR. Results showed, for

Table 1. Selected demographic characteristics of the sample

Demographic	Values	Frequency	Percent
Nation	United States	102	51.5%
	Mexico	96	48.5
Gender	Male	93	47.0
	Female	105	53.0
Age	18-34	67	33.8
	35-49	63	31.8
	50-64	65	32.8
	64 and over	3	1.5
Years of experience	0-1	9	4.5
	2-3	24	12.1
	4-5	27	13.6
	6-10	30	15.2
	More than 10	108	54.5
Educational level	High school or less	11	5.6
	Some college	47	23.7
	Bachelor's degree	90	45.5
	Some graduate studies	14	7.1
	Master's or doctorate	36	18.2
Training in philosophy	None	51	25.8
	Short-term workshop(s)	52	26.3
	One college course	32	16.2
	Multiple college courses	54	27.3
	College degree in philosophy	9	4.5
Position	Supervisor	32	16.2
	Mid-level manager	52	26.3
	Top-level manager	38	19.2
	Professional/staff	55	27.8
	Other	21	10.6

example, that participating managers scored lowest on the dimension of individualism ($M = 3.06$, $SD = 1.39$) and highest on long-term orientation ($M = 5.98$, $SD = 0.96$). For the dependent variable PRESOR, the overall score for all respondents was 5.99 ($SD = 0.89$) out of a total possible score of 7.00, where U.S. respondents scored 5.75 ($SD = 1.02$) and Mexican respondents scored 6.23 ($SD = 0.66$).

Table 2. Means and standard deviations for survey results

Variable	High Score	Low Score	M	SD
Power distance, total	7.00	1.00	3.75	1.12
U.S.	7.00	1.60	3.83	1.03
Mexico	7.00	1.00	3.60	1.20
Uncertainty avoidance, total	7.00	3.00	5.53	0.86
U.S.	7.00	1.00	5.43	0.95
Mexico	7.00	3.20	5.64	0.77
Individualism, total	7.00	1.00	3.06	1.39
U.S.	7.00	1.00	3.68	1.35
Mexico	6.33	1.00	2.45	1.14
Masculinity, total	7.00	2.50	5.56	1.04
U.S.	7.00	2.50	5.09	1.10
Mexico	7.00	3.50	6.03	0.73
Long-term orientation, total	7.00	2.50	5.98	0.96
U.S.	7.00	2.75	5.74	1.02
Mexico	7.00	2.50	6.22	0.84
PRESOR, total	7.00	2.57	5.99	0.89
U.S.	7.00	2.57	5.75	1.02
Mexico	7.00	4.00	6.23	0.66

Data Analysis

The culture and ethical attitude variables were analyzed as follows: The five components of the independent variable were measured using a set of questions. To normalize these into equivalent factors the scores for each variable were added together to obtain a total. Then, since each variable was measured using a different number of questions (three, four, or five), each total was divided by the number of questions to determine an average score. This was done to ensure that each question was evenly weighted as a variable in the regression analysis that was performed to determine the strength of each variable in predicting ethical attitudes.

The single dependent variable was the measure of attitudes called PRESOR, or "perceptions of [the] relative importance of ethics and social responsibility" (Vitell, Paolillo, & Thomas, 2003, p. 64). This was measured using a set of seven questions. Likewise, the protocol used with the independent variables was used to reduce all seven questions to a single score, which was the average score of the seven questions.

Findings on Research Question 1

The first research question asked to what extent, if any, do Hofstede's five cultural dimensions (power distance, uncertainty avoidance, individualism, masculinity-femininity, and long-term orientation) correlate with ethical attitude levels among business managers in Mexico and the United States, as measured by PRESOR? Survey results were analyzed separately for the managers of the two countries, the United States and Mexico. For the U.S. managers, for the full set of five variables that make up total national culture, the R-square statistic indicates that 46.1% of PRESOR can be explained by the combination of cultural dimensions. There was a significant correlation between national culture and ethical attitudes, as measured by PRESOR, $F(5, 92) = 15.77, p < .001$, providing evidence to support the hypothesis that there is a significant correlation between Hofstede's cultural dimension of national cultures and ethical attitude level.

In reducing the five elements of culture into each of the individual dimensions and correlating them with ethical attitudes, the correlations were revealed (see Table 3). Three of the cultural dimensions were shown to support the hypotheses that they significantly correlate with the level of ethical attitudes. Uncertainty avoidance (with a P-value significance level of .010) is a significant predictor of PRESOR. Masculinity (with a significance level of .049) is a significant predictor of PRESOR. Long-term orientation (with a significance level of .004) is a significant predictor of PRESOR. Evidence therefore exists to support the correlation between these dimensions of culture and ethical attitudes, as measured by PRESOR.

Conversely, two of the individual dimensions of culture showed no significant correlation with PRESOR. Power distance (with a significance level of .263) is not a significant predictor of PRESOR. Individualism (with a significance level of .738) is also not a significant predictor of PRESOR.

Survey results were also analyzed separately for the managers of from Mexico. Results show that for the full set of five variables of culture, R-square indicates that

Table 3. Regression results, U.S. managers

Variable	B	Std. Error	*t*	*Sig.*
Constant	1.722	.703	2.450	.016
Power distance	-.093	.083	-1.126	.263
Uncertainty avoidance	.319	.121	2.633	.010
Individualism, total	-.022	.065	-.336	.738
Masculinity, total	.187	.094	1.992	.049
Long-term orientation, total	.310	.104	2.972	.004

46.6% of PRESOR can be explained by the combination of cultural dimensions. There was a significant correlation between national culture and ethical attitudes, as measured by PRESOR, $F(5, 94) = 16.39, p < .001$, providing evidence to support the hypothesis that there is a significant correlation between Hofstede's cultural dimension of national cultures and ethical attitude level (see Table 4).

This analysis revealed the following correlations: Masculinity (with a significance level of .000) is a significant predictor of PRESOR. Long-term orientation (with a significance level of .001) is also a significant predictor of PRESOR. Uncertainty avoidance (with a P-value significance level of .059), likewise, is a significant predictor of PRESOR.

The other two dimensions of culture, taken separately, however, did not show a significant correlation with PRESOR. Power distance (p=. 367) is not a significant predictor of PRESOR. Individualism (p=. 529) is also not a significant predictor of PRESOR.

Findings on Research Question 2

The second research question asked to what extent, if any, does the relationship between Hofstede's five cultural dimensions (power distance, uncertainty avoidance, individualism, masculinity-femininity; and long-term orientation) and ethical attitude levels differ between business managers in Mexico and the United States?

The methodology for this comparison was to perform a T-test for each hypothesis comparing the two samples of U.S. and Mexican managers to determine the significance of the differences between the two groups. For the combination of all five cultural dimensions, representing total culture, there was a statistically significant difference between the U.S. and Mexican groups. The U.S. sample revealed a lower mean PRESOR score ($M = 5.75$, $SD = 1.02$) than the Mexican sample ($M = 6.22$, $SD = .66$, $t(196) = -3.92$, $p < .001$).

Table 4. Regression results, Mexican managers

Variable	B	Std. Error	t	Sig.
Constant	2.585	.611	4.230	.000
Power distance	-.038	042	-.906	.367
Uncertainty avoidance	.047	.075	.632	.529
Individualism, total	-.089	.047	-1.909	.059
Masculinity, total	.382	.078	4.899	.000
Long-term orientation, total	.230	.065	3.562	.001

While Mexican participants scored higher than U.S. participants, there was a greater standard deviation for the U.S. sample. Each individual dimension of culture was also tested to determine the significance of the difference between U.S. and Mexican managers.

There was no significant correlation between U.S. and Mexican managers in the cultural dimension of power distance ($F(27, 170) = 1.23$, $p = .21$). However, there were a number of significant differences. There was a significant correlation between U.S. and Mexican managers in the cultural dimension of uncertainty avoidance ($F(20,177) = 5.84$, $p < .001$). There was a significant correlation between U.S. and Mexican managers in the cultural dimension of individualism ($F(17,180) = 3.51$, $p < .001$). There was a significant correlation between U.S. and Mexican managers in the cultural dimension of masculinity ($F(18,179) = 5.89$, $p < .001$). Finally, there was also a significant correlation between U.S. and Mexican managers in the cultural dimension of long-term orientation ($F(16,181) = 9.78$, $p < .001$).

Evaluation of Findings

The two theoretical foundations for the proposed research were (a) national culture and (b) ethical attitudes. While many other factors have proven to influence ethical attitudes in the workplace, culture has proven to be a significant one. The research for this study showed considerable support for the correlation with ethical attitude levels among business managers in Mexico and the United States. This bolsters the existing research (Davis, Bernardi & Bosco, 2013) and adds to the body of knowledge built from Hofstede's research concerning national culture showing the correlation of culture with ethical attitudes among managers in the United States and Mexico..

Total culture (a composite of all five dimensions of culture), uncertainty avoidance, masculinity, and long-term orientation were all shown to be significant predictors of PRESOR. Evidence therefore exists to support the correlation between these dimensions of culture and ethical attitudes. Power Distance and Individualism were shown by the research not to be significant predictors. Interestingly, this pattern held true for both U.S. and Mexican managers, demonstrating some evidence contrary to the Hofstede research, which has indicated in many studies that they tend to be positively correlated.

Regarding the significance of the differences between managers in the two cultures of the U.S. and Mexico, the research supports the hypothesis that there is a significant difference between the two national cultures. There was a significant effect for total culture, with Mexican managers receiving higher scores than U.S. managers. The difference between managers from the two countries was also significant in the comparisons with each dimension of culture with one exception. That exception was power distance ($F(27) = 1.231, p = .213$). Uncertainty avoidance, individualism, masculinity, and long-term orientation showed a significant difference.

The most surprising result of the research is that Mexican managers scored higher than U.S. managers in mean scores of PRESOR, where U.S. managers scored an overall mean of 5.75 and Mexican managers scored a mean of 6.22. Participants in other studies from the United States have been consistently higher than most other cultures used for comparison purposes (Axinn, et al., 2004; Vitell & Paolillo, 2004). In a study of 13 different countries that included the United States and Mexico, Ardichvili et al. (2010) found that Mexican ethical practices, in the area of human resource development, lay in what they called the middle group of ethicality, while the United States was in the high grouping. In a study that covered business students in 36 countries, however, Peterson et al. (2010) found that Mexican subjects scored higher than the United States in its ethicality score. Weeks et al. (2006) found that an ethical climate among salespeople positively affected organizational commitment for American managers, but not significantly for Mexican managers.

Reasons for these conflicts with previous research may include changes to culture over time; the fact that a higher proportion of subjects in the present study had high levels of experience (54.5% had more than 10 years of experience), reflecting greater experience that would tend to moderate or improve ethical decision making; and a high educational level (70.8% had a bachelor's degree or a more advanced college degree), indicating a more well-rounded background in understanding all aspects of business that would include ethical decision making. The sample also had a high level of training in philosophy (74.2%), indicating a higher-than-average background in abilities to understand the philosophical and ethical aspects of decision making. Such high levels of achievement in each of these areas may have led to a sample that is not fully reflective of the populations of managers as a whole.

Additional possible explanations for deviance from hypothesis on PRESOR may include that the survey was offered only online. Many potential respondents may not have had access to technology, especially in the country of Mexico (Internet Live Stats, n.d.). Secondly, business cultures change over time. With more managers and employees receiving ethical training in recent years, there has been a boost in ethical awareness, especially in the country of Mexico.

The study results showed a positive relationship between national culture and ethical attitudes. Overall national culture and ethical attitudes were correlated (r $(97) = 0.461, p < .001$) resulting in the null hypothesis being rejected at the .05 level in favor of the alternative hypothesis. Sub-hypotheses were similarly tested for the effect of each dimension of culture, resulting in rejecting the null hypotheses for the cultural dimensions of uncertainty avoidance, masculinity, and long-term orientation. These results held for both U.S. and Mexican samples.

The research also showed that there was a significant difference between the cultures in their overall ethical attitudes. The results (t (196) = -3.924, $p < .001$) showed a significant difference between the ethical attitudes of the U.S. and Mexican subjects. Subset hypotheses concerning the correlation of the two sample groups also showed significant differences in the cultural dimensions of uncertainty avoidance, individualism, masculinity, and long-term orientation, but no significant difference for the power distance dimension. When measured as an overall model, the findings support the positive correlation of national culture with ethical attitudes of managers in the two countries of the United States and Mexico, while showing that differences between the two cultures are significant.

IMPLICATIONS, RECOMMENDATIONS, AND CONCLUSION

Scholars have discussed the importance of antecedents to ethical decision-making including that of national culture. To promote better understanding and improved management, managers need knowledge of the similarities and differences across country borders in improving trade among businesses in this important market (Doh et al., 2010; Franke & Nadler, 2008). Addressing the problem of the deficiency in this knowledge base will assist managers and scholars to find ways of enhancing the corporate legitimacy, profitability, and competitive advantage in international business in North America (Ahmad & Ramayah, 2012; Zheng, Luo, & Wang, 2014). These advantages include improved collective organizational commitment and citizenship behaviors (Chun et al., 2013), improved legitimacy and financial performance (Harris 2007), positive linkage between a company's social responsibility and business performance (Buciuniene & Kazlauskaite, 2012), competitive advantage in international business (Takei, 2011), and corporate strategies that include moral values that are more successful in global business (Wieland, 2010).

Limitations

There were several limitations to the study's generalization to a larger population of managers in specific industries or other countries. Limitations included the size of the sample studied, which was relatively small (n=198). The fact that this research examined populations of only two countries also limits the generalization of conclusions to other national cultures. The nature of the sample, a purposive sample, was another limitation of this study. A random sample of managers in both countries would yield more reliable results.

The study used the assumption that the sample of managers in both the United States and Mexico was representative of the population of such managers in the two countries. Age distribution of the sample was quite uniform, with 33.8% in the 18-34 group, 31.8% in the 35-49 group, and 32.8% in the 50-64 group. Only 1.5% were from the 64 and over group (Vogt, 2007). The survey sample was also limited to users of the Internet, which restricted the sample and excluded other managers who may not have such access (Internet Live Stats, n.d.).). In the U.S., 86.75% of the population had access to the Internet as of 2014, while 41.13% of the Mexican population had Internet access in 2014.

Another possible limitation to the study is response bias, which may occur when a respondent has an overly positive or negative response, either conscious or subconscious, that differs from his or her actual intended response. This could happen due to a fear of information not being confidential or may present harm to his or her job. With sensitive issues such as those of an ethical nature, social desirability bias could also be limiting (Singh et al., 2004).

Implications

That ethical behavior is essential for the well-being of an organization has been established (Buciuniene & Kazlauskaite, 2012; Chun et al., 2013; Harris 2007; Takei, 2011; Wieland, 2010), and that ethical attitudes and culture are antecedents to such behavior (Resick et al., 2006; Schepers, 2006). This research lends credence to the positive correlation of national culture and its related ethical attitudes among business managers. This finding was true for both U.S. and Mexican managers in this research. Not all of the five dimensions of culture were shown to be significant, but uncertainty avoidance, masculinity, and long-term orientation were shown to contribute enough to the correlation to mitigate the lack of correlation with power distance and individualism for both Mexican and U.S. managers.

Implications of this finding, which mostly corroborated existing research on other national cultures (e.g., Davis et al., 2013), are that managers should realize the importance of cultural aspects that employees bring to the workplace and find ways to take advantage of the positive views they bring to inform ethical attitudes and decisions. Along with this, finding ways of improving those attitudes can positively impact organizational outcomes.

National culture as an antecedent to ethical attitudes and good ethical decision-making has been shown by this research to be important at a statistically significant level. Further implications of this research include enabling a deeper understanding of the culture-ethical attitude linkage, which can lead to better managerial decision-making regarding employee training and policies. Additionally, improved professional standards and human resource practices that improve the environment for making ethical decisions can better be accomplished (Smith & Hume, 2005). Finally, knowing that uncertainty avoidance, masculinity, and long-term orientation are the most important dimensions of national culture that lead to enhanced ethical attitudes, organizational performance can be enhanced. Focusing on these most important antecedents can lead to better managerial decisions and policies.

While it should not be used as a litmus test for employment or other human resource practices, findings from this research indicate a deeper understanding of an employee's culture can lead to better employment decisions. This, in turn, can lead to enhanced, on-the-job ethical behaviors and organizational outcomes that can be tailored to individuals within an organization. Knowing the differences among employees can be advantageous in this way. Employee training, in particular, can become more targeted and effective when equipped with the results of this research.

Management decision-making and policy-making can be improved in several ways as a result of the findings of this and related research. It can guide policy development, professional standards, and guidelines for human resource action that improve ethical decision-making (Smith & Hume, 2005). Managers who better understand the culture-ethics correlation are better prepared to develop effective ethics strategies (MacNab, 2007). Specific programs of ethics training and human resource management practices, based on the common elements of culture between the U.S. and Mexican subjects of uncertainty avoidance, masculinity, and long-term orientation dimensions of culture, are can be better formulated.

This research enhances the knowledge concerning the correlation of national culture with ethical attitudes among managers in the United States and Mexico. The findings support the statistically significant correlations between national culture and ethical attitudes for managers in both nations. The study also supports the hypothesis that there is a statistically significant difference between the managers of the two countries. Overall culture was shown to be a significant predictor of ethical attitudes. Implications of the research are to enable improvement in the understanding of workplace ethical attitudes and decision-making and how this improved knowledge can enhance organizational outcomes.

RECOMMENDATIONS AND FUTURE RESEARCH

The need for more focused future research in the correlation of culture with ethical attitudes includes identifying which cultural dimensions are most significant in influencing ethical attitudes, whether more specific elements of national cultures have influenced ethical attitudes, and how changing cultures have changed these attitudes. A time-series study into how things have changed in another five or ten years would be helpful. Future research might be able to identify other factors that affect ethical attitudes that were not recognized in the present study and a study with a larger or more random sample would enhance knowledge in this area. Finally, more research is advisable in correlating culture with ethical attitudes for specific demographic groupings: there may be a significant difference in ethical attitudes in the same culture between males and females, among age groups, or among educational levels.

REFERENCES

Ahmad, N., & Ramayah, T. (2012). Does the notion of 'doing well by doing good' prevail among entrepreneurial ventures in a developing nation? *Journal of Business Ethics, 106*(4), 479–490. doi:10.1007/s10551-011-1012-9

Alas, R. (2006). Ethics in countries with different cultural dimensions. *Journal of Business Ethics, 69*(3), 237–247. doi:10.1007/s10551-006-9088-3

Andreoli, N., & Lefkowitz, J. (2009). Individual and organizational antecedents of misconduct in organizations. *Journal of Business Ethics, 85*(3), 309–332. doi:10.1007/s10551-008-9772-6

Ardichvili, A., Jondle, D., & Kowske, B. (2010). Dimensions of ethical business cultures: Comparing data from 13 countries of Europe, Asia, and the Americas. *Human Resource Development International, 13*(3), 299–315. doi:10.1080/13678 868.2010.483818

Axinn, C., Blair, M., Heorhiadi, A., & Thach, S. (2004). Comparing ethical ideologies across cultures. *Journal of Business Ethics, 54*(2), 103–119. doi:10.1007/s10551-004-0663-1

Beekun, R., & Westerman, J. (2012). Spirituality and national culture as antecedents to ethical decision-making: A comparison between the United States and Norway. *Journal of Business Ethics, 110*(1), 33–44. doi:10.1007/s10551-011-1145-x

Blodgett, J., Bakir, A., & Rose, G. (2008). A test of the validity of Hofstede's cultural framework. *Journal of Consumer Marketing, 25*(6), 339–349. doi:10.1108/07363760810902477

Bremer, J. (2008). How global is the global compact? *Business Ethics (Oxford, England), 17*(3), 227–244. doi:10.1111/j.1467-8608.2008.00533.x

Buciuniene, I., & Kazlauskaite, R. (2012). The linkage between HRM, CSR and performance outcomes. *Baltic Journal of Management, 7*(1), 5–24. doi:10.1108/17465261211195856

Bureau of Labor Statistics. (2012). *Labor force statistics from the current population survey*. Retrieved from http://www.bls.gov/cps/cpsaat11.htm

Carroll, A., & Buchholtz, A. (2008). *Business and society: Ethics and stakeholder management* (7th ed.). Mason, OH: South-western.

Chun, J., Shin, Y., Choi, J., & Kim, M. (2013). How does corporate ethics contribute to firm financial performance? The mediating role of collective organizational commitment and organizational citizenship behavior. *Journal of Management*, *39*(4), 853–877. doi:10.1177/0149206311419662

Chung, K. Y., Eichenseher, J. W., & Taniguchi, T. (2008). Ethical perceptions of business students: Differences between East Asia and the USA and among "Confucian" cultures. *Journal of Business Ethics*, *79*(1), 121–132. doi:10.1007/s10551-007-9391-7

Davis, J., Bernardi, R., & Bosco, S. (2013). Examining the use of Hofstede's uncertainty avoidance construct in a major role in ethics research. *International Business Research*, *6*(1), 63–75. doi:10.5539/ibr.v6n1p63

Doh, J., Husted, B., Matten, D., & Santoro, M. (2010). Ahoy there! Toward greater congruence and synergy between international business and business ethics theory and research. *Business Ethics Quarterly*, *20*(3), 481–502. doi:10.5840/beq201020331

El-Astal, M. (2005). Culture influence on educational public relations officers' ethical judgments: A cross-national study. *Public Relations Review*, *31*(3), 362–375. doi:10.1016/j.pubrev.2005.05.019

Everhart, S., Vazquez, J. M., & McNab, R. M. (2009). Corruption, governance, investment and growth in emerging markets. *Applied Economics*, *41*(13), 1579–1594. doi:10.1080/00036840701439363

Ferrell, O., Fraedrich, J., & Ferrell, L. (2008). *Business ethics: Ethical decision making and cases*. Boston, MA: Houghton Mifflin.

Franke, G., & Nadler, S. (2008). Culture, economic development, and national ethical attitudes. *Journal of Business Research*, *61*(3), 254–264. doi:10.1016/j.jbusres.2007.06.005

Gift, M., Gift, P., & Zheng, Q. (2013). Cross-cultural perceptions of business ethics: Evidence from the United States and China. *Journal of Business Ethics*, *114*(4), 633–642. doi:10.1007/s10551-013-1709-z

Godos-Díez, J., Fernández-Gago, R., & Martínez-Campillo, A. (2011). How important are CEOs to CSR practices? An analysis of the mediating effect of the perceived role of ethics and social responsibility. *Journal of Business Ethics*, *98*(4), 531–548. doi:10.1007/s10551-010-0609-8

Harris, J. (2007). Do firms do 'worse' by doing 'bad'? Financial misrepresentation and subsequent firm performance. *Academy of Management Proceedings*, 1-6. doi: 10.5465/AMBPP.2007.26508370

Hofstede, G. (2001). *Culture's consequences: Comparing values, behaviors, institutions, and organizations across nations* (2nd ed.). Thousand Oaks, CA: Sage.

Holland, D., & Albrecht, C. (2013). The worldwide academic field of business ethics: Scholars' perceptions of the most important issues. *Journal of Business Ethics*, *117*(4), 777–788. doi:10.1007/s10551-013-1718-y

Internet Live Stats. (n.d.). *Internet users*. Retrieved from www.internetlivestats.com

Jacobs, K. (2011). *Assessing the relationship between servant leadership and effective teaching in a private university setting* (Doctoral dissertation). Northcentral University. Retrieved from http://library.ncu.edu/ncu_diss/default.aspx

Khera, I. (2010). Ethics perceptions of the U.S. and its large developing-country trading partners. *Global Management Journal*, *2*(1), 33–41. Retrieved from http://globalmj.eu/wp-content/uploads/2012/02/GMJ_No1_2010.pdf#page=33

Kohlberg. (1984). *The psychology of moral development: The nature and validity of moral stages*. San Francisco, CA: Harper and Row.

Li, N., & Murphy, W. (2012). A three-country study of unethical sales behaviors. *Journal of Business Ethics*, *111*(2), 219–235. doi:10.1007/s10551-012-1203-z

Lian, H., Ferris, D. L., & Brown, D. J. (2012). Does power distance exacerbate or mitigate the effects of abusive supervision? It depends on the outcome. *The Journal of Applied Psychology*, *97*(1), 107–123. doi:10.1037/a0024610 PMID:21766996

MacNab, B., Brislin, R., Worthley, R., Galperin, B. L., Jenner, S., Lituchy, T. R., & Bess, D. et al. (2007). Culture and ethics management: Whistle-blowing and internal reporting within a NAFTA country context. *International Journal of Cross Cultural Management*, *7*(1), 5–28. doi:10.1177/1470595807075167

Marta, J., Heiss, C. M., & De Lurgio, S. A. (2008). An exploratory comparison of ethical perceptions of Mexican and US marketers. *Journal of Business Ethics*, *82*(3), 539–555. doi:10.1007/s10551-007-9575-1

Nielsen, R. P. (2010). High-leverage finance capitalism, the economic crisis, structurally related ethics issues, and potential reforms. *Business Ethics Quarterly*, *20*(2), 299–330. doi:10.5840/beq201020222

Pearce, C. L., Manz, C. C., & Sims, H. P. Jr. (2008). The roles of vertical and shared leadership in the enactment of executive corruption: Implications for research and practice. *The Leadership Quarterly*, *19*(3), 353–359. doi:10.1016/j. leaqua.2008.03.007

Peterson, M., & Søndergaard, M. (2011). Traditions and transitions in quantitative societal culture research in organization studies. *Organization Studies*, *32*(11), 1539–1558. doi:10.1177/0170840611421255

Rakas, S. (2011). Global business ethics - Utopia or reality. *Megatrend Review*, *8*(2), 385-406. Available from http://connection.ebscohost.com/c/articles/70970531/ global-business-ethics-utopia-reality

Resick, C., Hanges, P., Dickson, M., & Mitchelson, J. (2006). A cross-cultural examination of the endorsement of ethical leadership. *Journal of Business Ethics*, *63*(4), 345–359. doi:10.1007/s10551-005-3242-1

Robertson, C., Olson, B., Gilley, K., & Bao, Y. (2008). A cross-cultural comparison of ethical orientations and willingness to sacrifice ethical standards: China versus Peru. *Journal of Business Ethics*, *81*(2), 413–425. doi:10.1007/s10551-007-9504-3

Schepers, D. (2006). Three proposed perspectives of attitude toward business' ethical responsibilities and their implications for cultural comparison. *Business and Society Review*, *111*(1), 15–36. doi:10.1111/j.1467-8594.2006.00259.x

Scholtens, B., & Dam, L. (2007). Cultural values and international differences in business ethics. *Journal of Business Ethics*, *75*(3), 273–284. doi:10.1007/s10551-006-9252-9

Schumacher, E., & Wasieleski, D. (2013). Institutionalizing ethical innovation in organizations: An integrated causal model of moral innovation decision processes. *Journal of Business Ethics*, *113*(1), 15–37. doi:10.1007/s10551-012-1277-7

Shafer, W. E., Fukukawa, K., & Lee, G. M. (2007). Values and the perceived importance of ethics and social responsibility: The US versus China. *Journal of Business Ethics*, *70*(3), 265–284. http://hdl.handle.net/10.1007/s10551-006-9110-9. doi:10.1007/s10551-006-9110-9

Sheng, C., & Sheng, Q. (2004). *A defense of utilitarianism*. Lanham, MD: University.

Simha, A., & Cullen, J. (2012). Ethical climates and their effects on organizational outcomes: Implications from the past and prophecies for the future. *The Academy of Management Perspectives*, *26*(4), 20–34. doi:10.5465/amp.2011.0156

Singh, N. (2004). From cultural models to cultural categories: A framework for cultural analysis. *The Journal of American Academy of Business, Cambridge*, 92–101. Retrieved from http://www.jaabc.com/journal.htm

Singhapakdi, A., Vitell, S., Rallapalli, K., & Kraft, K. (1996). The perceived role of ethics and social responsibility: A scale development. *Journal of Business Ethics*, *15*(11), 1131–1140. doi:10.1007/BF00412812

Smith, A., & Hume, E. C. (2005). Linking culture and ethics: A comparison of accountants' ethical belief systems in the individualism/collectivism and power distance contexts. *Journal of Business Ethics*, *62*(3), 209–220. doi:10.1007/s10551-005-4773-1

Stedham, Y., & Beekun, R. (2013). Ethical judgment in business: Culture and differential perceptions of justice among Italians and Germans. *Business Ethics (Oxford, England)*, *22*(2), 189–201. doi:10.1111/beer.12018

Stephens, G., & Greer, C. (1995). Doing business in Mexico: Understanding cultural differences: New field research clarifies how cultural differences play a role in U.S.-Mexican business alliances. *Organizational Dynamics*. Retrieved from http://www.journals.elsevier.com/organizational-dynamics/

Strubler, D., Park, S., Agarwal, A., & Cayo, K. (2012). Development of a macro-model of cross cultural ethics. *Journal of Legal, Ethical & Regulatory Issues, 15*(2), 25-34. Available from http://law-journals-books.vlex.com/vid/development-macro-model-cross-cultural-ethics-370762482

Su, S. (2006). Cultural differences in determining the ethical perception and decision-making of future accounting professionals: A comparison between accounting students from Taiwan and the United States. *The Journal of American Academy of Business, Cambridge*, *9*(1), 147. Retrieved from http://www.jaabc.com/journal.htm

Takei, H. (2011). Strategic frameworks of ethic management in MNEs: Theoretical discussions and model development. *Journal of Management Research*, *3*(2), 1–15. doi:10.5296/jmr.v3i2.560

Thorne, D. M., Ferrell, O. C., & Ferrell, L. (2011). *Business and society: A strategic approach to social responsibility and ethics*. South-Western Cengage.

Torluccio, G. (2012). *Economics, social responsibility and consumers. The ethical perception*. Bologna, Italy: Silvano Pagani.

U.S. Census Bureau. (n.d.). *Foreign Trade*. Retrieved from https://www.census.gov/foreign-trade/balance/c2010.html

U.S.-Chile Free Trade Agreement. (2009). *United States Department of Agriculture Foreign Agricultural Service website*. Available from https://www.fas.usda.gov/data/free-trade-agreements-and-us-agriculture

Vitell, S., & Paolillo, J. (2004). A cross-cultural study of the antecedents of the perceived role of ethics and social responsibility. *Business Ethics (Oxford, England)*, *13*(2-3), 185–199. doi:10.1111/j.1467-8608.2004.00362.x

Vitell, S., Paolillo, J., & Thomas, J. (2003). The perceived role of ethics and social responsibility: A study of marketing professionals. *Business Ethics Quarterly*, *13*(1), 63–86. doi:10.5840/beq20031315

Westerman, J., Beekun, R., Stedham, Y., & Yamamura, J. (2007). Peers versus national culture: An analysis of antecedents to ethical decision-making. *Journal of Business Ethics*, *75*(3), 239–252. doi:10.1007/s10551-006-9250-y

Whitaker, B., & Godwin, L. (2013). The antecedents of moral imagination in the workplace: A social cognitive theory perspective. *Journal of Business Ethics*, *114*(1), 61–73. doi:10.1007/s10551-012-1327-1

Wieland, J. (2010). Ethics and economic success: A contradiction in terms? Zeitschrift für Psychologie. *The Journal of Psychology*, *218*(4), 243–245. doi:10.1027/0044-3409/a000034

Zheng, Q., Luo, Y., & Wang, S. (2014). Moral degradation, business ethics, and corporate social responsibility in a transitional economy. *Journal of Business Ethics*, *120*(3), 405–421. doi:10.1007/s10551-013-1668-4

Chapter 5
Business Ethics and the Greek Healthcare System

Vaitsa Giannouli
Aristotle University of Thessaloniki, Greece

ABSTRACT

This chapter provides a review not only of classic literature on healthcare business and ethics, but also an introduction to the legal changes in the Greek healthcare system with ethical values on focus. A study examining in both a quantitative and qualitative way what the Greek healthcare experts think and feel about ethics and healthcare services presents the factors that shape attitudes towards ethical values from the viewpoint of the healthcare professionals. For this reason, 34 semi-structured interviews, accompanied by the administration of perceived cohesion scale, generalized immediacy scale, job affect scale, state anxiety inventory, Maslach burnout inventory, and the attitude towards business ethics questionnaire revealed that healthcare professionals do have knowledge of ethical values and moral responsibility, but no clear connections with specific emotional aspects were found. The chapter concludes with future directions on how business ethics can be further examined and applied.

ETHICS: AN INTRODUCTION TO ETHICAL VALUES

Ethical values are part of people's lives regardless of social, historical, spiritual, cultural and/or economic contexts (Weber, 2008). Values can be defined as the sum of the positive properties that reflect the importance of a good person or thing, which people recognize that they should try to acquire and recommend them to others (IGI Global Dictionary, 2017; Philosophical and Sociological Dictionary, 1995). For the

DOI: 10.4018/978-1-5225-2650-6.ch005

examination of the concept of ethical values, philosophy and social sciences have from time to time proposed various definitions. A fairly common approach is the separation in values related to material and economic dimensions of things (e.g. material goods, technical goods, work, money), political values (e.g. individual freedoms, democracy, egalitarianism, rule of law), social values (e.g. love, friendship, cooperation, peace), aesthetic values (coming from the different art movements), natural values (e.g. life, health, nature), and moral values (such as responsibility, honesty, conscientiousness, self-awareness, self-control, dignity) (Diamantopoulos, 2002). The hierarchy of these values depends on the cultural environment and may present differences both in terms of understanding the concepts of different values, and the importance given to each one of them by the individuals (Pletz, 1999).

The term 'ethical value' was originally used in the field of economics as a term not directly linked to financial-business matters, but today it's spread as a basic concept both in theoretical writings and in daily use, regarding all employees (leaders and subordinates) (Harris, 1990; Kanungo, 2001). Ethical values, inherently include, in their meaning, all relevant thoughts and actions in order to overcome the difficulties/barriers of the exterior world, and which are in contrast to everything that can be linked to the natural and effortless (Lalande, 1955). It seems, then, that values can be attributed to everything the conscious thought of a man can perceive and it seems to hold a special position, exerting substantial influence on all future (individual and group) thinking and action/behavior. Of course, there is a hierarchy of values based on (ir)rational or explicit rules of the group in which a person belongs (Landau & Osmo, 2003). So, it is understandable that historically there have been numerous ethical value systems in ancient civilizations, which generally do not show dramatic differences among them. The differences can be found in the varying degrees of importance that specific values may have in the system-society-culture, but most of the times (not without striking exceptions) special attention is given to the values that are positively linked to human life, freedom and justice regardless of the frame (Donnelly, 2013; Schwartz & Bardi, 2001).

HEALTHCARE BUSINESS AND ETHICAL VALUES IN MODERN SOCIETIES

The business activities of people render necessary the achievement of prosperity for the maintenance of societies (Carroll & Buchholtz, 2014; Wartenberg, 2011). Companies are not separate 'entities' and are probably directly influenced by developments in the social and economic environment. Thus, business organizations of all sizes depend on the attitudes, values and the internalized and externalized behavior of their shareholders, their employees, investors, consumers and the government/s of the country or countries in which they operate, which could lead to diversity in terms of attitudes and perceptions of ethical values (Biron, 2010; Liu & Lin, 2016; Peppas & Peppas, 2000; Segon & Booth, 2013; Valentine & Barnett, 2003; van Auken, 2016).

Nowadays, worldwide but also locally in Greece, there is a tendency to consider that there exists a generalized crisis of ethical values in healthcare settings (Kavali, Tzokas & Saren, 2001; Williams & Elliott, 2010), which along with the austerity measures has affected greatly the health of the Greek population and their access to public health services (Kentikelenis et al., 2014). The depreciation of the importance of moral values (as taken through philosophical and religious texts of earlier historical periods) in Greece seems to result from indifference or violation or even encouragement for violation of these ethical rules from the socialization entities, such as the family, school and the media, the prevalence of incoming foreign consumers' new life standards, and the uncontrolled rapid technological progress (Tzavaras, 2005).

During the recent period of the global financial crisis, the debate seems rekindled over the moral values-moral responsibility of both individuals and businesses (Arvidsson & Peitersen, 2013; Cardy & Servarajan, 2006; Gilmartin & Freeman, 2002; Gounaris, 2008). Acts, as a result, are always considered as a person's acts and include mental actions, (i.e. intentions, desires, beliefs, habits etc.).Notably many business theorists argue that since the companies are not natural persons, it is not necessary to have a moral responsibility for their actions, while other theorists argue that the business and the proposed philosophical theories of business ethics should be regarded in terms of a game, where there are some rules to obey or even some rules to defy (Bervesluis, 1987; Carr, 1968), while other theorists see values as a tool in the form of rules, but not necessarily as moral constraints to individual or group action (Friedman, 1962). This means that the reason for the existence of businesses is to increase profits, provided that they are playing according to the rules of the market game (fair play), following the open competition without deception or fraud (Friedman, 2007). This is considered necessary as in interactive situations, such as local and international markets, there seems to apply an inevitable (long-term or short-term) bilateral economic loss when one of the 'players' is harmed in a way that does not follow the rules of the game (French, 1995). It is clear, therefore, that to continue to have a business game in a viable market, the business organizations have the responsibility and obligation to adopt a behavior that will be literally 'moral' and will be governed by an honest spirit for an ethically pure game (Gounaris, 2012). Accordingly, the previous argument of business depersonalization does not hold true, as the operations-actions (or even the non-actions) are always considered as acts either from individuals or from groups-businesses (French, 1995).

The reflection on ethical values directly affects prioritization, action planning and operation of the various healthcare systems and the companies operating in these contexts (Hartman, DesJardins & MacDonald, 2014), while the lack of an 'ethical culture' in healthcare organizations risks breaking the public's trust, and potentially undermines patient care (Rushton, 2016). Although it is generally accepted that the existing relationships between healthcare providers and pharmaceutical or other health-related companies with commercial interests is ethically complex and may end up in biased influences on decision-making, and more specifically on the independent objective judgment of the health professionals (Weber, Wayland & Holton, 2001), the fight for quality services in the healthcare sector (mainly from companies related to the production of drugs and suppliers of medical services) leads more and more managers and specialists of public relations mainly from the private companies in the healthcare sector to strive beyond the economic activity of their companies, and to take care of (usually through advertising) the ethical values of the company they represent. Although this is a superficial approach to the issue of ethical values in business, as the main objective of managers and business owners is just to strengthen the 'social profile of the organization' in order again to have a profit by informing (potential) customers for the (real or not) commitment of the organizations in matters regarding ethical values, the issue of ethical values does not seem in reality to be given any importance from the way that businesses in healthcare choose what they eventually will follow as practice and in the ethical behavior of their employees (Deshpande, Joseph & Prasad, 2006; Simou & Koutsogeorgou, 2014), while it seems to prevail under this pretense, a generalized disregard for compliance with any practices that follow the generally accepted moral values in this field of business (Giannouli, 2014a).

THE PROBLEMS OF THE GREEK HEALTHCARE SYSTEM

The most pressing problems of the Greek National Health System are associated with primary care and related administration, organization, funding, staffing and operation. Characteristic structural and functional problems are the unjust and inefficient fragmentation of the system because of the numerous and different public and private providers, who do not cooperate with a formally established way together and operate without an 'input filter system' (Mossialos, Allin & Davaki, 2005; Oikonomou & Tountas, 2011; Tountas & Karnaki, 2005).

More specifically, according to the literature the main reasons for the high cost and low quality of primary healthcare in Greece is the repetition of diagnostic tests and the unjustified drug prescriptions. The recurrent nature of these activities is based (intentionally or not) on problems in information distribution between the individual provider and the rest of the healthcare services providers, and the induced demand, which is caused primarily by poor government control of doctors' activity and the establishment of the powerful and numerous qualified medical professionals (the numerically largest proportion in the OECD countries), and the cloudy private business network around them. Thus, even if the expenditure is dramatically high, this is not followed by the corresponding health effects. This calls into question the role of primary health care in Greece as an effective care based on methods that are scientifically and socially acceptable and which are accessible to all individuals and community groups (Benos, 1996). In addition to that, the role of the primary healthcare worker is canceled, and as a consequence there is no "concierge-filter-keeper" to the system. The absence of the family doctor leads to overloading of outpatients in hospitals, while the uncontrolled numbers of patient input is degrading the content and quality of care. As a result, the expenditure is not restrained and the system cannot achieve the reduction of the unnecessarily induced/latent demand for specialist (and therefore expensive) services (Benos, 1996; Khorasani et al., 2014; Moraitis, 1996).

The proposed solutions to overcome the foregoing problems, because of the nature of the healthcare services, should be based not only on public policy initiatives, but also on general social consensus on the changes (Oikonomou & Tountas, 2011). According to Oikonomou and Tountas (2011), this can be done through control of all agents and professionals in the primary healthcare, by establishing inter-professional teams of primary care providers and strengthening of the family doctor's role as prime responsible for the «patients' itinerary» (when and only when necessary) for further testing, and/or for further diagnosis and treatment to specialized doctors and hospitals. Furthermore, it is necessary to introduce and implement formal diagnostic and treatment guidelines in daily practice (such as the already used ICD and DSM), and control the number of trainee doctors (based on real market needs).

The previous solutions-changes are mechanisms for control and cost containment through control of the medical procedures, such as the drug prescription and by using new advances of technology, while controlling the medical demography in the context of a single, new effort to upgrade the policy and planning for primary health care. These reforms can help to overcome previous problems only if done in parallel, since each of them has its own advantages and disadvantages. Also, there is no point to simply copy foreign efforts, as the Greek system has its own economic, political and social quirks, but need to be made in cooperation and with the support of international organizations.

UNDERSTANDING ETHICS IN THE GREEK HEALTHCARE SYSTEM

Within this generalized dysfunctional healthcare system in recent years the phenomenon of induced demand (supplier-induced demand, SID) has become a serious problem. The demand that does not correspond to existent real healthcare needs, but is caused by other factors, the most important of which are the physicians, who are causing an increase in demand for medical services for the purpose of direct or indirect increase in personal financial remuneration. Usually the phenomenon of induced demand occurs in healthcare systems, where the physician is remunerated by each act, and is more acute in cases where the costs are covered by insurance providers. Among the causes are the educational and research purposes, the need for vacant hospital beds, or in order to satisfy the patients themselves, especially when they are not properly informed. An important factor in this situation is the direct or indirect advertising of medical "products" of the private sector in order to increase the profitability of the medical and pharmaceutical companies (Tountas, 2007).

Crucial to the examination of this phenomenon is the asymmetry of information between physicians and patients, as the physicians-providers act as patient representatives taking decisions on the diagnosis and treatment to be followed. Thus, in the field of healthcare services (where the majority of the decisions to be made come from the medical staff), there is a high tendency to excessive 'service consumption', and the physicians seem to encourage intentionally this abuse of services (with the sole aim of economic profit) that leads to higher treatment costs than the patients would choose themselves if they had perfect information (e.g. if they were physicians themselves) (Folland, Goodman & Stano, 2012; Richardson & Peacock, 2006). Physicians, therefore, because of information asymmetry, can change the demand for healthcare services expressed by consumers-patients (Arrow, 1963; Karimi et al., 2015). This influence by physicians implies demand changes on the part of the patients for usually more (or even fewer) services-medical products (Folland, Goodman & Stano, 2016; Richardson, 1981), with the increase in demand being the most common trend in the Greek Healthcare System. The explanation of this behavior that some physicians demonstrate may be related to their desire-motivation to have, maintain or achieve a certain level of financial rewards. So, when they do not succeed the desired income, they modify their behavior in order to reach the desired amount of money-income. Of course, aside from the obvious economic factor, it has been suggested that this phenomenon may be due to the different attitudes that physicians as individuals-scientists have on the suitability and effectiveness of the quality that they offer to their patients (Wennberg, Barnes & Zubkoff, 1982). Unfortunately nowadays, this is not the case, because of the introduction of scientifically based and commonly accepted, clear guidelines and diagnostic and treatment protocols that do not necessary require superfluous expenses.

Although the empirical verification of induced demand in the healthcare services market is considered to be difficult (Matsaganis, 1999), resulting in difficulties in implementing policy solutions to this problem (LaBelle, Stoddart & Rice,1994), it is expected to be higher in remuneration systems that involve physicians who are paid according to the medical acts that they perform, in hospital compensation schemes based on the cost, in healthcare systems where there is a complete or comprehensive insurance coverage for diseases with large clinical uncertainty, and in healthcare systems where there is a high-proportion of specialist physicians in the population, and in countries where there are many emergencies (Aletras, 2012).

In Greece, two examples that serve as good examples of the phenomenon of induced demand are: 1) the additional diagnostic tests, which physicians recommend, even if they know that they are useless or that they will not provide factual information to diagnose medical problems and/or 2) the order of therapeutic procedures (e.g. surgery) and pharmaceutical products, for which physicians know that the international scientific medical community supports that they will not help to cure or alleviate a specific medical problem. The knowledge on the part of the physicians of the minimum benefit for the patient is crucial. In the first example, the use of modern technology in Greece (especially with the particularly high consumption indicators for imaging techniques-like CTs and MRIs- compared with other countries), with repetitive and mostly unnecessary CT scans or other tests (e.g. blood testing) has created in Greece chaos in the public sector with delays in conducting those tests for patients that are really in need, and economic maximization of the debt in the laboratories of public hospitals, which negatively impact on the profitability and create in parallel other side problems in hospitals not only in specific clinics, but to the entire operation of the organization. Also, apart from the creation of patient lists that will not really be helped by the proposed high-cost medical tests, and who will be not satisfied with the quality of the services because of the non-diagnosis of their problem due to the delay that they will have to face and the fatigue due to the multiple medical tests, the subsequent delay to the onset of substantial care or the deterioration of their health status due to the effects of the excessive use of diagnostic techniques can exacerbate their health problems, so that subsequent treatment efforts will not have the desired therapeutic effects. Still, out of the hospital environment, a huge and mostly non-controlled private sector (with centers, which systematically cooperate with specific physicians in the public and private sector) has been nurtured the last decades to the detriment of patients and the state.

In the second example of induced demand that raises ethical questions, the unnecessary and arbitrary choice of medical procedures in public (and private) hospitals not only bring profit to the physicians and to their colleagues, but causes problems to the number of vacant hospitalization beds for those who really need them and this creates a climate of dissatisfaction with the waiting lists, the lack of simultaneous large-scale admission to hospitals. As a result, these people are turning to the private sector or to healthcare services abroad. A recent example of induced demand is the unnecessary increase in the numbers of cesarean sections in women who do not need and even do not want to follow this surgical procedure. In this case, the impact of this unethical behavior is not only economic (for gynecologists and maternity clinics), but this medical act may have possible negative effects to the health status for both the mother and the infant, it increases the length of stay in hospital after the birth and the risk of bleeding, infections and complications from anesthesia, while it makes difficult the breastfeeding and the subsequent maternal and child health status (Foura, 2012). Finally, the overprescription of drugs (mostly regarding elderly people), seems to lead to profit for the pharmaceutical industry, excessive pharmaceutical expenditure which could not and cannot be covered by the state, and serious consequences of polypharmacy with the most well-known the deteriorating health of patients from the excessive drug consumption. Possible economic policies to address overconsumption, because of induced demand, can be the user's participation in the cost, the per capita payments, the use of global budgets and/or the perspective financing (Kil & Houlberg, 2014; Niakas, 1999), but all the above have not yet diminished the number of overconsumption since the roots of the problem are not only financial, but also ethical.

LEGAL CHANGES FOR THE GREEK HEALTHCARE SYSTEM: ETHICS ON FOCUS

Conventional ideologies across the world have traditionally supported that any individual or organization involved in the healthcare sector has special duties of beneficence and distributive justice with respect to the impoverished, who are in dire need of their services and products. This way of understanding ethics in the healthcare may also be influenced by religion or ethical views that are directly linked to religion (Ashley, DeBlois & O'Rourke, 2006). In the legal arena, the knowledge of the specific characteristics of 'health care' and the relating problems (e.g. induced demand) is essential for the management, organization, operation and financing of the National Health Service in any country. In particular taking the above into consideration, legal measures for induced demand are necessary, since the internalized values - moral code (not knowledge) of physicians are sacrificed for the economic benefit and it is difficult to bridge the information gap, because it is time-consuming to educate in scientific-medical matters all the clients-patients

(Dranove, 1988; Giannouli, Mistraletti, & Umbrello, 2017), something that would create a society of physicians, while the majority of patients in the Greek society are elderly and non-physicians. Therefore, the changes must be achieved through public policy interventions and strict legislation, particularly for the states that face financial difficulties (Ahmed & Shaikh, 2009).

Thus, the aim of the reforms envisaged by the law do not directly focus on ethical-moral wrongdoings, but only on their legal consequences (Fisher & Lovell, 2009). The recent Law 3918 (Government Gazette of the Hellenic Republic, 2011) is one more attempt to reform the Greek National Health System, which from its establishment in 1983, is in a state of continuous crisis (Davaki & Mossialos, 2005; Tountas, Karnaki & Pavi, 2002). The main idea behind the reform is that the creation of a single National Organization for the Provision of Healthcare Services (Εθνικός Οργανισμός Παροχής Υπηρεσιών Υγείας -E.O.P.Y.Y.), will make legal control easier. This improvement requires operational coordination and achieving cooperation between all entities constituting the primary healthcare network (e.g. health centers and regional clinics, physicians and rural service providers, the primary units care of local authorities and health service units E.O.P.Y.Y.). Achieving cooperation will be achieved through the establishment of a common code of communication, namely the common rules for quality standards and effectiveness for health services, with particular emphasis on the management and control of funding and the rational utilization of available sources. The establishment of criteria and contract terms for providing primary and secondary healthcare (in particular, the conditions, procedures, manner and the time of provision of primary healthcare services, and the level and administration of compensation) with public organizations, private practitioners, as well as the revision and modification of these terms where and when necessary (Article 18) could affect the issue of induced demand, and everyone involved will be subject to the same rules of strict control.

In the same direction of putting emphasis on control of overconsumption (because of the overpopulation in the medical profession) is the creation of a strong board of directors, which, according to the information that they will get from each and every unit belonging or related to the E.O.P.Y.Y. services (Article 23), will become capable of monitoring the provision of primary healthcare and manage according to current market conditions and the behavior of parties involved, as well as the E.O.P.Y.Y. estate and thus act accordingly in order to authorize contracts with third-party healthcare providers (such as hospitals, private clinics, diagnostic centers, rehabilitation centers, pharmacists, private physicians) (Article 22). The problematic relationship between costs and services is therefore expected to be addressed in various ways. For example, the introduction and establishment of e-prescription and e-referrals for medical examinations, which are already in use (Article 25), can serve as a quite effective effort of direct control of operations of the medical profession. Many legal changes will result in more control, such as the responsibility for the drafting of contracts with all parties of healthcare providers, monitoring compliance with these conditions by the Human Resources Management Division of E.O.P.Y.Y., the establishment of criteria and evaluation of contracts with external suppliers, and the special provision for accounting and business operation issues (Article 28). The current dramatic situation in healthcare economics in Greece can drastically change by controlling prescribing via electronic prescriptions, with clear guidelines and prescribing instructions, protocols for medical practices and the continuous training of physicians, and not with funds from drug companies. In conclusion, the current financial crisis requires strict analysis of the administrative and legal dimensions of financial and moral problems, while prompt implementation of legislative reforms are needed.

ETHICAL VALUES AND HEALTHCARE EMPLOYEES: QUALITATIVE AND QUANTITATIVE PERSPECTIVES

Methodology

Based on the above, one of the key questions that could clarify the current situation should focus on the identification of the ethical values that are considered to be most important by companies operating in the health sector (public and private) and their employees. Following the study methodology adapted by Giannouli (2014a), an empirical study was conducted by using both quantitative and qualitative semi-structured interviews on the issue of ethical values (ethics) and healthcare services in Greece. The main question to be answered was "What are the ethical values that are considered to be vital for companies active in the health sector services according to the employees who work in these organizations, and how the employees experience this situation?".

The Quantitative Approach

Six questionnaires were administered: a modification of the five-point scale Attitude Towards Business Ethics Questionnaire (ATBEQ) (Neumann & Reichel, 1987)(see questions in Table 1). The Job Affect Scale (JAS), which measures emotions that people have felt in their work during the last week (active, elated, excited, relaxed, happy, energetic, calm, serene, strong, nervous, scared, sad, contemptuous, hostile, angry, sleepy, inert) (Brief, Burke, George, Robinson, & Webster, 1988).The Generalized Immediacy Scale, which measures how emotionally close the participants perceive

Table 1. Means and standard deviations for the questions from ATBEQ

Questions	Mean	Standard Deviation
1. The only moral for business is making money.	1.05	.23
2. Act according to the law, and you can't go wrong morally.	2.82	.52
3. Business decisions involve a realistic economic attitude and not a moral philosophy.	1.64	.59
4. Moral values are irrelevant to the business world.	1	.00
5. I view sick days as vacation days that I deserve.	1.82	.62
6. If an employee in the company is caught for fraud, corruption and / or theft, should not necessarily be dismissed or punished.	1.08	.28
7. Ethical values in business aim only at creating a good image to the outside and for financial gain.	1.14	.35
8. Investing in society is the best way to realize the values in business.	4.52	.61
9. "Business ethics" is a concept for public relations only.	1.02	.17
10. A person who is doing well in business does not have to worry about moral problems.	1	.00
11. The lack of public confidence in the ethics of business people is not justified.	1.11	.32

the director of the company (direct-not direct, near-distant, warm- cold, friendly-not friendly) (Andersen & Andersen, 2005). The Maslach Burnout Inventory (MBI), which measures the three dimensions of burnout: emotional exhaustion, lack of personal achievements, and depersonalization (Anagnostopoulos & Papadatou, 1992). The Perceived Cohesion Scale which measures how the individual evaluates how it feels like being in the workgroup (Chin, Salisbury, Pearson, & Stollak, 1999), and the State Anxiety Inventory (SAI) which measures how anxious people feel right now.

The Qualitative Approach

The Grounded Theory was developed by sociologists who argue that the data is often distorted (misrepresented) to verify existing theoretical assumptions and supports that the researchers do not develop or modify their theory in the light of new data. For these reasons, they suggest using interviews to investigate social phenomena instead of already developed questionnaires. As a methodological tool, semi-structured interviews were initially conducted in a neutral space that was not the participants' workplace (in order to have more comfort during the interview and then be able to complete and quantitative questionnaires with more honesty). The themes on which the interviews were based were: a) description of the general state-behavior regarding ethical values of the employees (including leaders and subordinates) in public and private companies active in the field of healthcare, b) ways of communication with others for ethical values issues, c) the ethical values and the everyday life of the employees at work and out of work in relation to the family and other people, d) the support from colleagues and / or other people out of work, e) the psychological-social consequences of the presence of a working environment where there is no interest or even devaluation of ethical values, and f) the management of present situation and thoughts about the future.

All interviews were recorded, transcribed from the recordings and analyzed according to the principles of the Grounded Theory. It was necessary to conduct semi-structured interviews, because it would be wrong to start with a pre-formulated hypothesis for an issue that is not investigated in Greece. Because of scarce research in Greece, the adoption of assumptions that are based on findings from other socio-cultural contexts in the field of social psychology would be risky (Sigma-Muga, Daly, Oukal & Kavut, 2005). So, in this research it seemed more appropriate to collect data with a variety of methods. For the interviews, from the information gathered, the key points are marked with a series of codes, which are extracted from the text. The codes are grouped into similar concepts, to make them more appropriate in the analysis procedure. From these concepts, categories are formed, which are the basis for the creation of a theory. This contrasts with the traditional model of the survey, where the researcher selects a theoretical framework, and then applies this model to the phenomenon to be studied (Allan, 2003). The objective, therefore, with this chosen method of data analysis was to develop a complete theoretical understanding of the experiences reported by the participants.

Participants

Thirty-four individuals (21 women), who worked full-time in healthcare businesses and who had a permanent residence in Northern Greek cities, participated in the study. About half of the participants (22) were employed during the conduct of their individual interview in private health services companies, and the rest of the participants were working in the public healthcare sector. The selection of this type of business was made on the basis of scarce previous relevant research and because the investigation of the situation of the companies in the healthcare sector is particularly crucial not only for the workers themselves, but also for the welfare of the whole society.

The average age of the participants was 49.2 years (SD = 4.74), all were of Greek origin, the majority (31) had university and postgraduate education: 23 in business and economics or 8 in medicine (mean education 18.5 years), while 5 were high school graduates and marital status in all participants was: 26 married (6 with a minor child and 20 with two minor children), and were 8 non-married. The average length of working in the same organization was 8.44 years (SD = 3.19), while their superiors in the company was at least 10 years. None of the participants had a managerial position in the healthcare businesses where they worked.

RESULTS AND CONCLUSION

For interviews after repeated reading of transcripts and keeping extensive notes, it became possible to identify some issues - categories which were initially 104. Then the aforementioned categories were grouped and their number reduced to 12 categories. Finally, in the third level, 3 categories were formed as follows:

1. The interaction of ethical values in the working environment and their impact on the personal life-mental health of the employees;
2. Methods of finding balance for the discrepancy of ethical values of the workplace and the personal life;
3. Consideration of the ethical values of the business in the health sector for the future.

The majority of the participants during the interviews placed great emphasis on the impact of the company when it does not recognize the importance of ethical values, primarily to themselves and then to the community. It was clear, therefore, that the recognition of the violation of ethical values is important mainly for the individual and then to the community-group. That the health companies do not put as their primary objective the establishment and existence of social welfare, but only aim at the economic prosperity of their shareholders, seems to be one of the basic patterns in the interviews of all participants in the current study. The exclusive focus on production and consumption of health-related goods and/or services and the creation of needs that do not really exist and that are potentially dangerous for people or for the society (induced demand phenomenon) were at the center of the interviews-narratives of the participants. They say (mainly the employees in health enterprises, especially those who are in positions related to the handling of economic issues) that they largely perceive the issue of ethical values in companies that are active in healthcare as a personal and secondary as a social failure to achieve prosperity. The participants say that they feel 'pressure', not so much from the program and the workload, but they feel stress that is caused by the fear not to 'trample during business hours (as they say) the values espoused in their personal lives. In addition to that, they are afraid that they will not be able to respond to their role as honest, objective and independent individuals, as they will have to comply with the 'values' of any employer. A similar finding is presented in the relevant literature for the society's expectations for employees (Libby & Thorne, 2007).

The sensed mismatch of work and personal life regarding the issue of ethical values leads people to negative feelings of guilt and worthlessness and lack of autonomous moral action for themselves, because they believe that their actions at work partially alter their personal identity. This sensed 'moral loss within the workplace' is described as a particularly painful experience daily, while the reported mood swings are mainly related to pleasurable experiences not relevant to moral issues within and outside the workplace. Participants also reported that they feel guilty about the ethical values issue, while the majority of them (27/34) describe a cycle of negative thoughts that prolong the despair of 'moral decadence-misery' and yet again they tend to focus and cut off this experience from the rest of their lives. They even express feelings of stress and anger - even hatred - for their superiors at work (who create this indifference towards ethical values and the equation of social welfare with the sum of the financial surpluses for themselves and/or the company). This seems consistent with the identification of a new syndrome (hubris syndrome), which refers to the tendency of leaders (whether they come from the world of politics, either from the business world) to become arrogant, presumptuous and contemptuous not only against individuals, but also towards the value system that they are expected to accept and follow, taking decisions without considering the consequences for the society and considering themselves above all authority and ethics systems (Anderson et al., 2008). Beyond that, participants express negative emotions (especially sadness and hate) towards their colleagues who deliberately comply with the demands of the superiors and accept the absence of even a basic system-code of ethical values in the healthcare business (22/34).

All the above findings are connected as shown by the interview quotes with the reduction of personal interest in work and with various physical symptoms. None of the participants mentioned the term "depression" (although the type and frequency of the described symptoms) could be described as such. The strange thing is that the employees refer that they automatically limit the 'personal and moral disagreement' in their workplace (21/34). Specifically, the participants who have their own families with children report that their main concern is how their children and parents will accept the fact that they do not always act in a faithful way and according to their own personal values. It is also very interesting that all the participants spontaneously mentioned at this point of the interviews that they do not see ethical issues in relation to the possible future legal implications (e.g. legal punishment) (Loeb, 1975).

From the analysis of the collected information, it appears that participants believe that there are universal ethical values, and for the companies-organizations in the healthcare sector they refer to the following themes related to values without a specific hierarchy: 1) altruism –care mainly for man and secondarily for the natural environment, 2) social justice through the recognition of basic human rights, 3) public recognition and support through practical methods of equality between people (customers and non-customers), 4) respect of the freedom of individuals/patients/customers, 5) truth-honesty for both financial management and the quality and suitability of products and services, and 6) the reliability are accountability that the healthcare business must demonstrate towards the individual customers and the state. It also appears under this qualitative approach that in modern Greek markets the ethical values are generally ignored, negated and replaced by just the opposite, for the sake of financial gain as evidenced by the interview excerpts of the participants, a fact that is largely attributed to the economic crisis. Thus, the position of Adam Smith that people act in the financial world not based on humanitarianism but by selfishness, is confirmed by the current qualitative findings (in addition to the quantitative approach to this phenomenon as described by Falk, & Szech (2013).

The participants when asked whether they believe that in the future they will adopt the values that they reported and will not engage in 'immoral behavior' in their work, responded in a positive way and in contrast to previous findings of quantitative research from other countries (McCabe, Ingram & Data-On, 2006; Peterson et al., 2010) in a similar way (both men and women) and in contrast to similar studies coming from abroad with quantitative methods (Gill, 2009; Valentine & Page, 2006; Tanveer et al., 2012; Peterson et al., 2010; Woodbine, 2006). In general, women and men of this sample during the interviews and during the completion of the quantitative questionnaires showed similar compliance to the above mentioned values (and in agreement with some other findings from studies of non-western countries: Dellaportas, 2006; Gholipour et al, 2012).

Of particular interest is that all participants, regardless of their educational level described in various ways a non-ethical behavior expression in the workplace (by others and not by themselves as they stated) that is the phenomenon of induced demand, i.e. any kind of action that increases directly or indirectly the personal financial profit of the employee or the company at the expense of the patient, of course or another company or the state.

There is not a specific pattern in the participants' interviews and therefore they do not appear to differ or be related to a systematic manner according to their feelings about how they feel themselves at work (as measured by the Job Affect Scale). No statistically significant differences were found in the way that they feel tied to the group in which they work (Perceived Cohesion Scale), their state anxiety (as measured by the State Anxiety Inventory) and their experience of burnout (Maslach Burnout Inventory). In addition, there was not a statistically significant correlation between these questionnaires and the Attitude Towards Business Ethics Questionnaire (ATBEQ), while the mean scores and deviations for each of the questions in the

ATBEQ revealed that the participants do have knowledge of ethical values and moral responsibility (see Table 1).

During the interview participants were asked to state in their words, the possible ways that particularly unfavorable circumstances or states, of ethical values could be improved in the health business. Their responses were formulated in the form of proposals concerned two main strategies: 1) learning through relevant educational-information programs that would focus on raising awareness on ethical value issues and business, and 2) selection of senior executive managers who would be trained to raise awareness and to promote the issue of ethical values in business. Even if these suggestions were not accepted or implemented as guidelines for action, they quite clearly demonstrate the presence of a common approach that employees could use to address the issue of ethical values. It is noteworthy that the participants propose during their interviews the above two strategies, however, it seems that although employees accept their personal responsibility and the need for action, they do not want to start these actions in order to change the situation and postpone the personal action (as they consider themselves 'unprepared for such an initiative'). The intention not to take independent action depends as mentioned again by the majority of the participants (28/34) on the refusal of the management of their businesses to deal with the moral issue. Additionally, some employees (25/34) reported that they avoid the risk of an open discussion or even public complaint on the matter with the managers (unless this initiative is launched by their own superiors), and say they do not trust their superiors handling ethical issues in the workplace and would prefer to remain silent or even leave the company, instead of an open conflict with the team and especially with the leader of the working group (21/34). As a way to manage the problem, all the participants reported finding emotional support from the family and friends network, as they fear that disclosure of further information from the workplace and their working relationships could be misunderstood or used in an uncontrolled manner by third persons - not close relatives (including spouse, parents, etc.).

The initial findings of this investigation, come to cover both the theoretical and the research gap regarding ethical values and how we experience and think about these employees in companies operating in the healthcare sector in Greece. The fact that even this small number of examined employees in such enterprises do not differ in their views on the subject regardless of their demographic characteristics and despite their workload, seems to make clear that they are aware and very concerned about the issue of ethical values. The idea that there is an observed immoral behavior-corruption-commitment due to the importance that economic values impose, while there is a full depreciation of ethical values of people when operating in the market, because they focus exclusively on competition and profits and not on the ethical parameters (Falk & Szech, 2013). The participants express in their interviews that they know very well that the focus on the economic factor is not in agreement with the idea of the importance of the value that man has over everything else, especially for the health sector. Apart from the short-term and/or long-term psychological effects of actions or non-actions of immoral behavior in the same interviews there is concern about the impact of this kind of attitudes and behavior on the mental and especially the physical health of the business customers and at the macro-level, in the general welfare of the society. From all the interviews, we can also find that the best way to improve the existing 'discount' of ethical values and for reconstructing a 'culture of ethics' in daily business operations (especially for healthcare business) it is necessary to ask for an informative or even invasive action of a third party in order to raise awareness and improve the whole attitude change procedure through learning techniques especially at the workplace. The only way for the employees of the study to achieve long-term sincere adoption of behaviors in order to achieve social welfare (which will bring beneficial effects both for the employees themselves in the healthcare companies -with reduction of moral inconsistency experienced) is to raise awareness and learning (as in school environments) regarding ethics and business matters initially for managers and then or even parallel for the subordinate business employees in order to incorporate this diverse set of core values in the daily life of the healthcare organization.

FUTURE RESEARCH DIRECTIONS

Thus, the importance of the above findings for the general audience is focused on the fact that managers according to employees can play a significant part in ethics-related initiatives in the workplace. Therefore, future research attempts should further clarify and investigate cross-culturally the 'ethical' role of managers in healthcare settings (Buttigieg et al., 2015). Generally, in business, the role of managers is considered to be of great importance as primarily through their very actions (e.g. organization of training-sensitization programs), they can ensure that an ethical climate fostering organizational ethical integrity will be created, communicated and sustained for the whole organizational team (Demirtas & Akdogan, 2015; Dracopoulou, 2006; Liaropoulos, 1998; Silverman, 2000; Stevens, 1999). Tomorrow's healthcare management in Greece should utilize modern organizational tools to manage human resources not only with a focus on financial matters (Minogiannis, 2016), but also by incorporating ethical leadership, that is the ways that leaders can follow in order to influence the ethical culture of units at various levels, and therefore influence employees' ethical cognitions and behavior (Brown & Treviño, 2006; Mayer et al., 2012; Schaubroeck et al., 2012).

It should be mentioned that the main limitation of this research is the small number of participants, as characterized by the qualitative method compared to quantitative research. Nonetheless, a smaller sample imposed little or no limitations in our efforts to collect rich information on a new dual approach to the study of ethical values in business. A new perspective that combines both quantitative and qualitative methods on human resource management was attained. Future challenges and directions that relate to the inability to simultaneously gather qualitative and quantitative data, at both the individual and the organizational level (Giannouli, 2014b), are highly linked to the above research methodological impediments. Generalizability in the application of this knowledge in the world of international business, and especially in healthcare management, is necessary in order to achieve optimum understanding and use of values across healthcare professionals that will help improve interprofessional teamwork and decision-making (Falkenström, Ohlsson & Höglund, 2016; Moyo et al., 2016).

REFERENCES

Ahmed, J., & Shaikh, B. T. (2009). The many faces of supplier induced demand in health care. *Iranian Journal of Public Health*, *38*(2), 139–141. Retrieved from https://www.researchgate.net/publication/233864600_The_Many_Faces_of_Supplier_Induced_Demand_in_Health_Care

Aletras, V. (2012). *Health, healthcare and healthcare business.* Retrieved from Hellenic Open University DMY60 Economic and Financial Management of Health Care Services: https://study.eap.gr/login/index.php

Allan, G. (2003). A critique of using grounded theory as a research method. *Electronic Journal of Business Research Methods*, *2*(1), 1–10. Retrieved from http://citeseerx.ist.psu.edu/viewdoc/download?doi=10.1.1.464.1384&rep=rep1&type=pdf

Anagnostopoulos, F., & Papadatou, D. (1992). Factor composition and internal consistency of the questionnaire for recording burnout in a sample of nurses. *Psihologijske Teme*, *5*(3), 183–202. doi:10.5281/zenodo.44229

Andersen, P. A., & Andersen, J. F. (2005). Measurements of perceived nonverbal immediacy. In V. Manusov (Ed.), *The sourcebook of nonverbal measures: Going beyond words* (pp. 113–126). Mahwah, NJ: Erlbaum.

Anderson, C., Ames, D. R., & Gosling, S. D. (2008). Punishing hubris: The perils of overestimating one's status in a group. *Personality and Social Psychology Bulletin*, *34*(1), 90–101. doi:10.1177/0146167207307489 PMID:18162658

Arrow, K. J. (1963). Uncertainty and the welfare economics of medical care. *The American Economic Review*, *53*(5), 941–973. Retrieved from http://www.jstor.org/stable/1812044

Arvidsson, A., & Peitersen, N. (2013). *The ethical economy: Rebuilding value after the crisis*. New York, NY: Columbia University Press.

Ashley, B. M., DeBlois, J., & O'Rourke, K. D. (2006). *Health care ethics: A Catholic theological analysis*. Washington, DC: Georgetown University Press.

Benos, A. (1996). Competition or solidarity: The proposal of primary health care. In G. Kyriopoulos & T. Filalithis (Eds.), *Health policy in Greece: The crossroads of choices* (pp. 43–53). Athens: Themelio.

Beversluis, E. H. (1987). Is there "no such thing as business ethics"? *Journal of Business Ethics*, *6*(2), 81–88. doi:10.1007/BF00382021

Biron, M. (2010). Negative reciprocity and the association between perceived organizational ethical values and organizational deviance. *Human Relations*, *63*(6), 875–897. doi:10.1177/0018726709347159

Brief, A. P., Burke, M. J., George, J. M., Robinson, B. S., & Webster, J. (1988). Should negative affectivity remain an unmeasured variable in the study of job stress? *The Journal of Applied Psychology*, *73*(2), 193–198. doi:10.1037/0021-9010.73.2.193 PMID:3384771

Brown, M. E., & Treviño, L. K. (2006). Ethical leadership: A review and future directions. *The Leadership Quarterly*, *17*(6), 595–616. doi:10.1016/j.leaqua.2006.10.004

Buttigieg, S. C., Rathert, C., D'Aunno, T. A., & Savage, G. T. (2015). International research in health care management: Its need in the 21st century, methodological challenges, ethical issues, pitfalls, and practicalities. *Advances in Health Care Management*, *17*, 3–22. doi:10.1108/S1474-823120140000017001 PMID:25985505

Cardy, R., & Servarajan, T. (2006). Assessing ethical behaviour: The impact of outcomes on judgment bias. *Journal of Managerial Psychology*, *21*(1), 52–72. doi:10.1108/02683940610643215

Carr, A. (1968). Is business bluffing ethical? *Harvard Business Review*, *46*, 143–153. Retrieved from https://hbr.org/1968/01/is-business-bluffing-ethical

Carroll, A. B., & Buchholtz, A. K. (2014). *Business and society: Ethics, sustainability, and stakeholder management*. Stamford, CT: Nelson Education.

Chin, W. W., Salisbury, W. D., Pearson, A. W., & Stollak, M. J. (1999). Perceived cohesion in small groups: Adapting and testing the Perceived Cohesion Scale in a small group setting. *Small Group Research*, *30*(6), 751–766. doi:10.1177/104649649903000605

Davaki, K., & Mossialos, E. (2005). Plusça change: Health sector reforms in Greece. *Journal of Health Politics, Policy and Law*, *30*(1-2), 143–168. doi:10.1215/03616878-30-1-2-143 PMID:15943391

Dellaportas, S. (2006). Making a difference with a discrete course on accounting ethics. *Journal of Business Ethics*, *65*(4), 391–404. doi:10.1007/s10551-006-0020-7

Demirtas, O., & Akdogan, A. A. (2015). The effect of ethical leadership behavior on ethical climate, turnover intention, and affective commitment. *Journal of Business Ethics*, *130*(1), 59–67. doi:10.1007/s10551-014-2196-6

Deshpande, S. P., Joseph, J., & Prasad, R. (2006). Factors impacting ethical behavior in hospitals. *Journal of Business Ethics*, *69*(2), 207–216. doi:10.1007/s10551-006-9086-5

Diamantopoulos, D. (2002). *Modern dictionary of the basic concept of the material-technical, spiritual and ethical civilization*. Athens: Patakis.

Donnelly, J. (2013). *Universal human rights in theory and practice*. Ithaca, NY: Cornell University Press.

Dracopolou, S. (Ed.). (2006). *Ethics and values in healthcare management*. New York, NY: Routledge.

Dranove, D. (1988). Demand inducement and the physician/patient relationship. *Economic Enquiry*, *26*(2), 281–298. doi:10.1111/j.1465-7295.1988.tb01494.x PMID:10287407

Falk, A., & Szech, N. (2013). Morals and markets. *Science*, *340*(6133), 707–711. doi:10.1126/science.1231566 PMID:23661753

Falkenström, E., Ohlsson, J., & Höglund, A. T. (2016). Developing ethical competence in healthcare management. *Journal of Workplace Learning*, *28*(1), 17–32. doi:10.1108/JWL-04-2015-0033

Felce, D., & Perry, J. (1995). Quality of life: It's definition and measurement. *Research in Developmental Disabilities*, *1*(4), 51–74. doi:10.1016/0891-4222(94)00028-8 PMID:7701092

Fisher, C. M., & Lovell, A. (2009). *Business ethics and values: Individual, corporate and international perspectives*. Harlow, UK: Pearson.

Folland, S., Goodman, A., & Stano, M. (2012). *The economics of health and health care* (7th ed., pp. 305–308). Boston, MA: Pearson.

Folland, S., Goodman, A. C., & Stano, M. (2016). *The economics of health and health care: Pearson international edition*. Routledge.

Foura, G. (2012). *Profitable unnecessary industry of caesarean sections*. Retrieved from http://news.kathimerini.gr/4dcgi/_w_articles_ell_1_15/01/2012_469283

French, P. A. (1995). *Corporate ethics*. New York: Harcourt.

Friedman, M. (1962). *Capitalism and freedom*. Chicago, IL: University of Chicago Press.

Friedman, M. (2007). The social responsibility of business is to increase its profits. In R. F. Chadwick & D. Schroeder (Eds.), *Corporate ethics and corporate governance* (pp. 173–178). Berlin: Springer; doi:10.1007/978-3-540-70818-6_14

Gholipour. T., Nayeri, H., & Mehdi. (2012). Academic journal investigation of attitudes about corporate social responsibility: Business students in Iran. *African Journal of Business Management, 6*(14), 5105-5113. doi: 10.5897/AJBM11.2699

Giannouli, V. (2014a). The moral values for social welfare: The importance of moral values for companies in the health sector. *European Business Ethics Network*, 1-26. Retrieved from http://www.eben.gr/wp-content/uploads/2014/12/hthikes_axies_sto_xwro_tis_ygeias_vaitsa_giannouli.pdf

Giannouli, V. (2014b). *Emotional leadership in health care units: Relationships of leaders-subordinates* (Unpublished master's thesis). Hellenic Open University, Patras, Greece.

Giannouli, V., Mistraletti, G., & Umbrello, M. (2017). ICU experience for patients' relatives: Is information all that matters? *Intensive Care Medicine, 43*(5), 722–723. doi:10.1007/s00134-017-4723-2 PMID:28236257

Gill, S. (2009). Is gender inclusivity an answer to ethical issues in business? An Indian stance. *Gender in Management, 25*(1), 37–63. doi:10.1108/17542411011019922

Gilmartin, M. J., & Freeman, R. E. (2002). Business ethics and health care: A stakeholder perspective. *Health Care Management Review, 27*(2), 52–65. doi:10.1097/00004010-200204000-00006 PMID:11985291

120

Gounaris, A. (2008). Business and moral responsibility. *CRS Review,* 3. Retrieved from http://www.academia.edu/456272/Business_and_Moral_Responsibility

Gounaris, A. (2012). From business ethics to the compulsory 'fair play'. *Corporate Social Responsibility*, 16-17. Retrieved from http://www.academia.edu/456270/ From_Business_Ethics_to_Forced_Fair_Play_

Government Gazette of the Hellenic Republic. (2011). *N. 3918* (ΦΕΚ Α' 31/2-3-2011 τεχ. Α'). Retrieved from http://www.eopyy.gov.gr/Home/StartPage?a_ HomePage=Index

Harris, J. R. (1990). Ethical values of individuals at different levels in the organizational hierarchy of a single firm. *Journal of Business Ethics*, 9(9), 741–750. doi:10.1007/ BF00386357

Hartman, L. P., DesJardins, J. R., & MacDonald, C. (2014). *Business ethics: Decision making for personal integrity and social responsibility*. New York, NY: McGraw-Hill.

Ibrahim, N., Howard, D., & Angelidis, J. P. (2008). The relationship between religiousness and corporate social responsibility orientation: Are there differences between business managers and students? *Journal of Business Ethics*, 78(1-2), 165–174. doi:10.1007/s10551-006-9321-0

IGI Global Dictionary. (2017). *What is ethical value.* Retrieved from https://www. igi-global.com/dictionary/ethical-value/10274

Kanungo, R. N. (2001). Ethical values of transactional and transformational leaders. *Canadian Journal of Administrative Sciences/Revue Canadienne des Sciences de l'Administration, 18*(4), 257-265. doi: 10.1111/j.1936-4490.2001.tb00261.x

Karimi, S., Khorasani, E., Keyvanara, M., & Afshari, S. (2015). Factors affecting physicians' behaviors in induced demand for health services. *International Journal of Educational and Psychological Researches, 1*(1), 43–51. doi:10.4103/2395-2296.147469

Kavali, S., Tzokas, N., & Saren, M. (2001). Corporate ethics: An exploration of contemporary Greece. *Journal of Business Ethics*, 30(1), 87–104. doi:10.1023/A:1006215311621

Kentikelenis, A., Karanikolos, M., Reeves, A., McKee, M., & Stuckler, D. (2014). Greece's health crisis: From austerity to denialism. *Lancet, 383*(9918), 748–753. doi:10.1016/S0140-6736(13)62291-6 PMID:24560058

Khorasani, E., Keyvanara, M., Karimi, S., & Jazi, M. J. (2014). Views of health system experts on macro factors of induced demand. *International Journal of Preventive Medicine, 5*(10), 1286–1298. PMID:25400888

Kil, A., & Houlberg, K. (2014). How does copayment for health care services affect demand, health and redistribution? A systematic review of the empirical evidence from 1990 to 2011. *The European Journal of Health Economics, 15*(8), 813–828. doi:10.1007/s10198-013-0526-8 PMID:23989938

LaBelle, R., Stoddart, G., & Rice, T. (1994). A re-examination of the meaning and importance of supplier-induced demand. *Journal of Health Economics, 13*(3), 347–368. doi:10.1016/0167-6296(94)90036-1 PMID:10138860

Lalande, A. (1955). *Dictionary of philosophy.* Athens: Papyrus.

Landau, R., & Osmo, R. (2003). Professional and personal hierarchies of ethical principles. *International Journal of Social Welfare, 12*(1), 42–49. doi:10.1111/1468-2397.00007

Liakos, A., & Giannitsi, S. (1984). The reliability and validity of the amended Greek Spielberger anxiety scale. *Encephalos, 21,* 71–76.

Liaropoulos, L. (1998). Ethics and the management of health care in Greece. In S. Dracopoulou (Ed.), *Ethics and values in health care management* (pp. 148–171). London, UK: Routledge.

Libby, T., & Thorne, L. (2007). The development of a measure of auditors' virtue. *Journal of Business Ethics, 71*(1), 89–99. doi:10.1007/s10551-006-9127-0

Liu, C. M., & Lin, C. P. (2016). Corporate ethical values and turnover intention. *Journal of Leadership & Organizational Studies, 23*(4), 397–409. doi:10.1177/1548051816632358

Loeb, S. E. (1978). *Ethics in the accounting profession.* New York, NY: Wiley.

Matsaganis, M. (1999). Public intervention in the health sector. In V. Aletras, M. Matsaganis, & D. Niakas (Eds.), *Economic and financial management of healthcare services* (Vol. A, pp. 15–39). Patras: Hellenic Open University Publishing.

Mayer, D. M., Aquino, K., Greenbaum, R. L., & Kuenzi, M. (2012). Who displays ethical leadership, and why does it matter? An examination of antecedents and consequences of ethical leadership. *Academy of Management Journal, 55*(1), 151–171. doi:10.5465/amj.2008.0276

Mccabe, A. C., Ingram, R., & Data-On, M. C. (2006). The business of ethics and gender. *Journal of Business Ethics, 64*(2), 101–116. doi:10.1007/s10551-005-3327-x

Minogiannis, P. (2016). Tomorrow's public hospital in Greece: Managing health care in the post crisis era. *Social Cohesion and Development, 7*(1), 69-80. Retrieved from http://ejournals.epublishing.ekt.gr/index.php/SCAD/article/viewFile/8990/9184

Moraitis, E. (1996). A realistic proposal for the creation of a modern primary health care system in Greece. In G. Kyriopoulos & T. Filalithis (Eds.), *Primary health care in Greece* (pp. 180–185). Athens: Themelio.

Mossialos, E., Allin, S., & Davaki, K. (2005). Analysing the Greek health system: A tale of fragmentation and inertia. *Health Economics, 14*(1), S151–S168. doi:10.1002/hec.1033 PMID:16161195

Moyo, M., Goodyear-Smith, F. A., Weller, J., Robb, G., & Shulruf, B. (2016). Healthcare practitioners' personal and professional values. *Advances in Health Sciences Education: Theory and Practice, 21*(2), 257–286. doi:10.1007/s10459-015-9626-9 PMID:26215664

Neumann, Y., & Reichel, A. (1987). *The development of attitudes toward business ethics questionnaire (ATBEQ): Concepts, dimensions, and relations to work values.* Working Paper, Department of Industrial Engineering and Management, Ben Gurion University of the Negev, Israel.

Niakas, D. (1999). Methods of compensation and financing of suppliers. In V. Aletras, M. Matsaganis, & D. Niakas (Eds.), *Economic and financial management of healthcare services* (Vol. A, pp. 87–98). Patras: Hellenic Open University Publishing.

Oikonomou, N., & Tountas, Y. (2011). The Greek economic crisis: A primary health-care perspective. *Lancet, 377*(9759), 28–29. doi:10.1016/S0140-6736(10)62336-7 PMID:21195247

Peppas, S. C., & Peppas, G. J. (2000). Business ethics in the European Union: A study of Greek attitudes. *Management Decision, 38*(6), 369–376. doi:10.1108/00251740010373070

Peterson, R. A., Albaum, G., Merunka, D., Munuera, T. L., & Smith, S. M. (2010). Effects of nationality, gender and religiosity on business related ethics. *Journal of Business Ethics, 96*(4), 573–587. doi:10.1007/s10551-010-0485-2

Philosophical and Sociological Dictionary. (1995). Athens: Kapopoulos.

Pletz, J. (1999). *Being ethical.* New York, NY: Nova.

Richardson, J. (1981). The inducement hypothesis: That doctors generate demand for their own services. In J. Van der Gaag & M. Perlmand (Eds.), *Health, economics and health economics* (pp. 189–214). Amsterdam: North-Holland.

Richardson, J., & Peacock, S. (2006). Supplier-induced demand: Reconsidering the theories and new Australian evidence. *Applied Health Economics and Health Policy*, *5*(2), 87–98. doi:10.2165/00148365-200605020-00003 PMID:16872250

Rushton, C. H. (2016). Creating a culture of ethical practice in health care delivery systems. *The Hastings Center Report*, *46*(S1), 28–31. doi:10.1002/hast.628 PMID:27649916

Schaubroeck, J. M., Hannah, S. T., Avolio, B. J., Kozlowski, S. W., Lord, R. G., Treviño, L. K., & Peng, A. C. et al. (2012). Embedding ethical leadership within and across organization levels. *Academy of Management Journal*, *55*(5), 1053–1078. doi:10.5465/amj.2011.0064

Schwartz, S. H., & Bardi, A. (2001). Value hierarchies across cultures taking a similarities perspective. *Journal of Cross-Cultural Psychology*, *32*(3), 268–290. doi:10.1177/0022022101032003002

Segon, M., & Booth, C. (2013). Values based approach to ethical culture: A case study. In M. Schwartz, H. Harris, & S. Cohen (Eds.), *Ethics, values and civil societies, Research in ethical issues in organizations* (Vol. 9, pp. 93–118). Bingley, UK: Emerald. doi:10.1108/S1529-2096(2013)0000009011

Sigma-Muga, C., Daly, B. A., Oukal, D., & Kavut, L. (2005). The influence of nationality and gender on ethical sensitivity: An application of the issue-contingent model. *Journal of Business Ethics*, *57*(2), 139–159. doi:10.1007/s10551-004-4601-z

Silverman, H. J. (2000, September). Organizational ethics in healthcare organizations: Proactively managing the ethical climate to ensure organizational integrity. HEC Forum, 2(3), 202-215. doi:10.1023/A:1008985411047

Simou, E., & Koutsogeorgou, E. (2014). Effects of the economic crisis on health and healthcare in Greece in the literature from 2009 to 2013: A systematic review. *Health Policy (Amsterdam)*, *115*(2), 111–119. doi:10.1016/j.healthpol.2014.02.002 PMID:24589039

Spielberger, C. D. (1983). *State-trait anxiety inventory: A comprehensive bibliography*. Palo Alto, CA: Consultant Psychologists.

Stevens, B. (1999). Communicating ethical values: A study of employee perceptions. *Journal of Business Ethics*, *20*(2), 113–120. doi:10.1023/A:1005869431079

Tanveer, M. A., Gill, H., & Ahmed, I. (2012). Why business students cheat? A study from Pakistan. *American Journal of Scientific Research, 78*, 24–32. Retrieved from http://search.proquest.com/openview/67e22ad71eac4b7ea0d8075e9d1e91df/1?pq-origsite=gscholar

Timms, N., & Timms, R. (1982). *Dictionary of social welfare*. London, UK: Routledge.

Tountas, Y. (2007). *Induced demand and excessive use of health services*. Retrieved from http://panacea.med.uoa.gr/topic.aspx?id=813

Tountas, Y., Karnaki, P., & Pavi, E. (2002). Reforming the reform: The Greek National Health System in transition. *Health Policy (Amsterdam), 62*(1), 15–29. doi:10.1016/S0168-8510(01)00217-2 PMID:12151132

Tountas, Y., Karnaki, P., Pavi, E., & Souliotis, K. (2005). The "unexpected" growth of the private health sector in Greece. *Health Policy (Amsterdam), 74*(2), 167–180. doi:10.1016/j.healthpol.2005.01.013 PMID:16153477

Tzavaras, G. (2005). *The depreciation of values*. Athens: Indiktos.

Valentine, S., & Barnett, T. (2003). Ethics code awareness, perceived ethical values, and organizational commitment. *Journal of Personal Selling & Sales Management, 23*(4), 359–367. doi:10.1080/08853134.2003.10749009

Valentine, S., & Page, K. (2006). Nine to five: Skepticism of women's employment and ethical reasoning. *Journal of Business Ethics, 63*(1), 53–61. doi:10.1007/s10551-005-7714-0

Van Auken, S. (2016). Assessing the role of business faculty values and background in the recognition of an ethical dilemma. *Journal of Education for Business, 91*(4), 211–218. doi:10.1080/08832323.2016.1160021

Wartenberg, J. (2011). Human well-being at the heart of economics. *The Global Women's Project-Advancing human well-being and ecological sustainability*. Retrieved from https://www.coc.org/files/Briefing-Paper-5-Human-Wellbeing(1).pdf

Weber, E. T. (2008). Religion, public reason, and humanism: Paul Kurtz on fallibilism and ethics. *Contemporary Pragmatism, 5*(2), 131–147. doi:10.1163/18758185-90000095

Weber, L. J., Wayland, M. T., & Holton, B. (2001). Health care professionals and industry: Reducing conflicts of interest and established best practices. *Archives of Physical Medicine and Rehabilitation, 82*(12), S20–S24. doi:10.1016/S0003-9993(01)65648-X PMID:11805916

Wennberg, J., Barnes, B., & Zubkoff, M. (1982). Professional uncertainty and the problem of supplier-induced demand. *Social Science & Medicine, 16*(7), 811–824. doi:10.1016/0277-9536(82)90234-9 PMID:7100999

Williams, R., & Elliott, L. (2010). *Crisis and recovery: Ethics, economics and justice*. Hampshire, UK: Palgrave Macmillan. doi:10.1057/9780230294912

Woodbine, G. (2006). Gender issues impact the role of the moral agent in a rapidly developing economic zone of the People's Republic of China. *Journal of Asia-Pacific Business, 7*(3), 79–103. doi:10.1300/J098v07n03_05

ADDITIONAL READING

Dracopolou, S. (Ed.). (2006). *Ethics and values in healthcare management*. New York, NY: Routledge.

Runciman, B., & Walton, M. (2007). *Safety and ethics in healthcare: A guide to getting it right*. Burlington, UK: Ashgate.

Thompson, D. F. (2005). *Restoring responsibility: Ethics in government, business, and healthcare*. Cambridge, UK: Cambridge University Press.

KEY TERMS AND DEFINITIONS

Burnout: The psychological stress that is related to the job of the individual, and which is mainly characterized as feeling exhausted, lacking enthusiasm-motivation, and feeling ineffective at work.

Ethical Leadership: Leadership that is based on the respect for ethical values and for the dignity and rights of others.

Ethical Values: The set of principles that an individual, team or the whole society follow, and which are considered to govern "virtuous" behavior.

Healthcare Management: Theory and practice that are related to the combined field of management in healthcare, that is, in structures and services related to the prevention, diagnosis, and treatment of a mental or physical impairment that can occur in humans.

Healthcare System: All involved professionals, institutions and other resources that meet the healthcare needs through relevant organized provision of services to the population in a country.

Job Affect: The various positive and negative emotional states felt by the employees at work.

Perceived Cohesion: The perception of an individual regarding the bonds linking members of a social group to one another and to the group as a whole.

Perceived Immediacy: The perception of an individual regarding the verbal and nonverbal signs of closeness and willingness to communicate in interpersonal settings.

State Anxiety: The feelings of unease, worry, tension, and stress that are related to a specific state-condition, in contrast to the stable (trait) anxiety tendency of an individual.

Chapter 6

Interactions Between Personality Traits of Law Enforcement and Corrections Officers, and Attitudes Toward Felony Drug Offenders:
Best Practices for Interventions

Karin Celosse
CDCR, USA

ABSTRACT

Punitive attitudes in criminal justice staff towards felony drug offenders, as related to level of social dominance orientation, right wing authoritarianism, protestant work ethic orientation, and openness to change were examined. These traits were hypothesized to be factors contributing to continued acceptance of a paradigm emphasizing use penalties and punishment to address substance abuse. The study utilized 28 law enforcement officers, 14 corrections officers, and 58 non-criminal justice individuals. Data was collected using Altemeyer abbreviated RWA scale, SDO-6 scale, Miles and Garrett protestant work ethic scale, attitudes to organizational change, officer's attitude survey, and researcher designed survey. Results indicated both moderating and mediating effects between variables, except in the case of openness to change. To reduce unwanted behaviors, focus needs to be on assisting criminal justice staff with challenges in a more psychologically healthy manner.

DOI: 10.4018/978-1-5225-2650-6.ch006

INTRODUCTION

With the events in Ferguson, Missouri and other similar high-profile events involving law enforcement and citizens in recent years, the appropriateness of examining potentially contributing personality factors in law enforcement and corrections officers continues to be relevant. This is especially relevant comparative to how the majority of the remainder of non-low income nations approach law enforcement, criminal justice, and corrections. Of specific interest to this research are personality factors related to an individual's level of identification with a Social Dominance Orientation (SDO), Right Wing Authoritarianism (RWA), Protestant Work Ethic (PWE), along with openness to change. Using a critical theory lens, this research sought to explain "what is wrong with current social reality, identify the actors to change it, and provide both clear norms for criticism and achievable practical goals for social transformation" (Malpas, 2012). Despite being an unethical practice, law enforcement and corrections officers have historically been proven to treat felony drug offenders differently, particularly in instances where it is permitted to seize the assets of the alleged offender (Champion, 2001). Specific attitudes related to officers having a higher percentage of these personality traits (greater identification with a higher level of SDO, RWA, and a stronger philosophical adherence to the idea of PWE) were hypothesized to be significant factors.

These factors perpetuate the continued acceptance of a paradigm that emphasizes the use of restrictions, penalties, and punishment to discuss substance abuse and addiction, despite a growing body of research contrary to the efficacy of these practices. Continued adherence to this approach towards felony drug offenders has a negative impact on the criminal justice system. For example, it contributes to the overcrowding of jails and prisons. Excessive emphasis on penalties, punishment and the like also perpetuate the problem of recidivism. This then becomes an issue of ethics, as it does nothing to ease the process of rehabilitation of these incarcerated individuals and yet we expect them to reintegrate into society in a successful manner. In the United States, responsibility for poverty, crime, and drug use are attributed to the communities suffering from these symptoms, and society at large is exonerated from any responsibility. As Sidanius and Liu (2001) explain, the idea that inequality is moral, fair, and unavoidable is maintained. If assistance is offered, it is often under extremely restrictive circumstances. In the United States, state spending on addiction across the nation averages around 11% of state budgets. Of this 11%, only between 1 to 4 cents on each dollar is spent on prevention and treatment. The rest is spent on the consequences of addiction, and this includes incarceration (CASA Columbia.org, 2015).

Within the larger criminal justice field, there is a lack of understanding in the process of addiction, recovery, and mental health (Silverstone, Krameddine, DeMarco,

& Hassel, 2013). Punitive measures such as those currently in effect do not have a deterrent effect on engaging in drug-related criminal activity (Chiang, Chan, Chen, Sun, Chang, Chen, & Chen, 2006; De Wree, De Ruyver, & Pauwels, 2009; Drucker, 1999; Fellner, 2009; Goldstein, Bigelow, McCusker, Lewis, Mundt, & Powers, 2001; Kinner & Milloy, 2011; Mccarty, Aussenberg, Falk, & Carpenter, 2013; Miller, 2009; Topalli, Brezina, & Bernhardt, 2012). Individuals drawn to this field of work have a higher than usual level of SDO and RWA, and the nature of the job itself serves to exacerbate these traits within them (Crawford, Brady, Pilanski, & Erny, 2013). The institutional normative police environment promotes the organization of all social relations into a hierarchy in which conventionalism, authoritarian submission, and authoritarian aggression are salient (Euwema, Kop, & Bakker, 2004). After only one month's immersion in the police environment provides evidence in support of the role of group socialization on the transmission of negative intergroup attitudes and ideological beliefs (Gatto & Dambrun, 2012; Gatto, Kerbrat, & Oliveira, 2010).

People with a conservative personality (as defined by their need for order, structure, closure, resistance to change, intolerance of uncertainty, discomfort with ambiguity and change, identification with higher levels of SDO, higher levels of identification with RWA, and higher levels of identification with support of the idea of the PWE have certain values that they use to approach the world. People with these personality traits have certain values that form the schema with which they approach the world. Their age, gender, sexual orientation, and level of education do not affect this schema. They feel strongly that some individuals are superior to others. They feel strongly that rules should be followed no matter what. Within the framework of the ideals of the PWE, they feel strongly that all individuals are personally accountable for success in life, or lack thereof (Nam, Jos & Van Bavel, 2003; Boer-Jacobs & Fischer, 2013). It was hypothesized that individuals who measure high on conservative personality traits would have a certain level of resistance to changing attitudes towards less punitive interventions for felony drug offenders and supporting programs that provide help for people that served time in prison or jail for drug offenses (serious or not). The research sought to explore if the independent variable of criminal justice employment moderates was or was not mediated by levels of SDO, RWA, adherence to the idea of the PWE, and level of resistance to change, relative to the dependent variable of punitive attitudes towards felony drug offenders.

People employed in the field of law enforcement or corrections present as having higher than average rates of conservative personalities (Euwema, Kop & Bakker, 2004; Gatto & Dambrun, 2012; Gatto, Goldbrun & Oliviera, 2010). Individuals employed in the criminal justice field have also been shown to have higher than average rates of low levels of agreement with understanding the protective factors (Langeliers, Amin & O'Toole, 2010; Silverstone et al., 2013) involved in recidivism prevention, as well as the protective factors involved in the recovery process as related to substance abuse. This contributes to the continued acceptance of a paradigm that emphasized the use of restrictions, penalties, and punishment to address substance abuse and addiction despite a growing body of research contrary to the efficacy of these practices.

According to data gathered on the Bureau of Justice Statistics, the governmental agency in the United States that gathers and compiles data on all things related to law enforcement and criminal justice in the nation, 51.5% of individuals with a history of felony conviction were arrested for a new crime within one year and 75.3% were arrested for a new crime within 3 years of release. (Bureau of Justice Statistics [BJS], 2003). These figures can be directly correlated to lack of available rehabilitation programs in the correctional system and accessible community support programs upon exit (Sherman et al., 1998). The status of available rehabilitation programs, their structure and organization, and their funding has remained a problematic issue and has thus far still not resulted in any widespread change in a positive direction. Although currently there is a slight move towards decriminalizing substance abuse, it remains limited in scope and lacking in general organization.

BACKGROUND

Social Dominance Theory (SDT) developed out of Social Identity Theory (SIT). SIT assumes that the dynamics of intergroup contact are what result in the establishment and maintenance of social hierarchies. SDT "assumes that the complex dynamics of intergroup relations and structural inequality result from individuals' psychological dispositions" (Schmitt, Branscombe, & Kappen, 2003; Wilson & Liu, 2003; Tajfel & Turner, 1986). Individuals in the U.S. who are high on the Social Dominance Orientation (SDO) measurement scale identify strongly with the idea that individuals who exist in less than fortunate circumstances are solely responsible for this, and indeed should even be punished for it (Schmitt, Branscombe, & Kappen, 2003; Green, Thomsen, Sidanius, Staerklé, & Potanina, 2009; Schmitt, Branscombe, & Kappen, 2003). A high Social Dominance Orientation (SDO) is related to a variety of social hierarchy-maintaining systems, including support for harsh criminal sanctions, as well as to deterrence and retribution beliefs (Sidanius & Liu, 2001).

Similarly, individuals that score high on measures of PWE are far more likely to blame people for their circumstances, as opposed to assigning any influence to external contexts. There are also positive correlations between attitudes towards low SES individuals, authoritarianism, regular church attendance and PWE scores, and to situational locus of control (Furnham, 1982; Dombrink, 2012; Jones, 2009; Minguic, 2010). Individuals who score high on PWE measures placed low value on

Figure 1. Graphic of people incarcerated in U.S.

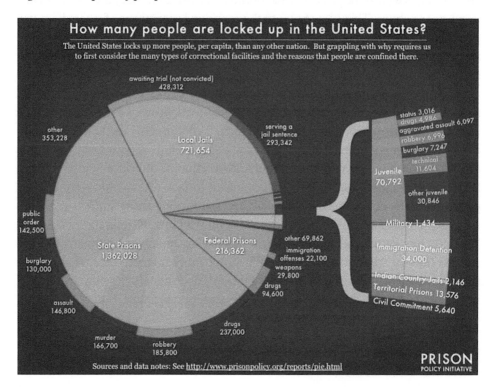

ideas such as equality, open mindedness, imagination and creativity, but place high value on ambition and self-control (Furnham, 1982). Jones, Furnham, and Deile (2010) stated that "conservative beliefs are used for controlling internal feelings and resisting irrational impulses...very much in accord with the already-noted PWE tendency to defer gratification and to favor the future over the present".

Biological Influences

There is a biological connection between high versus low religiosity and conservative versus liberal political attitudes (Smith, Oxley, Hibbing, Alford & Hibbing, 2011). There appears to be a combination of social influence and genetic predisposition for thought processing preference that contributes to a conservative world-view, as well as the converse (Crowson & Michael, 2009). Additionally, Settle, Dawes, and Fowler (2009) also found that heritability accounted for over half of the variation in political party preference (when divided into general conservative versus general liberal ideas). Studies by Bardi and Schwartz (2003), Mondak and Canache (2013), Settle, Dawes, and Fowler (2009), Crowson (2009), and Malka et al., (2012) serve to further support this idea. Heritability accounts for close to 50% of the variance in strength of partisan attachment, demonstrating a significant role of biology in the expression of important political behaviors. Banks and Valentino (2012) further found that humans hold genetically based and strong emotions connected with idea of deviance, which in turn activates beliefs about the perceived deviance. This then shifts support for relative policies and biology and politics become intertwined. There also exist physiological indicators for unconscious influences on behavior (Smith et al., 2011) and it is possible that this physiological response carries over to an aversion towards people with perceived lack of discipline or self-control.

Aversion to perceived deviance in humans is dealt with primarily through the use of moral codes at a societal level. The inherent values and tendencies that characterize religiosity as related to world-view approach naturally seem to steer people towards conservative social outcomes and policies (Malka et al., 2012). There is great weight placed on internal attributions to individual circumstances, stemming from the heavy emphasis of an attempt the gauge the moral condition of a person's soul (Huang & Liu, 2005). Festinger's Cognitive Dissonance Theory (1958) suggests that all people have an inner drive to keep attitudes and beliefs congruent, so as to avoid an unpleasant state of dissonance. Considering that most individuals will experience some distress at seeing the plight of others, a high SDO may function as a way to reduce this cognitive dissonance for the individual. In this context people seem motivated to view existing social arrangements as legitimate, justifiable, and perhaps even part of the natural order of things (Nam, et al., 2013). Support for the biological basis of organization of culture or society into a hierarchical structure based on dominance can also be seen in the social group organization of most animals and is not limited to primates (Stevens et al., 2007; Paz-y- Miño et al., 2004).

Psychological/Personality Influences

Those who perceive and identify themselves as individualists and persons with a conservative world-view have been shown to demonstrate a preference for simpler ideas (Van Lange, Bekkers, Chirumbolo, & Leone, 2012) and have also been shown to be less comfortable with things that cause cognitive dissonance. This presents a challenge, which in turn results in a tendency to avoid non-confirming information (Malka & Lelkes, 2010; Malka & Lelkes 2012; Nam, et al., 2013) and only to seek out information that confirms their ideas/ideals (Nam, et al., 2013). Considering the strength of identity formation and its resistance to change (Crowson & Michael, 2009; Smith et al., 2011), and how various studies have demonstrated that traits in the areas of individualism and collectivism are established at this level, the influence of being or becoming a more critical thinker appears to have a potential connection to cognitive ability, flexibility, and education (Malka & Lelkes, 2010;

Malka & Lelkes, 2012; Nam, et al., 2013). While conservatism and liberalism, or individualism and collectivism appear be stable personality traits, multiple studies (Redmond, 2009; Smith, et al., 2011; Malka & Lelkes, 2010 & 2012) support that it is possible to find windows of opportunity to change the level of concern a person can have for disadvantaged persons.

Social/Group Influences

Pro-socials (Penner, Fritzsche, Craiger, & Freifeld,1995) tend to weigh things in terms of morally good and bad. But the term is more specific in reference to a "universal good" as opposed to taking a position of judgment, whereas individualists and competitors view things more in terms of power/might (Van Lange, et al., 2012). Mondak and Canache (2013) found differences in personality as measured by the Big-5 traits observed at the cross-national and subnational levels, and political culture corresponding with a wide array of important social and political phenomena. Ishio (2010) found that when "socially hierarchical structures are based on race/ethnicity, religion, age or socioeconomic class, members of socially dominant groups are more emotionally attached to their country than are socially subordinate groups". Emotions that have a cognitive component attached to them are encoded into memory more readily with the in-group than with the out-group. This phenomenon results in the in-group perceiving that they alone hold emotions that are somehow uniquely human relative to the out-group (Leyens, 2007; Paladino & Vaes, 2009).

Van Lange et al., (2012) found that social value orientation affects political preferences strongly, and the need for structure correlates strongly with the need for structure and political preferences. "Authoritarian individuals are inclined to submit to authority, adhere to conventional norms, and promote group cohesion. These characteristic tendencies of the authoritarian individual in turn promote survival, by encouraging the use of collective action and the pooling of resources" (Hastings & Shaffer, 2008). In Blake, Mania, and Gaertner (2006) not only did out-group status moderate relationships between attitudes towards degree of threat, but all of the tested types of threats (group esteem, distinctiveness, realistic, and symbolic threats, as well as intergroup anxiety and negative stereotypes) were positively related to a negative attitude towards the "out group". In Nicholson, Duncan, White, & Watkins, (2012), subjects displayed an element of moral emotional involvement when relating to one's perceived in-group. Additionally, Bardi and Schwartz (2003) found that values seem to motivate behaviors. That is to say, behaviors that demonstrate tradition and values are strongly related (Schwartz, 2006). Graham, Nosek, and Haidt (2012) found that moral stereotypes were predictive regarding conservative and liberal differences in political core beliefs.

Cohrs, Moschner, Maes, & Kielmann, (2005) found that the Protestant Work Ethic (PWE) connects the idea of sustained effort and hard work with the belief that you can accomplish anything despite circumstances. Levy, Velilla, and Hughes (2010) found a pervasive attitude among subjects that clings to the idea of people being able to pull themselves up by their proverbial bootstraps. The Huang and Liu (2005) findings strengthened the idea that even though the Protestant and Calvinist inheritance may be distant in terms of time, it is still reflected in people's daily judgment and political behavior. In a meta-analysis spanning almost 40 years Rosenthal, Levy, and Moyer (2011) confirm the idea that PWE is used as a justification of disadvantage.

Attitudes Towards Felony Drug Offenders

Lack of support for the belief in rehabilitative potential of ex-offenders, and in particular drug offenders, applies to a large percentage of the rank and file within the field of law enforcement and correctional staff. The environment in which they function promotes organization of all social relationships into a hierarchy where submission, aggression, and authoritarianism are encouraged, as are negative intergroup attitudes and beliefs (Gatto, & Dambrun, 2012; Gatto, Kerbrat, & Oliviera, 2010; Haley, & Sidanius, 2005; Haslam, & Reicher, 2012). Individuals drawn to this field of work present with higher levels of both SDO and RWA attitudes, as well as a possible associated belief in the PWE interpretation of success (Crawford, et al., 2013). The very job environment within which they work serves to exacerbate these traits within these individuals (Langeliers, Amin, & Toole, 2010; Larsson, Bjorklund, & Backstrom, 2012; Sidanius, et al., 2001; Sidanius, Liu, Shaw, Pratto, 1994).

Problem

The dominant narrative of contemporary American penal culture holds that the United States stands unmatched in the western world in its harsh treatment of lawbreakers (Green, et al., 2013). Changing the level of understanding in the process of substance use, abuse, and addiction, as well as the recovery process and potential associated mental health issues is key for more successful outcomes (Silverstone, 2013b). Being able to accept the benefits of best practices as related to harm-reduction, providing a nurturing-healing support paradigm, and strengthening social bonds as well as using programs such as the assertive community treatment model will have a significant impact on the process (Hearn, 2010; Clayton, O'Connell, Bellamy, Benedict, & Rowe, 2013; Nicholson et al., 2012; Sacks, Sacks, McKendrick, Banks, & Stommel, 2004; Silverstone, et al. 2013). Current practices and approaches within the criminal justice system in terms of dealing with felony drug offenders suffers from the misconception of seeing felony drug offenders as struggling with not trying

Figure 2. Graphic of prison populations around the world

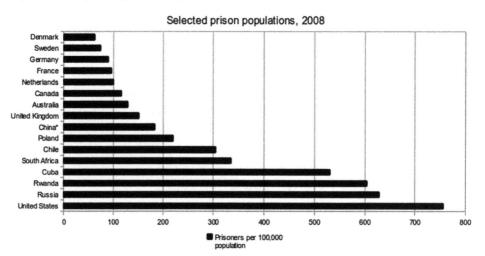

hard enough to overcome their addiction. These misconceptions have consistently led to a continued punitive approach to substance abuse and addiction, even in the case of supervised release such as occurs in drug court diversion programs. The punitive measures currently in effect across most of the nation do not have a deterrent effect on individuals engaging in drug-related criminal activity (Chiang et al., 2006; DeWree et al., 2009; Drucker, 1999; Fellner, 2009; Goldstein et al., 2001; Kinner, & Malloy, 2011; McCarty et al., 2013; Miller, 2009; Topalli, Brezina, & Bernhardt, 2012). It is within this environment that criminal justice staff must currently function, for better or worse.

Question

This study sought to establish the level of punitive attitudes towards the population under study (felony substance abuse offenders), specifically as related to high level of SDO, RWA, PWE orientation, and low openness to change in criminal justice employed individuals.

Background

People employed in the field of law enforcement or corrections present as having higher than average rates of conservative personalities (Euwema, Kop & Bakker, 2004; Gatto & Dambrun, 2012; Gatto, Goldbrun & Oliviera, 2010). Individuals employed in the criminal justice field have also been shown to have higher than average rates of low levels of agreement with understanding the protective factors

(Langeliers, Amin & O'Toole, 2010; Silverstone, 2013a) involved in recidivism prevention, as well as the protective factors involved in the recovery process as related to substance abuse. This contributes to the continued acceptance of a paradigm that emphasized the use of restrictions, penalties, and punishment to address substance abuse and addiction despite a growing body of research contrary to the efficacy of these practices.

Hypothesis

It was hypothesized that individuals who measure high on conservative personality traits would have a certain level of resistance to changing attitudes towards less punitive interventions for felony drug offenders and supporting programs that provide help for people that served time in prison or jail for drug offenses (serious or not). The research sought to explore if the independent variable of criminal justice employment moderates was or was not mediated by levels of SDO, RWA, adherence to the idea of the PWE, and level of resistance to change, relative to the dependent variable of punitive attitudes towards felony drug offenders.

Research

The study included 28 law enforcement officers, 14 corrections officers, and 58 non-criminal justice individuals, who were at least 18 years of age, U.S. Citizen, had voted in 1 election, and had a history of working =/>20 hrs. Social media was used to recruit participants. Posts on the social media sites were accompanied by a brief introduction to the study. The study took place remotely, via phone administration.

Subjects completed multiple survey instruments designed to measure level of SDO, level of RWA, level of PWE, level of Openness to Change, and projected voting behavior on specific issues related to community reintegration support programs for felony drug offenders. Participants were followed up via email with within a month of data collection completion to debrief and offered the opportunity to accept contact information for local counseling resources should they so desire.

After ascertaining if the potential subject qualified for the study, wished to participate, and had been given informed consent, a simple data gathering form was used to obtain demographics including age, gender (male, female or other), self-identification with church affiliation, and level of education. The study utilized the Altemeyer (1998) Abbreviated RWA scale, the 16 item SDO-6 scale, the 19 item Miles and Garrett (1971) Protestant Work Ethic Scale, the 50-item Attitudes to Organizational change (Neiva, Ros, & da Paz, 2005), the 32-item Officer's Attitude Survey (Durmaz, 2007), and a researcher-developed 5-item survey on projected voting behavior on specific questions related to funding community support and reintegration for felony drug offenders.

The data was analyzed to explore to what degree (how well) the different independent variables predicted the variance in the dependent variable "punitiveness", specifically as related to felony drug offenders once the re-enter the community after being incarcerated. First, a linear regression analysis was conducted to determine if the models were significant and if the amount of variance accounted for in Model 2 (with the interaction between religiosity, age, sexual orientation, gender, voting, education, criminal justice employment status, and openness to change, SDO, RWA, and PWE level) was significantly more than Model 1 (religiosity, age, sexual orientation, gender, voting, education, and criminal justice employment status only and without the interaction).

Model 1 (without the interaction with openness to change, SDO, RWA, and PWE level being included) was not significant $F (7, 99) = 1.673$, $p = .125$, but model 2 (with the interaction) was significant $F (11, 99) = 3.961$, $p = .000$. This was attributed to there being a significant interaction within Model 2 that Model 1 lacks.

Model 2 with the interaction between religiosity, age, sexual orientation, gender, voting, education, and criminal justice employment status, and openness to change, SDO, RWA, and PWE level accounted for significantly more variance than just religiosity, age, sexual orientation, gender, voting, education, and criminal justice employment status level by themselves:

$$R^2\Delta= .331, p = .000$$

indicating that there is potentially significant moderation between religiosity, age, sexual orientation, gender, voting, education, and criminal justice employment status, and openness to change, SDO, RWA, and PWE level.

To further test the hypothesis that a high level of punitiveness in criminal justice employed individuals is a function of multiple factors (and more specifically whether level of openness to change, SDO, RWA, and PWE moderate the relationship between criminal justice employment status and high level of punitiveness), first a moderation and then a mediation analysis was completed using the PROCESS plugin for SPSS/SAS by Andrew Hayes, PhD. PROCESS runs the regression on centered terms to examine effect. The analysis sought to examine the potential moderation and mediating effects of level of SDO, RWA, PWA\E, and openness to change on level of punitiveness in criminal justice and non-criminal justice employed individuals, while controlling for age, gender, sexual orientation, voter status, level of education, and identified level of religiosity.

Model 3 tested for basic moderating effects of the proposed moderators: level of SDO, level of RWA, and level of PWE on the outcome of level of punitiveness in individuals employed in the criminal justice field. SDO with openness to change had a significant moderating effect on punitiveness $F (13, 86) = 3.1650, p < .01$, $R^2 = .2672$.

The conditional effect of X (punitiveness) on Y (criminal justice employment status) at the values of the moderator showed a mild effect of criminal justice employment status on punitiveness at 1.309 among individuals with low openness to change and low SDO ($m_1 = .4094$, $w_1 = -.4932$), $t (100) = 1.8903, p = .0621$, and a significant effect of criminal justice employment status on punitiveness at .9031 among individuals with neutral openness to change and low SDO ($m_1 = -.4094$, $w_1 = 0$), $t (100) = 2.312, p = .0221$.

RWA with openness to change had a significant moderating effect on punitiveness $F (13, 86) = 4.8751, p < .01, R^2 = .3293$. The conditional effect of X (punitiveness) on Y (criminal justice employment status) at the values of the moderators showed no significant effect.

PWE with openness to change had a significant moderating effect on punitiveness $F (13, 86) = 4.0614, p < .01, R^2 = .2715$. The conditional effect of X (punitiveness) on Y (criminal justice employment status) at the values of the moderators showed no significant effect. To confirm a mediating variable and its significance in the model, it needed to be shown that while the mediator was caused by the initial independent variable (IV) and was a cause of the dependent variable (DV), the initial IV lost its significance when the mediator was included in the model.

Criminal justice employment status had a significant relationship with level of punitiveness ($X \rightarrow Y$), $F (7, 92) = 2.1235, p = .0486, R^2 = .1129$. Criminal justice employment status (X) did not have a significant relationship with openness to change alone, $F (7, 92) = .7483, p = .6318, R^2 = .0583$, but did have a significant relationship with level of PWE, $F (7, 92) = 3.9901, p = .0007, R^2 = .2176$; a significant relationship with level of RWA, $F (7, 92) = 3.1949, p = .0045, R^2 = .2176$; and a significant relationship with level of SDO, $F (7, 92) = 2.4878, p = .0219, R^2 = .1130$. The relationship between criminal justice employment status and PWE, RWA, and SDO level was significant ($X \rightarrow M$). The proposed mediators of openness to change, PWE, RWA, and SDO together with level of punitiveness in criminal justice employment status ($M|X \rightarrow Y$) had a significant relationship; $F (7, 92) = 5.1247, p = .0000, R^2 = .3311$.

Finally, there was meaningful reduction in effect of the relationship between the criminal justice employment status and the level of punitiveness in the presence of the proposed mediators openness to change, PWE, RWA, and SDO ($X|M \rightarrow Y$); $F (7, 92) = 2.1235, p = .0486, R^2 = .1129$. The mediating variables of PWE, RWA, and SDO have therefore been confirmed as significant in this model, the total effect size of criminal justice employment status on level of punitiveness ($X \rightarrow Y$) is greater than zero (ULCI=1.2381) and the indirect effect of criminal justice employment status on

Figure 3. Likelihood of incarceration in the U.S.

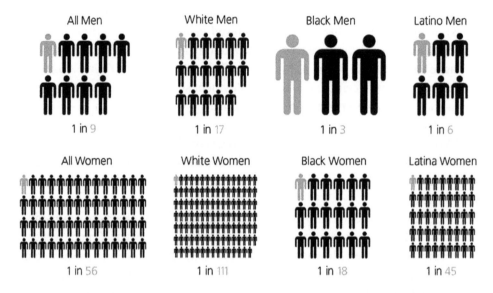

Lifetime Likelihood of Imprisonment of U.S. Residents Born in 2001

Source: Bonczar, T. (2003). *Prevalence of Imprisonment in the U.S. Population, 1974-2001*. Washington, DC: Bureau of Justice Statistics.

level of punitiveness is also greater than zero (BootULCI=1.2331). Criminal justice employment status alone accounted for 11% of the variance in level of punitiveness, but when the mediating variables of openness to change, level of SDO, RWA, and PWE were included, criminal justice employment status accounted for 33% of the variance in level of punitiveness. The model did not show that criminal justice had a significant relationship to openness to change indicating that openness to change was not a significant mediator in this model.

RESULTS

The data was initially analyzed to obtain information to ultimately be able to facilitate the process of targeting officers with training messages perceived as more relevant to them. The data analysis here partially supported the alternative hypothesis (H_1) that there is a relationship between the variables of SDO, RWA, PWE, employment status (criminal justice or other), level of resistance to change, and punitiveness after controlling for respondents age, gender, and level of education, sexual orientation, and voting status. The one finding that diverged from full mediation of the moderating variables (SDO, RWA, PWE, and openness to change) as a function of punitive attitudes in criminal justice employed individuals was that of openness to change. This variable was found to not have a significant mediating effect when examined independent of SDO, RWA, and PWE. It was also found to be the only variable not moderated by criminal justice employment status.

This study did find some interaction specifically between employment, gender, level of punitiveness, and openness to change. There were interactions between openness to change along with SDO, RWA, and PWE relative to level of punitiveness in criminal justice staff. All four were shown to be significant moderators in this model.

However, criminal justice employment status was not found to have a significant relationship with openness to change alone but did have a significant relationship with level of PWE, a significant relationship with level of RWA, and a significant relationship with level of SDO. As indicated in research literature in the fields of biological psychology, social psychology, and evolutionary biology, an individual's personality is an inherent part of how they perceive and interact with the world and people around them. Attempting to change individuals at this level is both highly impractical, and potentially unethical as it ventures into the realm of social engineering.

DISCUSSION

What the results from this study appear to partially support is the presence a factor of environment and group interactions (employment in the criminal justice field in this particular study's case) that brings to the surface the "darker" side of human behavior when there are certain personality traits present. The key seems to lie in the interaction of personality and situation of the individual who is manifesting the cruel, callous, or uncaring behavior, where he/she views the object as not equal to them self, as the "other" and justified as "deserving" of the treatment they are exposed to.

The findings that there were interactions between openness to change along with SDO, RWA, and PWE that moderated of level of punitiveness in criminal justice employed individuals were consistent with Euwema, Kop & Bakker, 2004, who found higher level of stress to correlate with not only higher levels of SDO in officers, but also with higher levels of depersonalization and poorer treatment of law breaking individuals with which they interacted with. It was also consistent with Nam, et al. (2013) who found that that individuals align with conservatism because it "serves to reduce fear, anxiety, and uncertainty; to avoid change, disruption, and ambiguity; and to explain, order, and justify inequality among groups and individuals".

In contrast to the results of present study, Green, et al. (2013) presented data that supported that individuals who identify themselves as staunchly conservative actually use their religiosity as justification for more rehabilitative, gentle attitudes toward individuals who have histories of criminal justice involvement (substance related or other). He also pointed out that "religiously rooted rationales and goals have contributed to the success of the Second Chance Act and to a range of other progressive reforms, including the Prison Rape Elimination Act of 2003 and the Fair Sentencing Act of 2010". Haslam and Reicher (2012) explained that it is not the actual personality traits of an individual that affects their behavior towards the "other". They pointed out that malignant treatment of the "other" is "conditional on identification with the authority in question and an associated belief that the authority is right". While this concept of the "other" is more generic, it is within this description that individuals who have a history of involvement with the criminal justice system fit. The study by Hastings and Shaffer (2008) found that individuals' behavior towards the "other" is more determined by evolutionary processes related to threat, real or perceived, and not due to personality traits. Euwema, Kop, and Bakker (2004) even went so far as to state criminal justice staff that are "burned out" behave more leniently and in a less punitive manner towards individuals in their custody. This finding might suggest it is more the job itself, as opposed to the individual and their personality traits, which influences how the "other" is treated.

Factoring in the contrasting results of existing literature, the understanding that can be gained from the results of this study point in the direction of a more complex picture of the reasons behind how criminal justice staff interacts with the individuals in their charge. One school of thought may operationalize behavior as externally influenced by dominance and power, whereas another may attribute this behavior to an external or internal reaction to perceived threat. Yet others operationalize behavior as a factor of genetics, and then others as a factor of personality traits.

SOLUTIONS AND RECOMMENDATIONS

Zimbardo (1971) and the Stanford Prison Experiment demonstrated that even the most educated and self-aware have within them the capacity to act in a manner that is incongruent with their supposed values and ideals. During the Nuremberg trials post-WW2, Nazi war criminals over and over again attempted to justify their atrocities by stating they were "simply following orders". Additionally, Milgram (1962) demonstrated that even individuals who see themselves incapable of cruelty could be coaxed into committing acts that are incongruent with their sense of who they are as a human being. However, Milgram's results were not the same when he attempted the same experiment with individuals who were close, i.e. subjects who were family members or friends of each other as in Milgram's unpublished "Relationship Condition" (Russell, 2014). The results of the original experiment were replicated, although to an only slightly lesser degree decades later (Berger, 2009), in order to address the critique that individuals were more blindly conforming in the 1960s versus the present. Somewhat more recently, the behaviors demonstrated by soldiers at Abu Graib served to reinforce both Milgram and Zimbardo's findings. What this may imply, and what the results from this study appear to partially support, is the presence a factor of environment and group interactions (employment in the criminal justice field in this particular study's case) that brings to the surface the "darker" side of human behavior when there are certain personality traits present. The key seems to lie in the interaction of personality and situation of the individual who is manifesting the cruel, callous, or uncaring behavior, where he/she views the object as not equal to them self, as the "other" and justified as "deserving" of the treatment they are exposed to.

Consider that perhaps part of the issue related to acting out behaviors on the part of law enforcement and corrections is connected to specific factors related to what they see and experience, day in and day out. The traumatic and often violent events those involved in the field of criminal justice are exposed to may elicit a shutting down of sorts. This reaction has been hypothesized to be psychologically protective (Bekhtereva & Cambarova, 1985) and in order to remain in this shut down emotional state, distancing of the self from others is necessary. Distancing of the self from others can serve to facilitate an internal blind spot to maltreatment of individuals encountered in the course of a work shift. Cognitive dissonance (Festinger, 1958) results from this and this emotional state is untenable over the long term. The results are maladaptive compensatory behaviors such as substance use, self-harm, harmful behaviors towards others, and increased levels distressing mental health symptoms (up to and including suicide). This state of mental health distress is however very much treatable. As such, it provides support for the focus on decreasing the stigma of getting psychological help within the field of criminal justice work needs to be intensified.

An intervention that demonstrates the possibility of a two-fold benefit is that of compassion focused therapy. Compassion focused therapy could facilitate the process of reducing the impact of distressing mental health symptoms resulting from exposure to repeated vicarious trauma in criminal justice staff. In turn, a decrease in maladaptive behaviors towards individuals that criminal justice staff interact with on a regular basis could result. This is important because McBeth and Gumley (2012) found a large effect size for the relationship between compassion and psychopathology ($r = 2\ 0.54$ (95% CI= 0.57 to 0.51; $Z=34.02$; $p < .0001$). Neff, et al. (2007) reported that an important buffer against one form of psychopathology (anxiety) is the concept of self-compassion. Psychological well-being was increased as well, and language use focused more on the idea of connected as opposed to separate. Neff and Germer (2013) explained that self- compassion allows an individual to see their pain and suffering as a part of the greater human experience. It allows an individual to be gentle and understanding towards themselves, to avoid being self-critical and isolating themselves. It permits individuals to recognize they are part of a shared humanity, is akin to unconditional positive regard and allows individuals to accept themselves more readily, and therefore become more acceptant of the "other". The initial goal of this study had been to focus the presence of certain personality traits and what the relationship was with how criminal justice staff interacts with felony drug offenders. This information was then proposed to serve as a base for potential training program development. After analyzing the data, it became clear that attention would more effectively be shifted mainly to intervention in currently employed criminal justice staff.

The present study found were varying interactions between specific personality traits, openness to change, and punitiveness within criminal justice staff. The interaction might potentially be due to the more individuals with specific personality traits (SDO, RWA, etc.) are immersed in the criminal justice work environment, the more they may need to "ramp up" these traits as a psychologically protective mechanism. Compartmentalization becomes their defense. This may unfortunately have several harmful effects. It affects the individual working in the field of criminal justice through experiencing PTSD (Post Traumatic Stress Disorder), substance abuse, depression, anxiety, and increased suicide risk. These issues translate into changing how criminal justice staff interacts with individuals around them. This includes the individuals they encounter on a daily basis through the workplace (i.e. felony drug offenders). There is a need for a focus on addressing the mental health issues that criminal justice staff face as a result of their daily, repeated experiences of vicarious and first hand trauma, and there is an even deeper need to reduce the perceived stigma of (a) admitting you hurt emotionally, and that (b) you need help to work through it.

The concept of self-compassion needs to be incorporated in initial criminal justice staff training and in regular mandatory CE's and in-service trainings. Such an approach also needs to have a component that addresses the de-stigmatization of mental health issues (such as stress, anxiety, depression, PTSD) in criminal justice staff so that they will be more open to admitting need for help. Motivational interviewing techniques are a non-threatening way to get past the initial resistance of admitting there is a need for help, and to facilitate motivation to be compassionate. More experienced and emotionally healthy criminal justice staff should be encouraged to be mentors.

FUTURE RESEARCH DIRECTIONS

The presence of economic factors such as the current state of the economy may have been significant in the context of this study, and present as an additional area of research to be explored. Two questions on the hypothetical voting questionnaire were specifically worded so as to elicit a conscious choice on the part of the subject to choose an item that would potentially have a legislative financial impact. Considering that hypothesized voting behavior on issues was examined and used as a measure of level of punitiveness in law enforcement and corrections officers, whether there is a correlation between level of intergroup willingness to vote for funding (new or continued) for supportive community programs and the presence of poor economic conditions may have been a factor. The use of the PWE scale measurement has limited studies that demonstrate adequate validity of the scale and the application of such constructs across contexts (Geren, 2009). The 50-item Attitudes to Organizational change (Neiva, Ros, & da Paz, 2005) may not be as relevant for criminal justice staff as had been assumed. Gender differences in proneness to punitiveness and lower levels of openness to change were not addressed. Additionally, it may also be that it would have been more appropriate to measure and compare variance based on instruments that measure personality traits themselves as a group, such as the Minnesota Multiphasic Personality Inventory-2 (MMPI-2) and Millon Clinical Multiaxial Inventory-III (MCMI-III). More focused research based on general personality traits is an added area in need of exploration, especially since the specific personality traits this researcher chose to measure may not be the personality traits that accounted for the variance, and might have been conceptualized at too much of a micro-level or focused on traits that do not have a significant influence when taken in isolation.

CONCLUSION

Instead of only focusing on individuals with a specific group of personality traits being attracted to employment in the field of criminal justice, it is important to instead consider that it may be the field of work itself that affects the individual with high levels of punitiveness and potentially exacerbates or magnifies this state. In order to examine this possibility, further research and refinement in research design is needed. In the meanwhile, direct interventions focused on reducing the stigma aimed at the level of criminal justice rank and file staff needs to be implemented. Individuals employed in the field of criminal justice that score high on these "conservative" personality traits struggle with the effects of exposure to trauma as well. One way of coping with this is to dehumanize the "other" to prevent cognitive dissonance when

Figure 4. Effect of war on drugs

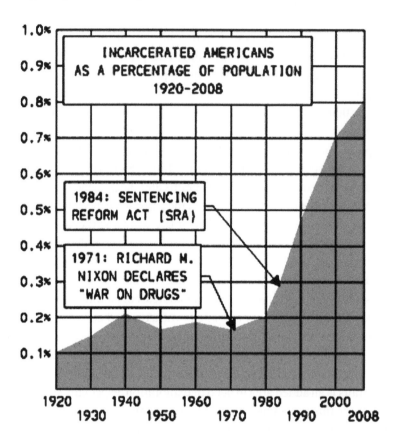

presented with the painful emotions that can arise from interactions. An additional manner in which this emotional state is dealt with is through emotional blunting brought on by excessive drinking or other substance use. Some serious effects that result are maltreatment of the "other", increased rates of PTSD, depression, anxiety, and suicide among criminal justice staff. These results are aggravated by the stigma surrounding admitting a need for and asking for psychological assistance among criminal justice staff. Approaching the problems created by events such as those in Ferguson, Missouri[1] and other similar high-profile events involving law enforcement and citizens from a lens focused on healing the front-line staff – individuals employed in the field of criminal justice – can have far reaching, positive effects on all parties involved.

In addition to staff improvement), the importance of phasing in and implementing reforms within the criminal justice system and patterns of incarceration in the U.S. should be modeled on those of the Netherlands and the Nordic countries (Sweden,

Figure 5. Ratio of incarceration

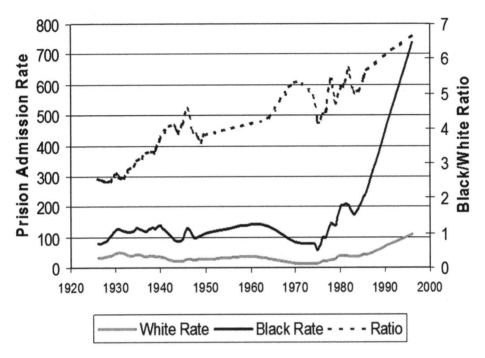

Norway, Denmark, and Finland). This would contribute greatly to reducing recidivism even more, thereby providing real chance in the rehabilitation of previously incarcerated individuals to reintegrate into the community successfully. Those who continue to defend the highly punitive prison system in the U.S. often respond with the argument that the Nordic attitude toward prisons in general is naive in assuming that prisoners can be treated as normal humans who can improve. However, societies in Nordic countries continue to remain quite safe after allowing people who have committed the most severe crimes to return back in society, generally after far shorter sentences than in the U.S.:

While high-security prisons in the U.S. often involve caging and dehumanizing inmates, prisons in Nordic countries are designed to treat them as people with psychosocial needs that are to be carefully attended to. Prison workers fulfill a dual role of enforcer and social worker, balancing behavioral regulation with preparation for re-entry into society. (Johnsen, Granheim, & Helgesen, 2011)

Finally, recognizing that the "war on drugs" that began with President Nixon in the U.S. during the 1970's and continues to this day, despite being an abysmal failure, will assist in recognizing the fallacy of criminalizing substance use and incarcerating users and addicts. Using the Netherlands as a longstanding success and workable model, Reinarman (2000) clearly outlines how liberal drug laws can be beneficial, as do Drucker (1998) and De Wree, De Ruyver, and Pauwels (2009).

REFERENCES

Adams, G., & Mullen, E. (2013). Increased voting for candidates who compensate victims rather than punish offenders. *Social Justice Research*, *26*(2), 168–192. doi:10.1007/s11211-013-0179-x

Bailey, C. (2011). Does the Defining Issues Test measure ethical judgment ability or political position? *The Journal of Social Psychology*, *151*(3), 314–330. doi:10.1080/00224545.2010.481690 PMID:21675184

Banks, A., & Valentino, N. (2012). Emotional substrates of white racial attitudes. *American Journal of Political Science*, *56*(2), 286–297. doi:10.1111/j.1540-5907.2011.00561.x

Bannon, D. (2003). Voting, non-voting and consumer buying behaviour: Non-voter segmentation (NVS) and the underlining causes of electoral inactivity. *Journal of Public Affairs*, *3*(2), 138–151. doi:10.1002/pa.142

Bechtereva, N., & Kambarova, D. (1985). Neurophysiology of emotions and some general brain mechanisms. In B. D. Kirdcaldy (Ed.), *Individual differences in movement* (pp. 169–192). Springer Netherlands; doi:10.1007/978-94-009-4912-6_8

Berger, J. (2009). Replicating Milgram: Would people still obey today? *The American Psychologist*, *64*(1), 1–11. doi:10.1037/a0010932 PMID:19209958

Bischoff, I., Neuhaus, C., Trautner, P., & Weber, B. (2013). The neuroeconomics of voting: Neural evidence of different sources of utility in voting. *Journal of Neuroscience, Psychology, and Economics*, *6*(4), 215–235. doi:10.1037/npe0000016

Blumstein, A., Fabelo Martin, T., Horn, J., Lehman, D., Tacha, R., & Petersili, J. (2005). *Commentaries on: Sentencing and corrections in the 21st Century: Setting the stage for the future.* Retrieved from https://www.ncjrs.gov/pdffiles1/nij/189106-2a.pdf

Boer-Jacobs, D., & Fischer, R. (2013). How and when do personal values guide our attitudes and sociality? Explaining cross-cultural variability in attitude-value linkages. *Psychological Bulletin*, *139*(5), 1113–1147. doi:10.1037/a0031347 PMID:23339521

Bowles, M., DeHart, D., & Webb, J. R. (2012). Family influences on female offenders' substance use: The role of adverse childhood events among incarcerated women. *Journal of Family Violence, 27*(7), 681–686. doi:10.1007/s10896-012-9450-4

Celosse, K. (2015). *Interactions between personality traits of law enforcement and corrections officers, and attitudes toward felony drug offenders* (Unpublished doctoral dissertation). Chicago School of Professional Psychology, Los Angeles, CA.

Champion, D. (2001). Criminal courts: Structure, process, and issues (3rd ed.). Upper Saddle River, NJ: Academic Press.

Chiang, S.-C., Chan, H.-Y., Chen, C.-H., Sun, H.-J., Chang, H.-J., Chen, W. J., & Chen, C.-K. (2006). Recidivism among male subjects incarcerated for illicit drug use in Taiwan. *Psychiatry and Clinical Neurosciences, 60*(4), 444–451. doi:10.1111/j.1440-1819.2006.01530.x PMID:16884446

Clayton, A., O'Connell, M. J., Bellamy, C., Benedict, P., & Rowe, M. (2013). The Citizenship Project part II: Impact of a citizenship intervention on clinical and community outcomes for persons with mental illness and criminal justice involvement. *American Journal of Community Psychology, 51*(1-2), 114–122. doi:10.1007/s10464-012-9549-z PMID:22869206

Cohrs, J. C., Moschner, B., Maes, J., & Kielmann, S. (2005). The motivational bases of right-wing authoritarianism and social dominance orientation: Relations to values and attitudes in the aftermath of September 11, 2001. *Personality and Social Psychology Bulletin, 31*(10), 1425–1434. doi:10.1177/0146167205275614 PMID:16143673

Cooper, C. S. (2007). Drug courts - just the beginning: Getting other areas of public policy in sync. *Substance Use & Misuse, 42*(2-3), 243–256. doi:10.1080/10826080601141982 PMID:17558929

Crawford, J. T., Brady, J. L., Pilanski, J. M., & Erny, H. (2013). Differential effects of Right-Wing Authoritarianism and Social Dominance Orientation on political candidate support: The moderating role of message framing. *Journal of Social and Political Psychology, 1*(1), 5–28. doi:10.5964/jspp.v1i1.170

Crowson, H. M. (2009). Are all conservatives alike? A study of the psychological correlates of cultural and economic conservatism. *The Journal of Psychology, 143*(5), 449–463. doi:10.3200/JRL.143.5.449-463 PMID:19943397

De Wree, E., De Ruyver, B., & Pauwels, L. (2009). Criminal justice responses to drug offences: Recidivism following the application of alternative sanctions in Belgium. *Drugs Education Prevention & Policy*, *16*(6), 550–560. doi:10.3109/09687630802133632

Deus Ex Machina: The influence of polling place on voting behavior. (n.d.). *Political Psychology, 31*(2), 209–225. doi:*3*(2).10.1111/j.1467-9221.2009.00749.x

Drucker, E. (1999). Drug prohibition and public health: 25 years of evidence. *Public Health Reports*, *114*(1), 1–17. doi:10.1093/phr/114.1.14 PMID:9925168

Elff, M., & Rossteutscher, S. (2011). Stability or decline? Class, religion and the vote in Germany. *German Politics*, *20*(1), 107–127. doi:10.1080/09644008.2011.554109

Euwema, M., Kop, N., & Bakker, A. (2004). The behaviour of police officers in conflict situations: How burnout and reduced dominance contribute to better outcomes. *Work and Stress*, *18*(1), 23–38. doi:10.1080/0267837042000209767

Fellner, J. (2009). Race, drugs, and law enforcement in the United States. *Stanford Law & Policy Review*, *20*(2), 257–291. Available from http://heinonline.org/HOL/ LandingPage?handle=hein.journals/stanlp20&div=20&id=&page=

Gatto, J., & Dambrun, M. (2012). Authoritarianism, social dominance, and prejudice among junior police officers. *Social Psychology*, *43*(2), 61–66. doi:10.1027/1864-9335/a000081

Gatto, J., Kerbrat, C., & Oliveira, P. D. E. (2010). Prejudice in the police: On the processes underlying the effects of selection. *European Journal of Social Psychology, 269*, 252–269. doi:10.1002/ejsp

Goldstein, R. B., Bigelow, C., McCusker, J., Lewis, B. F., & Mundt, K. a, & Powers, S. I. (2001). Antisocial behavioral syndromes and return to drug use following residential relapse prevention/health education treatment. *The American Journal of Drug and Alcohol Abuse, 27*(3), 453–82. Retrieved from http://www.ncbi.nlm. nih.gov/pubmed/11506262

Goodrich, B. *The Calvinist work ethic and consumerism* [Lecture]. Retrieved from http://carbon.ucdenver.edu/~bgoodric/The%20Calvinist%20Work%20Ethic%20 an%20 Consumerism.htm

Graham, J., Nosek, B., & Haidt, J. (2012). The moral stereotypes of liberals and conservatives: Exaggeration of differences across the political spectrum. *PLoS One*, *7*(12), e50092. doi:10.1371/journal.pone.0050092 PMID:23251357

Green, E. G. T., Thomsen, L., Sidanius, J., Staerklé, C., & Potanina, P. (2009). Reactions to crime as a hierarchy regulating strategy: The moderating role of social dominance orientation. *Social Justice Research, 22*(4), 416–436. doi:10.1007/s11211-009-0106-3

Haley, H., & Sidanius, J. (2005). Person organization congruence and the maintenance of group-based social hierarchy: A Social Dominance perspective. *Group Processes & Intergroup Relations, 8*(2), 187–203. doi:10.1177/1368430205051067

Haslam, S. A., & Reicher, S. D. (2012). Contesting the "nature" of conformity: What Milgram and Zimbardo's studies really show. *PLoS Biology, 10*(11), e1001426. doi:10.1371/journal.pbio.1001426 PMID:23185132

Hearn, N. (2010). Theory of desistance. *International Journal of Criminology*, 1–48. Retrieved from http://www.search.org/files/pdf/Hearn_Theory_of_Desistance_IJC_Nov_2010.pdf

HM Inspectorate of Prisons and HM Inspectorate of Constabulatory. (2012). *Expectations for Police Custody: Criteria for assessing the treatment of and conditions of detainees in police custody* (version 2, 2012). Retrieved from https://www.justiceinspectorates.gov.uk/hmicfrs/media/police-custody-expectations-full-document-20120118.pdf

HM Inspectorate of Prisons and HM Inspectorate of Constabulatory. (2014). *Criteria for assessing the treatment of prisoners and conditions in prisons.* Retrieved from https://www.justiceinspectorates.gov.uk/hmiprisons/

Johnsen, B., Granheim, P. K., & Helgesen, J. (2011). Exceptional prison conditions and the quality of prison life: Prison size and prison culture in Norwegian closed prisons. *European Journal of Criminology, 8*(6), 515–529. doi:10.1177/1477370811413819

Jones, H. B. Jr, Furnham, A., & Deile, A. J. (2010). Religious orientation and the Protestant Work Ethic. *Mental Health, Religion & Culture, 13*(7-8), 697–706. doi:10.1080/13674670802111862

Kinner, S. A., & Milloy, M.-J. (2011). Collateral consequences of an ever-expanding prison system. *CMAJ: Canadian Medical Association Journal = Journal de l'Association Medicale Canadienne, 183*(5), 632. doi:10.1503/cmaj.101848

Kleinig, J., & Murtagh, K. (2005). Disenfranchising Felons. *Journal of Applied Philosophy, 22*(3), 217–239. doi:10.1111/j.1468-5930.2005.00307.x

Knowles, E. D., Lowery, B. S., Shulman, E. P., & Schaumberg, R. L. (2013). Race, ideology, and the Tea Party: A longitudinal study. *PLoS One, 8*(6), e67110. doi:10.1371/journal.pone.0067110 PMID:23825630

Langeliers, A. L. A. I., Amin, S., & Toole, S. K. O. (2010). Correctional officers and attitudes toward mental illness. American Psychological Association 2010 Convention Presentation.

Larsson, M., Bjorklund, F., & Backstrom, M. (2012). Right-wing authoritarianism is a risk factor for torture-like abuse, but so is social dominance orientation. *Personality and Individual Differences, 53*(7), 927–929. doi:10.1016/j.paid.2012.06.015

Lattimore, P. K., Barrick, K., Dawes, D., Steffey, D., & Visher, C. A. (2012). *Prisoner reentry services: What worked for SVORI evaluation participants? Final Report.* Retrieved from https://www.nij.gov/topics/corrections/reentry/pages/evaluation-svori.aspx

MacBeth, A., & Gumley, A. (2012). Exploring compassion: A meta-analysis of the association between self-compassion and psychopathology. *Clinical Psychology Review, 32*(6), 545-552. 10.1016/j.cpr.2012.06.003

Malka, A., & Lelkes, Y. (2010). More than ideology: Conservative–Liberal identity and receptivity to political cues. *Social Justice Research, 23*, 156–188. doi:10.1007/s11211-010-0114-3

Malka, A., Lelkes, Y., Srivastava, S., Cohen, A. B., & Miller, D. T. (2012). The association of religiosity and political conservatism: The role of political engagement. *Political Psychology, 33*(2), 275–299. doi:10.1111/j.1467-9221.2012.00875.x

Malpas, J. (2012). In *The Stanford Encyclopedia of Philosophy.* Retrieved from http://plato.stanford.edu/archives/win2012/entries/davidson/

Mccarty, M., Aussenberg, R. A., Falk, G., & Carpenter, D. H. (2013). Drug testing and crime-related restrictions in TANF, SNAP, and housing assistance. Washington, DC: Academic Press.

Miller, E. J. (2009). Drugs, courts, and the new penology. *Stanford Law & Policy Review, 20*(2), 417–461. Retrieved from https://ssrn.com/abstract=1464353

Mondak, J. J., & Canache, D. (2013). Personality and political culture in the American States. *Political Research Quarterly.* doi: 10.1177/1065912913495112

Morrison, K. R., & Ybarra, O. (2009). *Symbolic threat and social dominance among liberals and conservatives: SDO reflects conformity to political values.* Academic Press. doi:10.1002/ejsp

Nam, H. H., Jost, J. T., & Van Bavel, J. J. (2013). "Not for all the tea in China!" political ideology and the avoidance of dissonance-arousing situations. *PLoS One*, *8*(4), e59837. doi:10.1371/journal.pone.0059837 PMID:23620724

Natarajan, N. et al.. (2008). *Substance abuse treatment and public safety*. Washington, DC: Justice Policy Institute.

Neff, K. D. (2011). Self-compassion, self-esteem, and well-being. *Social and Personality Psychology Compass*, *5*(1), 1–12. doi:10.1111/j.1751-9004.2010.00330.x

Neff, K. D., & Germer, C. K. (2013). A pilot study and randomized controlled trial of the mindful self-compassion program. *Journal of Clinical Psychology*, *69*(1), 28–44. doi:10.1002/jclp.21923 PMID:23070875

Neff, K. D., Kirkpatrick, K. L., & Rude, S. S. (2007). Self-compassion and adaptive psychological functioning. *Journal of Research in Personality*, *41*(1), 139–154. doi:10.1016/j.jrp.2006.03.004

Nicholson, T., Duncan, D. F., White, J., & Watkins, C. (2012). Focusing on abuse, not use: A proposed new direction for US drug policy. *Drugs Education Prevention & Policy*, *19*(4), 303–308. doi:10.3109/09687637.2012.682231

Panagopoulos, C. (2013). Positive social pressure and prosocial motivation: Evidence from a large-scale field experiment on voter mobilization. *Political Psychology*, *34*(2), 265–275. doi:10.1111/pops.12007

Pratto, F., Sidanius, J., & Levin, S. (2006). Social dominance theory and the dynamics of intergroup relations: Taking stock and looking forward. *European Review of Social Psychology*, *17*(1), 271–320. doi:10.1080/10463280601055772

Ramírez, L., Levy, S. R., & Hughes, J. M. (2010). Considering the roles of culture and social status: The Protestant Work Ethic and egalitarianism. *Revista latinoamericano de piscologica*, *42*(3), 381-390. doi:.10.14349/rlp.v42i3.580

Rattinger, H., & Steinbrecher, M. (2011). Economic voting in times of economic crisis. *German Politics*, *20*(1), 128–145. doi:10.1080/09644008.2011.554111

Redmond, B. (2009). Lesson 8 commentary: Intergroup theories: How do the people around me influence me? In *Work Attitudes and Motivation*. The Pennsylvania State University World Campus.

Reinarman, C. (2000). The Dutch example shows that liberal drug laws can be beneficial. In S. Barbour (Ed.), *Drug legalization: Current controversies* (pp. 102–108). San Diego, CA: Greenhaven.

Rosenthal, L., Levy, S., & Moyer, A. (2011). Protestant work ethic's relation to intergroup and policy attitudes: A meta-analytic review. *European Journal of Social Psychology*, *41*(7), 874–885. doi:10.1002/ejsp.832

Rule, N. O., Freeman, J. B., Moran, J. M., Gabrieli, J. D., Adams, R. B. Jr, & Ambady, N. (2009). Voting behavior is reflected in amygdala response across cultures. *Social Cognitive and Affective Neuroscience*, *5*(2-3), 349–355. doi:10.1093/scan/nsp046 PMID:19966327

Russell, N. (2014). Stanley Milgram's obedience to authority "relationship" condition: Some methodological and theoretical implications. *Social Sciences*, *3*(3), 194–214. doi:10.3390/socsci3020194

Rutchick, A. M. (2010). Deus ex machina: The influence of polling place on voting behavior. *Political Psychology*, *31*(2), 209–225. doi:10.1111/j.1467-9221.2009.00749.x

Sacks, S., Sacks, J. Y., McKendrick, K., Banks, S., & Stommel, J. (2004). Modified TC for MICA offenders: Crime outcomes. *Behavioral Sciences & the Law*, *22*(4), 477–501. doi:10.1002/bsl.599 PMID:15282836

Satcher, D. (1996). *1994: Ten leading causes of death in the United States*. Atlanta, GA: Centers for Disease Control, National Center for Injury Prevention Control. Retrieved from http://www.cdc.gov/injury/wisqars/leadingcauses.html

Schoen, H. (2011). Merely a Referendum on Chancellor Merkel? Parties, Issues and Candidates in the 2009 German Federal Election. *German Politics*, *20*(1), 92–106. doi:10.1080/09644008.2011.554107

Settle, J. E., Dawes, C. T., & Fowler, J. H. (2009). The heritability of partisan attachment. *Political Research Quarterly*, *62*(3), 601–613. doi:10.1177/1065912908327607

Sidanius, J., & Liu, J. (2001). The Gulf War and the Rodney King beating: Implications of the general conservatism and social dominance perspectives. *The Journal of Social Psychology*, *132*(6), 685–700. doi:10.1080/00224545.1992.9712099

Sidanius, J., Liu, J., Shaw, J., & Pratto, F. (1994). Social dominance orientation hierarchy attenuators and hierarchy enhancers: Social dominance theory and the criminal justice system. *Journal of Applied Social Psychology*, *24*(4), 338–366. doi:10.1111/j.1559-1816.1994.tb00586.x

Siegel, M., & Lotenberg, L. (2007). *Marketing public health: Strategies to promote social change*. Sudbury, MA: Jones and Bartlett.

Silverstone, P. (2013a). A Novel approach to training police officers to interact with individuals who may have a psychiatric disorder. *The Journal of the American Academy of Psychiatry and the Law*, *41*(3), 344–355. PMID:24051586

Silverstone, P. (2013b). Police training mental illness.pdf. *The Journal of the American Academy of Psychiatry and the Law*, *41*(3), 344–355. PMID:24051586

Silverstone, P. H., Krameddine, Y. I., DeMarco, D., & Hassel, R. (2013). A novel approach to training police officers to interact with individuals who may have a psychiatric disorder. *The Journal of the American Academy of Psychiatry and the Law*, *41*(3), 344–355. PMID:24051586

Smith, K. B., Oxley, D., Hibbing, M. V., Alford, J. R., & Hibbing, J. R. (2011). Disgust sensitivity and the neurophysiology of left-right political orientations. *PLoS One*, *6*(10), e25552. doi:10.1371/journal.pone.0025552 PMID:22039415

Topalli, V., Brezina, T., & Bernhardt, M. (2012). With God on my side: The paradoxical relationship between religious belief and criminality among hardcore street offenders. *Theoretical Criminology*, *17*(1), 49–69. doi:10.1177/1362480612463114

Torellia, C., & Kaikati, A. (2009). Values as predictors of judgments and behaviors: The role of abstract and concrete mindsets. *Journal of Personality and Social Psychology*, *96*(1), 231–247. doi:10.1037/a0013836 PMID:19210077

Van Lange, A., Bekkers, R., Chirumbolo, A., & Leone, L. (2012). *Are conservatives less likely to be prosocial than liberals? From games to ideology, political preferences and voting.* Academic Press. doi:10.1002/per

Van-Tienen, M., Scheepers, P., Reitsma, J., & Schilderman, H. (2011). The role of religiosity for formal and informal volunteering in the Netherlands. *Voluntas*, *22*(3), 365–389. doi:10.1007/s11266-010-9160-6

Wilson, M. S., & Sibley, C. G. (2013). Social dominance orientation and right-wing authoritarianism: Additive and interactive effects on political conservatism. *Political Psychology*, *34*(2), 277–284. doi:10.1111/j.1467-9221.2012.00929.x

Zimbardo, P. (1971). The Stanford Prison Experiment: A simulation study of the psychology of imprisonment conducted August 1971 at Stanford University [Slideshow]. Manuscripts and archives, Stanford University, Stanford, CA.

Zimbardo, P. (2007). The Lucifer Effect: Understanding how good people turn evil. *Journal of the American Medical Association, 298*(11), 1338–1340. Available from http://go.galegroup.com/ps/anonymous?id=GALE%7CA179132813&sid=googleScholar&v=2.1&it=r&linkaccess=fulltext&issn=01200534&p=AONE&sw=w&authCount=1&isAnonymousEntry=true

KEY TERMS AND DEFINITIONS

Authoritarianism: An attitude consisting of the favoring of complete obedience or subjection to authority as opposed to individual freedom.

Conventionalism: An attitude consisting of the adherence to or advocacy of conventional attitudes or practices.

JWB: Just world belief, defined as interpreting the societal status quo by blaming disadvantaged groups for their own situation.

Prejudice: An unfavorable opinion or feeling formed beforehand or without knowledge, thought, or reason, or any preconceived opinion or feeling, either favorable or unfavorable, or unreasonable feelings, opinions, or attitudes, especially of a hostile nature, regarding an ethnic, racial, social, or religious group.

PWE: Protestant work ethic, defined as the belief that hard work leads to success.

RWA: Right wing authoritarianism, defined as a personality trait which predicts prejudice towards disadvantaged and stigmatized groups (e.g., racial minorities and prisoners). This construct includes three dimensions: authoritarian aggression, authoritarian submission, and conventionalism.

SDO: Social dominance orientation, defined as values, attitudes, causal attributions, and ideologies that provide moral and intellectual justification for existing hierarchical social orders, unequal distributions of social value, and social policies that promote hierarchy.

ENDNOTE

[1]   In 2014, protests in Ferguson, MO followed Michael Brown's death and a grand jury declined to charge the officer with murder. A justice department investigation also found widespread alleged racial bias in the police force.

Chapter 7
Mother America:
Cold War Maternalism and the Origins of Korean Adoption

Shawyn C. Lee
University of Minnesota – Duluth, USA

ABSTRACT

After the Korean War, it became acceptable and expected that American families would adopt Korean children into their homes, symbolizing American prosperity and security. As significant a role as social work played in this process, there currently exists no research that examines the activities of the profession and the origins of Korean adoption. This chapter discusses the maternalist nature of adoption efforts during the 1950s by one international social welfare agency after the Korean War: the American Branch of International Social Service (ISS-USA). Predicated on maternalist ideologies that shaped the social work profession during the Progressive Era, in what the author calls Cold War maternalism, the gendered notions of motherhood were expanded to genderless notions of parenthood. Anticommunist sentiments thrust adoptive parenthood into the political spotlight on an international level, thus serving the best interests of adoptive parents and the nation long before serving those of the children.

INTRODUCTION

In 1953, an armistice temporarily suspended the Korean War, a three-year civil war between what is now the Democratic People's Republic of Korea (North Korea) and the Republic of Korea (South Korea) (Cumings, 2010). Those left behind in

DOI: 10.4018/978-1-5225-2650-6.ch007

the aftermath of the war included hundreds of thousands of widows and children (Korean Institute of Military History, 2001). According to the Ministry of Social Affairs (ca. 1956), "The number of children's institutions is three times as many and the number of children in the institutions is four times as many as before the war" (p. 2). Many of the children in desperate need of help were mixed-blood children—those born of Korean mothers, primarily fathered by American servicemen. Given their urgent situation, many Americans, including professional social workers, began devising safe and expeditious methods of child removal, thereby institutionalizing intercountry adoption.

Using historical research methods situated within a maternalist framework, this chapter provides a critical analysis of social-work child-rescue efforts in postwar South Korea during the 1950s, as embodied by one international social welfare agency: the American Branch of International Social Service (ISS-USA). This social work organization established and institutionalized intercountry adoption practices in the aftermath of the Korean War, in response to the plight of mixed-blood Korean children orphaned by the war. It was the premier expert on intercountry adoption of foreign children to the United States during the 1950s.

BACKGROUND

Described as a "hermit nation," (Dr. Bob Pierce, as cited in Wagner, 1956), Korea was a "poor and primitive country" with towns that were "sordid and dirty," and homes that were "hovel-like" (Wagner, 1956, p. 1). Agencies attempting to help the children left abandoned or deserted after the war had to deal with a complete lack of social welfare. As Far East Representative Florence Boester (1957) reported, there was "inadequacy of feeding, housing, and medical facilities; lack of trained leadership; maddening difficulties in the means of communication and travel; absence of coordinated social resources" (p. 4). The families of the birth mothers of mixed-blood Korean children had deserted them. According to Valk (1956), "Missionaries who work up near the 38th parallel where there are stationed many foreign servicemen describe the woods being full of girls with such children" (p. 3). The children were described as animal-like. They were "dirty, untrained, and not properly fed" (Pettiss, 1955c, p. 1). American assistance was desperately needed.

After the war, virtually no social welfare structure at any level existed in Korea (International Social Service Korea Project, n.d.) . There were "not even half a dozen fully trained Korean social workers in the country," as social work had not been established as a profession (Boester, 1957b, p. 4). Until its connection with ISS-USA in 1954, Child Placement Service (CPS) had been the only government-affiliated child-placement service in South Korea after the war. But Susan Pettiss (1955c) reported that "no one on staff knows the first things about American adoption practices" (p. 1). The director, Mrs. Hong, was "an untiring and devoted individual"; however, she was found to be "unsatisfactory in preparing adequate case histories on the children and in operating organizationally" (Young, 1958, p. 1).

Reports from many International Social Service (ISS) correspondents revealed the urgent situation in South Korea. Senior Case Consultant of the American Branch of International Social Service (ISS-USA), Margaret A. Valk (1956), reported the alleys being "cluttered with women and children, beasts and debris" (p. 2). Mrs. John M. Burnside (1956), Chairman of the Korean Adoption Program of the Joint Committee, reported that while any orphan institutionalized in Korea faces a harsh life, "the orphan of mixed parentage carries on his innocent shoulders the burdens of being unwanted, resented and unclaimed" (para. 4).

Correspondents also wrote of what they witnessed in the many overcrowded orphanages: "For the most part they lack heat, adequate water supply, and adequate staff. Children come and go; they die" (Valk, 1956, p. 2). Mrs. Burnside (1956) wrote:

It is difficult to speak dispassionately of the children whom we saw in many institutions. We saw children with the swollen bellies and match-stick legs of malnutrition; we saw children with sores and skin diseases on faces and heads and with eye infections, nearly all were suffering from colds; we saw children dressed in thin rags, their feet and hands purple from the cold; we saw dying babies lying in rags on cold floors; we saw scores of apathetic children who sat silent and motionless; we saw children with solemn, searching looks on their faces; we saw children who played quietly and silently and unsmilingly. (p. 3)

Dr. Bob Pierce, director of World Vision Inc., recalled:

Last Sunday night a Korean girl with a child about 2 years old came to a World Vision orphanage asking to leave the child there. When asked why, she said the father was an American soldier who left her, and her Korean parents would not allow her to stay in the home with the baby. There was a Korean man willing to marry her if she would get rid of the child. The orphanage, already crowded, advised the girl it was not possible to accept the baby and sent the girl away. At 5 a.m. the next morning, the orphanage officials found the baby half frozen on the steps outside the building. (Wagner, 1956, p. 1)

Part of a letter quoted in *The Waiting Children*, by Pearl Buck (n.d.), implored the American public to do something to help these suffering children:

We have more than forty babies now on bottles, tiny babies, and others are coming in every day. We have toddlers everywhere, sleeping wherever we can bed them down. The older children try to help, but the summer heat is upon us and disease is rife. Many of the little ones will die. We know that. We know, too, that good families in the United States want to adopt such children. Why doesn't your country let them in? (p. 1)

The reports coming from South Korea ignited the humanitarian efforts to save the children of war that characterized the midcentury Cold War years. Rhetoric of rescue spoke to the benevolent and religious aspects of 1950s life, as American citizens began chasing their desires to save these poor, suffering children (Herman, 2008). With Cold War America absorbed in family making across racial and national boundaries, "'Adopting' a child enabled a sense of participation in U.S. foreign policy" that every American could experience (Klein, 2003, p. 158).

In 1953, Congress passed the Refugee Relief Act, which allowed 4,000 orphans under the age of 10 to be adopted by American citizens in the U.S. (Kim, 2010). A major limitation of the Refugee Relief Act was that it would expire at the end of 1956. Another limitation was that the Refugee Relief Act allowed one family to adopt no more than two orphans at a time. Because of the immense need to rescue the many destitute children in South Korea, individuals and organizations desperately worked to find ways to get the children quickly to the United States, before the Refugee Relief Act expired.

Postwar Korean adoption initiatives in the 1950s marked the first time that more formal intercountry adoption practices were implemented. Whereas foster homes and orphanages had been used during World War II as temporary aid, those involved in the intercountry adoption of Korean children understood it as permanent removal of these children from their families and country (Marre & Briggs, 2009). With the urgent situation in postwar South Korea, many individuals and organizations worked quickly to devise best practices for quickly removing mixed-blood orphansm. Various organizations, especially Christian organizations such as World Vision, Inc., Save the Children Federation, and Christian Children's Fund, joined forces with ISS-USA in order to build and strengthen institutions and resources for orphaned children (Oh, 2005).

Painstaking efforts were undertaken to ensure that the best interests of the Korean child were served. However, in recent years, historians and adoption scholars have begun to question whether the best interests of the child were truly served. *Outsiders Within* is an anthology of writings by transracial adoptees, many of them Korean adoptees. Trenka, Oparah, & Shin (2006), editors of the collection, proclaim that the book is a "corrective action" against adoptive parents and professionals, such as social workers and psychiatrists, who have long dominated the literature on adoption.

As experts in their fields, they "have been the ones to tell the public—including adoptees—'what it's like' and 'how we turn out'" (p. 1). Consequently, this has become the dominant narrative that many adoptees have come to know about themselves. One of the contributing authors is well-known scholar and activist in adoptee communities, Kim Park Nelson. In her piece titled "Shopping for Children in the International Marketplace," Park Nelson (2006) disrupts the long-standing clinical narrative, and brings to light the business transactions and compensations—monetary, material, or social—involved in international adoption. She asserts, "The growing practice of transnational adoption can be understood through a simple supply and demand equation" (p. 89). Similarly, in her analysis of how Korean orphans were made into marketable objects, scholar SooJin Pate (2014) posits that the orphan is reduced "into an object or product that can fill orders and be collected" (p. 90).

Race has also been an important factor in adoption narratives. Locked into the business of such adoptions is the fact that often, children from other countries have racial and cultural identities that are different from their white adoptive families. Even though clinical experts have acknowledged these racial differences in transracial adoptions, rarely has race—and more importantly, racism—been factored into more macro-level understandings of international adoption. Park Nelson (2006) argues that the hierarchical differences in adopting children domestically or abroad, and the superiority that white parents feel in terms of their parental abilities when compared to parents in poor countries, justify transnational adoption. Park Nelson also contends that white adoptive parents are able to perpetuate their white privilege through the act of adoption, as transracial children assimilate white American values, behavior, and ideals.

In her book *Global Families: A History of Asian International Adoption in America*, ethnic studies professor Catherine Ceniza Choy (2013) examines the creation of the global family through adoption. She defines "global family making" as "the process involving the decisions made and actions taken by people who create and sustain a family by consciously crossing national and often racial borders" (p. 9). Choy asserts that while social workers were sensitive to race and racism in Korea and the United States, the lived experiences expressed by adult adoptees, through memoirs, visual arts, and documentary films, reveal how detrimental the absence of discussions of race and racism in the broader adoption narrative has been. The mark of a successful adoption was the proper Americanization of the Korean adoptee (Choy, 2007). Americanization has been synonymous with Christianization (Oh, 2005; Pate, 2014). With many adoptees growing up in white, Christian families, identifying culturally as American and isolated from each other, racial discrimination has been particularly challenging. Korean adoptees often express feelings of not being American enough as racial minorities, and not being Korean or Asian enough in South Korea and Korean-American communities (Kim, 2007). Considering the

161

intersections of race, culture, and religion, scholar and activist JaeRan Kim (2006) says:

White parents may feel that they are exempt from being racist; after all, they adopted a child of another race. Yet through promoting the 'we are all God's children' mentality, Christianity breeds a sort of colorblindness that is often as dangerous to a child of color as overt racism. (p. 158)

Arissa Oh (2015) also discusses the ways in which Korean adoptees were assimilated as American citizens through Christian indoctrination. The religiosity of 1950s America, which she terms *Christian Americanism*, drove many American families to adopt the orphaned children of South Korea. Positioning the salvation of these children as missionary work, Oh demonstrates how the fusion of religious and patriotic sensibilities affirmed the Christian goodness and "Americanness" of adoptive families. Through the adoption of mixed-blood Korean orphans, Americans responded to the Korea situation in three ways. According to Oh, the adoption of these children served as an ideological victory of the Korean War, since there had been no obvious defeat of North Korea. The expansion of American families through intercountry adoption reinforced this intimate and vital unit of containment (May, 2008). Stable homes with married parents and children offered a sense of stability and security. The situation in Korea, with the many desperate and abandoned children, made Americans realize just how fragile the notions of home and family were. As Oh (2015) states, "Seeing the plight of Korean orphans was like seeing their own nightmares made real" (p. 88).

INTERNATIONAL SOCIAL SERVICE

International Social Service (ISS) is an international social welfare organization with headquarters in Geneva, Switzerland. The organization's name comes from the three-pronged definition of *international social service*—social work within one country with individuals not originally from that country; social work requiring work across national borders; and social workers of one country conducting their work in another country (Northcott, Rosicky, Elvin, Ayoub, & Lambert, 2012). The American Branch of International Social Service (ISS-USA) offers a number of psychosocial and legal services to children and families who have been separated by migration, always keeping the best interests of the child as a top priority (ISS, 2015; Northcott, et al., 2012).

For almost a century, ISS has utilized intercountry casework in its service to children and families, a practice it developed and refined over the years since it was founded in 1924 (Northcott et al., 2012). While ISS dealt with the many problems brought to the organization using casework methods locally, the worldly reach of its services led to its application of casework on an international level (ISS, n.d.). In 1959, then director of ISS, Edna Weber, defined intercountry casework as "a method of extending individualised social services to persons whose problems require study or action in another country; a method of interagency co-operation designed to bring together on behalf of a client social services in more than one country" (Weber, 1959, p. 44). However, applying social casework methods on a global scale was no easy task. According to a publication issued by ISS (n.d.) titled, *International Social Service, a History, 1921-1955*, differences in socio-cultural, political, and economic backgrounds and attitudes in different countries caused ISS to recognize that casework meant different things in different countries. Furthermore, as an intermediary between social agencies in different countries, ISS was limited in how much direct contact it had with the individuals that its services directly affected. In order to establish an effective intercountry casework method, the various ISS branches had to figure out how to establish a close working relationship with one another, despite the distance. They also had to learn how to share the knowledge they were gaining with local social workers.

ISS began its intercountry adoption work after World War II, when it was tasked with helping the many children left abandoned or orphaned (ISS, 1957). As stated in *International Social Service, a History, 1921-1955* (ISS, n.d.):

Because many of these children, coming without prior social inquiry, are not subject to any of the safeguards customary in local adoptions, the ISS has become acutely aware of the wide divergence in national laws, attitudes and placement practices, and the scant international coordination in protective measures. Indeed, in no one field had intercountry consultation seemed more urgent than about these children transplanted from one cultural and legal setting to another. (p. 60)

The ultimate goal of ISS in the development of its intercountry adoption program was to establish sound practices that resulted in children being adopted into homes within their birth countries whenever their natural parents could not care for them (ISS-USA, 1957b). The principles of intercountry adoption, established by ISS in 1957, laid out the specificities in regard to child welfare. In particular, Principle 2 stated that "sufficient consideration should be given to possible alternative plans for the child within his own country before intercountry adoption is decided upon since there are various hazards inherent in transplanting a child from one culture to another" (Dodds, 1961, p. 2). However, while ISS worked with social agencies in other countries to increase and improve the services it provided to children in need of adoption, the Korean War brought a new kind of problem—mixed-blood children.

Because most mixed-blood Korean children adopted after the war went to homes in the United States, it was the work of ISS-USA that exemplified the intercountry casework method of *case conference by correspondence*—casework through writing and sending descriptive letters to social welfare agencies, politicians, and other organizations nationally and internationally. In 1955, ISS-USA Assistant Director Susan Pettiss (1955b) stated, "We provide service to all the social agencies throughout the United States and correspond with almost all the countries around the world" (p. 1). At that time, ISS-USA had eight social workers plus clerical staff (Pettiss, 1955b). In the immediate aftermath of the Korean War, ISS-USA, under the direction of William T. Kirk, set out to use its intercountry casework methods to rescue the many mixed-blood Korean War orphans, whose situations were dire and futures bleak, at best.

Constantly changing orphan legislation, bound up in policies regulating immigration, heavily dictated the work of ISS-USA. There was no intercountry adoption law. After World War II, with the passage of the Displaced Persons Act of 1948, intercountry adoption grew in popularity in the United States (Pettiss, 1958; Krichefsky, 1958). However, capitalizing on American expansion into Asia during the early Cold War years, and subsequent U.S.-Asia integration, Christina Klein (2003) argues that the sentimental discourse developed by intellectuals and policymakers forged bonds between Americans and Asians both domestically and internationally. Within the United States, these bonds were manifest in the reform of immigration and naturalization laws that allowed Asians to more easily enter the country and become naturalized citizens.

The Refugee Relief Act of 1953 serves as a prime example of the integration to which Klein referred. With its passage, Korean adoption would leave an indelible mark on immigration policy. Congress granted responsibility to the U.S. State Department for implementing the Orphan Program under the Refugee Relief Act (Pettiss, 1958). The Orphan Program allowed for 4,000 nonquota visas for orphans under the age of 10, who could be adopted abroad or in the U.S. if a citizen couple gave assurances that they would legally adopt the orphan and provide proper care. A prospective adoptive couple had to select a recognized welfare agency to underwrite their assurance of adoption (Krichefsky, 1958). The Refugee Relief Act required the involvement of an authorized or licensed U.S. child welfare agency before a child could enter the country. In her article in *Child Welfare* on the effects of foreign adoptions on U.S. adoption standards, Susan Pettiss (1958) indicated that the U.S. government recognized two major national agencies for the Orphan Program: the Catholic Committee for Refugees of the National Catholic Welfare Conference and ISS. She maintained that both of these organizations worked closely with the U.S. Children's Bureau, the Child Welfare League of America, and the American Public

Welfare Association to continually review procedures and practices in intercountry adoptions.

The best interest of the child has long been a slogan of social work in the realm of child welfare. Certainly ISS-USA was committed to the child's best interest in its design and implementation of intercountry adoption practices. By 1954, ISS-USA had pieced together a procedural outline of how it would apply intercountry casework methods to the intercountry adoption of Korean children. The American Branch of International Social Service worked with Korea and other U.S. agencies to establish a program that would find homes in other countries for mixed-blood children (ISS, 1967). Eugenie Hochfield (1963) reported that after it was determined that a child was available for adoption overseas, child welfare agencies would begin the placement process. A long-distance relationship of sorts was started between the potential adoptive parents and the child. Social workers in both countries involved mediated the relationship.

Home Studies

In a 1957 document titled "Home Study Material for Intercountry Adoption Applications," ISS-USA provided an explanation of the home study, including capture of information about the adoptive parents for "matching" purposes. The descriptive and evaluative information that ISS-USA received during the home study assisted in the decision-making process as to the suitability of prospective adoptive parents to adopt a foreign child. The information gave the agency "a picture of the family, the setting and community in which they live, and their hopes and expectations for an adoptive child" (ISS-USA, 1957a, p. 2). Some of the information collected described all family members, including such items as physical appearance, personality, education, and ambitions. Family attitudes toward home and community were also assessed. Medical information of the adoptive parents was necessary. If infertility was a reason for intercountry adoption, the home study narrative had to include the prospective adoptive parents' reaction to that reality. The prospective adoptive parents' experience with handling children, including those from other cultural backgrounds, was discussed, as was their motivation for adopting a foreign child (ISS-USA, 1957a).

Formalities in Korea

In a document titled "Rules of Procedure for Adoption of Korean Child by American Adoptive Parent" (ca. 1954-1955) from the Child Placement Service (CPS) in South Korea, American parents had to submit a written statement of adoption to whichever administrative authority had jurisdiction over the registered domicile of the child. This was in accordance with the Korean Family Registration Act, the closest statute the country had to an intercountry adoption law. In addition, a certificate assuring the eligibility of the prospective adoptive parents had to be submitted by a recognized social welfare agency from the state in which the adoptive parents lived (CPS, ca. 1954-1955).

Supervision

After a Korean child came into an American home, there was a period of six months to a year in which a social worker from the local social welfare agency supervised the family. In "Guide for Supervisory Reports," ISS-USA (n.d.) outlined the procedure and information collected. Supervision reports captured such information as the child's health, development, interactions with siblings and classmates, language adjustment, and personality and emotional needs. In terms of the parent-child relationship, first reports included information on such aspects as parents' initial reaction to the child; handling of the language barrier; day-to-day experiences with feeding, sleeping, and playing; discipline; complex issues that came up concerning racial differences between parents and child, and within the community; and the parents' ability to help the child work through feelings of his or her past life. Progress of adjustment was captured in the child's experiences with new day-to-day activities, as well as any comparative comments regarding past and present life, and the parents' handling of this. Finally, the later reports served to describe the overall development and acceptance of both the parental role and integration of the child into the family.

In 1957, three years after ISS-USA began formalizing intercountry adoption from South Korea, ISS created a set of principles that governed its intercountry adoption practices. The commitment of ISS to the best interest of the child was exemplified in the following principles:

Principle 1: That adoption is the best substitute for care by the child's own parents or close relatives, provided that adoption is based fundamentally on the welfare of the child. (Dodds, 1961, p. 1)

Principle 2: That sufficient consideration should be given to possible alternative plans for the child within his own country before intercountry adoption is decided upon since there are various hazards inherent in transplanting a child from one culture to another. (Dodds, 1961, p. 2)

Principle 7: That an adequate home study of the prospective adopters should be completed before a child is suggested to or placed with a couple in view of intercountry adoption, as well as an adequate study of the child's background, physical conditions, and personality development. (Dodds, 1961, p. 5)

Principle 9: That before legal adoption is completed, there must be a trial period of not less than six months under the supervision of a social worker attached to a qualified agency. (Dodds, 1961, p. 6)

MATERNALISM

Maternalism becomes a useful framework in which to examine child-placing practices through adoption, particularly in its fit with the pronatalist attitudes of midcentury Cold War America. According to historian Molly Ladd-Taylor (1994), maternalism is an ideology that combines a unique feminine value system of care and nurturance with a woman's capacity for motherhood and duty to care for future generations of citizens. Koven and Michel (1993) assert that maternalism has its roots in social reform movements of the early 19th century, when women organized around issues pertaining to moral purity. Domestic ideologies that differentiated men and women drove women's humanitarian concerns for child welfare, and activist interpretations of religious and moral values associated with the gospel. The moral and compassionate qualities, and the capacity to nurture, became linked with a woman's motherliness.

During the Progressive Era in particular, maternalism was understood primarily as a political movement, and allowed many women to have great political influence. Reformers identified mothers and their quality of care as central to child welfare. As Skocpol (1995) states, "By the progressive era, indeed, women's associations had concluded that women should act as 'housekeepers for the nation'" (p. 27). Women entered into the political arena to advocate and develop "a policy template to inspire a 'higher,' more 'American' quality of motherhood" (Mink, 1995, p. 5). Social policies were developed by, and carried the moral values of upper- and middle-class women, "for the good of" women of less privileged classes (Skocpol, 1995, p. 72).

In 1912, the United States Children's Bureau was established as a research agency to coordinate and regulate various child welfare policies and initiatives. As Ladd-Taylor (1994) asserts, it "underscored how thoroughly women's work of childcare was politicized in early twentieth century America" (p.74). The Children's Bureau became the lead authority on the welfare of children and families (Trattner, 1999). Maternalist measures such as the U.S. Children's Bureau were considered by political coalitions as "extensions of mother love into the public sphere" (Skocpol, 1995, p. 261).

Even though the political arm of maternalist social movements fell away at the end of the 1920s, maternalist ideologies have remained prominent fixtures in the profession of social work. Laura Curran (2005) states that midcentury social workers were focused on the welfare of children and continued to prioritize notions of motherhood. She asserts that maternalist ideologies underwent a transformation in the early Cold War years, due to the changing sociocultural attitudes toward sustaining middle-class families. History professor Rebecca Jo Plant (2010) maintains that maternalism has continued to be used in other contexts to report on almost any political activity in which women have asserted their roles as mothers. In her book *Mom: The Transformation of Motherhood in Modern America,* Plant stretches Ladd-Taylor's definition of maternalism to encompass the cultural representations of maternal subjectivity, in addition to the gendered aspects of motherhood, and motherhood as a familial and civic duty. American motherhood emerged from the belief that mothers had the ability to transform children. It was conceptualized as an institution, and was likened to "a branch of government, charged with reproducing the populace and upholding the nation's guiding principles" (Plant, 2010, p. 5). The institution of American motherhood would have a significant effect on adoption.

The construction of adoptive motherhood began in the early 1900s with a publication called the *Delineator,* a popular women's magazine. Julie Berebitsky (2000) discusses the influence of the "Child-Rescue Campaign" in the *Delineator* on women who were interested in adopting children. Even before the institutionalization of American motherhood to which Plant refers, the *Delineator* urged women to adopt "by appealing to their sense of patriotic and civic duty, in addition to their motherly instinct" (p. 55). The value of motherhood was elevated through the positioning of adoptive mothers as selfless women choosing to adopt children in order to have a family. Motherhood was based on love and nurturance, not the blood tie. Berebitsky continues by explaining that the *Delineator* provided a platform on which adoptive motherhood could be built and shared. It offered practical information for women interested in finding children to be adopted. It normalized adoption, and offered descriptions of the experience of adoptive mothering.

In sharp contrast to the goodness and priority of the adoptive mother, there was the Korean mother—the Korean unwed mother. Korean unwed mothers were cast in a negative light and deemed unfit to care for their own children (Pate, 2014). However, especially for those who were prostituted in camptowns surrounding U.S. military bases in Korea, their fall from virtue and chastisement as "Yankee whores" (Cho, 2008, p. 120) elevated American adoptive parents into Christ-like status, as they essentially forgave the birthmother's transgression by saving her child via adoption (Pate, 2014). The South Korean government and adoption agencies encouraged prostituted Korean women to put their mixed-blood children up for adoption (Kim, 2007). Those born from the U.S.-Korea relationship were bodies bearing the marks of militarization. These children were viewed as "bastards of the Western princess," "seeds sown by GIs," and "darkies" or "niggers" (Cho, 2008, p. 118). In desperate attempts to escape camptown life by way of marriage to an American soldier, the women tried to sever themselves from their pasts as prostituted women in order to become more marriageable, even if it meant getting rid of the mixed-blood child that served as material evidence of her past:

GI babies were found in every conceivable place – at missions, churches, and orphanages; in train stations, shops...public toilets, the market place, and on doorsteps. In the most desperate cases, the babies were left to die in garbage dumps or on mountainsides, or worse, some little blonde-haired babies were washed up on the seashore. (Holt, 1956 as cited in Oh, 2005)

Hurdis (2007) asserts that international adoption privileges "First World nations through the exploitation of Second and Third World nations, specifically women and children" (p. 177). She maintains that we must understand the ways in which children continue to be commoditized into resources that First World nations can afford to purchase. Seen through this framework, Hurdis argues that there is a price placed on motherhood, and a separation of legitimate and illegitimate mothers. Consider terms such as "orphan" or "imploring waif." Contrast that language with descriptions of camptown prostituted women. They were considered *fallen women* who long ago lost social status and self-respect by deviating from the traditional, strictly prescribed roles of dutiful and obedient girls, women, daughters, and wives (Moon, 1997). They were "shy Korean maiden[s]" turned "into brazen Western whores" (Cho, 2008, p. 93). Whether her deviations, such as sex outside of marriage, rape, incest, or divorce, were seen as choice or as inflicted upon her did not matter. In a society characterized by classist distinctions and racial and cultural homogeneity, having had sexual relations with foreigners cast these women as pariahs—a disgrace to themselves and to Korea (Moon, 1997). Because these women lacked social status and financial resources to keep their children, giving them up willingly or having them forcibly taken bestows upon them an identity of illegitimacy in terms of motherhood. Meanwhile, because First World women can afford these children, they were designated as legitimate mothers (Hurdis, 2007).

COLD WAR MATERNALISM

In what the author calls *Cold War maternalism*, the definitions of maternalism put forth by Ladd-Taylor and Plant are expanded to look at a genderless notion of motherhood, encapsulated in the idea of a particular kind of parenthood—adoptive parenthood. Cold War maternalism also moves apolitical parenthood to the very political concept of national parenthood that was the pronatalist response to the threat of Communist takeover during the early Cold War years. Finally, by virtue of its definition, Cold War maternalism questions the belief that intercountry adoption from Korea served the best interest of the child. In considering the maternalist nature of the origins of Korean adoption, the author argues that the interests of American parents, and thus the country, were of the greatest importance, while the interests of the children were subsumed under issues of national security.

In her book, *Kinship by Design,* Ellen Herman (2008) discusses the unprecedented and ambitious goal of creating families "safely and well by making them public, on purpose, and according to plan" (p. 1). Herman goes on to argue that researchers of early adoption placements "attempted to naturalize adoption, convinced their discoveries about nature, nurture, attachment, and identity would refine policies related to qualifications for adoption, placement timing, and failed adoptions" (p. 3). In this sense, the adoption methods practiced and endorsed by ISS-USA center the attention on the adoptive family. Also, in considering contextual pieces of 1950s Cold War America that privileged white, middle-class, nuclear families, all of the policies and practices established by policymakers and professionals ensured that adoption, and therefore family-making, was governable (Herman, 2008). As ISS-USA (1957a) outlined:

The family, in signing the immigration forms, and the agency, in approving placement, [have] formally agreed to ensure proper care to the child under the agency's supervision until legal adoption has been completed. This agreement, which is included on the forms used to apply for the child's admission to the United States, is made to the United States government. In addition to this accepted responsibility, the family and the agency have an obligation to inform the child's legal guardian abroad, and the cooperating agency in the child's country, about the child's welfare and progress. Close cooperation, by the family with the local agency, and among the agencies here and abroad involved in the adoption plan, is required. (p. 2)

As adoption became more and more publicly accepted and practiced, child welfare agencies largely abandoned their mission of serving the best interests of the child, instead focusing their services on couples who wanted babies. In this sense, social workers served as brokers for couples interested in adoption (May, 1995). In *Children of Calamity,* John Caldwell (1957) discussed the ways in which orphan children were conveyed as products for purchase. Citing cables that came into the Christian Children's Fund, Caldwell offered some of their headlines: "Rush me 500 orphans," or "Need 200 Korean, 10 Japanese mixed-blood, 50 Chinese, 10 Arabs" (p. 29). Christina Klein (2003) likened this to department store backorders. Kim Park Nelson (2006) explains this in terms of the supply and demand aspect of international adoption, whereby white parents adopt children from foreign countries, an exchange that involves not only money, but also "white parents' desire to enrich their lives by parenting a child from a foreign culture" (p. 89). The American Branch of International Social Service certainly fulfilled the dreams of white American parents wishing to adopt Korean children. As an intermediary between local welfare agencies in the United States and South Korea, the organization filtered the "department store backorders," filled with specific children American couples wished to adopt.

Because of the urgent situation, some social welfare agencies actually relaxed their screening standards for prospective adoptive parents. In a memo to district supervisors from Hilmer Olsen (1961), the Wisconsin State Department of Public Welfare indicated that while their screening of prospective adoptive couples wishing to adopt a Korean child would follow the same procedures as domestic adoptions, they were willing to "approve the marginal applicant for these children," even though in a domestic situation, the "marginal applicant" would be rejected (p. 1). This is a primary example of how the best interest of the child was relaxed to benefit more parents, given the situation in South Korea. In a document titled "Home Study Material for Intercountry Adoption Applications," ISS-USA (1957a) stated that couples "with humanitarian or spiritual motivations," and "those with a highly developed interest in, or ties with other cultures predominate among the families recommended for the adoption of a foreign child" (p. 2). Considering the contextual factors of 1950s Cold War America with respect to American religiosity, and Christina Klein's (2003) notion of Cold War Orientalism, the privileging of prospective adoptive parents whose values and moral investments fit with the larger needs and interests of the United States is exemplified here. Hyde & Hyde (1958) also alluded to this when they suggested, "When the wishes of prospective parents rather than the child are the primary concern, however well-intentioned the parents may be, the adoption process becomes skewed, and children's needs will not be met" (p. 20).

The work of ISS-USA also demonstrated the ways in which the children were positioned as potential deviants, thus potentially jeopardizing national image. Gaither Warfield (1958), of the Methodist Committee for Overseas Relief, expressed similar concerns when he stated:

One must always remember that an unloved child growing up in the wrong home can easily become delinquent. With oriental features this child will be known in the American community, and any misconduct—natural under the circumstances—will be held against Korea and other Far Eastern countries. (p. 2)

Here, the presumption is that mixed-blood Korean children are likely to act up in their American communities. Because they stand out racially, their delinquency will reflect poorly on South Korea. The main concern here is on the image of the country, rather than the best interests of the child.

The ways in which intercountry adoption from South Korea privileged the United States can be understood within the pronatalist attitudes of 1950s America, and the recrafting of adoptive motherhood as adoptive parenthood. Adoptive parenthood represented the vehicle by which the United States could reinforce its resistance to Communism. Christina Klein (2003) writes of American expansion into Asia during the Cold War. She suggests that the Cold War was presented to Americans as "something that ordinary Americans could take part in, as a set of activities in which they could invest their emotional and intellectual energy" (p. 7). Intercountry adoption from Korea after the war became one of the activities in which Americans partook. Because of the voluntary nature of formation, as opposed to coercion and violence, racial integration, and a justification for permanent U.S. extension of power across the world, the multiracial and multinational families that were formed by intercountry adoption represented a model of postwar integration (Klein, 2003).

The extent to which American social work had been established in South Korea, and informed the mass removal of mixed-blood Korean children to white American homes, also represents the ways in which the interests of the United States were privileged at the expense of the child's best interest, even though the profession claimed its practices were meant to serve the best interest of the child. In this way, the profession of social work became a kind of official gatekeeper of national security. Since World War II, the needs of soldiers and their families had shaped midcentury social work. Casework offered to the middle class became a feature of postwar social work practices (Trattner, 1999). As adoption pushed beyond national boundaries, and ISS implemented intercountry casework practices on a global level, American social work practices expanded into South Korea through ISS-USA.

Margaret Valk (1956) reported that after the war, there was no governmental welfare, and certainly no general child welfare program in South Korea. With much of the Korean budget spent on the military, the Korean Ministry of Health and Social Affairs did not have enough money to begin such a program. Valk also reported that the directors of the orphanages had no special training or experience in child welfare. The Korean Ministry of Social Affairs reported that a lack of trained staff in the field made this work particularly challenging. It was felt that an American social worker needed to be in South Korea to help advise the government and CPS, especially in terms of further developing its body of knowledge of American child welfare practices (Pettiss, 1955a). A number of American-trained social workers thus went to Korea to help set up a coordinated system of child-placing through what eventually came to be the South Korean branch of the ISS. In particular, Miss Helen McKay, Mr. Ed Francel, and Mrs. Ellen Trigg Visser were trained child welfare workers, and also had considerable related experience in the U.S. and in Europe (Chamberlin, 1956). Additionally, in 1955, three Korean social workers were sent to the University of Minnesota to complete their education in social work. The Korean social workers were on a fellowship developed by then director of the University of Minnesota School of Social Work, John Kidneigh, and the Unitarian Service Committee, to advance social work training in South Korea by improving practice through in-service training (Unitarian Service Committee, Inc., 1956).

American social workers worked directly with CPS and the Ministry of Social Affairs in South Korea to coordinate intercountry adoption. They recommended to Dr. Pierce, of World Vision, Inc., the employment of an American social worker to work with the doctor on site at the Reception Center, a World Vision orphanage. The American Branch of International Social Service also conducted demonstration projects designed to not only establish sound intercountry practice, but also show how to maintain such practices in the best interests of all involved. Moreover, the American Branch of ISS aimed to strengthen the knowledge and skills of Korean workers, so that they could eventually provide the services themselves (ISS, 1967). Although Korean workers did increasingly become involved in the coordinated efforts of ISS-USA and ISS-Korea, the American Branch recognized that many of the foreign welfare services being brought into South Korea were American.

Many Third World nations rely extensively on Western social work models (Midgley, 1990). Postwar South Korea was no exception. Even though ISS-USA desired to indigenize international casework in South Korea, American models of intervention became the reference point for Korean social work (Khinduka, 1971). Because case conference by correspondence was derived from the casework practices of American social work, intercountry casework represented the "exportability of American casework methods to foreign settings" (Pettiss, 1956, p. 1). While these services helped alleviate the needs of many needy groups, the overall effect actually discouraged Korean authorities from taking responsibility in meeting the social needs of their people (ISS-USA, 1962).

Europe and the United States both have involved histories in the colonization of poorer and underdeveloped nations. The establishment of social work in these countries occurred largely under Western influences, rather than from indigenous sources. Unfortunately, this has called into question the relevance of curricula and practices in non-Western countries (Lyons et al., 2012). Healy (2012) asserts that this has associated the profession of social work with imperialism and colonialism. Lyons et al. (2012) similarly suggest that, historically, the forces of colonialism that privileged whiteness and oppressed indigenous populations were instrumental in the establishment of the profession in poorer countries abroad. In attempts to unravel and define inclusion and exclusion in the context of other countries, "international exchange has at times been characterized by unselective imposition and borrowing of foreign models of education and practice" (Healy, 2012, p. 13). This has led to the establishment and maintenance of a superior-inferior relationship between the West and non-Western nations (Healy, 2012). Unfortunately, according to Khinduka

(1971), "the current conception of professional social work, which is undoubtedly dominant and the most fully elaborated conception, is generally irrelevant and sometimes dysfunctional to the resolution of the major issues that beset the poor nations" (p. 64).

IMPLICATIONS FOR SOCIAL WORK PRACTICE AND RESEARCH

This research can have a number of influences on future social work practice and research. First, it is important to point out that much of the extant literature on intercountry adoption has examined the experiences of children and adolescents (e.g., Brooks & Barth, 1999; Burrow & Finley, 2004; Grotevant, 1997; Hamilton, Samek, Keyes, McGue, & Iacono, 2015; Howe, 2001; Swim, Saltsman, Deater-Deckard, & Petrill, 2007; Weinberg, Waldman, van Dulmen, & Scarr, 2004). More research needs to be done with adult adoptees (Finley, 1999). The experiences of adult Korean adoptees have often been quite different from the grand adoption narrative constructed in part by existing adoption research (e.g., Choy, 2013; Kim, 2010; Pate, 2014). Using an historical trauma lens can provide a valuable framework from which we can understand the history of Korean adoption and the effects it has had on the lived experiences of many adult adoptees today. Sloth (2006) states:

[R]esearch influences—or should influence—adoption policy and practice. Research results interpret adoptees' realities. They inform our assumptions about what is right and wrong in adoption. Therefore it is vital that intercountry adoptees, as the "objects" of performed research, assess research results and compare them with lived experiences to ensure their validity and reliability. We cannot leave this task to nonadopted academics alone. (p. 253)

This is especially useful to adoption agencies or other organizations providing pre- and post-adoption services. It is imperative that professionals be able to connect the histories of their clients with present-day realities and challenges, in order to work effectively with those seeking assistance (Knight, 2015). Adoption professionals should be discussing with prospective adoptive parents the long history of Korean adoption, and the discrepancies between what clinical research has shown and the actual lived realities of adoptees as they move beyond childhood and adolescence, into adulthood. For those Korean adoptees who seek counseling services, trauma-informed practice methods that focus on client-centered and client-driven interventions (e.g., Harper, Stalker, Palmer, & Gadbois, 2008) can help, in that they consider the holistic perspective on the person, including his or her history, and allow for client control over treatment. These practice implications can extend beyond Korean adoptees to include all transracial or transnational adoptees. As scholar and activist John Raible (2006) states, "Finite, outcome-oriented research ignores the ongoing, lifelong impact of the adoption experience itself on adoptees.... Most of the existing research has failed to capture the continual negotiation and performance of fluid racial identities over the course of the life span" (p. 181).

Second, even though the practice standards ISS-USA established in the 1950s claimed to have the child's best interest in mind, there are myriad aspects to intercountry adoption that can have profound effects on all involved. As Hübinette (2006) explains of the history of Korean adoption, at one end is the contextual story of migration, both historically and in relation to other child-placing schemes. At the other end is the social control aspect of adoption, particularly with respect to regulating and controlling Korean women's bodies in the name of social development and national security. Applying this spectrum to the role of social work in intercountry adoption, at one end the profession needs to understand its own historical child-placing stories, both from an historical context and situated within larger narratives of international child rescue. At the other end, the profession needs to disrupt the social control aspect of intercountry adoption. This calls into question the profession's commitment to culturally appropriate practices.

Finally, the profession of social work should seek to understand the complex political factors associated with intercountry adoption. Does social work truly have the child's best interest at heart when, so often, it seems to maintain complex political obligations literally through the sale of children from poorer nations to wealthier ones? How does the profession reconcile this colonial aspect of its own history? As Hübinette (2006) points out, in the larger narrative of the genocidal aspects of forced migrations, "Only international adoption remains largely uncontested, made legal through various 'international' conventions that in reality privilege Western concepts of adoption" (p. 143). Furthermore, how does the profession understand its role in a multibillion-dollar moneymaking industry fraught with corruption? Joyce (2013) states, "People with good intentions have become a market, the demand side of an industry that can be as profit-driven as any other, and they have significant cash to spend" (p. xiii). Because the supply side—the number of available children—is comparatively smaller than the demand side, it has resulted in children's records being laundered, turning them into "manufactured" orphans with no family, at least on paper (Joyce, 2013).

These are hard questions the profession must ask itself. It must turn introspective and retrospective, not only to revisit the story of professionalization and child placing, but also to critically assess this history in order to make changes. One major area in which this work could be done is in social-work curricula. Relatively few schools of social work offer a standalone social welfare history course at the graduate level. In addition to increasing the numbers of schools offering such courses, the design of the curriculum should critically engage students in the history of their profession. More specific to bridging the past to the present with respect to intercountry adoption (though this certainly could apply to other stories that have been left in the margins of social work history), the perspectives of those whose lived experience it was and still is should be central. Linda Smith (2012) writes, "To resist is to retrench in the margins, retrieve 'what we were and remake ourselves'" (p. 4). Adoptees are indeed beginning to retrench themselves in the margins in order to discover their personal and collective pasts, and disrupt prevailing discourses that have continued to disregard their perspectives. They have known all too well, and for far too long, "what it means, what it feels like, to be present while [our] history is erased before [our] eyes, dismissed as irrelevant, ignored" (Smith, 2012, p. 31).

CONCLUSION

The intercountry adoption work by ISS-USA was imbued with maternalist ideologies that have long permeated the profession of social work. The early Cold War years were predominantly characterized by rigid gender roles and "domestic banality" (Curran, 2005, p. 112). Elaine Tyler May (2008) reports that the roles of breadwinner and homemaker were embraced during the post-World War II family boom, and the 1950s considered the "last gasp of time-honored family life" (p. 7). Career-oriented male breadwinners provided for their families, while housewives took care of the home and childrearing responsibilities (May, 1995). With the social-work profession focused on child welfare issues, including specific notions of motherhood, the situation in postwar Korea reimagined motherhood across national and international boundaries.

During the postwar and early Cold War years, national security went hand in hand with domesticity, an ideology realized in the focus on the nuclear family and what it represented in terms of hope for the nation's future (May, 1995). The nuclear-family-focused maternalism espoused by midcentury social workers was a revision of its Progressive Era predecessor. It still clung to the importance of the mother-child relationship, but excluded the political movement that allowed women to break into the public sphere and influence policies affecting mothers and children (Curran, 2005). The postwar white, middle-class ethos asserted that the only occupation for women was motherhood. In addition, fatherhood also became a measure of good citizenship (May, 1995). Adoption thrust the family into the public eye where its very meaning, and the meaning of parenthood, was crafted and recrafted (Berebitsky, 2000).

Following Progressive Era maternalist ideologies pertaining to nation-building and the Americanization or Christianizing especially of immigrant populations and persons of color, what the author calls Cold War maternalism was infused in the child-rescue efforts of midcentury social workers involved with intercountry adoption efforts in postwar South Korea. Cold War maternalism reconstructed notions of motherhood, moving motherhood to the broader category of parenthood, and even to nationhood. M. M. Slaughter (1995) redefines "Mother" to include the person who rears the child, and not necessarily the one who also bears the child, suggesting, "In this usage, there is nothing in nature that requires women to Mother, or prevents men from doing so" (p. 73). Slaughter's reframing of "Mother" leads Cold War maternalism to parenting—the construction of parenting from a maternalist perspective. That is, maternalist parenting still carries the hierarchical Progressive Era ideologies, in which demographic characteristics etch out the best parents, and the assimilative features of good "mothering" that shape future responsible citizens.

Cold War maternalism puts parenting within a national and international scope, by asserting that the adopted Korean child became the joint childrearing project of American parents, and therefore the nation, as Third World countries were "mothered" out of the grips of Communism and into modernity. *State maternalism*, a term coined by Yvonne Zylan (2000), refers to the state's responsibility to care for mothers and children. It shared with Progressive Era maternalism the importance of the mother-child relationship, and the impact of that relationship on maintaining a healthy society. Cold War maternalism carries on this ideology, and expands it to the "national family," with the familial relationship as the litmus test for a healthy society. By ensuring that Korean children would become "'American' by unlearning their cultures" (Mink, 1995, p. 79), social workers of ISS-USA ensured that the national security of their country was stable by creating a system of intercountry, transracial adoption that encapsulated the primacy of international mothering through two-parent nuclear families. Miss Bessie C. Irvin (1955) of the State of California Department of Social Welfare, an agency well connected with ISS-USA, stated, "we do not feel that a single woman is able to offer a real 'family' to a child . . . Children will have a better opportunity to adjust to a strange country if they are able to be placed with both a mother and a father in their substitute home" (p. 1).

Cold War maternalism represents yet another shift in maternalist ideologies. With a focus on the nuclear family, and pronatalist attitudes of midcentury Cold War America (May, 2008), the adoption of Korean children into American homes became one way of creating and sustaining the middle-class family. Furthermore, with the expansion of American powers into postwar South Korea (Klein, 2003), including American social-work practices (Pettiss, 1956), Cold War maternalism not only continued to reinforce adoptive motherhood as a symbol of patriotism (Berebitsky, 2000), but also held the adoptive family responsible for properly raising transracial adoptees as American citizens. From a cultural standpoint, this meant that in terms of nation building, the citizenry would be "white, Christian, and modern" (Jacobs, 2009,

p. 26). As scholars such as Arissa Oh (2005, 2015) and SooJin Pate (2014) assert, Korean orphans were inculcated with American and Christian morals and values both before they came to the U.S., and certainly after placement in their families. From children's welfare needs to subsequent American policies and practices, the maternalist nature of child-rescue efforts in postwar South Korea crafted suffering children into malleable objects, to be recreated in the American image, all in the name of national security. As Jacobs (2009) states, white Americans "wished to create a white nation, their model of cultural assimilation suggested that one was not necessarily born white, but could become so" (p. 73). South Korea was the child, in multiple senses, and white America its mother.

REFERENCES

Berebitsky, J. (2000). *Like our very own: Adoption and the changing culture of motherhood, 1851-1950*. University Press of Kansas.

Boester, F. (1957). *Summary report of initial organization, ISS delegation: Korea. International Social Service – American Branch (Folder: ISS 1957, box 4). Social Welfare History Archives, Elmer L.* Minneapolis, MN: Anderson Library, University of Minnesota.

Buck, P. S. (n.d.). *The waiting children.* International Social Service – American Branch (Folder 34: Associations: Welcome House, 1955-, box 23). Social Welfare History Archives, Elmer L. Anderson Library, University of Minnesota, Minneapolis, MN.

Burnside, J. M. (1956). *International Social Service – American Branch (Folder: ISS-Branches, 1-1956-Dec. 1956, Korea "RRA-5," Box 35). Social Welfare History Archives, Elmer L.* Minneapolis, MN: Anderson Library, University of Minnesota. [Letter]

Caldwell, J. C. (1957). *Children of calamity.* The John Day Company.

Chamberlin, L. (1956). *Letter to Susan Pettiss dated February 2, 1956. International Social Service – American Branch (Folder: ISS-Branches, Korea, "RRA-5" 1-1956-December 1956, box 35). Social Welfare History Archives, Elmer L.* Minneapolis, MN: Anderson Library, University of Minnesota.

Child Placement Service. (ca. 1954-1955). Rules of procedure for adoption of Korean child by American adoptive parent. International Social Service – American Branch (Folder: ISS-Branches, Korea, "RRA-5" Refugee Relief Program, 1954-Dec. 1955, box 35). Social Welfare History Archives, Elmer L. Anderson Library, University of Minnesota, Minneapolis, MN.

Cho, G. M. (2008). *Haunting the Korean diaspora: Shame, secrecy, and the forgotten war*. Minneapolis, MN: University of Minnesota Press.

Choy, C. C. (2007). Institutionalizing international adoption: The historical origins of Korean adoption in the United States. In K. J. S. Bergquist, M. E. Vonk, D. S. Kim, & M. D. Feit (Eds.), International Korean adoption: A fifty-year history of policy and practice (25-42). Haworth Press, Inc.

Choy, C. C. (2013). *Global families: A history of Asian international adoption in America*. New York University Press. doi:10.18574/nyu/9780814717226.001.0001

Cumings, B. (2010). *The Korean War: A history*. New York, NY: The Random House Publishing Group.

Curran, L. (2005). Social work's revised maternalism: Mothers, workers, and welfare in early Cold War America, 1946-1963. *Journal of Women's History, 17*(1), 112–136. doi:10.1353/jowh.2005.0005

Dodds, D. (1961). *Fundamental principles in intercountry adoption. International Social Service – American Branch (Folder 34: Children: Intercountry Adoption General, 1954-1962, box 10) Social Welfare History Archives, Elmer L.* Minneapolis, MN: Anderson Library, University of Minnesota.

Finley, G. E. (1999). Children of adoptive families. In W. K. Silverman & T. H. Ollendick (Eds.), Developmental issues in the clinical treatment of children (pp. 358-370). Boston: Allyn & Bacon.

Healy, L. M. (2012). The history and development of social work. In L. M. Healy & R. J. Link (Eds.), Handbook of international social work: Human rights, development, and the global profession (55-62). Oxford University Press.

Herman, E. (2008). *Kinship by design*. Chicago: The University of Chicago. doi:10.7208/chicago/9780226328072.001.0001

Hochfield, E. (1963). Across national boundaries: Problems in the handling of international adoptions, dependency and custody cases. *Juvenile Court Judges Journal, 14*(3), 3–7. doi:10.1111/j.1755-6988.1963.tb00251.x

Hübinette, T. (2006). From orphan trains to babylifts: Colonial trafficking, empire building, and social engineering. In J. J. Trenka, J. C. Oparah, & S. Y. Shin (Eds.), Outsiders within: Writing on transracial adoption (pp. 139-149). South End Press.

Hurdis, R. (2007). Lifting the shroud of silence: A Korean adoptee's search for truth, legitimacy, and justice. In K. J. S. Bergquist, M. E. Vonk, D. S. Kim, & M. D. Feit (Eds.), International Korean adoption: A fifty-year history of policy and practice (pp. 171-185). Haworth Press, Inc.

Hyde, L., & Hyde, V. P. (1958). A study of proxy adoptions. International Social Service – American Branch (Folder 14: Child Welfare League or America & International Social Service (American Branch), box 11). Social Welfare History Archives, Elmer L. Anderson Library, University of Minnesota, Minneapolis, MN.

International Social Service – American Branch. (1957a). *Home study material for intercountry adoption applications. International Social Service – American Branch (Folder 3: Miscell. Forms for Adoption Proceedings, box 11). Social Welfare History Archives, Elmer L.* Minneapolis, MN: Anderson Library, University of Minnesota.

International Social Service – American Branch. (1957b). *Report on September 27*[th]*, 1957 workshop on intercountry adoptions.* International Social Service – American Branch (Folder 36: Children: Intercountry Adoption Conferences and Workshops, box 10). Social Welfare History Archives, Elmer L. Anderson Library, University of Minnesota, Minneapolis, MN.

International Social Service – American Branch. (1962). *A report to child welfare agencies on the placement of children from Korea into the United States. International Social Service – American Branch (Folder 25: Korea Adoptions Questions, box 34). Social Welfare History Archives, Elmer L.* Minneapolis, MN: Anderson Library, University of Minnesota.

International Social Service – American Branch. (n.d.). *Guideline for supervisory reports.* International Social Service – American Branch (Folder 3: Miscell. Forms for Adoption Proceedings, box 11). Social Welfare History Archives, Elmer L. Anderson Library, University of Minnesota, Minneapolis, MN.

International Social Service, Inc. (1957). *In a world they never made: The story of International Social Service. International Social Service – American Branch (Folder 3: Miscellaneous Folder, box 47). Social Welfare History Archives, Elmer L.* Minneapolis, MN: Anderson Library, University of Minnesota.

International Social Service, Inc. (1967). *Results of leadership, demonstrations, and training in South Korea by International Social Service 1954-1966. International Social Service – American Branch (Folder: To Korea, Reports & Visits, box 35). Social Welfare History Archives, Elmer L.* Minneapolis, MN: Anderson Library, University of Minnesota.

International Social Service, Inc. (2015). *Vision and mission.* Retrieved from http://www.iss-ssi.org/index.php/en/home/mission

International Social Service, Inc. (n.d.). *International Social Service, a history, 1921-1955.* International Social Service – American Branch (Folder 23, box 3). Social Welfare History Archives, Elmer L. Anderson Library, University of Minnesota, Minneapolis, MN.

International Social Service Korea Project (n.d.). [document summarizing ISS-Korea project]. International Social Service – American Branch (Folder 25: Korea Adoptions Questions, box 34). Social Welfare History Archives, Elmer L. Anderson Library, University of Minnesota, Minneapolis, MN.

Irvin, B. C. (1955). *Letter to Mrs. Oak Soon Hong dated June 21, 1955. International Social Service – American Branch (Folder: ISS-Branches, Korea, "RRA-5," Refugee Relief Program, 1954-December 1955, box 35). Social Welfare History Archives, Elmer L.* Minneapolis, MN: Anderson Library, University of Minnesota.

Jacobs, M. D. (2009). *White mother to a dark race: Settler colonialism, maternalism, and the removal of indigenous children in the American West and Australia, 1880-1940.* University of Nebraska Press.

Joyce, K. (2013). *The child catchers: Rescue, trafficking, and the new gospel of adoption.* Public Affairs.

Khinduka, S. K. (1971). Social work in the Third World. *The Social Service Review, 45*(1), 62–73. doi:10.1086/642647

Kim, E. (2007). Remembering loss: The Koreanness of overseas adopted Koreans. In K. J. S. Bergquist, M. E. Vonk, D. S. Kim, & M. D. Feit (Eds.), International Korean adoption: A fifty-year history of policy and practice (pp. 115-129). Haworth Press, Inc.

Kim, E. J. (2010). *Adopted territory: Transnational Korean adoptees and the politics of belonging.* Durham, NC: Duke University Press. doi:10.1215/9780822392668

Kim, J. R. (2006). Scattered seeds: The Christian influence on Korean adoption. In J. J. Trenka, J. C. Oparah, & S. Y. Shin (Eds.), Outsiders within: Writing on transracial adoption (pp. 151-162). South End Press.

Klein, C. (2003). *Cold War orientalism: Asia in the middlebrow imagination, 1945-1961*. Berkeley, CA: University of California Press.

Knight, C. (2015). Trauma-informed social work practice: Practice considerations and challenges. *Clinical Social Work Journal*, *43*(1), 25–37. doi:10.1007/s10615-014-0481-6

Korean Institute of Military History. (2001). *The Korean War*. Lincoln, NE: University of Nebraska Press.

Koven, S., & Michel, S. (Eds.). (1993). *Mothers of a new world: Maternalist politics and the origins of welfare states*. Routledge.

Krichefsky, G. D. (1958). Immigrant orphans. I & N Reporter [Article]. International Social Service – American Branch (Folder: Immigration: Re: Admission of Foreign Orphans to US (proposed by INS), box 13). Social Welfare History Archives, Elmer L. Anderson Library, University of Minnesota, Minneapolis, MN.

Ladd-Taylor, M. (1994). *Mother-work: Women, child welfare, and the state, 1890-1930* (Vol. 88). Urbana, IL: University of Illinois Press.

Lyons, K. H., Hokenstad, T., Pawar, M., Huegler, N., & Hall, N. (Eds.). (2012). *The Sage handbook of international social work*. Sage.

Marre, D., & Briggs, L. (Eds.). (2009). *International adoption: Global inequalities and the circulation of children*. NYU Press. doi:10.18574/nyu/9780814791011.001.0001

May, E. T. (1995). *Barren in the promised land: Childless Americans and the pursuit of happiness*. Basic Books.

May, E. T. (2008). *Homeward bound: American families in the Cold War Era*. New York, NY: Basic Books.

Midgley, J. (1990). International social work: Learning from the Third World. *Social Work*, *35*(4), 295–301.

Ministry of Social Affairs. (ca. 1956). *Social welfare in Korea*. [Document]. International Social Service – American Branch (Folder: ISS-Branches, 1-1956-Dec 1956, Korea "RRA-5," Box 35). Social Welfare History Archives, Elmer L. Anderson Library, University of Minnesota, Minneapolis, MN.

Mink, G. (1995). *The wages of motherhood: Inequality in the welfare state, 1917-1942*. Cornell University Press.

Moon, K. H. S. (1997). *Sex among allies: Military prostitution in U.S.–Korea relations*. New York, NY: Columbia University Press.

Northcott, F., Rosicky, J. G., Elvin, A., Ayoub, J., & Lambert, C. (2012). International Social Service: Addressing the need for intercountry casework. In L. M. Healy & R. J. Link (Eds.), Handbook of international social work: Human rights, development, and the global profession (pp. 95-101). Oxford University Press.

Oh, A. H. (2005). A new kind of missionary work: Christians, Christian Americans, and the adoption of Korean GI babies, 1955-1961. *Women's Studies Quarterly*, *33*(3/4), 161–188.

Oh, A. H. (2015). *To save the children of Korea: The Cold War origins of international adoption*. Stanford University Press.

Olsen, H. (1961). *Memo to district direct service supervisors from Hilmer Olsen, Chief of Direct Services, Wisconsin State Department of Public Welfare, Division for Children and Youth. International Social Service – American Branch (Folder: ISS-Branches, Korea, "RRA-5" 1-1956 – December 1956, box 35). Social Welfare History Archives, Elmer L.* Minneapolis, MN: Anderson Library, University of Minnesota.

Park Nelson, K. (2006). Shopping for children in the international marketplace. In J. J. Trenka, J. C. Oparah, & S. Y. Shin (Eds.), Outsiders within: Writing on transracial adoption (pp. 89-104). South End Press.

Pate, S. (2014). *From orphan to adoptee: U.S. empire and genealogies of Korean adoption*. Minneapolis, MN: University of Minnesota Press. doi:10.5749/minnesota/9780816683055.001.0001

Pettiss, S. T. (1955a). *Letter to Ellen Trigg Visser dated June 2, 1955. International Social Service – American Branch (Folder: ISS-Branches, Korea, "RRA-5" Refugee Relief Program 1954-December 1955, box 35). Social Welfare History Archives, Elmer L.* Minneapolis, MN: Anderson Library, University of Minnesota.

Pettiss, S. T. (1955b). *Letter to Mrs. Oak Soon Hong dated February 3, 1955. International Social Service – American Branch (Folder: ISS-Branches, Korea, "RRA-5" Refugee Relief Program 1954-December 1955, box 35). Social Welfare History Archives, Elmer L.* Minneapolis, MN: Anderson Library, University of Minnesota.

Pettiss, S. T. (1955c). *Letter to Ellen Trigg Visser received January 15, 1955. International Social Service – American Branch (Folder: ISS-Branches, Korea, "RRA-5" Refugee Relief Program 1954-December 1955, box 35). Social Welfare History Archives, Elmer L.* Minneapolis, MN: Anderson Library, University of Minnesota.

Pettiss, S. T. (1956). *Special aspects of casework with families separated by national boundaries* [Paper presented at the 1956 National Conference of Social Work]. International Social Service – American Branch (Folder: Associations: National Conference on Social Welfare (formerly on Social Work) 1954-1959, box 22. Social Welfare History Archives, Elmer L. Anderson Library, University of Minnesota, Minneapolis, MN.

Pettiss, S. T. (1958). *Effect of adoptions from foreign children on U.S. adoption standards and practices, Child Welfare, July 1958. International Social Service – American Branch (Folder 9: Adoption Manual and Other Printed Material, box 11). Social Welfare History Archives, Elmer L.* Minneapolis, MN: Anderson Library, University of Minnesota.

Plant, R. J. (2010). Mom: The transformation of motherhood in modern. University of Chicago Press.

Raible, J. (2006). Lifelong impact, enduring need. In J. J. Trenka, J. C. Oparah, & S. Y. Shin (Eds.), Outsiders within: Writing on transracial adoption (pp. 179-188). South End Press.

Skocpol, T. (1995). *Social policy in the United States: Future possibilities in historical perspective.* Princeton University Press.

Slaughter, M. M. (1995). The legal construction of "Mother." In M. A. Fineman & I. Karpin (Eds.), Mothers in law: Feminist theory and the legal regulation of motherhood (pp. 73-100). Columbia University Press.

Sloth, K. H. (2006). Researching adoption: Whose perspective and what issues? In J. J. Trenka, J. C. Oparah, & S. Y. Shin (Eds.), Outsiders within: Writing on transracial adoption (pp. 253-258). South End Press.

Smith, L. T. (2012). *Decolonizing methodologies: Research and indigenous peoples* (2nd ed.). Zed Books.

Trattner, W. I. (1999). *From poor law to welfare state: A history of social welfare in America.* The Free Press.

Trenka, J. J., Oparah, J. C., & Shin, S. Y. (Eds.). (2006). *Outsiders within: Writing on transracial adoption.* South End Press.

Unitarian Service Committee, Inc. (1956). *International Social Service – American Branch (Folder, 13: Unitarian Universalist Service Committee, Inc., box 23). Social Welfare History Archives, Elmer L.* Minneapolis, MN: Anderson Library, University of Minnesota. [Document introducing three Korean social workers on fellowship at the University of Minnesota School of Social Work]

Valk, M. A. (1956). *American Branch ISS: Adoption program – Korea, descriptive report by M. A. V., visit to Korea, November 21st–30th, 1956.* International Social Service – American Branch (Folder: Reports & Visits to Korea, 1956, box 35). Social Welfare History Archives, Elmer L. Anderson Library, University of Minnesota, Minneapolis, MN.

Wagner .(1956). *Report of Meeting with Dr. Pierce of World Vision.* International Social Service – American Branch (Folder 29: Children: Independent Adoption Schemes – World Vision 1955–1960, Box 10). Social Welfare History Archives, Elmer L. Anderson Library, University of Minnesota, Minneapolis, MN.

Warfield, G. P. (1958). *Letter from Gaither P. Warfield dated April 4, 1958. International Social Service – American Branch (Folder: Associations: Methodist Committee for Overseas Relief 1955-", box 22). Social Welfare History Archives, Elmer L.* Minneapolis, MN: Anderson Library, University of Minnesota.

Weber, E. (1959). The practice of intercountry casework. International Social Work, April 1959, 44-49. International Social Service – American Branch (Folder 3: Miscellaneous Folder, box 47). Social Welfare History Archives, Elmer L. Anderson Library, University of Minnesota, Minneapolis, MN.

Young, H. (1958). *Letter to Susan Pettiss dated September 15, 1958. International Social Service – American Branch (Folder 14, box 10). Social Welfare History Archives, Elmer L.* Minneapolis, MN: Anderson Library, University of Minnesota.

Zylan, Y. (2000). Maternalism redefined: Gender, the state, and the politics of day care, 1945-1962. *Gender & Society, 14*(5), 608–629. doi:10.1177/089124300014005002

KEY TERMS AND DEFINITIONS

Casework: The work of a professional social worker with an individual or family. This work can include intake, assessment, intervention, monitoring, and evaluation.

Cold War: The period after World War II through the early 1990s. It was characterized by the fear of the spread of communism and nuclear warfare. Americans relied on domestic containment ideologies, such as the nuclear-family model, to bolster the country's resistance to communism. The United States also took a keen interest especially in East Asian countries, in order to stop the threat of global communism.

In the Best Interest of the Child: A long-standing aim of professional social work in child welfare matters. Interventions are designed to guarantee the least amount of disruption to the positive development and healthy functioning of the child.

Intercountry Adoption: The formal and legal adoption of a foreign-born child by American citizens. It marks a permanent removal of the child from their country of origin, and their natural families. The process is overseen by social workers and social welfare agencies in both countries; the national governments of both countries; and local governmental authorities in the state in which the child will live. Intercountry adoption is also referred to as international adoption, overseas adoption, or transnational adoption.

International Social Service – American Branch (ISS-USA): The American branch of International Social Service, an international casework organization that began after World War I to help persons displaced by the war. The American branch was crucial in the development and institutionalization of intercountry adoption practices in the 1950s in the aftermath of the Korean War.

Maternalism: A set of gendered ideologies that intersected with race, class, sex, and religion, maintaining that especially white, American, middle- and upper-class Christian women were the most suitable mothers in raising children to be productive citizens. It was also a political movement during the Progressive Era in which women had profound influence over policies and institutions that served the unique needs of women and children.

Pronatalism: A values-based belief during the early Cold War that prioritized parenthood and the creation and maintenance of nuclear families as a national responsibility in order to present the spread of communism.

Social Work: A profession characterized today by a strengths-based and ecological person-in-environment perspective. Its roots are in the early twentieth century, emerging from the "friendly visitors" of the Charity Organization Society and the more policy-driven Settlement House Movement, both of which sought to improve the lives of the poor.

Chapter 8

Reconfiguring Responsibility in International Clinical Trials:
A Multicultural Approach

Ike Valentine Iyioke
Michigan State University, USA

ABSTRACT

This chapter aims to prominently position the African philosophical notion of the self within the clinical trials context (and the larger bioethics project). As opposed to autonomy-based principlism, this other-regarding or communalist perspective is proposed as the preferred alternative model. The intent is to draw further attention to the inadequacy of the principlist approach particularly in multicultural settings. It also engenders a rethink, stimulates interest, and re-assesses the failed assumptions of universal ethical principles. As a novel attempt that runs against much of the prevailing (Euro-American) intellectual mood, this approach strives to introduce the African view point by making explicit the import of the self in a re-contextualized (nay, globalized) arena. Viewed as such, research ethics is guided to go beyond autonomy-based considerations for the individual with absolute right to self-determination; to embrace more holistic-based approach, recognizing that the individual is embedded in his/her family, community, and the environment.

INTRODUCTION

The collective progress in the field of biomedical research is astonishing, thanks to R&D. This feat represents the heights human brain power has attained in making dreams a reality and in improving our physical, emotional, and material conditions.

DOI: 10.4018/978-1-5225-2650-6.ch008

However, scientific research has sometimes become more a search for material gains, absolute control and might, and less a quest for the truth. When science fashions a project to serve such agendas, the avowed goal of dominating nature can turn into domination of the human person, and ethical problems of enormous proportions may result. The very essence of humanity stands the risk of being compromised, sometimes irreversibly. In that instance, science might become self-deprecating, with no clue, much less an answer (Okere, 2005).

Indeed, R&D in biomedicine greatly relies on clinical trials. But what may not be so obvious are the dynamics involved; they include, the admixture of scientific, technological, socio-cultural and environmental factors that collide in the process.

The present analysis of a multi-cultural approach to clinical trials is borne out of interests that interlink bioethics, multiculturalism, environmental and global studies. This is exemplified in the attempt to string together seemingly disparate subject matters such as *responsibility*, *clinical trials*, and *selfhood* (African notion of it),[1] to make them cohere.[2] To some readers, certain questions might arise: What do these have in common? Is there an African philosophy?[3] And, an "African self," what is that?

It suffices to clarify that this topic occupies a tricky terrain at the confluence of research in biomedical attitudes, the discipline of philosophy, and the disciplines of multiculturalism, including sociology and ecology. Evidently, the task is rare, even herculean, but it is desirable to make the connection (between the tripartite themes of responsibility, clinical trials, and selfhood) to provide a complete understanding of the trajectory of this discussion. It is hoped that readers will be willing to stretch their capacities beyond their accustomed bounds in readiness to accommodate the uncommonly offered lines of reasoning that follow.

The aim of this chapter is to prominently position the African philosophical notion of personhood within the clinical trials context (and the larger bioethics project). As opposed to the Euro-American autonomy-based principlism in research ethics, this chapter will propose an 'other-regarding' or communalist[4] perspective as the preferred alternative model. Hence, this chapter attempts to explore the ethics of public health, specifically, responsibility in clinical trials. It re-conceptualizes responsibility in clinical trials with the insight of the African understanding of the human person. By inference, it strives to complement scholarly literature dealing with cross-cultural biomedical research ethics, and emphasizes the African perspective, which is rare or even non-existent in some cases. This tactic draws further attention to the inadequacy of the principlist approach particularly in multicultural settings. Hence, it aims to stimulate interest, engender a rethink, and present a re-assessment of the failed assumptions of universal ethical principles.

Background

There has long been this earworm of an issue: the 1996 drug experimentation in Nigeria by Pfizer, Inc., which caused significant public health uproar in that part of the world. For people unfamiliar with this case, it is hardly a blip in the annals of international biomedical research and nothing worth fussing about. For the current task, however, the challenge is to revisit the event not as a clichéd issue but as a formidable topic of interest reborn and relevant; after all, the likes of Nuremburg and Tuskegee trials still reverberate today.

This was a case of the experimental drug Trovan, an antibiotic. Its development coincided with concurrent outbreaks of cerebro-spinal and bacterial meningitis, measles, and cholera that were affecting some pediatric patients in the northern Nigerian city, Kano. Pfizer dispatched a research team to a local hospital providing treatment and quickly recruited over 100 kids among the long lines of people seeking care and administered the trial drug to determine its effectiveness. The drug had never been tested on children. An investigative report later blamed the drug trial for a catalogue of effects ranging from adverse drug reaction, adverse events, to serious adverse events including the immediate death of 11 children. Several more suffer (ongoing) permanent disabilities such as brain damage, paralysis, muteness, slurred speech, and blindness. A series of law suits by the victims and the Nigerian government (filed in the U.S. under the Alien Tort Claims Act) commenced in 2001 but were aborted in the U.S. Supreme Court in the fall of 2010. Pfizer had struck a $75-million out-of-court settlement for claims related to the experiment.

The Nigeria-Pfizer incident is here reexamined from a different angle to challenge all bioethicists to reconsider and reground their arguments about the application of clinical trials principles. Analysts would be able to recognize that the psychological and philosophical thinking behind the research ethics principles which guide responsibility in clinical trials as currently conceived flows from some sort of a faulty logic. This is especially so when, as it is sometimes the case, clinical investigators go from the Global North to conduct studies in the Global South.

The current research ethics principles (of autonomy, non-maleficence, beneficence, and justice)[5] aim specifically for the good of the individual. It emphasizes his/her autonomy as a dominant theme, not community/population health (Callahan & Jennings, 2002). However, whenever this autonomy-cum-individual right-based ideology encounters communitarian ideology, there is the constant tendency for head butting.

This has prompted the present suggestion for the revamping of our understanding of responsibility, much like Maier's proposition (2012), when he called for a better reasoning about nature's value. Clearly, adopting this viewpoint is to alienate oneself from the *status quo* which is largely built on the economics of biomedicine. But, as an ethical relativist, it is better to join forces in declaring the Emperor naked rather than shirk the role or delay the chance any further. With enough conviction and no reason to keep one's intuition from rationalizing in any other way, this feels to me like a comfortable intellectual posture.

To repeat, what is under scrutiny here is the psychology which informed the dominant viewpoint about principlism. As a sign post, I intend to use that understanding to pivot to another way of thinking about responsibility in clinical research in a broader form. Hence, the following questions which are shaped by realities of globalization will serve as guides: What new ways can human research subjects be protected, and who should provide them protection as transnational borders continue to disappear? Also, how can we ensure compliance, guideline consistency, and checks and balances across borders as well as recognize and respect multicultural systems? While most clinical studies today are initiated and registered in the Global North (predominantly in the U.S.), many of the actual trials are sometimes outsourced and offshored (Petryna, 2009; NIH, 2013); often to the Global South (Rehnquist, 2001).

Coupled with the changing geography is the fact that private sector research by, for example, pharmaceutical companies, has led the way since the 1980s. And foremost in their approach is speed and profitability (Rehnquist, 2001, p. 12). That is a concern that triggers further questions: If they are so disposed, would responsibility for study subjects be paramount on their minds? Even so, would they in addition, be bound by the local systems at the study sites (socio-cultural, political, and legal systems where available), and/or would they abide only by international codes of research ethics like they should if they were in their home turfs where enforcements are stricter? And even those guidelines are autonomy-based. Caveat: answers to these questions will not be easy to come by. But, if the inquiry can catalyze enough buzz, positive changes are only a matter of time.

Since its inception, the autonomy-based set of research ethics principles with Euro-American[6] origins, has largely been useful in transforming clinical trial protocols for good. When applied properly the individual patient-subject enjoys a pride of place, his rights and dignity are protected. However, because of its extreme individualist emphasis, it has been particularly deficient in communalist settings. In opposition to the autonomy-based practice, an all-encompassing communalist model is proposed here. The supporting argument in favor of a new paradigm is that, because of the mazy connectedness and complex relatedness of human persons and indeed of everything else in nature, whatever happens to the individual patient-subject happens to the family/community in which he/she belongs, including his physical environment. This is apparent given that the individual is integrally located and anchored in a mesh of relationships within the family, village and clan (living and dead), all of whom are primordial sources of that person's physical, psychic,

Figure 1. Balancing mainstream with multi-cultural practices

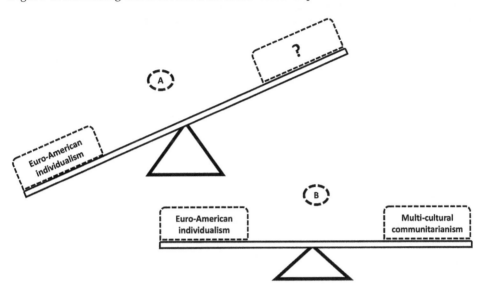

and spiritual wellbeing. By implication, if you are responsible for one, you are responsible for all in varying degrees. It is thus viewed in this chapter as a one-in-all paradigm and labeled bio-eco-communalism, BEC. If clinical investigators and other scholars are versed in this understanding, they would be better equipped to plan and conduct trial protocols accordingly and adequately.

The claim here is not simply that the collectivist or holistic view is novel. Rather, it is believed that as the movement towards cultural diversity in global bioethics gathers steam, researchers would have to face up to the fact about the African and other multicultural world view on for instance, morality; and in the reality that the devolution of the individual into his/her community is key. Biomedical researchers are hereby challenged to recognize that principlism is not a one-size fits all model. In fact, the principle of BEC may be preferable given that it incorporates into its fold the salient aspects of mainstream principlism.

Hubris or disrespect can fuel social tension; studies suggest it can also harm public good. The authors of Callahan and Jennings (2002) acknowledge in their research that "There has always been an undercurrent of resistance to the individualistic, autonomy-driven mainstream orientation within bioethics, and that orientation has held sway," (p. 170). This is understandably so because the communitarian orientation whose philosophical underpinnings align with the goals of public health, is increasingly becoming a force to be reckoned with and is effectively turning the argument on its head, namely that the absolute freedom of the individual can no longer be seen to *forever* trump the common good or the public interest.

Calls have been increasing for the balancing of individualism with some multicultural approach, example, communalism. Currently, individualism is the view that drives much of bioethics, weighing disproportionately in favor of Euro-Americanism (in Figure 1 above, compare Part 'A' to Part 'B'). In agreement with these calls, the purpose here is to insert the African epistemology about personhood, a major perspective in African philosophical understanding that changes the equilibrium in deliberations pertaining to responsibility for research subjects in clinical trials.

Heart of the Matter

The illustrative test case in this chapter remains the Pfizer experimental drug *Trovan*, and the negative effects it has continued to exert. Such an event, though a couple of decades old, never ceases to force the mind into reflective moments, examining our understanding of what to do or how to respond when ethical issues with biomedical situations arise. The Pfizer case is only but a placeholder; other ethical issues of various relative magnitudes may not be hard to find around the world.

In revisiting the meaning of bioethics, a poignant analysis by the US Public Broadcasting Service highlights its diverse areas of inquiry, describing it as the systematic study of the ethical and moral implications of new biological discoveries and biomedical advances, particularly in drug research and genetic engineering (PBS, *Our genes, our choices*). To engage this hydra-headed task, bioethicists try to provide ethical guidelines for doctors, patients, and families faced with complex quality-of-life decisions. Their skills apply to a wide range of medical and moral issues like the definition of death, the process of organ donation and transplantation, international surrogacy and adoption, the appropriate use of fetal tissue, genetic engineering, and guidelines for research on human subjects, and so on.

Ultimately, the focus or the essential ingredient of bioethics is the human person. It does not matter whether we are laboring to establish thematic issues in medical policy, practice, and research, or dissecting ethical questions that relate to the life sciences, biotechnology, medicine, politics, law, culture, religion and philosophy; the primary task essentially pertains to values of the human person. The objective of bioethics revolves around sorting out the ethical tension between the social world and the health of persons who inhabit it. At issue are the philosophical and cultural perspectives pertaining to personhood. Which is why, in research ethics the cardinal concern is human subject protection, the responsibility of which is primarily borne by clinical investigators.

Now, let me tease apart each of the triadic themes of 'responsibility,' 'clinical trials,' and 'African personhood;' and establish their meeting points in this analysis.

Responsibility

For so long, 'responsibility' has remained a conceptual theme theorists claim to have shredded into tiny analyzable pieces and cobbled back. But regardless of this presumption, it continues to challenge philosophers, neuroscientists and psychologists as they try to understand our drives and motivations. Here, the intention is not to reinvent the wheel. As a practical matter, responsibility is a term that describes actions involving moral agents and/or persons on a day-to-day basis. It suggests as well as assumes a form of moral, including social and legal obligation which we owe to ourselves, to others, to the society and to the environment within a given circumstance. The obligation to be responsible can at times be formal, i.e., codified into laws as in laws guiding business transactions or traffic; as well as ingrained in the society's mores to guide conduct.

Attention is also drawn to the fact that responsibility ought to be conceived of in terms of a virtue. The virtue of responsibility conjures up the reasoning that goes with both individual and collective responsibility including the discussion that focuses on public health responsibility for certain social actions such as (in the case under review) biomedical clinical trials. Not surprisingly, most of the relevant philosophies that provide the background for this analysis exhibit some trappings that relate with virtue ethics.[7] Virtue ethics emphasizes the acquisition of moral character, an attribute that harks back to Aristotle and Plato, but more accurately, to the ancient African mystics of Egypt and the Nubia region (Diop, 1974, Onywuenyi, 1991).

The understanding of the virtue of responsibility extends to all 'persons' be they human persons or persons/entities in the legal sense. Thus, just as virtue can be cultivated and habituated in persons with flesh and blood, so too can it be embedded or inculcated in the formations of legal entities or organizations in ways that are action-guiding. If the pursuit of the good life is the ideal for humans, one can as well see a parallel application of responsibility to legal persons in a performative sense. If the primary pursuit for legal entities is profit making, call it pursuit of the 'good life', it ought to be within a social, not a self-centered context. In other words, it ought to aim for a win-win, not a zero-sum outcome. After all, corporate entities seek to be, for instance, reliable and even trustworthy. Just like responsibility, these are attributes of moral appraisals or normative notions by which entities are judged or assessed in the space of social norms.

The U.S. legal system contains instances where corporations are protected as legal entities, à la the 14th amendment to the Constitution. That amendment, which came on the heels of the Civil War, gave the freed slaves the standing and protection accorded other natural persons. And from 1886, the Supreme Court decided in *Santa Clara County vs. Southern Pacific Railroad* to give a comparable standing to corporations. More recently, some have argued that corporations can even "vote" by other means. They invoke for instance, the 2010 U.S. Supreme Court affirmation of the right of corporations to express their political views in the unrestricted campaign contributions they make to political parties (*Citizens United vs. FEC* case).

Other views indicate that this claim may be a bit stretched. Nonetheless, what is undebatable is the impact political war chest can sometimes have on election outcomes. Perhaps a far more exerting anthropomorphization of corporations is the June 2014 decision of the U.S. apex court in the case of *Burwell vs. Hobby Lobby, Inc*. The Supreme Court ruled 5-4, that requiring family-owned corporations to pay for insurance coverage for contraception under the Affordable Care Act violated a federal law protecting religious freedom.[8]

But, personification brings responsibility on a host of issues. As White (2005) suggests, it cannot be tolerated when corporate entities engage in unethical and/or unlawful practices such as defrauding customers, lying and deceiving in advertising, and producing unsafe and lethal products, all for the pursuit of profits. Similarly, democratic societies should not condone organizations that make offensive policies/ public statements to customers, minorities, or social groups; or pollute the environment with toxic chemicals. Regarding our case study, biomedical corporations such as Pfizer, Inc., should be held to similar ethical standards when they conduct research with human subjects. The conduct of such large Multi-National Corporations need to be both in compliance with international research ethics principles and with sensitivity to other ethical and cultural norms as well.

Clinical Trials

Obviously, clinical trials of drugs, medical devices and biologics, provide the link between R&D and public use of products. Hence, advances in biomedical research epitomize the dizzying strides in applied science. As stated earlier, this quintessential character represents the unleashing of human brain power in making dreams a reality and in improving our physical, emotional, and material conditions.

Thus, the 'clinical trials' theme, both as the fulcrum of research ethics and as a concept that has endured since the dawn of experimentation, presents a platform for analyses on a wide range of issues. That platform is probably more critical today than it has ever been. The 1996 clinical trials by Pfizer, Inc., in Nigeria provide both the catalyst and a test case for this analysis. The citing of this case serves to illustrate two things, first the imposition of the mainstream autonomy-based philosophical principles on other cultures (e.g., the African milieu). Second, and very importantly, it points to the unbridled expansion and exploitation of scientific and biotech markets; to the point that even the minimum that international research ethics principles demanded were apparently unmet. In light of this, it could be seen to buoy the multicultural argument by unintentionally presenting an opportunity that exposes excessive individualism in clinical testing and need to acknowledge and integrate other philosophical and cultural systems.

Thus, there is need to view responsibility in clinical trials as that character trait or ideal that facilitates moral agents, including legal 'persons,' in their duty to serve the common good while recognizing multiculturalism. According to Meara, Schmidt, and Day (1996), because virtue ethics is "rooted in the narratives and aspirations of specific communities, [it] can particularly be helpful to professionals in discerning appropriate ethical conduct in multicultural settings and interactions" (p. 4).

African Personhood

In African thought and culture, a person is fundamentally regarded as an 'essential energy' or 'vital force' which exists within a hierarchy of forces. Within these forces, there is a bond or intimate ontological relationship in ranking order, from the highest (Supreme Deity or God, the spirits, founding fathers, the dead; the living, according to their rank in terms of seniority), to the lowest (animals, vegetables, and minerals), which are in turn categorized in relative importance in their own classes.

Mbiti (1970) captures the constitutive make-up of this perspective in these trenchant words,

... in traditional life, the individual does not and cannot exist alone except corporately. He owes his existence to other people, including those of past generations and his contemporaries. He is simply part of the whole ... [and] depends on the corporate group. The individual can only say: 'I am because we are; and since we are, therefore I am.' This is a cardinal point in the understanding of the African view of personhood/selfhood (p. 108).

To illustrate, we know from physics that if an object or a person is elevated spatially (say, on a 10-foot stool in an open field); it would be impossible to visually perceive or detect his acuity without a backdrop. Put otherwise, without a contrasting background, gratings of different waveforms and spatial frequencies make it impossible for the human visual system to measure the band-pass characteristics of the environing channels for the eye to pick out an object/subject in thin air. Likewise, in the African communitarian view, a person cannot exist independent of or, without a bearing to the community which provides him/her cogency. That is also to say that no one exists in a vacuum. We are who we are both because of what we are made of and because of where we belong.

In contrast, the Euro-American approach presents the person as autonomous, propertied, self-interested, accumulative and having independent agency which is measured in terms of his power of control over others. "[The] individual's interest is

195

opposed to both the interest of other individuals and that of the larger social whole" (Piot, 1999, p.18). This is the theoretical basis upon which principlism was founded.

Thus, the opposing conceptions in the two views (Western vs. African) are quite profound and are here typified by Menkiti's (1984) illustration. As shown in Figure 2, while the African view allocates ontological independence to human society, and moves from society to individuals, the Euro-American perspective asserts autonomy and moves instead from the individual to the society.

To apply the communalist suggestion to public health is a recognition of (1) the pre-eminence of group over the individual, and (2) the interconnectedness and interweavement of human persons and indeed of everything else in nature, such that whatever happens to the individual happens to the community in which he belongs. By implication, if you are responsible for one, you are responsible for all at least in some varying degrees. Research ethics is right, just, proper, and culturally sensitive so long as it expresses respect for communal relationships in which people both identify with each other and exhibit solidarity with each other and with their environment.

Because of this communal disposition in multi-cultural settings, it follows that almost every issue with the individual is correspondingly regarded as the affair of the extended family, sometimes to the point that, as Metz (2010, p. 382) says, "the family (or community) has a stake in becoming aware of another's illness/wellbeing and having a role in the decisions regarding their treatment or upkeep." This is a phenomenon that conflicts with the Euro-American proclivity for individual right to confidentiality. The benefit of this comparative analysis should be a teaching moment for researchers, clinicians, bioethicists, students and academics as they confront the African philosophical perspective.

Making the Case

As indicated earlier, the approach to this subject matter was informed by the vantage position of having a diverse background in philosophy, international studies, et al. But despite this multidisciplinary cultivation, it's not hard to see that true responsibility in

Figure 2. The polar opposites of selfhood

African

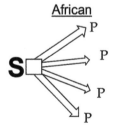

Euro-American

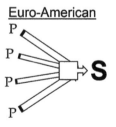

any clinical trial enterprise could not exclusively be for the individual patient-subject alone. True, most clinical trials deal directly with the individual but, ultimately, they transcend him/her hence, the proposition for a BEC framework.

The argument here reiterates the deficiency in principlism. Given that the origin of mainstream ethical principles was based chiefly on individualistic terms, supreme emphasis is laid on personal rights, autonomy, self-determination, privacy, self-interest, the tendency to accumulate and the excessive quest to possess independent agency with power of control over others. Thus, conflicts between individual interests and those of the larger social group are inherently unavoidable. In terms of ethical theory and for instrumental reasons, this translates to creating a duality between the *object* of morality, the individual, to the neglect of the *subject*, the agent.

Not surprisingly, John S. Mill might be influencing this thought process. Mill speaks in *Logic*, of things as 'non-substances' and 'attributes' as *objects* and appearing to seek an alternative term which diminishes the 'perceived ontic burden,' or contains rather less obvious metaphysical weight. By extension, this might be likened to Wittgenstein's 'pure concept object' which has no empirical content; or in a related sense the Aristotelian abstract and concrete objects. However, the nub of Mill's suggestion is that for certain purposes, "any implicature of substantiality ought to be detached, meaning nothing more than something, anything, to which one may be counted as one" (Stanford Encyclopedia of Philosophy).

Contrast that with my preferred model: BEC, which is rooted in the African philosophical tradition. This multicultural perspective presents the individual not as a self-interested loner who is obsessed with privacy, status and control, but a vivacious, unique entity who is ceaselessly waxing and waning within himself/herself but more within the dynamic interplay of relationships with forces around him/her both on the physical and the supernatural plains. As an analogy, the African self could be compared to a being (vital force or vital energy) that is hooked on a grid. The energy that he/she generates serves his/her individual needs, but is also shared with other forces around him/her. But as the need arises, he/she also supplements his/her individual energy with those of other elemental forces. In other words, though existing as a power point in an interconnected network, he/she is a generator, a supplier as well as a consumer of the voltage energy of the distribution network.

The self is capable of this interpersonal dynamism due to his/her attributes of being a vital force who is imbued and animated with a vital principle and above all, is anchored in the communal operations of other forces. As such, he/she is a force in the hierarchy of forces, habitually in intimate consanguinity with other forces above and below him/her. The fulfillment of his/her life is predicated on the support of other forces (humans, spirits, the biota). Thus, consideration for the community of other forces is always in the mix whenever ethical, juridical, ontological, epistemological, and other decisions are made. It is upon this platform that the argument for reconfiguration of responsibility stands (Iyioke, 2016).

Like a self-fulfilling prophecy, this understanding is wholly shared by the *Guidance framework for testing of genetically modified mosquitoes*, GMM, project (World Health Organization, 2014).[9] Its recommendations literally validate the essence of the African philosophical viewpoint (for thousands of years), namely the intricate bonding between the individual and his/her immediate family, community and the environment as well as the interweavement and interrelatedness of all reality. For instance, notwithstanding that the WHO transgenic mosquitoes' study had no primary human subjects, yet it is unprecedented how it considered the need to deal head on with possible resultant pathogens in a way that does not harm either the environmental or human health (along with anything else in-between, e.g., the health of non-human animals). In addition, it recommends that the overarching ethical goal in human subject research should be to respond to obligations to individuals being asked to participate, in this case, people living within the trial site who are classified as 'human research subjects.' Included too are the adjoining communities being asked to host trials. Above all, it proposes an approach that maintains transparent and respectful channels of communication, and protection plans throughout and long after the trial period.

Thus, to accept the GMM recommendations for biomedical clinical trials, particularly the linkage between human and environmental health, is to commit (in a gradient process) to the widely shared African philosophical perspective. That view expresses first, the intrinsic value of the human person and his/her affinity or interconnectedness with family; his/her community; his/her environment, and indeed the unity of the ecosystem at large. To scope it further, this would include both the physical and metaphysical/ontological realms of existence.

The GMM's special attention to ethics and public engagement in research is particularly a welcome boost to earlier suggestions about the need for a respectful approach towards research communities, the role of effective education, communication of goals and methods, and opportunities for follow-up discussions. The community engagement approach takes on a concentric relational web: from the core traditional and non-traditional human research subjects, to families, neighbors, communities, and so on. The outer spectrum recognizes individuals who do not typically fall within the definition of human subjects but might be affected by the conduct of the research in some way. It is scarcely surprising that this suggestion lends support to the community permission model that have long been prescribed by many authors. It is a model that requires *permission* and *approval* (emphasis) from local authorities before biomedical studies are conducted (Diallo, et al., 2005). As a practical and ethically appropriate approach, you wonder why it hadn't been made

Figure 3. The intermix of GMM framework, environmental/human health, and African holism

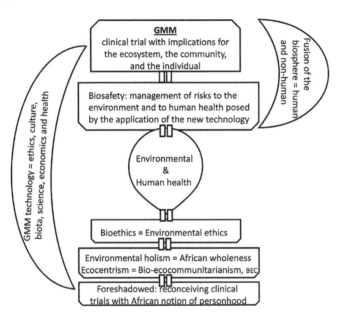

a gold standard, given its potential to minimally reduce and ultimately eliminate the tendency to disrupt traditional social structure and customs of host communities.

The GMM model is in lockstep with my fundamental argument here. Its suggestion for biosafety reveals the need to improve the links between research and health care delivery and to promote the environmental, cultural, socio-political and economic processes that are involved so we can assimilate the vicissitudes of the impacts of public health research (or any other research for that matter). Also, as it is implied here, the GMM framework as a public health initiative shrewdly recognizes that clinical trials ought to be applied within the context of prevailing social, cultural, legal, regulatory and political institutions at the local level. Couched within the philosophical commitment to evaluate clinical trials in terms of ecological and human health, my suggestion aims to rejig our thinking and spark a healthy debate.

That debate might well be tried out, for instance, when we view the issue of corporate responsibility as part of the day-to-day corporate affairs and pursuit of profits. When an organization such as Pfizer, Inc., can begin to adopt a (layered) philosophical commitment that caters for the diverse elements in any given clinical trial (individuals, family, 'communicology') as part of the economics of biomedicine; only then shall it be deemed fit and willing to tackle the challenges head on.

It is here claimed that in public health, just as in medical ethics generally, responsibility is both subliminal as well as overt. In the case of population-based research the concern is that some biomedical scientists, while riding on readily available trust, might sometimes be inclined to renege on their responsibility and force unwanted procedures on the public. In doing so, patient-subjects are made to sacrifice personal dignity, autonomy, safety, liberty, and above all, cultural identity in the name of participating in research for the public good. This seems to be the case with the trial drug, *Trovan*. The Pfizer experiment may be emblematic of all that should not happen particularly when clinical trials travel abroad: hubris, disrespect for other cultures, apparent emphasis on profit, use of patient-subjects solely as means, disregard for local authority, and betrayal of trust; all of which are hallmarks of irresponsibility.

Numerous authors have tangled with aspects of principlism, among them Ryan (2004), De Vries, et al. (2010) and Kukla (2014). As is apparent, the part of principlism that is most antithetical to the present exegesis is its excessive emphasis on individualism, focusing on individual rights and autonomy, at the expense of everything else. In that way, much is left to be desired. Interestingly, the many interpretations and reversals of these principles through the years even in Western research ethics practice, clearly point to obvious inbred difficulties in their application. That, in and of itself, further buttresses the argument for my BEC approach.

It has increasingly become clear that the assumptions implicit in the mainstream framework that makes claim to universal validity about those principles are not shared particularly by non-Western cultures. If not addressed, the concern seems to be that the dominant approach is bound to globalize a less than global view of the world and reality. As already demonstrated, the mainstream set of guidelines for research (principlism), is itself inherently linked to Euro-American individualistic notions of personhood, whereas the rest of the world, particularly Africa, sees the person not as an isolated individual, but as a part of the community. More disappointingly, the holism of the African world-view in which the people's ethics is rooted, and the societal activities which center on the promotion of vitality and fertility of human beings, livestock, and the land on which their livelihood depends, are entirely missed by principlism ("Using APA," 2011).

Some striking similarities exist between the Tuskegee Syphilis Study and the Trovan experiment. Both were conducted on poor illiterate cohorts. While one was on a select group of rural black men, the other was on local pediatric patients, but the racial subjugation of subjects of both experiments cannot be missed; and so on. Beyond all that, the Trovan trials are quite foreboding. To appreciate the full impact of this experiment, one must look beyond the fact that victims were mere children (and that point alone echoes eerie feelings). Children in an agrarian African context such as Kano, are indispensable social capital. They represent a set of assets that produces a stream of many benefits. Before Coleman's (1988) formalization of the social capital theory, it had long been a mainstay social concept and practice in Africa for thousands of years. More recently, authors such as Grootaert and van Bastelaer (2002) have further written persuasively about the role of social capital in development. The stream of benefits from social capital, or the channel through which it affects development includes mutually beneficial collective actions that lead to high incomes and upliftment of households, communities and nations (p. 4).

The dictum that you are better off surrounded by people than by wealth (*onye nwere madu, ka onye nwere ego*), holds supreme in African social thought and culture. More specifically, the significance of children in the family markedly differs in African setting from the Euro-American counterpart. Nothing 'warms up' a household better than the presence of children. Better still, beyond mere species regeneration, families rely on children to cultivate the farms, tend the livestock, conduct commercial enterprises, run errands, hunt, and do home chores. In Kano, the trial site for Trovan drug where the Hausa and Fulani form the majority ethnic demography, commerce and farming are the main forms of livelihood. In this Sahel region, provision of forage for livestock and protection against erosive desert encroachment, to name just two, can only be possible largely with the help of children. Unlike in most Euro-American traditions, African parents are usually not eager to declare an empty nest. Indeed, children are insurance policy for old age. Such a model ultimately benefits both sides mutually, leading to incalculable net worth of socio-economic ends.

Given all that I have discussed thus far, the reader can appreciate the depth of disruption this drug experimentation has caused in the lives of the people. Without the proper knowledge of the communalist posture of African societies and about how communal practices are interwoven with nature, things can only be expected to go wrong and they have. It would be hard for the uninformed to fathom how this type of drug trial can have seething consequences that envelop the community and even the environment for generations. When investigators with individualistic mindset lead foreign-sponsored clinical trials such as this one, they are most likely to miss the point. It amounts to imposing a foreign conceived and incompatible idea on the multicultural community, depriving them of the right to direct their lives. Note, the basic premise is that it is not merely the assumption of a superior scientific knowledge of the health crisis that justifies interference. It is also the acceptance that the local communities would agree that such actions preserve or promote, not harm or distort, their ways of living.

It is thus worth restating that the African world-view in which the people's ethics is rooted, and the societal activities which center on the promotion of vitality and fertility of human beings, livestock, and the land on which their livelihood depends, are entirely left in the cold by principlism. Kelbessa (2005) made a case for this holistic concept in his espousal of ethical dialogue, an attempt that builds unity and harmonious coexistence and sustenance of all facets of nature. As a practical matter, Africans habitually maintain a harmony with all other creatures in the natural environment and in promoting ecological balance. Appreciation for nature is thoroughly ingrained in the culture. "For instance, trees are valued as sources of diversity, food, medicine, construction materials, forage for livestock and protection against erosion. The forest can be admired for its aesthetics; trees are protected for their majestic size" (pp. 10-11).

SOLUTIONS AND RECOMMENDATIONS

Present among the numerous public health and biomedical scenarios across Africa are challenges besetting public policies and programs that cry for more articulate formulation and approach. The attempt here has been to use the unique notion of personhood in African thought to bridge the bioethics discourse. This trend of thought is bucked up by the argument that global bioethics will succeed *only* to the extent that it is culturally relevant. Consequently, bioethics must expand its vision.

In light of this, a reappraisal of sorts about the place of responsibility for human subjects in research becomes necessary. More specifically, as some clinical trials are off-shored abroad (to the Global South), it may be an opportunity to weigh in on the extreme emphasis on individualism and thus acknowledge the cultural systems of other peoples, for instance, communitarianism. While opposing individualism (the Euro-American mantra), the African perspective (here expressed as BEC) stresses communitarianism. This collectivist philosophical view point instantly recognizes that ethical issues with biomedical studies are far more broad-based. Therefore, responsibility in clinical trials *must* in tandem, be broad-based.

Ditto, research studies impact the individual no doubt, but that impact extends in varying degrees to everyone else around him/her – family, neighborhood, community and even his/her physical and spiritual environments. Put otherwise, responsibility in biomedical studies particularly, those dealing with human subjects, must be seen to surpass the individual person and to encompass the individual's family, the community and the entire environment within which the individual resides. Because the African notion of selfhood is collectivist and broad-based, it is adequately structured to address some of the shortcomings in the mainstream individualist perspective. As such, responsibility for (and by) the individual can only make sense through the community in which he/she is rooted. When this is done, responsibility for the human subject in research (particularly in adequately suited cultural environments), will henceforth mean responsibility for the individual rights and autonomy, plus, those of his family, community, and the ecosystem.

I have no illusions that the overarching suggestion here about the relevance of ethico-cultural relativity, nay, re-conceptualizing responsibility from an African perspective (particularly for research projects in Africa), is certain to clash with mainstream accounts within bioethics. Refuters of this argument are likely to question for instance, the rationale for 'erecting another layer of rules;' and to doubt whether it would change much, if anything. But a more balanced assessment will recognize that the four principles are not an all-purpose set of tools fitting enough to sufficiently serve the global bioethics enterprise. At best, the principles can be handy as a convenient lever that steers different value judgments close enough so everyone can express their opinion and identity.

CONCLUSION

It is said that in ancient Greece (which is foundational in shaping Western thought), philosophy was a search for the truth about nature and truth about man. In African thought (the *Numero Uno* philosophical tradition), it is about the search for the meaning of being, existence, life – all life in their order, interrelated as one continuum that finds fulfillment in the creator (God).

That theme of uninterrupted non-spatial wholeness continues here. This analysis was initiated to prominently position the African philosophical notion of the self within the clinical trials context (and the larger bioethics project). Contrary to the mainstream autonomy-based notion, an 'other-regarding' perspective is here being put forward and touted as the preferred alternative model. This tactic draws further attention to the inadequacy of the principlist approach, particularly in multicultural settings. It also engenders a rethink, stimulates interest, and re-assesses the failed assumptions of universal ethical principles.

As an attempt that runs against much of the prevailing (Euro-American) intellectual mood, this approach strives to prop up the African view point by making explicit the import of the individual vis-a-vis the community in clinical trials particularly under a re-contextualized global setting. As such, research ethics is guided to go beyond autonomy-based, *exclusive* considerations for the individual with absolute right to self-determination; and towards a more holistic-based approach that highlights the tie between the individual and his/her family, community and the environment.

As a corollary, this reconceptualization move implicitly captures the comprehensive fields of bioethics and environmental ethics as one unified field of philosophical inquiry, encouraging the development of a reliable and appropriate framework of analysis for the field made whole. It is hoped that Africanists particularly, native African thinkers would find reason to be more engaged in shaping the discussion and promoting authentic and home-grown philosophical and multicultural values from this perspective.

A re-formulated understanding of responsibility in clinical trials transcends mere principlism and concentrically addresses the interests of *all stakeholders* in their order: the human subject, family, host community, the physical environment, animals, minerals and everything in the biota.

In the final analysis, responsibility in clinical trials is aimed to cover the interest of not just the traditionally defined human subjects, it includes by extension responsibility for family members, friends, neighbors, immediate community, extended community, interest groups, the health and lives of non-human animals, and the physical environment. Indeed, it is farcical to think that individuals can continue to act without considerations for things and other humans environing them. We are who we are because of what makes us whole; and we are not just part of nature, we are nature. Ultimately, we ought to see beneficence, non-maleficence, justice and respect for the individual's autonomy; as beneficence, non-maleficence, justice, and respect for autonomy of everyone, and everything around him (in varying degrees). In this way, the interconnectivity and inter-dependability, as well as the wholeness of reality are underscored, along with attendant socio-cultural, political, and economic ramifications.

The main take-home point is that when clinical trials (much of which are currently conceived in the Global North) involve other cultures (particularly Africa – in the Global South, where many of the tests are sometimes offshored to), there is need to reframe the thinking and apply additional considerations. The current practice has yet to contemplate this option to properly formulate an appropriate rubric. As already articulated, the philosophical/cultural significance of the person in the African setting differs markedly from the Western perspective. Therefore, the suggestion to re-conceptualize responsibility from an understanding of the African perspective is a landmark point at which to address myriad bioethical issues, one of which is responsibility in clinical trials. This course of action provides a path to head off unnecessary philosophical, cultural and ideological tensions that are still lurking ahead.

FUTURE RESEARCH DIRECTIONS

The focus of this discussion is clearly framed within the confines of redefining or reconfiguring responsibility in clinical trials with the understanding of personhood in African traditional philosophy and culture. Surely, it could not have covered every aspect of the subject area or conclusively settled every matter in this regard. The analysis here is meant to join forces with scholarly discussions that have been gathering steam on the topic of cultural diversity in global bioethics. Hence, I align with the momentum with the purpose of forging an appropriate rubric for practice, with reference to Africa. The chapter submits that the autonomy-based bioethical principles are too narrow and urges for a more comprehensive consideration for the individual – the substrate of clinical trials and the larger bioethics project. Here, the African philosophical insight about selfhood is suggested. Identified below are a handful of topics that were either partly covered or not covered at all in this chapter but, which demand some more attention:

1. I urge for relentless energy to resist the wool over our collective eyes on the question of ethical universalism. Evidence is mounting that even the dominant Euro-American stance on principlism does not capture enough, including some subtle and specific European cultural structures. At best the research ethics principles may function as reflective guidelines on important values in Euro-American culture but they can no longer be assumed to be universal everlasting ideas or transcendental truths (Rendtorff, 2002). More objections to Beauchamp and Childress' version of common morality have continued to find it dubious that "we could convincingly show that there are general rules of principles that 'everyone' accepts" (Kukla, 2014, p. 79). It behooves us therefore to harness the newfound energy and stand clear of the tall shadow of universalism in principlism.

2. It is a given that environmental health is the basis of human health. In other words, it is trite to say that the state of the natural world determines the state of everything residing in it. In the same token, environmental health ethics is ethics of healthcare or bioethics. There is a crying need to frame environmental discourses in ways that connect with public health discourses (or vice versa – as it was originally intended when bioethics emerged on the scene), to provide more holistic understanding of health issues. For instance, the clinical trials process can never be sufficiently made fully meaningful without reference to environmental ramifications (be they physical, social, or even spiritual).

3. In numerous African settings (rural and urban), traditional or ethno- medicine has played a significant role in the healthcare delivery since the emergence of time. More recently it has complemented the modern medical practice. But it is almost inconceivable to put in the same bucket list the modern form of clinical trial protocols along with traditional (alternative) medical practice. However, it would be worth the effort to elevate the notion of self in indigenous biomedical practice and discourse by researching it further. Thus, examining this notion in the traditional medical practice will contribute to and authenticate African values by highlighting many of its unexplored dimensions. It will also help to articulate its theoretical basis and render research in indigenous medicine more ethically grounded.

REFERENCES

Akabayashi, A., & Slingsby, B. (2003). Biomedical ethics in Japan: The second stage. *Cambridge Quarterly of Healthcare Ethics*, *12*(3), 261–264. doi:10.1017/S0963180103123079 PMID:12889330

Anderson, M. S., & Steneck, N. H. (Eds.). (2011). *International research collaborations: Much to be gained, many ways to get in trouble*. Routledge.

Beauchamp, T., & Childress, J. (2012). *Principles of biomedical ethics* (7th ed.). New York, NY: Oxford University Press.

Callahan, D., & Jennings, B. (2002). Ethics and public health: Forging a strong relationship. *American Journal of Public Health*, *92*(2), 169–176. doi:10.2105/AJPH.92.2.169 PMID:11818284

Coleman, J. S. (1988). Social capital in the creation of human capital. *American Journal of Sociology*, *94*, S95–S120. doi:10.1086/228943

De Vries, R., Rott, L. M., & Paruchuri, Y. (2010). Normative environment in international science. In M. S. Anderson & N. H. Stencek (Eds.), *International research collaborations: Much to be gained, many ways to get in trouble* (pp. 105–120). New York, NY: Routledge.

Diallo, D. A., Doumbo, O. K., Plowe, C. V., Wellems, T. E., Emanuel, E. J., & Hurst, S. A. (2005). Community permission for medical research in developing countries. *Clinical Infectious Diseases*, *41*(2), 255–259. doi:10.1086/430707 PMID:15983925

Diniz, D., & Velez, A. C. (2001). Feminist bioethics: the emergence of the oppressed. In R. Tong (Ed.), *Globalizing feminist ethics* (pp. 62–72). Boulder, CO: Westview.

Diop, C. A. (1974). *The African origin of civilization: Myth or reality*. Chicago, IL: Lawrence Hill.

Grootaert, C., & van Bastelaer, T. (2002). Introduction and overview. In C. Grootaert & T. Bastelaer (Eds.), The role of social capital in development: An empirical assessment (p. 4). New York, NY: Cambridge University Press. doi:10.1017/CBO9780511492600.002

Iyioke, I. V. (2016). *Re-conceptualizing responsibility in clinical trials: An insight with the African notion of self* (Unpublished doctoral dissertation). Michigan State University, East Lansing, MI.

Kelbessa, W. (2005). *The utility of ethical dialogue for marginalized voices in Africa*. Retrieved from http://pubs.iied.org/pdfs/13508IIED.pdf?

Kukla, R. (2014). Living with pirates: Common morality and embodied practice. *Cambridge Quarterly of Healthcare Ethics*, *23*(1), 75–85. doi:10.1017/S0963180113000480 PMID:24256603

Maier, D. S. (2012). *What's so good about biodiversity?* New York, NY: Springer. doi:10.1007/978-94-007-3991-8

Mbiti, J. S. (1970). *African Religions and Philosophy*. London, UK: Longman.

Meara, N., Schmidt, L., & Day, J. (1996). Principles and virtues: A foundation for ethical decisions. *The Counseling Psychologist*, *24*(1), 4–77. doi:10.1177/0011000096241002

Menkiti, I. (1984). Person and community in African traditional thought. In R. Wright (Ed.), *African Philosophy* (pp. 171–181). New York, NY: University Press of America.

Metz, T. (2010). Recent work in African ethics. *Journal of Moral Education*, *39*(3), 381–391. doi:10.1080/03057240.2010.497618

Object. (n.d.). In *Stanford Encyclopedia of Philosophy online*. Retrieved from http://plato.stanford.edu/entries/object/

Okere, T. (2005). *Philosophy, culture, and society in Africa*. Afro-Orbis.

Onyewuenyi, I. (2005). *The African origin of Greek philosophy: An exercise in Afrocentrism*. University of Nigeria Press.

Onywuenyi, I. (1991). Is there an African philosophy? In T. Serequeberhan (Ed.), *African Philosophy: The essential readings* (pp. 29–46). Minneapolis, MN: Paragon.

Our genes, our choices (n.d.). *Science sidebars*. Retrieved from http://www.pbs.org/inthebalance/archives/ourgenes/science_sidebars.html

Petryna, A. (2009). *When experiments travel: Clinical trials and the global search for human subjects*. Princeton, NJ: Princeton University Press. doi:10.1515/9781400830824

Piot, C. (1999). *Remotely global: Village modernity in West Africa*. Chicago, IL: The University of Chicago Press.

Rehnquist, J. (2001). *The globalization of clinical trials: A growing challenge in protecting human subjects*. Washington, DC: Department of Health and Human Services. Retrieved from https://oig.hhs.gov/oei/reports/oei-01-00-00190.pdf

Rendtorff, J. D. (2002). Basic ethical principles in European bioethics and biolaw: Autonomy, dignity, integrity and vulnerability – Towards a foundation of bioethics and biolaw. *Medicine, Health Care, and Philosophy*, 5(5), 235–244. doi:10.1023/A:1021132602330 PMID:12517031

Ryan, M. A. (2004). Beyond a Western bioethics? *Theological Studies*, 65(1), 158–177. doi:10.1177/004056390406500105 PMID:15515232

Santa Clara County v. Southern Pacific R. Co., 118 U.S. 394. (1886). Retrieved August 29, 2015, from https://supreme.justia.com/cases/federal/us/118/394/case.html

White, J. (2005). *Contemporary moral problems*. Belmont, CA: Cengage.

World Health Organization. (2014). *Guidance framework for testing of genetically modified mosquitoes*. Retrieved from http://www.who.int/tdr/publications/year/2014/Guidance_framework_mosquitoes.pdf

KEY TERMS AND DEFINITIONS

Adverse Drug Reaction (ADR): A response to a drug that is noxious and unintended and occurs at doses normally used in a person for the prophylaxis, diagnosis or therapy of disease, or for modification of physiological function. Adverse drug reactions are classified into six types (with mnemonics): dose-related (augmented), non-dose-related (bizarre), dose-related and time-related (chronic), time-related (delayed), withdrawal (end of use), and failure of therapy (failure).

Adverse Event (AE): Any untoward medical occurrence in a patient or clinical investigation subject to whom a pharmaceutical product is administered. An AE can therefore be any unfavorable and unintended sign (including an abnormal laboratory finding), symptom, or disease temporally associated with the use of a medicinal (investigational) product, if related to the medicinal (investigational) product.

All-in-One (One-in-All): A term I have coined to depict the suffusion and inseparability of the individual into his/her community and environment.

BEC: Bio-eco-communalism just like one-in-all, refers to the inseparability of the individual within his/her community and environment.

Biota: All species of plants and animals occurring in a specific area.

CRS: Corporate social responsibility is a duty or an in-built commitment by corporate bodies to uphold ethical values and ensure quality of life of the workforce, the local community and the physical environment, while earning profits.

Ecosystem: A biological system composed of a community of organisms and the nonliving environment with which it interacts (same for environment and ecology).

Global North: Also known as the industrialized world, Western, or Euro-American – refers to the 57 countries with high human development that have a Human Development Index above .8 as reported in the United Nations Development Program Report 2005. Most, but not all, of these countries are in the Northern Hemisphere.

Global South: The industrializing world or the Global South refers to the countries of the rest of the world, most of which are in the Southern Hemisphere. It includes both countries with medium human development index, HDI (88 countries with an HDI less than .8 and greater than .5) and low human development index (32 countries with an HDI of less than .5). Thus, the Global South is made up of some 133 countries out of a total of 197. Most of the Global South is in South and Central America, Africa, and Asia.

GMM: Genetically modified mosquitoes, also called genetically engineered mosquitoes, transgenic mosquitoes, or living modified mosquitoes – mosquitoes that have heritable traits derived through use of recombinant DNA technology, which alter the strain, line, or colony in a manner usually intended to result in reduction of the transmission of mosquito-borne human diseases.

Holism: The interconnectivity and interdependence of all things.

Serious Adverse Event, SAE, or Serious Adverse Drug Reaction, Serious ADR: Any untoward medical occurrence that at any dose results in death, is life-threatening, requires inpatient hospitalization or prolongation of existing hospitalization, results in persistent or significant disability/incapacity, or is a congenital anomaly/birth defect.

ENDNOTES

[1]   Person, man, self, individual, human being/person, and to a lesser extent, identity, are used interchangeably in this chapter to mean the same thing (following existing literary corpus). However, there may be cases where exceptions are made.

[2]   There is effort to blend these seemingly disparate themes (even as they are full-fledge concepts in their own rights), to justify why it makes sense to couple them together in this essay. Also, it is easy to misconstrue the reference to 'African notion of personhood,' as essentializing. It is not an overgeneralization. In fact, beneath the apparent multiplicity of African philosophical expressions of the self, is a fundamental and undisputed uniformity. As with many other African concepts, the understanding of the self sometimes seems to vary from one milieu to another, but under close analysis, particularly in terms of its functions, the cream usually rises to the top and a unifying grain of unanimity

emerges. Abundant literature supports this fact across much of Africa, from the 'Arab' North to the southern-most tip.

3   This question seems to persist despite irrefutable evidence that all philosophies, just like the origin of all mankind, emerged out of ancient African philosophical tradition. For more, see Onyewuenyi, I. (2005) and Diop, C. (1974).

4   Communitarianism, collectivism and bio-eco-communalism (BEC), are here considered synonymous.

5   The four principles of bioethics (a.k.a., principlism) for mainstream practice are: respect for autonomy (a norm of respecting the decision-making capacities of autonomous person); non-maleficence (a norm of avoiding the causation of individual harm); beneficence (a group of norms for providing benefits and balancing benefits against individual risks and costs); and, justice (a group of norms for distributing individual benefits, risks, and costs fairly).

6   "Western" and "Euro-American" mean the same thing in this analysis and the reason may be obvious. For instance, in bioethics, a field that took off in the U.S. in the 1960s – 70s, its philosophical principles are Eurocentric (deriving for instance, from the deontological theories of Kant and Mill-Bentham utilitarian principles). Further still, while bioethics is traditionally practiced in the West within the four-corner stone principles of autonomy, non-maleficence, beneficence, and justice; in other parts of the world, incongruities with these principles usually emerge at the local level when their West-centric orientation fail to fit with established traditions. Examples can be found in Akabayashi, A. & Slingsby, B. (2003); and Diniz, D. & Velez, A. C. (2001).

7   These include thoughts by Godfrey Tangwa, Tsenay Serequeberhan, Leopold Senghor, Christopher Gowans, Emmanuel Levinas, James Gustafson, James Laney, Richard Niebuhr and Bernard Haring.

8   The court ruled that some corporations (for instance, the ones that are owned/ controlled by religious groups/families) have religious beliefs, just like ordinary "flesh and blood" persons. Such corporations cannot be required to provide contraceptive coverage for their female employees against the beliefs of their owners. At issue are regulations promulgated by the Department of Health and Human Services under the Patient Protection and Affordable Care Act of 2010, which requires specified employers' group health plans to furnish preventive care and screenings for women without any cost sharing requirements. However, opponents assert that this decision violates Religious Freedom Restoration Act, of 1993 which prohibits the Government [from] substantially burden[ing] a person's exercise of religion even if the burden results from a rule of general applicability...

9   The GMM project is a public health intervention tool that was framed to address the problem of mosquito vectors *ab initio*, hence, the most effective way to eliminate transmission of malaria and dengue diseases in endemic areas. The mechanics of the technology works when lab-hatched genetically modified mosquitoes are ... made sterile before being introduced to the environment they are unable to pass on the genetic makeup to future generations through mating. Also, the GMM are meant to mate and introduce the effect briefly into the local mosquito population, but the modification will gradually be diluted out by crossing with local mosquitoes over several generations until it is lost.

Chapter 9
Standardizing Ethics East and West:
The Need to Conform to a One World Standard

F. Sigmund Topor
Keio University, Japan

ABSTRACT

A basic element that separates primates from us Homo sapiens is language, which serves as a socializing catalyst for interpersonal and intercultural communication. Linguistic rules can be regarded as the ethics of communication. Without such rules, encoding and decoding of communication between a speaker/writer and a listener/reader would be impossible. Etiquette and the social emotion of shame, which have dissimilar connotations in Confucian heritage cultures of the East and Socratic or Judeo-Christian cultures of the West, are examples of moral qualities having different attributes and applications for diverse peoples. Whereas distinctive societies, cultures, and civilizations define morality based on their particular history and culture, including religion, humans everywhere are the same. Thus, drawing on Jean-Jacques Rousseau's 1762 Social Contract, the current reality of globalization requires a cultural contract that harmonizes the morals and ethics of Eastern and Western civilizations.

DOI: 10.4018/978-1-5225-2650-6.ch009

INTRODUCTION

The need for global ethics that can guide international and intercultural research is not a new phenomenon. In 1996, James Bretzke wrote about a then-growing appeal for global ethics, which led to a habitude of scholars to employ hermeneutical and communicative theories that were thought to represent workable models for Christian ethics. Since then, communicative modalities employed by various cultures have failed to curtail misunderstandings in the global arena of intercultural epistemology.

In light of the pervasive nature of ethics, which is applicable without exception to all of human activities, this chapter excludes other areas of ethical concern and highlights cultural epistemology as an example of an aspect of human characteristics that tend to distinguish one people from another. Such divisive attributes include geographic orientation, political persuasion, economic ideology, religious doctrine, and language. Such a notion is exemplified in health care (Cooper & David, 1986; LaVeist, 1994) and human biology (Scarr, 1993). Given the unity of humanity, as medical sciences have proven, it is easier to argue in favor of a single morality and ethical epistemology, using the health care domain as justification. Our contemporary civilization, as a global society, bestows different conditions upon humankind compared with the original human condition (Cartwright, 2016; Krutch, 1959) in the Aristotelian animalistic human environment.

Information is scarce, if accessible, regarding the ethics requirements in health care that are applicable in a global research methodology. Such scarcity belies the fact that different societies, cultures, and nations apply their modes of ethics in medicine in conformity with their respective traditions, moral epistemologies, religious beliefs, and civil codes of behavior. There are ample reasons for dissatisfaction with the prevailing ethical modus operandi. One basic reason for the need to change from local to global is that events occurring in one country or culture impact events and people in other countries and cultures; such is a consequence of globalization.

The descriptive reference or application of the notion of morality is one that is used by socio-anthropologists when they report on the moral comportment of the societies that they study (Howell, 2005; Milesi & Alberici, 2016; Robbins, 2004; Rydstrøm, 2003). A descriptive explanation should suffice as a micro definition for the purpose of associating the notions of ethics and morality with the conduct of individuals on the basis of membership affiliation. A normative definition that is applicable to all human beings would depict a macro or universal account. Gert and Gert (2016) specified that a condition of rationality is almost always a requirement for moral agency. Normative codes of morality and ethics are neither mutually exclusive nor necessarily complementary given the numerous dissimilarities of the cultures that comprise the global arena in which human activities are conducted.

BACKGROUND

Did morality originate in the animal kingdom to satisfy a need for physiological and sociopolitical advancement? A basic element separating primates from us *homo sapiens* is said to be language (Arbib, 2005; Stanley Greenspan & Shanker, 2009), which serves as a socializing catalyst (Rizzolatti & Arbib, 1998) for interpersonal and intercultural communication. Linguistic rules can be regarded as the ethics of communication. Without such rules comprehension it would be impossible for a listener or reader to understand or comprehend what a speaker or writer encoded. Flannery and Marcus (2012) maintained that language is the decisive factor that distinguishes apes from humans and that the use of visceral, irrational force in regulating the affairs of humans has been averted by the natural gift of language. Nevertheless, other forces also converged to impose cohabitation. Social contract theory (Baker, 2013; Dunfee, Smith, & Ross, 1999; Hampton, 1988; Skyrms, 2014; Timmermann, 2009) is a Western moral and/or ethical theory that is associated with philosophers such as David Hume (1711–1776), Immanuel Kant (1724–1804), Jean-Jacques Rousseau (1712–1778), John Locke (1632–1704), and Thomas Hobbes (1588–1679), among others.

Modern moral and ethical theories are derivatives of ancient moral philosophical tenets, which originated in Ancient Egypt (Assmann, 2008; Griffiths, 1991) and Ancient Greece. De Waal (2003) explained that our human ancestors were forced to adopt moral and ethical standards in response to the insufferable consequences of continuous battles, conflicts, struggles, and needless scuffles. They desired peaceful coexistence. Hobbes (1660) adopted a different view. In Leviathan, Hobbes argued that the nature of humans is to use language to assign names to ideas that are combined into propositions and used to understand one another in communication. Drawing on Jean-Jacques Rousseau's 1762 Social Contract, the current reality of globalization requires a cultural contract that harmonizes the ethics of Eastern and Western civilizations.

Defining the concepts of *ethics* and *morality* is an immense undertaking. *Merriam-Webster's* defines *moral* in terms of the principles of right and wrong behavior. Gert and Gert (2016) suggested that such a definition encompasses the identification of numerous theories of morality at the micro/local level as well as on a global level. The micro level describes the ways and means by which institutions, nations, and civilizations attend to the distinction between right and wrong behavior. Morality evolved with evolutionary changes that occurred as a result of the transformation from brute culture, when ape shrewdness and chimpanzee troupes (Flannery & Marcus, 2012) ruled over primates and the weak failed to survive as being unfit (Claeys, 2000) for civil society (Rousseau, 1775).

Morality refers to an individual's inclination to act or behave in a particular manner towards other individuals (Sharp, 1989). For cognitive developmentalists, the determination of moral rectitude is a function of individuals' sense of cooperative reciprocity together with what they perceive or consider as being just (Kohlberg, 1969; Piaget, 1932/1965). For example, in Tokyo, Japan, it is typically unethical for a younger person to sit in the section on a passenger train that is designated for the elderly, expecting mothers, or the handicapped. However, the same restrictions do not apply in other sections of the train and refusing to give up one's seat for an elderly person or a pregnant women there would not be unethical, although a person with a higher moral character would tend to observe the same mannerism as the ethics prescribed in the designated sitting areas on the train. Thus, one can see that morality is more related to individual inclination whereas ethics are established rules that regulate individuals in their dealing with others.

The distinction between moral rectitude and ethical responsiveness is perhaps akin to Hobbes's (1651) distinction between command and counsel. Hobbes argued that one is following an ethical principle, which he named *command*, when acting upon an obligation delineated by an authority (for a critical assessment, see Morris, 2000). Such authorities may include God for religious institutions or individuals; the Hippocratic oath for physicians (Miles, 2005); the American Institute of Certified Public Accountants Code of Conduct for public accountants (Cosmo, 2017); business management ethics (B. J. White & Montgomery, 1980); academic research (Bird, 1996), and so on. Moral precepts are more often than not informally established expectations of the behavior of individuals that are members of a given organization, culture, or civilization. Different societies, cultures, and civilizations define *morality* based on their particular history and culture, including religion. Etiquette and the social emotion of shame, which have dissimilar connotations for Confucius and Aristotle (Cua, 2003), are examples of moral qualities that have different attributes and applications for different institutions or organizations such as the church. It is important to note that the notion of shame as a social emotion is refuted by some authors (see, for example, Deonna & Teroni, 2011).

THE NEED FOR A GLOBAL/UNIVERSAL CODE OF ETHICS

Ethics is required, if not integrated, in nearly all areas of human interaction involving contact, communication, or other collaborative activities. Examples include sports, entertainment, education, and business administration. Although virtually all activities have some business implications in a utilitarian sense, some activities involve fewer people than others. Soccer is a good example of activities that involve more people, including players, spectators, facilities, number of countries, tournaments, and the Olympics. Soccer is the world's most popular sports (Kuper, 2010, 2011; Wood, 2010). According to Wood (2010), 3.5 billion people watch soccer worldwide. The least popular sports include shooting, bowling, darts, and weightlifting (Sam Greenspan, 2014). Taking the same factors involving soccer into account, fewer people are affected by unethical acts in, say, bowling or any of the least popular sports, whereas more people affected by unethical acts in soccer. Soccer provides the greatest amount of happiness for the greatest number of people. In much the same way that all players in every country must abide by the same rules in soccer, it is possible to implement similar standard rules for other areas such as business and health care. Ethics in business administration affects each and every person universally as all human activities, including sports and health care, even at the family level and between husband and wife (Margolin, 1982; Sherman, 2006) involve some level and degree of management.

Source of Moral and Ethical Epistemology

Aristotle (384–322 B.C.E.) recognized that humans are endowed with selfish instincts, a condition that facilitates antipathic demeanor towards others. Such human conditions led Aristotle to deem humans as less than accommodating and likened them to animals (Ambler, 1985). Human nature encapsulates the emotional predispositions such as interest, joy, surprise, sadness, anger, disgust, contempt, fear, shame/shyness, and guilt (Izard & Buechler, 1980).

As social animals (Frith & Frith, 2007), humans are persistently involved in multitudes of activities, including the formation of a distinct autobiographical self (Dautenhahn, 2001) while fostering and maintaining transactional processes and social interactions for various purposes, such as economic, academic, health, and entertainment. Global ethics is needed in the complex and expanding societies of the global community. Coexistence necessitates complex social evolutionary activities such as the need and ability to predict, influence, manipulate, and decipher the functions and intentions of individuals and organizations that are part and parcel of the social structure. Rules, procedures, and other established regulations are needed to normalize an otherwise chaotic sociocultural existence (Baumeister, 2005). Proponents of the Aristotelian human nature affirm the sociopolitical nature of humans as natural and that Aristotle's characterization of humans as political animals is true (Ambler, 1985; Arnhart, 1990, 1994, 1995; Davis, 1996; Masters, 1989a, 1989b; Mulgan, 1974; Saxonhouse, 1992; J. Q. Wilson, 1993; Yack, 1985). Rules that regulate intercultural and interpersonal behavior facilitate peace, improve stability, promote harmony, and maximize utility.

The current reality of the ethical realm in today's world is that individual cultures, nations, and civilizations base their morality and ethics on their specific sociocultural institutions and histories. Sociocultural institutions, which provide the basis for the moral ethical foundation for its members, include those relating to economy, kinship, religion, politics, law, and education (Ingram & Clay, 2000; Olsen, 1991; Turner, 1997). According to Parboteeah and Cullen (2003), sociocultural institutions "provide individual actors with sense making and taken-for-granted heuristics to know what is legitimate, reasonable, and appropriate" (p. 138). Sociocultural institutions ascribe moral values, norms, and beliefs (Parboteeah & Cullen, 2003) and provide teleological solace to individuals as a group. In some cultures, individuals are advised, as to which goals to pursue and which ones to avoid (Ingram & Clay, 2000; Smith & Schwartz, 1997). Schwartz's (1999) definition of *social institutions* implies social structures that shape individual activities around work, to coincide with broader sociocultural values, and to provide individuals with economic relationships (Scott, 1995; Turner, 1997).

The Violence of Religious Morals

The association of violence with religion (Chang, 1983; Magnani, 2011; Reinhart, 2015a) has beleaguered all of humanity for centuries. Assmann (2008) expounded on the evolution of apocalyptic martyrdom as eventual consequences in response to violence perpetuated by political leaders in Ancient China, Egypt, Persia, Rome, and beyond. Holy wars, militant martyrdom, and human sacrificial rites exemplify the dark side of religion. As Juergensmeyer, Kitts, and Jerryson (2013) acknowledged, "religious violence and the adulation of its prophets continue to confound scholars, journalists, policy makers, and members of the general public" (p. 2). Nevertheless, a workable meaning and/or definition of the phenomenon of religion remains fleeting while unrelenting scholarly debate persists among anthropologists, ethologists, philosophers, psychologists, sociologists, theologians, and others.

Ample accounts of religious killing by political leaders in Ancient China (Chang, 1983, 1994; Flad, 2008; Fung, 2000; Keightley, 2012; Liu, 1996, 2000; Reinhart, 2015a; Underhill, 2002) reveal the origin of present-day confusion over the classification of Confucianism as a religion or a philosophy. Given the power of charismatic religious leadership (Reinhart, 2015b) in commanding the allegiance of people who are vulnerable and defenseless against supernatural phenomena such as illness and death, political leaders have been enticed to adopt religious ceremonies and rituals as a means of commanding reverence the like of which followers bestow upon ecclesiastic leadership. Religious rituals exhibiting powers of divination are obvious imitations for political leaders who are keen on administrative and political legitimacy and obsessed with the total allegiance of the masses. De Bary (1988) acknowledged that "Confucianism still lurks as the specter of a reactionary and repressive past, surviving in antidemocratic, 'feudal' features [attributed to] the current regime" (p. 133).

False Differences Accentuated

The ethics underlying Western individualism sharply contrasts with those of the East. These differences are accentuated in the rhetoric of some highly influential intellectuals with the effect of dampening any expectations of the adoption of a single moral and epistemology in this one world. Notable attributes of Western civilization that are different from Eastern attributes include reverence of individual differences (Hofstede, 2001; Kateb, 1992); promotion of independent critical thinking; equality and nondiscrimination based on age, social status, and gender; and other attributes as spelled out in the United Nations (1999) Universal Declaration of Human Rights and by the United Nations Educational, Scientific and Cultural Organization (2005). Contrasting cultural attributes of Eastern civilization include collectivism, particularism, power distance, and uncertainty avoidance. (For detailed distinctive Eastern and Western cultural attributes, see Gratier, 2003; Hofstede, 2011; and Nisbett et al., 2001.)

Mahbubani (2011) berated divergent epistemologies and alluded to the need for democratic principles in his pronouncement thus: "Sadly, instead of a convergence of views, there is a growing divide between the 12% of the world's population who live in the West and the 88% who make up the rest of the world" (p. 131).

As with everything else that changes, including individuals (Prochaska, 1991; Prochaska, DiClemente, & Norcross, 1992) and organizations (Washington & Ventresca, 2004), so do civilizations and societies. Friend (2004) illustrated that such a definitional change is reflected in the meaning ascribed to *individual* taking into account the occasion, location, and/or epistemic context. For Hobbes, an individual is said to be a contractor; for Locke, a proprietor; for Rousseau, a noble savage. Friend would concur that the current milieu of globalization transforms the status of individuals from local to global ascendency wherein such stigmas as age, class, race, and sex are of minor consequence. Confucian ethics integrates the strategic use of language, which is shown in the rectification of names (Steinkraus, 1980).

Normative individualism, which is epistemically and ontologically attributed to Western culture and ethics, posits a world comprised of individuals belonging to various organizations or groups in the environment of social institutions. Such institutions include family, marriage, professional associations, and the church. Not only are individual differences (Byrne, 1997; Cacioppo & Petty, 1982; Maxwell-Smith et al., 2015) acknowledged but also such differences are promoted in rudimentary Western ethics and epistemology (Stanovich & West, 1997). What is more, Stanovich and West (2000) explained that "those individuals with cognitive/ personality characteristics more conducive to deeper understanding would be more accepting of the appropriate normative principles for a particular problem" (p. 652). Hence, sociocultural characteristics such as collectivism and individualism are not entirely exclusive to Eastern and Western civilizations as the literature relates (Gratier, 2003; Hindriks, 2014; Hofstede, 2011; A. Hwang & Francesco, 2010; Kateb, 1992; Nisbett et al., 2001). There are many instances on personal individualism in China, Japan, Korea, and other Confucian heritage cultures. For example, it is individuals who must take so-called meritocratic civil service exams in China (Suen & Yu, 2006) and high-stakes university entrance exams in Japan (Topor, 2014). Similar to all births, ailments, and deaths, social obligations and responsibilities in Confucian societies are often assigned on an individual basis. Discounting groups, individuals are typically prosecuted for crimes committed. Conversely, collectivism is also practiced in Western civilizations. Apart from institutions such as the church, synagogues, athletic teams, and entertainment organizations that serve the benefit of their members, others such as Doctors Without Borders (Redfield, 2013) serve under a distinct *modus operandi*, serving the interests of people other than its members. These organizations are but a few examples of communal practices in what is generally regarded as the individualistic society of the West.

As Nussbaum (1999) acknowledged, Kantianism and utilitarianism cannot have ascribed any meaningful description to their respective ethical theories deprived of virtue. To this extent, one might accept that the virtues of the East and West are, to some extent, intricately linked. Still, apologists of Eastern moral and ethical culture owe no apologies for defending and promoting Confucianism, although it is fair to opine that harmonization of the two, namely Eastern and Western ethical traditions, deserves attention within the context of a converging world and exemplifies a courageous portrayal of utilitarianism. Urgent remedial action is wanting in circumstances in which elevated emotional sentimentality is buttressed by commending one culture on the one hand while at the same time condemning the other. Literature is replete with descriptive and factual accounts of the attributes that distinguish Eastern and Western cultures (Hofstede, 2001; Nisbett, Peng, Choi, & Norenzayan, 2001). Further emphasis can best be described as superfluous.

A welcome dawning of the *Asian Century* (Mahbubani, 2014) allows for a contemplative assessment of the ethical and moral implications for the rest of the world. An Asian century, which, for all intents and purposes, is dominated by China, constitutes and espouses Eastern civilization, with Confucianism as the basis of moral and ethical epistemology. For some authors (H. White, 2005), unrestrained emphasis on the abilities and debilities of civilizations constitutes overindulgence. In the case of China, H. White (2011) stated that "many people will still see this as conceding too much . . . as it will seem like appeasement" (p. 87).

Critical Thinking and Morality

Emotional sentiments such as empathy can be understood as derivative of shared cultural attributes, beliefs, and customs of individual members of a group with a collective historical experience (Schooler, 1996). In Confucian heritage cultures, such normative cultural values (Kumagai & Lypson, 2009) and assumptions are reinforced (Huang & Harris, 1973) through collective mental and psychological programming (Hofstede, 1984) combined with the prominence of *li*-divinatory rituals (Ebrey, 2014) and ceremonial rituals (Billioud & Thoraval, 2009). Critical thinking, which questions unverified beliefs and assumptions (Chun & Evans, 2016), tends to nullify or negate these cultural mechanisms that are designed to ensure conformity in group-oriented cultures. Whereas enforcement and observance of group or organizational directives are more often than not accomplished with individual cognitive repose, Cacioppo, Petty, Feinstein, and Jarvis (1996) observed that different individuals employ and manifest varying degrees of intrinsic motivations requiring cognitive information processing. Individual self-reflection and critical analysis involving such cognitive processing as cost–benefit analysis (Larrick, Nisbett, & Morgan, 1993) may be less necessary, particularly in group-oriented cultures (D. B. Wilson, Bouffard, & MacKenzie, 2005) such as China and Japan. To safeguard group outcome, individual decisions are typically guarded by cultural epistemic cognition (A. Hwang & Francesco, 2010; Pillai, 2012) in Confucian heritage societies (K. K. Hwang, 2001); recognition and tolerance of individual differences allow for the unbiased and critical acceptance of dispositions that are antithetical to one's own (Lipman, 1991; Norris & Ennis, 1989; Perkins, 1995; Wade & Tavris, 1993; Zechmeister & Johnson, 1992).

Rather than maximize individual welfare, utilitarianism focuses on collective welfare and identifies goodness with the greatest amount of good for the greatest number of people, known as the *greatest happiness principle*. Therefore, maximizing benefits for the greatest number of people involves net assessments of benefit; utility is the net result of benefits and disbenefits, or costs. Utility has entered modern economics as a key quantitative concept. The concept of trade-offs is specifically embraced and social and environmental cost–benefit analyses are explicit utilitarian tools for assessing the goodness of an action. A simple balance sheet of costs and benefits can be drawn up to assess the overall utility of a decision.

One World Standard in Bioethics

Utilitarianism is a form of consequentialism. Utilitarianism promotes global consumption and global consumption produces the need for global treatment. Utilitarianism entails doing the best we can for the deontological end of achieving the truth. We are deontologically obligated to achieve the best and greatest satisfaction that can benefit the most people. The end result should be the achievement of epidemic truth.

Deontological ethics is best explained by means of Kant's categorical imperatives, which espouse a universal duty to perform or engage in virtuous deeds and activities regardless of individual egos, interests, or desires (Aune, 2014; Kant, 1879/2007). Kant argued that humans are duty bound to treat others in recognition of their intrinsic value, i.e., their individual existence, abilities, achievements, and potential, devoid of their connections to other persons or institutions. For Kant, it is unethical to treat others based on their instrumental value, as means to an end. Examples of duties that are entirely universal, in Kantian ethics, include the duty to not lie and the duty to tell the truth. Kant was not totally oblivious to the instinctive nature of humans; he maintained that humans are by no means flawlessly rational. For Kant, it is imperative that humans conform to a moral or ethical code of conduct. Imperfect and irrational human instincts have to be supplanted by duty and responsibility owned by oneself and others (Kant, 1879/2007). Other philosophers proclaimed their endorsement of Kant's rational argument (Hancey, 1976; Hobbes, 1651/1994; Locke, 2002), which underlies the nature of humans and eventually led to the creation of moral and ethical codes. Kantian virtues of the West, on the one hand, are conterminous with Confucian virtues of the Oriental East in ways that nullify Rudyard Kipling's dictum, East is East, West is West, and never the twain shall meet. Kipling's pessimistic poetic view of the world's two dominant civilizations is complemented by scholarly endorsements. Some authors prominently believe that Eastern and Western ethics, moral precepts, and epistemologies are irreconcilable (Dancy, 2006; Harman, 2000; Wong, 1984).

The morality of an act is determined by its utility. The utility of an act has consequences. This reality enhances the union of utilitarianism and consequentialism. The doctrine of utility is aimed at alleviating pain and suffering imposed upon humans by nature (Bentham, 1781/2000). It does not apply universally to all peoples, however; it seeks and confers pleasure to a specific individual or group of individuals, private organizations, and governments. Bentham (1781/2000) defined *utility* as a principle that defines the actions of individuals and/or organizations in which such actions cause or produce all desirable benefits, such as pleasure and happiness.

In health care, for example, the transfer and proliferation of health and medical services from local communities to a global audience happens worldwide, across countries, cultures, and linguistic groups. The movement of people in response to academic and medical needs foregrounds questions of academic and biomedical ethics. The practice of traveling from industrialized economies and societies to developing economies by individuals in search of affordable or cheaper health care and cosmetic surgeries is commonly known as medical tourism (Bookman

& Bookman, 2007). Medical tourism encompasses ethics that potentially includes diverse moral and civil codes, regulations or laws. Clark (2012, p. 28) found that local populations exhibit increasing disparities of health status and requirements that correspond to the diverse medical and health care composition in the global setting. The more people engage in medical tourism, the more urgent is the need for standardized ethical understanding and programs that can accommodate multicultural patients. Most medical tourists are typically from Western countries (i.e., Canada, Europe, Japan, and the United States). Most countries of destination are non-Christian and non-Western civilizations (Bergstrand & Landgren, 2011; Crooks, Kingsbury, Snyder, & Johnston, 2010). Given the fact that religion and other cultural elements form the basis of moral and ethical codes, medical tourists face real consequences.

As the medical tourism phenomenon along with the global-centered outsourcing of medical records become more entrenched in national health care programs and policies, individual medical records take flight from local repositories to global databases away from home countries such that remote x-ray and medical transcription are conducted (Bergstrand & Landgren, 2011) by personnel other than individuals' personal physician.

SOLUTIONS AND RECOMMENDATIONS

Standardizing ethics across civilizations and cultures cannot be regarded as an easy task. Nevertheless, we can celebrate the reality of globalization, which has so far resulted in the convergence of an academic, economic, and global lingua franca that makes intercultural communication easier. Harmonizing cross-cultural academic and medical ethics should be of little or no negative consequence given the overwhelming benefits that are enjoyed by both Eastern and Western societies. The first solution to the seemingly illusive ethical solution to intercultural harmony is to recognize the basic commonalities that are now in place.

Worldwide transcivilization and transcultural socioeconomic advances are a utilitarian consequence of the convergence of knowledge that is facilitated by modern telecommunication and information technology. The ubiquitous World Wide Web and Internet have improved the lots of millions of people, although given the totality of the human race, optimum utility has yet to be achieved. Nevertheless, a lingua franca that allows intercultural and international academic research is a promising development. The ethics in this area can be harmonized further than the current reality.

Ethics education, which has been based predominately on Western philosophical tenets (Durbin, 2008; Mitcham, 2009), was infused into U.S. engineering pedagogy in the late 1970s (Hansson, 2011; Lynch, 1997). For various reasons, including funding, bidding, safety against risks, and security and environmental ramifications, ethics has become an essential component of engineering and technological education (Bird, 2003; McLean, 1993; Vanderburg, 1995; Whitbeck, 1998). There are sufficient pedagogical tools to facilitate the easy implementation of ethical education in engineering (Bird & Sieber, 2005; Felder & Brent, 2003; Harris, Pritchard, & Rabins, 2000; Herkert, 2002; Loui, 2005; Martin & Schinzinger, 2005; Peperzak, 2013). Carpenter (1978) stated that Max Black's 1976 technological ethics presentation at Cornell University could be regarded as prevenient to the widespread inclusion of ethics as a subject in engineering education in the United States.

Future research should investigate whether there is relationship between a writing system and creativity. For example, is there a relationship between creativity and a syllable writing system?

CONCLUSION

The term *ethics* connotes a moral code that designates the way or manner in which individuals ought to behave in a given profession or in society at large. Thus, there are codes of ethics for such institutions, including academia (Bullock & Panicker, 2003; Dill, 1982; Fisher, 2003, 2008; Koocher & Keith-Spiegel, 2008), medicine (American Medical Association & New York Academy of Medicine, 1848; Schumann & Alfandre, 2008), and business (Asgary & Mitschow, 2002; Ashkanasy, Falkus, & Callan, 2000; Carasco & Singh, 2003; Egels-Zandén & Merk, 2014).

A welcome dawning of the *Asian Century* (Mahbubani, 2014) allows for a contemplative assessment of the ethical and moral implications for the rest of the world. An Asian century (Mahbubani, 2008), which, for all intents and purposes, is dominated by China, constitutes Eastern civilization, which is epistemologically and ontologically Confucian in terms of moral and ethical principles espoused and in use. Some authors, including White (2005), have expressed their opinion concerning unrestrained emphasis on the abilities and/or debilities of civilizations as well as conceived imminent dominance by one civilization over the other. The convergence of economies, technologies, and other academic and sociocultural endeavors should allow one to deny doomsday prophecies as overindulgence. As White (2011) stated, "many people will still see this as conceding too much . . . as it will seem like appeasement" (p. 87).

It is cavalier to surmise that alleviating a time-honored moral, ethical, and epistemic regimen such as Confucianism (Bian, 1997; Tsui & Farh, 1997) would be an easy feat. World harmony does not necessarily require a whimsical repeal of a duty- and relationship-based ethical system with one that is rule based. Perhaps one key measure of the appropriateness of any system might be the utility it provides or the resultant consequence.

REFERENCES

Ambler, W. H. (1985). Aristotle's understanding of the naturalness of the city. *The Review of Politics, 47*(2), 163–185. doi:10.1017/S0034670500036688

American Medical Association & New York Academy of Medicine. (1848). *Code of medical ethics* (A. H. Byfield, Ed.). Retrieved from https://play.google.com/books/reader?id=chY6AQAAMAAJ&printsec=frontcover&output=reader&hl=en&pg=GBS.PP1

Arbib, M. A. (2005). From monkey-like action recognition to human language: An evolutionary framework for neurolinguistics. *Behavioral and Brain Sciences, 28*(2), 105–167. doi:10.1017/S0140525X05000038 PMID:16201457

Aristotle,. (2000). *Nicomachean ethics* (R. Crisp, Trans.). Cambridge, UK: Cambridge University Press. doi:10.1017/CBO9780511802058

Arnhart, L. (1990). Aristotle, chimpanzees and other political animals. *Social Sciences Information. Information Sur les Sciences Sociales, 29*(3), 477–557. doi:10.1177/053901890029003003

Arnhart, L. (1994). The Darwinian biology of Aristotle's political animals. *American Journal of Political Science, 38*(2), 464–485. doi:10.2307/2111413

Arnhart, L. (1995). The new Darwinian naturalism in political theory. *The American Political Science Review, 89*(2), 389–400. doi:10.2307/2082432

Asai, A., Kadooka, Y., & Aizawa, K. (2012). Arguments against promoting organ transplants from brain-dead donors, and views of contemporary Japanese on life and death. *Bioethics, 26*(4), 215–223. doi:10.1111/j.1467-8519.2010.01839.x PMID:20731646

Asgary, N., & Mitschow, M. C. (2002). Toward a model for international business ethics. *Journal of Business Ethics, 36*(3), 239–246. doi:10.1023/A:1014057122480

Ashkanasy, N. M., Falkus, S., & Callan, V. J. (2000). Predictors of ethical code use and ethical tolerance in the public sector. *Journal of Business Ethics, 25*(3), 237–253. doi:10.1023/A:1006001722137

Assmann, J. (2008). *Of God and gods: Egypt, Israel, and the rise of monotheism.* Madison, WI: University of Wisconsin Press.

Aune, B. (2014). *Kant's theory of morals.* Princeton, NJ: Princeton University Press.

Bagheri, A. (2009). Japan organ transplantation law: Past, present and future. *Asian Bioethics Review, 1*(4), 452–456. Available from https://muse.jhu.edu/article/416370/pdf

Baker, E. (Ed.). (2013). *Social contract: Essays by Locke, Hume and Rousseau.* London: Oxford University Press.

Baumeister, R. F. (2005). *The cultural animal: Human nature, meaning, and social life.* New York, NY: Oxford University Press. doi:10.1093/acprof:oso/9780195167030.001.0001

Bays, D. H. (2003, June). Chinese Protestant Christianity today. *The China Quarterly, 174*, 488–504. doi:10.1017/S0009443903000299

Bentham, J. (2000). *An introduction to the principles of morals and legislation.* Retrieved from http://socserv.mcmaster.ca/econ/ugcm/3ll3/bentham/morals.pdf (Original work published 1781)

Bergstrand, F., & Landgren, J. (2011, August). Visual reporting in time-critical work: Exploring video use in emergency response. In *Proceedings of the 13th International Conference on Human Computer Interaction With Mobile Devices and Services* (pp. 415–424). Academic Press.

Bian, Y. (1997). Bringing strong ties back in: Indirect ties, network bridges, and job searches in China. *American Sociological Review, 62*(3), 366–385. doi:10.2307/2657311

Billioud, S., & Thoraval, J. (2009). 'Lijiao': The return of ceremonies honoring Confucius in mainland China. *China Perspectives, 80*, 82–100. Available from http://search.informit. com.au/documentSummary;dn=371300199876172;res=IELHSS

Bird, S. J. (1996). The role of science professionals in teaching responsible research conduct. *Bioscience, 46*(10), 783–786. doi:10.2307/1312856

Bird, S. J. (2003). Ethics as a core competency in science and engineering. *Science and Engineering Ethics, 9*(4), 443–444. doi:10.1007/s11948-003-0042-9 PMID:14652897

Bird, S. J., & Sieber, J. E. (2005). Teaching ethics in science and engineering: Effective online education. *Science and Engineering Ethics, 11*(3), 323–328. doi:10.1007/s11948-005-0001-8 PMID:16190273

Black, M. (1976). Are there any philosophically interesting questions in technology? *PSA: Proceedings of the Biennial Meeting of the Philosophy of Science Association, 1976*(2), 185–193. Available from http://www.journals.uchicago.edu/doi/pdfplus/10.1086/psaprocbienmeetp.1976.2.192381

Bookman, M. Z., & Bookman, K. R. (2007). *Medical tourism in developing countries.* New York, NY: Palgrave. doi:10.1057/9780230605657

Brandt, R. B. (1959). *Ethical theory: The problems of normative and critical ethics.* Retrieved from https://babel.hathitrust.org/cgi/pt?id=uc1.b3423294;view=1up;seq=7

Bretzke, J. T. (1996). Cultural particularity and the globalisation of ethics in the light of inculturation. *Pacifica, 9*(1), 69–86. doi:10.1177/1030570X9600900106

Bullock, M., & Panicker, S. (2003). Ethics for all: Differences across scientific society codes. *Science and Engineering Ethics, 9*(2), 159–170. doi:10.1007/s11948-003-0003-3 PMID:12774648

Byrne, D. (1997). An overview (and underview) of research and theory within the attraction paradigm. *Journal of Social and Personal Relationships, 14*(3), 417–431. doi:10.1177/0265407597143008

Cacioppo, J. T., & Petty, R. E. (1982). The need for cognition. *Journal of Personality and Social Psychology, 42*(1), 116–131. doi:10.1037/0022-3514.42.1.116

Cacioppo, J. T., Petty, R. E., Feinstein, J., & Jarvis, W. (1996). Dispositional differences in cognitive motivation: The life and times of individuals varying in need for cognition. *Psychological Bulletin, 119*(2), 197–253. doi:10.1037/0033-2909.119.2.197

Carasco, E. F., & Singh, J. B. (2003). The content and focus of the codes of ethics of the world's largest transnational corporations. *Business and Society Review, 108*(1), 71–94. doi:10.1111/1467-8594.00007

Carpenter, S. R. (1978). Developments in the philosophy of technology in America. *Technology and Culture, 19*(1), 93–99. doi:10.2307/3103310

Cartwright, J. (2016). *Evolution and human behaviour: Darwinian perspectives on the human condition.* London: Palgrave Macmillan.

Chang, K. C. (1983). *Art, myth, and ritual: The path to political authority in ancient China.* Cambridge, MA: Harvard University Press.

Chang, K. C. (1994). Ritual and power. In R. E. Murowchick (Ed.), *Cradles of civilization: China: Ancient culture, modern land*. Norman, OK: University of Oklahoma Press.

Cheng, M. M. (2003). House church movements and religious freedom in China. *China. International Journal (Toronto, Ont.)*, *1*(01), 16–45. doi:10.1142/S0219747203000049

Chun, E., & Evans, A. (2016). Rethinking cultural competence in higher education: An ecological framework for student development. *ASHE Higher Education Report*, *42*(4), 7–162. doi:10.1002/aehe.20102

Clark, M. J. (2012). Cross-cultural research: Challenge and competence. *International Journal of Nursing Practice*, *18*(s2), 28–37. doi:10.1111/j.1440-172X.2012.02026.x PMID:22776530

Cooper, R., & David, R. (1986). The biological concept of race and its application to public health and epidemiology. *Journal of Health Politics, Policy and Law*, *11*(1), 97–116. doi:10.1215/03616878-11-1-97 PMID:3722786

Cosmo, V. A., Jr. (2017). Accounting plan plagiarism: Is it time to strengthen the CPA Code of Professional Conduct? *Pennsylvania CPA Journal, 88*(1), 14–16. Retrieved from https://www.picpa.org/articles/

Crooks, V. A., Kingsbury, P., Snyder, J., & Johnston, R. (2010). What is known about the patient's experience of medical tourism? A scoping review. *BMC Health Services Research*, *10*(1), 1–12. doi:10.1186/1472-6963-10-266 PMID:20825667

Cua, A. S. (2003). The ethical significance of shame: Insights of Aristotle and Xunzi. *Philosophy East & West*, *53*(2), 147–202. doi:10.1353/pew.2003.0013

Dancy, J. (2006). *Ethics without principles*. Oxford, UK: Oxford University Press.

Dautenhahn, K. (2001). The narrative intelligence hypothesis: In search of the transactional format of narratives in humans and other social animals. In M. Beynon, C. L. Nehaniv, & K. Dautenah (Eds.), *Cognitive technology: Instruments of mind* (pp. 248–266)., doi:10.1007/3-540-44617-6_25

Davis, M. (1996). *The politics of philosophy: A commentary on Aristotle's politics*. Savage, MD: Rowman & Littlefield.

De Bary, W. T. (1988). *The trouble with Confucianism. The Tanner lectures on human values*. Retrieved from http://tannerlectures.utah.edu/_documents/a-to-z/d/debary89.pdf

de Waal, F. B. (2003). *Morality and the social instincts: Continuity with the other primates.* Retrieved from http://courses.washington.edu/evpsych/de%20Waal%20 on%20morality %202005.pdf

Deonna, J., & Teroni, F. (2011). Is shame a social emotion? In A. K. Ziv, K. Lehrer, & H. B. Schmid (Eds.), *Self-evaluation: Affective and social grounds of intentionality* (pp. 193–212)., doi:10.1007/978-94-007-1266-9_11

Dill, D. D. (1982). The structure of the academic profession: Toward a definition of ethical issues. *The Journal of Higher Education, 53*(3), 255–267. doi:10.2307/ 1981746

Dunfee, T. W., Smith, N. C., & Ross, W. T. Jr. (1999). Social contracts and marketing ethics. *Journal of Marketing, 63*(3), 14–32. doi:10.2307/1251773

Durbin, P. T. (2008). Engineering professional ethics in a broader dimension. *Interdisciplinary Science Reviews, 33*(3), 226–233. doi:10.1179/174327908X366914

Ebrey, P. B. (2014). *Confucianism and family rituals in Imperial China: A social history of writing about rites.* Princeton, NJ: Princeton University Press.

Egels-Zandén, N., & Merk, J. (2014). Private regulation and trade union rights: Why codes of conduct have limited impact on trade union rights. *Journal of Business Ethics, 123*(3), 461–473. doi:10.1007/s10551-013-1840-x

Eng, I., & Lin, Y. M. (2002). Religious festivities, communal rivalry, and restructuring of authority relations in rural Chaozhou, Southeast China. *The Journal of Asian Studies, 61*(4), 1259–1285. doi:10.2307/3096442

Felder, R. M., & Brent, R. (2003). Designing and teaching courses to satisfy the ABET engineering criteria. *Journal of Engineering Education, 92*(1), 7–25. doi:10.1002/j.2168-9830.2003.tb00734.x

Feuchtwang, S. (2000). Religion as resistance. In E. J. Perry & M. Selden (Eds.), *Chinese Society: Change, conflict and resistance* (pp. 161–177). London: Routledge.

Fisher, C. B. (2003). Developing a code of ethics for academics. *Science and Engineering Ethics, 9*(2), 171–179. doi:10.1007/s11948-003-0004-2 PMID:12774649

Fisher, C. B. (2008). *Decoding the ethics code: A practical guide for psychologists* (2nd ed.). Thousand Oaks, CA: Sage.

Flad, R. (2008). Divination and power. *Current Anthropology, 49*(3), 403–437. doi:10.1086/588495

Flanagan, O. (1991). *Varieties of moral personality: Ethics and psychological realism*. Cambridge, MA: Harvard University Press.

Flannery, K., & Marcus, J. (2012). *The creation of inequality: How our prehistoric ancestors set the stage for monarchy, slavery, and empire*. Cambridge, MA: Harvard University Press. doi:10.4159/harvard.9780674064973

Friend, C. (2004). Social contract theory. In *Internet encyclopedia of philosophy*. Retrieved from http://www.iep.utm.edu/soc-cont/

Frith, C. D., & Frith, U. (2007). Social cognition in humans. *Current Biology, 17*(16), R724–R732. doi:10.1016/j.cub.2007.05.068 PMID:17714666

Fung, C. (2000). The drinks are on us: Ritual, social status, and practice in Dawenkou burials, North China. *Journal of East Asian Archaeology, 2*(1), 67–92. doi:10.1163/156852300509808

Gert, B., & Gert, J. (2016, Spring). The definition of morality. In E. N. Zalta (Ed.), *The Stanford encyclopedia of philosophy*. Retrieved from https://plato.stanford.edu/archives/spr2016/entries/morality-definition/

Gladney, D. C. (2009). Islam in China: State policing and identity politics. In Y. Ashiwa & D. Wank (Eds.), *Making religion, making the state: The politics of religion in modern China* (pp. 151–178). Palo Alto, CA: Stanford University Press.

Goossaert, V., & Palmer, D. A. (2011). *The religious question in modern China*. University of Chicago Press. doi:10.7208/chicago/9780226304182.001.0001

Gordenker, A. (2014, July 18). Organ donation. *The Japan Times*. Retrieved from http://www.japantimes.co.jp/news/2014/07/18/reference/organ-donation/#.WWATFNOGPGI

Gratier, M. (2003). Expressive timing and interactional synchrony between mothers and infants: Cultural similarities, cultural differences, and the immigration experience. *Cognitive Development, 18*(4), 533–554. doi:10.1016/j.cogdev.2003.09.009

Greenspan, S. I., & Shanker, S. (2009). The first idea: How symbols, language, and intelligence evolved from our primate ancestors to modern humans. Cambridge, MA: Da Capo.

Greenspan, S. (2014). *Eleven most popular sports in the world*. Retrieved from http://www.11points.com/Sports/11_Most_Popular_Sports_in_the_World

Griffiths, J. G. (1991). *The divine verdict: A study of divine judgement in the ancient religions*. Brill.

Hampton, J. (1988). *Hobbes and the social contract tradition*. New York, NY: Cambridge University Press.

Hancey, J. O. (1976). John Locke and the law of nature. *Political Theory, 4*(4), 439–454. doi:10.1177/009059177600400404

Hansson, S. O. (2011). Do we need a special ethics for research? *Science and Engineering Ethics, 17*(1), 21–29. doi:10.1007/s11948-009-9186-6 PMID:19941087

Harman, G. (2000). Moral relativism defended. In G. Harman (Ed.), *Explaining value and other essays in moral philosophy* (pp. 3–19). Oxford, UK: Clarendon. doi:10.1093/0198238045.003.0001

Harris, C. E., Pritchard, M. S., & Rabins, M. J. (2000). *Engineering ethics: Concepts and cases* (2nd ed.). Belmont, CA: Wadsworth/Thomson.

Hatemi, P. K., & McDermott, R. (Eds.). (2011). *Man is by nature a political animal: Evolution, biology, and politics*. University of Chicago Press. doi:10.7208/chicago/9780226319117.001.0001

Herkert, J. R. (2002). Continuing and emerging issues in engineering ethics education. *Bridge, 32*(3), 8–13. Retrieved from https://www.nae.edu/File.aspx?id=7378&v=f37740e0

Herman, B. (2013). Morality and everyday life. In The American Philosophical Association centennial series (pp. 655–670). Academic Press. doi:10.5840/apapa201396

Hindriks, F. (2014). How autonomous are collective agents? Corporate rights and normative individualism. *Erkenntnis, 79*(S9), 1565–1585. doi:10.1007/s10670-014-9629-6

Hobbes, T. (1651). *Leviathan or the matter, forme, and power of a commonwealth ecclesiasticall and civill* (R. Hay, Ed.). London, England: Andrew Crooke. Retrieved from http://socserv2.socsci.mcmaster.ca/econ/ugcm/3ll3/hobbes/Leviathan.pdf

Hobbes, T. (1660). *The leviathan*. Retrieved from http://coral.ufsm.br/gpforma/2senafe/PDF/b36.pdf

Hobbes, T. (1994). Leviathan. In E. Curley (Ed.), *Leviathan, with selected variants from the Latin edition of 1668*. Indianapolis, IN: Hackett. (Original work published 1651)

Hofstede, G. (1984). *Culture's consequences*. Thousand Oaks, CA: Sage.

Hofstede, G. (2001). *Culture's consequences: Comparing values, behaviors, institutions, and organizations across nations* (2nd ed.). Thousand Oaks, CA: Sage.

Hofstede, G. (2011). Dimensionalizing cultures-The Hofstede model in context. *Online Readings in Psychology and Culture, 2*(1). doi:10.9707/2307-0919.1014

Howell, S. (Ed.). (2005). *The ethnography of moralities.* London: Routledge.

Huang, K. (2014). Dyadic nexus fighting two-front battles: A study of the microlevel process of the official-religion-state relationship in china. *Journal for the Scientific Study of Religion, 53*(4), 706–721. doi:10.1111/jssr.12149

Hwang, A., & Francesco, A. M. (2010). The Influence of individualism-Collectivism and power distance on use of feedback channels and consequences for learning. *Academy of Management Learning & Education, 9*(2), 243–257. doi:10.5465/AMLE.2010.51428546

Hwang, K. K. (2001). The deep structure of Confucianism: A social psychological approach. *Asian Philosophy, 11*(3), 179–204. doi:10.1080/09552360120116928

Ingram, P., & Clay, K. (2000). The choice-within-constraints new institutionalism and implications for sociology. *Annual Review of Sociology, 26*(1), 525–546. retrieved from http://www.columbia.edu/~pi17/525.pdf. doi:10.1146/annurev.soc.26.1.525

Japan Times. (2007, February 18). *Scandal over Ehime doc's transplants grows wider.* Retrieved from http://www.japantimes.co.jp/news/2007/02/18/national/scandal-over-ehime-docs-transplants-grows-wider/#.WV6z09OGPGI

Juergensmeyer, M., Kitts, M., & Jerryson, M. (Eds.). (2013). *The Oxford handbook of religion and violence.* Oxford, UK: Oxford University Press.

Kant, I. (2007). *Fundamental principles of the metaphysic of morals* (N. Y. New York, Trans.). Dover: T. K. Abbott. (Original work published 1879)

Kateb, G. (1992). *The inner ocean: Individualism and democratic culture.* Ithaca, NY: Cornell University Press.

Keightley, D. (2012). *Working for his majesty.* Berkeley, CA: University of California Institute of East Asian Studies.

Kindopp, J. (2004). Fragmented yet defiant: Protestant resilience under Chinese Communist Party rule. In, J. Kindopp & C. L. Hamrin (Eds.), God and Caesar in China: Policy implications of church-state tensions (pp. 122–148). Washington, DC: Brookings.

Kohlberg, L. (1969). Stage and sequence: The cognitive-developmental approach to socialization. In D. Goslin (Ed.), *Handbook of socialization theory and research* (pp. 347–480). Retrieved from https://books.google.com/

Koocher, G. P., & Keith-Speigel, P. (2008). *Ethics in psychology and the mental health professions: Standards and cases* (3rd ed.). Oxford, UK: Oxford University Press.

Krutch, J. W. (1959). *Human nature and the human condition: Texte imprimé.* New York, NY: Random House.

Kumagai, A. K., & Lypson, M. L. (2009). Beyond cultural competence: Critical consciousness, social justice, and multicultural education. *Academic Medicine, 84*(6), 782–787. doi:10.1097/ACM.0b013e3181a42398 PMID:19474560

Kuper, S. (2010). *Soccer against the enemy: How the world's most popular sport starts and fuels revolutions and keeps dictators in power.* New York, NY: Nation.

Kuper, S. (2011). *Soccer men: Profiles of the rogues, geniuses, and neurotics who dominate the world's most popular sport.* New York, NY: Nation.

Laliberté, A. (2011). Buddhist revival under state watch. *Journal of Current Chinese Affairs, 40*(2), 107–134. Retrieved from https://journals.sub.uni-hamburg.de/giga/jcca/article/view/419/417

Larrick, R. P., Nisbett, R. E., & Morgan, J. N. (1993). Who uses the cost-benefit rules of choice? Implications for the normative status of microeconomic theory. *Organizational Behavior and Human Decision Processes, 56*(3), 331–347. doi:10.1006/obhd.1993.1058

LaVeist, T. A. (1994). Beyond dummy variables and sample selection: What health services researchers ought to know about race as a variable. *Health Services Research, 29*(1), 1. PMID:8163376

Lipman, M. (1991). *Thinking in education.* Cambridge, UK: Cambridge University Press.

Liu, L. (1996). Mortuary ritual and social hierarchy in the Longshan culture. *Early China, 21*, 1–46. Retrieved from http://www.jstor.org/stable/23351730

Liu, L. (2000). Ancestor worship: An archaeological investigation of ritual activities in Neolithic North China. *Journal of East Asian Archaeology, 2*(1/2), 129–164. doi:10.1163/156852300509826

Locke, J. (2002). *Essays on the law of nature: The Latin text with a translation, introduction and notes, together with transcripts of Locke's shorthand in his journal for 1676* (W. von Leyden, Trans. & Ed.). Oxford, UK: Oxford University Press.

Loui, M. C. (2005). Ethics and the development of professional identities of engineering students. *Journal of Engineering Education, 94*(4), 383–390. doi:10.1002/j.2168-9830.2005.tb00866.x

Lynch, W. T. (1997). Teaching engineering ethics in the United States. *IEEE Technology and Society Magazine, 16*(4), 27–36. doi:10.1109/44.642561

Madsen, R. (2007). *Democracy's dharma: Religious renaissance and political development in Taiwan.* Berkeley, CA: University of California Press. doi:10.1525/california/9780520252271.001.0001

Magnani, L. (2011). *Understanding violence: The intertwining of morality, religion and violence: A philosophical stance* (Vol. 1). 10.1007/978-3-642-21972-6

Mahbubani, K. (2008). The case against the West: America and Europe in the Asian century. *Foreign Affairs, 87*(3), 111–124. Retrieved from http://www.jstor.org/stable/20032654

Mahbubani, K. (2011). Can Asia re-legitimize global governance? *Review of International Political Economy, 18*(1), 131–139. doi:10.1080/09692290.2011.545217

Mahbubani, K. (2014, December 4). Why Asia is on the brink of a golden era. *Bangladesh – Audacity of Hope.* Retrieved from https://mygoldenbengal.wordpress.com/2014/12/04/why-asia-is-on-the-brink-of-a-golden-era/

Margolin, G. (1982). Ethical and legal considerations in marital and family therapy. *The American Psychologist, 37*(7), 788–801. doi:10.1037/0003-066X.37.7.788 PMID:7137697

Martin, M. W., & Schinzinger, R. (2005). *Ethics in engineering* (4th ed.). New York, NY: McGraw-Hill.

Masters, R. D. (1989a). Gradualism and discontinuous change in evolutionary theory and political philosophy. *Journal of Social and Biological Structures, 12*(2/3), 281–301. doi:10.1016/0140-1750(89)90051-1

Masters, R. D. (1989b). *The nature of politics.* New Haven, CT: Yale University Press.

Maxwell-Smith, M. A., Seligman, C., Conway, P., & Cheung, I. (2015). Individual differences in commitment to value-based beliefs and the amplification of perceived belief dissimilarity effects. *Journal of Personality*, *83*(2), 127–141. doi:10.1111/jopy.12089 PMID:24444458

McLean, G. F. (1993). Integrating ethics and design. *Technology and Society Magazine, IEEE*, *12*(3), 19–30. doi:10.1109/MTAS.1993.232282

Milesi, P., & Alberici, A. I. (2016). Pluralistic morality and collective action: The role of moral foundations. *Group Processes & Intergroup Relations*. doi:10.1177/1368430216675707

Mitcham, C. (2009). A historico-ethical perspective on engineering education: From use and convenience to policy engagement. *Engineering Studies*, *1*(1), 35–53. doi:10.1080/19378620902725166

Morris, C. W. (Ed.). (2000). *The social contract theorists: Critical essays on Hobbes, Locke, and Rousseau*. Toronto: Rowman & Littlefield.

Mulgan, R. G. (1974). Aristotle's doctrine that man is a political animal. *Hermes*, *102*(3), 438–445. Retrieved from http://www.jstor.org/stable/4475868

Nakamura, K., Shimai, S., Kikuchi, S., Takahashi, H., Tanaka, M., Nakano, S., & Yamamoto, M. et al. (1998). Increases in body mass index and waist circumference as outcomes of working overtime. *Occupational Medicine*, *48*(3), 169–173. doi:10.1093/occmed/48.3.169 PMID:9659726

Nakanishi, N., Yoshida, H., Nagano, K., Kawashimo, H., Nakamura, K., & Tatara, K. (2001). Long working hours and risk for hypertension in Japanese male white collar workers. *Journal of Epidemiology and Community Health*, *55*(5), 316–322. doi:10.1136/jech.55.5.316 PMID:11297649

Nisbett, R. E., Peng, K., Choi, I., & Norenzayan, A. (2001). Culture and systems of thought: Holistic versus analytic cognition. *Psychological Review*, *108*(2), 291–310. doi:10.1037/0033-295X.108.2.291 PMID:11381831

Norris, S. P., & Ennis, R. H. (1989). *Evaluating critical thinking*. Pacific Grove, CA: Midwest.

Nussbaum, M. C. (1999). Virtue ethics: A misleading category? *The Journal of Ethics*, *3*(3), 163–201. doi:10.1023/A:1009877217694

Olsen, M. E. (1991). *Societal dynamics: Exploring macrosociology*. Englewood Cliffs, NJ: Prentice-Hall.

Parboteeah, K. P., & Cullen, J. B. (2003). Social institutions and work centrality: Explorations beyond national culture. *Organization Science*, *14*(2), 137–148. doi:10.1287/orsc.14.2.137.14989

Peperzak, A. (Ed.). (2013). *Ethics as first philosophy: The significance of Emmanuel Levinas for philosophy, literature and religion*. New York, NY: Routledge.

Perkins, D. N. (1995). *Outsmarting IQ: The emerging science of learnable intelligence*. New York, NY: Free Press.

Piaget, J. (1965). *The moral judgment of the child* (M. Gabain, Trans.). New York, NY: Free Press. (Original work published 1932)

Pillai, P. (2012). Cultural directions and origins of everyday decisions. *Integrative Psychological & Behavioral Science*, *46*(2), 235–242. doi:10.1007/s12124-012-9196-9 PMID:22403021

Prochaska, J. O. (1991). Assessing how people change. *Cancer*, *67*(S3), 805–807. doi:10.1002/1097-0142(19910201)67:3+<805::AID-CNCR2820671409>3.0.CO;2-4 PMID:1986849

Prochaska, J. O., DiClemente, C. C., & Norcross, J. C. (1992). In search of how people change: Applications to addictive behaviors. *The American Psychologist*, *47*(9), 1102–1114. doi:10.1037/0003-066X.47.9.1102 PMID:1329589

Raz, J. (1986). *The morality of freedom*. Oxford University Press.

Redfield, P. (2013). *Life in crisis: The ethical journey of doctors without borders*. Berkeley, CA: University of California Press. Retrieved from http://www.jstor.org/stable/10.1525/j.ctt24hsw6

Reinhart, K. (2015a). Religion, violence, and emotion: Modes of religiosity in the neolithic and bronze age of Northern China. *Journal of World Prehistory*, *28*(2), 113–177. doi:10.1007/s10963-015-9086-4

Reinhart, K. (2015b). Ritual feasting and empowerment at Yanshi Shangcheng. *Journal of Anthropological Archaeology*, *39*, 76–109. doi:10.1016/j.jaa.2015.01.001

Rizzolatti, G., & Arbib, M. A. (1998). Language within our grasp. *Trends in Neurosciences*, *21*(5), 188–194. doi:10.1016/S0166-2236(98)01260-0 PMID:9610880

Robbins, J. (2004). *Becoming sinners: Christianity and moral torment in a Papua New Guinea society* (Vol. 4). Berkeley, CA: University of California Press.

Rousseau, J. J. (2002). *The social contract and the first and second discourses* (D. Dunn, Ed.). New Haven, CT: Yale University Press. (Original work published 1755)

Rydstrøm, H. (2003). *Embodying morality: Growing up in rural North Vietnam.* Honolulu, HI: University of Hawaii Press.

Saxonhouse, A. (1992). *The fear of diversity.* Chicago University Press.

Scarr, S. (1993). Biological and cultural diversity: The legacy of Darwin for development. *Child Development, 64*(5), 1333–1353. doi:10.2307/1131538 PMID:8222876

Schooler, C. (1996). Cultural and social-structural explanations of cross-national psychological differences. *Annual Review of Sociology, 22*(1), 323–349. doi:10.1146/annurev.soc.22.1.323

Schwartz, S. H. (1999). A theory of cultural values and some implications for work. *Applied Psychology, 48*(1), 23–47. doi:10.1111/j.1464-0597.1999.tb00047.x

Scott, W. R. (1995). *Institutions and organizations.* Thousand Oaks, CA: Sage.

Sharp, F. (1898). An objective study of some moral judgments. *The American Journal of Psychology, 9*(2), 198–234. doi:10.2307/1411759

Sherman, J. G. (2006). Prenuptial agreements: A new reason to revive an old rule. *Cleveland State Law Review, 53,* 359. Retrieved from http://scholarship.kentlaw.iit.edu/cgi/viewcontent.cgi?article=1561&context=fac_schol

Skyrms, B. (2014). *Evolution of the social contract.* Cambridge, UK: Cambridge University Press. doi:10.1017/CBO9781139924825

Smith, P. B., & Schwartz, S. H. (1997). Values. In J. W. Berry, M. H. Segall, & C. Kagitcibasi (Eds.), Handbook of cross-cultural psychology. Boston, MA: Allyn & Bacon.

Spurgeon, A., Harrington, J. M., & Cooper, C. L. (1997). Health and safety problems associated with long working hours: A review of the current position. *Occupational and Environmental Medicine, 54*(6), 367–375. doi:10.1136/oem.54.6.367 PMID:9245942

Stanovich, K. E., & West, R. F. (1997). Reasoning independently of prior belief and individual differences in actively open-minded thinking. *Journal of Educational Psychology, 89*(2), 342–357. doi:10.1037/0022-0663.89.2.342

Stanovich, K. E., & West, R. F. (2000). Individual differences in reasoning: Implications for the rationality debate? *Behavioral and Brain Sciences, 23*(5), 645–665. doi:10.1017/S0140525X00003435 PMID:11301544

Steinkraus, W. (1980). Socrates, Confucius, and the rectification of names. *Philosophy East & West, 30*(2), 261–264. doi:10.2307/1398850

Suen, H. K., & Yu, L. (2006). Chronic consequences of high-stakes testing? Lessons from the Chinese civil service exam. *Comparative Education Review, 50*(1), 46–65. doi:10.1086/498328

Timmermann, J. (Ed.). (2009). *Kant's groundwork of the metaphysics of morals: A critical guide*. Cambridge, UK: Cambridge University Press. doi:10.1017/CBO9780511770760

Topor, F. S. (2014). A sentence repetition placement test for ESL/EFL learners in Japan. In V. Wang (Ed.), *Handbook of research on education and technology in a changing society* (pp. 971–988)., doi:10.4018/978-1-4666-6046-5.ch073

Tsai, L. L. (2002). Cadres, temple and lineage institutions, and governance in rural China. *China Journal (Canberra, A.C.T.), 48*, 1–27. doi:10.2307/3182439

Tsui, A. S., & Farh, J. L. L. (1997). Where guanxi matters: Relational demography and guanxi in the Chinese context. *Work and Occupations, 24*(1), 56–79. doi:10.1177/0730888497024001005

Turner, J. H. (1997). *The institutional order*. New York, NY: Addison-Wesley.

Uehata, T. (1991). Long working hours and occupational stress-related cardiovascular attacks among middle-aged workers in Japan. *Journal of Human Ergology, 20*(2), 147–153. doi:10.11183/jhe1972.20.147 PMID:1842961

Underhill, A. (2002). *Craft production and social change in Northern China*. New York, NY: Kluwer; doi:10.1007/978-1-4615-0641-6

United Nations. (1999). U*niversal declaration of human rights. First adopted and proclaimed in 1948*. New York, NY: Author. Available at: http://www.un.org/Overview/rights.html

United Nations Educational, Scientific and Cultural Organization. (2005). Universal draft declaration on bioethics and human rights. SHS/ EST/05/CONF.204/3REV. Paris, France: Author.

Vanderburg, W. H. (1995). Preventive engineering: Strategy for dealing with negative social and environmental implications of technology. *Journal of Professional Issues in Engineering Education and Practice, 121*(3), 155–160. doi:10.1061/(ASCE)1052-3928(1995)121:3(155)

Wade, C., & Tavris, C. (1993). *Critical and creative thinking*. New York, NY: Harper Collins.

Washington, M., & Ventresca, M. J. (2004). How organizations change: The role of institutional support mechanisms in the incorporation of higher education visibility strategies, 1874–1995. *Organization Science, 15*(1), 82–97. doi:10.1287/orsc.1030.0057

Weber, M. (1951). *The religion of China: Confucianism and Taoism* (H. H. Gerth, Ed. & Trans.). Retrieved from https://books.google.com/

Whitbeck, C. (1998). *Ethics in engineering practice and research*. New York, NY: Cambridge University Press. doi:10.1017/CBO9780511806193

White, B. J., & Montgomery, B. R. (1980). Corporate codes of conduct. *California Management Review, 23*(2), 80–87. doi:10.2307/41164921

White, H. (2005). The limits to optimism: Australia and the rise of China. *Australian Journal of International Affairs, 59*(4), 469–480. doi:10.1080/10357710500367273

White, H. (2011). Power shift: Rethinking Australia's place in the Asian century. *Australian Journal of International Affairs, 65*(1), 81–93. doi:10.1080/10357718.2011.535603

Wickeri, P. (1989). *Seeking the common ground: Protestant Christianity, the three-self movement, and China's United Front*. New York, NY: Orbis.

Wilson, D. B., Bouffard, L. A., & MacKenzie, D. L. (2005). A quantitative review of structured, group-oriented, cognitive-behavioral programs for offenders. *Criminal Justice and Behavior, 32*(2), 172–204. doi:10.1177/0093854804272889

Wilson, J. Q. (1993). *The moral sense*. New York, NY: Free Press.

Wong, D. B. (1984). *Moral relativity*. Berkeley, CA: University of California Press.

Wong, D. B. (2009). Comparative philosophy: Chinese and Western. In E. N. Zalta (Ed.), *The Stanford encyclopedia of philosophy* (Fall 2011 ed.). Retrieved from http://plato.stanford.edu/archives/fall2011/entries/comparphil-chiwes/

Wood, R. (2010). *Top 10 list of the world's most popular sports*. Retrieved from http://www.topendsports.com/world/lists/popular-sport/fans.htm

Yack, B. (1985). Community and conflict in Aristotle's political philosophy. *The Review of Politics, 47*(1), 92–112. doi:10.1017/S0034670500037761

Yang, F. (2011). *Religion in China: Survival and revival under communist rule*. New York, NY: Oxford University Press. doi:10.1093/acprof:oso/9780199735655.001.0001

Zechmeister, E. B., & Johnson, J. E. (1992). *Critical thinking: A functional approach*. Pacific Grove, CA: Thomson Brooks/Cole.

Zuo, J. (1991). Political religion: The case of the cultural revolution in China. *SA. Sociological Analysis, 52*(1), 99–110. doi:10.2307/3710718

KEY TERMS AND DEFINITIONS

Civilization: The integrated overarching whole within which many cultures exist. Civilization is a complex aggregate of various cultures and societies that may be located in different geographic areas of the world, each of which may not necessarily share the same language. Nonetheless, cultures draw from civilizations many important attributes and features such as approach to knowledge, belief systems, morals and ethics, customs, and social institutions.

Culture: The integrated attributes of a people including their approach to knowledge, belief system, etiquette, food, language, pattern and communication, religion, rites, rituals, and customs. Culture may spread over a wider geographic area. The area may or may not be contiguous. Culture is a subset of civilization.

Eastern Civilization: A civilization characterized by Confucianism, the teachings and philosophy of the Chinese philosopher Confucius (551–479 BCE). Confucian teachings comprising Eastern civilization encompass social stratification, religion, politics, and education. Essential features of Eastern civilization that provide the basis for social order, harmony and collectivism include human relationships, filial piety, and individual obligations.

Instrumental: Something is instrumental when it is used as a means that leads to something else, and end. For example, it is believed that education is instrumental to wealth and happiness.

Intrinsic: The essence, true nature, or basic fundamental element of a thing. For example, learning, memory, and recollection are intrinsic to humans; all humans have the intrinsic attribute to learn, remember, and recall.

Normative: The term normative is an adjective used to modify or describe ethical principles. A normative code of ethics prescribes how individuals ought to behave in terms of right and wrong.

Rituals: A prescribed set of protocols used to perform a religious or other ceremonies.

West Civilization: Civilization based on Judeo-Christian norms, belief systems, traditions, and principles. Western civilization espouses individual differences and adopts an approach to knowledge that is based on empiricism, critical thinking, and self-reflection.

Chapter 10
The Ethical Dilemma of Early Global Childhood Education

F. Sigmund Topor
Keio University, Japan

June C. Hysell
Rowan Cabarrus Community College, USA

ABSTRACT

This chapter investigates ethical dilemmas associated with early childhood education in Confucian heritage countries. It draws on literature in philosophy, psychology, sociology, and anthropology in concluding that sociocultural differences between Eastern and Western civilizations amount to an ethical dilemma, which threatens to prevent a basic epistemology as well as a pedagogy for the education of children in the context of globalization and the information technology revolution. As evidenced by inventions, innovations, developments, and other technological and scientific breakthroughs, Western learners enroll in science and technology courses. It seems as though Eastern learners are duty-bound to fulfill a national or cultural objective, which calls for studies in the science and engineering disciplines at the expense of subjects in the arts, independent of individual desire or competency.

BACKGROUND

This chapter investigates the notion of ethical dilemma associated with early childhood education in Confucian Heritage countries. It draws on literature in philosophy, psychology, sociology, and anthropology in concluding that sociocultural distinctions between Eastern and Western civilizations amount to an ethical dilemma, which

DOI: 10.4018/978-1-5225-2650-6.ch010

threatens to prevent a basic epistemology as well as a pedagogy for the education of children in the context of globalization and the information technology revolution.

Curriculum designs and objectives vary by country and to some extent culture or civilization (Hatano & Inagaki, 1998; Lee, 1998; Stigler & Stevenson, 1992; Tweed & Lehman, 2002). Whereas Confucius and Socrates espoused the importance of knowledge or learning as virtue, Confucius cultures have weaponized learning through its instrumental implementation for socialization and control. Group orientation is seen as a Confucian Heritage cultural attribute, which is contrasted with the individualism of Western culture. Unlike students from Confucian cultures, Western students have not limited their educational objectives to subjects that maximize economic and financial utility. Most of the graduate degrees sought by Asian students are in science and engineering (Tweed & Lehman, 2002). The arts—dance, painting, music, philosophy, and the like—are often less pursued by learners from Confucius heritage countries than by learners from the West.

The social contexts in which learning takes place can and do vary in many ways. Lev Vygotsky was known for his sociocultural theory focusing on cultural development that is immersed in "values, beliefs, customs, and skills of a social group" (Berk, Mann, & Ogan, 2006, p. 24). Vygotsky's group learning has been adapted into group learning of social and academic skills. Gaskins and Labbo (2007) argued that Vygotsky's theory should be applied to early literacy learning through scaffolding of skills for students until they can accomplish them successfully on their own. Through carefully designed play activities, students begin to understand the authentic purpose behind reading and writing skills through a familiar context (Bodrova & Leong, 2006). Similarly, Urie Bronfenbrenner devised a theory of learning through relationships within a larger context of the environment as a series of nested structures, including but also extending beyond the home, school, and neighborhood settings in which children spend everyday lives. Children development is powerfully impacted by each layer of their environment (Berk et al., 2006).

As evidenced by inventions, innovations, developments, and other technological and scientific breakthroughs, Western learners enroll in science and technology courses. The subject of choice is often based on individual prerogative rather than state-sponsored directives as a means of competing with others in distant lands. It seems as though Eastern learners are duty-bound to fulfill a national or cultural objective, which calls for studies in the science and engineering disciplines at the expense of subjects in the arts, independent of individual desire or competency. Although the Confucian edict of sustained socialization of youth through learning and the duty to pass professional as well as academic exams may seem utilitarian, the unethical practice of cheating (Briggs, Workman, & York, 2013; O'Neill & Pfeiffer, 2012) has been a remedial approach by learners that have had particular course of studies forced upon them. By the same token, a high frequency of juvenile delinquency in

Western societies, particularly in the United States, might be mitigated through the implementation of Confucian socialization respecting learning.

In the United Kingdom, curriculum emphasizes literacy, mathematics, understanding the world, expressive arts, and design (U.K. Department of Education, 2014). The definitions of *early numeracy* and *number sense* goes together with development (van de Rijt et al., 2003). Scientific knowledge is an appealing prospect to international organizations, governments, and corporations pursuing an instrumental agenda (Dahlberg & Moss, 2005). In Poland, the curriculum changes the limits of the teaching of theory, the former curriculum, and places more emphasis on the practical and experimental skills of math and science (United Nations Educational, Scientific and Cultural Organization [UNESCO], 2015).

Because learning is typically situated—that is, contextual, no learning occurs in a vacuum. Local cultures face a dilemma when they have to conform both to local epistemology and at the same time implement global standards in response to globalization and the information technology age. A typical example of how globalization and technology influence 21st-century learning has to do with communicative competence, which entails learning a foreign language. Cultural differences (Genc & Bada, 2005; Nisbett, Peng, Choi, & Norenzayan, 2001) make it necessary that second or foreign language learning instruction (McKay, 2003; Scovel, 1978) be in conformity with curriculum objectives in the particular learning environment. Such an arrangement raises ethical questions and poses a dilemma for Confucius heritage countries that promote group epistemology at the expense of individual initiatives and critical thinking (Nisbett et al., 2001). A utilitarian approach to curriculum as well as a Confucian-oriented pedagogy pose considerable dilemmas for systems that espouse the predominance of local cultures while paying lip service to the need for a global curriculum that includes 21st-century educational features such as critical thinking, individual initiatives, and communication competence.

In the United States, the Head Start Program, a popular federal preschool program, was implemented in 1965 as an answer to the War on Poverty in the 1960s. Federal legislation supported this preschool program to give young children a head start in order to close the achievement gap for children entering school. Promoting the goal of school readiness of children is the crucial objective of Head Start (Zill & Resnick, 2006). Head Start is the nation's largest provider of childcare for low-income children. Head Start follows national early childhood education standards that exceed most state and local standards (Dickinson & Sprague, 2003; New, 2003).

In Russia, the Vygotskian approach provides a new perspective to this dilemma: "intentional instruction in preschool and kindergarten should foster prerequisites for academic skills . . . promoting unique preschool foundational competencies and promoting them through play" (Bodrova & Leong, 2006, p. 358). This promotes a systematic play intervention designed to provide play-based scaffolding. In terms of being child centered, play oriented, and cognizant of layers of the wider world, this approach resembles that of Maria Montessori (UNESCO, 2006a).

PARENTS VS. PROFESSIONALS

Early childhood educators need to be cognizant of both local and global educational requirements. Such knowledge is indispensable in the current information age and globalization. Confucius heritage cultures such as Japan, China, Taiwan, Korea, and others have instituted a practice whereby parents have more say and control as to what preschoolers' curriculum and pedagogy ought to be (Wang, Pomerantz, & Chen, 2007). However, the school systems in these countries demand that teachers undergo extensive exams and licensing qualifications in order to become teachers.

An ethical dilemma posed by this arrangement is the fact that although parents in Confucius epistemic cultures may be authoritarian, which has been found to negatively impact developmental outcomes (Eisenberg et al., 2001) albeit they pay the cost of the education of their children and should therefore have a say in what is taught and how it is taught, they may not be authoritative in educational matters (Collins, Madsen, & Susman-Stillman, 2002). Conversely, teachers are professionally trained to implement the educational objectives and goals set by the government in these Confucian-oriented countries. As such, teachers should be in the best position to know what learners need to know in school. Thus, in terms of Western epistemology, there exists a conflict between parental responsibility and educators' authority in the preschool education system in China, Japan, Korea, Taiwan, and other Confucius heritage countries. The information age as well as globalization has led to the imposition of additional requirements (i.e., cultural competence [Leon Siantz & Meleis, 2007] and communicative and ethical competence [Ananiadou & Claro, 2009]), thus contributing to an augmented definition of *education* for learners (Tompkins, Campbell, Green, & Smith, 2014) as well as educators (Darling-Hammond, 2006).

Current technological advances pose a dilemma for civilizations and societies that are still interested in retaining their age-old epistemologies. The balance between local requirements and global demands that accompany intercultural communication, information technology, and globalizations tends to confound local educational administrators as well as teachers in what can be best described as a dilemma. Constructivist learning theorists, including Dewey (1902/2011), Piaget (1964), and Vygotsky (1978), maintain that students build upon connections with prior knowledge. This framework of learning is a process that brings emotional, environmental, and cognitive influences together in a complex learning process.

Constructivists believe that knowledge is gained by learning new information by linking it to prior knowledge (Creswell, 2009; H. Gardner, 2011). A uniquely Confucian epistemology was echoed in Vygotsky's (1978) similar learning theory, which focuses on the social aspects of learning in groups.

In many countries, the only requirements for becoming an early childhood education head teacher are a certificate and some experience. Such low professional standards introduce ethical questions about equal access to quality education. Specialized training in early childhood education or child development can be a great benefit to early childhood code of ethics professionals (UNESCO, 2015). Preschool teachers should also be educated in current research strategies on children's emergent literacy and language development (Osgood, 2006). Early childhood code of ethics programs in Argentina are preschool teachers' responsibility and are overseen by the Federal Council of Culture and Education (UNESCO, 2006b).

Confucius heritage countries face a dilemma as globalization solidifies and expands to virtually all fabrics of society. It poses a dilemma for countries, cultures, or civilizations to insist on retaining and maintaining their internal cultural epistemologies (Joy & Kolb, 2009) while at the same time expect to benefit from external contributions that require different approaches to learning. Eastern cultures continue the importation, amalgamation, and implementation of Western educational theories and practices (Nguyen, Terlouw, & Pilot, 2006; Schulz, 1991) that incorporate individual differences (Brooks, 1995; Burns, 1995; Fink, 2013; Ginsburg & Opper, 1979; Knowles, 1990, 1995; Knowles, Holton, & Swanson, 2014; Mezirow, 1981; Piaget, 1972, 1988; Skinner, 1950). The quasiadoptions of individualistic learning theories that incorporate critical thinking and the Socratic epistemology along with collective or Confucian epistemology that exclude individualistic learning theories and methodologies of teaching (Schulz, 1991) will prove to be a dilemma as local epistemic tradition collides with a global orthodoxy.

Curriculum expectations and directives do not always coincide with cultural beliefs (Bleakley, Brice, & Bligh, 2008; Elliott & Grigorenko, 2007) and expectations that parents and governments want more accomplishments for the children. The key to adequate curriculum implementation is well-trained and experienced teachers that are able to inculcate learners with the appropriate skills and knowledge (U.K. Department of Education, 2014). Teaching teachers well, in order to entrust them with the professional responsibility and power to shape the curriculum, based on solid knowledge and careful child observation, would be an influential formula for honest reform in early childhood education (Hatch & Grieshaber, 2002) as well as alleviate associated ethical dilemmas.

It seems inconceivable, at least from Western epistemic perspectives, that the duty and responsibilities of early childhood education are assigned to parents or family members while forgoing those of professionally training educators. Now that the 21st century has imposed additional requirements for education (Darling-Hammond, 2006; García, 2011; Gay & Howard, 2000), formal education has become prominent and the assignment of childcare duties has taken on new priorities. Amidst these eventualities, industries have emerged that did not exist anywhere more than a century ago. A dilemma for Confucius heritage countries is the need to balance between requirements for the new science- and technology-driven economy and the desire to retain cultural institutions and elements such as filial piety, suppression of individual initiatives and freedoms, justice, and ethnocentrism.

Parents' preference for private schooling typically hinges on assumptions of the provision of optimum utility. As Figure 1 shows, students in private school programs typically score higher than students in other programs score. However, rather than type of school, selection bias resulting from the many advantages that wealthy children enjoy could be the cause of these differences. In fact, mounting evidence show that there are social benefits for shifting from private to public school for early childhood education (Levin, Belfield, Muennig, & Rouse, 2007). The United Kingdom provides longitudinal study evidence, based on a sample of over 3,000 children, that both wealthy and poor children receive great benefits from socialization (Barnett, 1995; Pew Center on the States, 2005).

Figure 1. Estimated marginal means of book and print assessment scores. From What Do They Know When They Get There? The Relationship of Head Start, More at Four/NC Pre-K, Private Preschool Programs and No Preschool Experiences to Kindergarteners' Reading/Literacy Readiness (p. 70), by J. C. Hysell, 2013, available from ProQuest Dissertations and Theses database. (UMI No. 3592597). Copyright 2013 by June C. Hysell. Reprinted with permission.

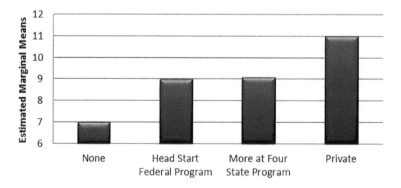

Estimated Marginal Means of Book and Print Assessment Scores

In South Korea, where private schools are seen as a path to better jobs and opportunities (Nambissan, 2012; UNESCO, 2015), the need for communicative competence in English attracts parents to private schools. In Japan, approximately 60% of all preschools are private. Japanese schools receive fewer public funds and must rely primarily on tuition and fees from parents (Ishikida, 2005). The public–private gap is likely attributable to the fact that students from wealthier and more advantaged backgrounds typically attend private schools (UNESCO, 2015). Quality preschools, however, are comparatively more costly (Bremberg, 2009; Ishikida, 2005). Cost is a major issue at the preprimary level, with some governments charging fees. China has an experimental program that provides tuition waivers and cash transfers for attendance (UNESCO, 2015). In the United Kingdom, many poor children are being left behind by low quality and low-end private preprimary facilities. Programs serving more affluent neighborhoods are generally equipped with better facilities and curriculum. In both Eastern and Western societies, schools that are available for parents to freely choose do not typically follow the utilitarian principle of the best utility. This is the case in China, New Zealand, Sweden, and the United States (UNESCO, 2015).

The ontologically sound solution that would avoid such dilemmas would involve early enrollment of children in school. Indeed, in some cases, commencing education at an earlier age could reduce the gap in school readiness, associated with student background, and thus make more life opportunities available to more children—a reference to Rawls's (1999) *veil of ignorance* thought experiment as justification. Traditional educational programs typically begin around age 5 and continue into adolescence, but such a model assumes that all 5-year-olds are similarly prepared for formal schooling. The variation in skills and knowledge at age 5 is substantial, even within countries, and highly correlated with parents' socioeconomic status (Janus & Duku, 2007; Lapointe, Ford, & Zumbo, 2007). Such variation leads to cohorts, and even classrooms, that are heterogeneous in terms of student abilities and behaviors, making instruction difficult and setting some students on trajectories of educational failure.

Although an efficiency dimension to the provision of early childhood education is evident, there is also an ethical dimension present. The financial means and associated resources needed for education are not always available to everyone as few are chosen from the many that call. Utilitarianism allows for some to be left behind as long as they are fewer than those who benefit. Amidst the burgeoning economic disparities within and among countries, the deprivation of so many people of the world cannot be a good example of utilitarian ethics as far as the provision of the ultimate utility in education is concerned. Maintaining the current practice amounts to the abandonment of the responsibilities of societies and nations to ensure harmony and understanding among all peoples of the world. Thus, shame and guilt should result by abdicating the duty of the state to provide adequate education of its citizens, specifically children. Intercultural education that allows individuals to conduct intercultural communication is a good example of adequate education in a globalized world. One does not have to relinquish local culture in order to participate in global affairs. Quality education is a classic example whereby only few wealthy people benefit.

Some countries have embarked upon programs that make private educational programs public. Adding to more than 4,000 existing private kindergartens, Jordan has established an excess of 500 public kindergartens as a part of the 2003 Education Reform for the Knowledge Economy (UNESCO, 2015). In Argentina, the autonomous city of Buenos Aires has provided public early education establishments. In addition, the government provides grants to many private centers for teacher salaries (UNESCO, 2006b). In 2004, the consolidated public expenditure for public education in Argentina was 3.8% and an estimated expenditure for private education was 1.1% (UNESCO, 2006b). Preschool/preprimary programs grew dramatically around the world between 1999 and 2012. Preschool/preprimary enrollment also globally increased during this period, significantly in some countries (see Figure 2).

Figure 2. Preprimary education systems and enrollment levels expanded rapidly in some countries (UNESCO, 2016)

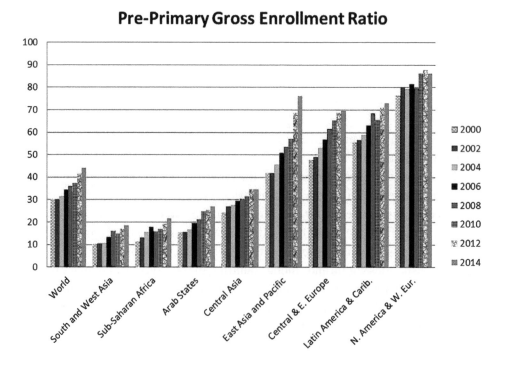

CONSEQUENCES OF UTILITARIAN PITFALLS

Although it may be tempting to argue in favor of a utilitarian approach to curriculum design and development, including the pedagogical implementation of educational objectives, utilitarianism is fraught with pitfalls and drawbacks.

Regulations are one means of leveling the playing field of education for everyone. Still, most often, government regulations do little to regulate private schools. In India, nongovernment organizations are established and placed under a combination of management orthodoxies, including private sole proprietorships, partnerships, corporations, and religious organizations (Ohara, 2013).

Albeit its pitfalls and drawbacks (William, 1973), utilitarianism affirms the collective good and welfare, taking into account the greatest amount of good benefiting the greatest number of people (Mill, 1861). Given the reality of globalization, which subjugates local curriculum with one that is global, it would seem difficult to live with the consequence of leaving behind a global epistemology in favor of one that is solely localized. Local curriculum would exclude communicative competence in the global lingua franca, English, in favor of local vernaculars.

This chapter discusses the ethics of education, specifically early childhood education with focus on the economic and cultural ramifications. The utility of education is maximized when children begin education early and their individual potentials are explored and enhanced through the application of appropriate educational theories. How the theories are delivered in terms of pedagogy and who does the delivery are also important ethical considerations. Professionally trained educators as well as educational administrators are all important pieces of an education system (Bath, 2013). Assuming society has a duty, in Kantian terms, and the obligation to educate its young, it is logical that society should do so in a utilitarian manner for the benefit of everyone in the long run. To ensure that all children are introduced to a foundation of knowledge and behaviors that will serve them in primary school and beyond, extending universal education from traditional grades to earlier ages promises be a necessary step. The next section develops the question of ethical justifications for early childhood education before getting to the primary objective, which is to compare the various ways in which nations currently provide, or fail to provide, such services to better understand the complexity of moving toward policies of universal early childhood education.

Ethical Lenses

Two approaches to applied ethics lend themselves well to a discussion of early childhood education and the question of making it universal. One approach is the Rawlsian tradition that can be traced to Immanuel Kant's categorical imperative

(Paton, 1971). This perspective recognizes that, from birth, individuals do not have equal opportunities and that it would be justifiable for society to provide early childhood education if such services would be universally desirable.

Given the complexity of the modern world, it is an easy step to see a utilitarian rationale for early childhood education, provided that its provision does not infringe too much on children's, parents', and taxpayers' freedoms. Identifying that balancing point requires good research into what education programs, including those in early childhood, would provide the greatest possible outcomes.

In both of these philosophical approaches, early childhood education is justifiable only if it is effective in improving educational outcomes. In Postman's (1995) words, "without a purpose, schools are houses of detention, not attention" (p. 7). Thus, early childhood education is not simply a question of whether to have it. The quality of the education must be established as well, and that can only be done if four questions are addressed: (a) When should formal education begin? (b) should it focus on meeting standards or following the child? (c) what makes an effective teacher? and (d) are these programs better provided through public or private resources? These questions are explored in the rest of this chapter.

The need to remain traditional vs. the requirement to meet global educational standards has proven enigmatic. The proper early childhood curriculum and pedagogy remains a controversial subject.

Nations and civilizations are almost always consistently involved in the improvement of their lot, including human capital, a feat that often seems competitive and engenders disagreements. Often, such disagreements are based on traditional values that inculcate antipathy and cultural bias, compared with theory-driven, empirically verified methodologies and pedagogies that espouse and esteem individualism (McMullen, 1998, 2001). In China, traditional teaching, which is based on Confucian traditions, has come into conflict with new discoveries about developmentally appropriate practices (McMullen et al., 2005). In the United States, the National Association for the Education of Young Children has a widely published policy statement on developmentally appropriate practices that some people criticize for implying that one and only one appropriate philosophy exists on early childhood education and childcare (McMullen et al., 2005).

Interest in educational reforms is often motivated by an emphasis on utilitarian principles. Maximizing students' academic achievement at all grade levels was a goal of primary importance to U.S. education policymakers in the 1980s. Perhaps no other documentation since then has illustrated this feeling more than *A Nation at Risk* (D. P. Gardner, 1983). Also, great pressure is caused by fears of children not being ready to start formal schooling and the difficulties they may face later on in school (Bodrova, 2008; Zigler & Bishop-Josef, 2006). Early childhood policymakers are constantly engaged in a back-and-forth discussion (Hatch, 2002).

The best educational opportunities for young children to reach their potentials are not created by early, accelerated instruction, the main effect of which is shortening childhood. Zaporozhets (1986) found that this type of instruction forces students into more formal educational settings before they are developmentally ready to do so (Bodrova & Leong, 2006). David Elkind, researcher of cognitive development, "argued that young children were being 'miseducated' in settings where they were experiencing stress from academic pressure for no apparent benefit" (Hatch, 2002, p. 230).

Once policymakers believe they have the appropriate age of schooling and curricular orientation, they often want to verify its success. "The need to regulate and control stems from the discursive construct of a 'crisis in education'" (Osgood, 2006, p. 6) that came from arguments such as those found in D. P. Gardner's 1983 *A Nation at Risk*. The logic of the accountability movement is based on the premise that children should be assessed on their performance in relation to a set of predetermined standards. All too often, a lack of clarity about responsibilities and accountability occurs that stems from systemic problems with accountability measures (Osgood, 2006). Educational autonomy requires a transfer in the role of school supervision from exercising administrative control to supporting educators while also holding them to standards (De Grauwe, 2007). Throughout education globally, there are proposals for a common core of skills and knowledge for children's workforce, a common assessment framework (Osgood, 2006). Although accountability is useful for guiding policy decisions, it could lead to more finger-pointing than educating as secondary teachers blame elementary teachers and elementary teachers blame early childhood teachers. The teaching profession is not accustomed to playing the blame game. Common values and beliefs are generally subsumed under cultural etiquettes, including religious beliefs that are grounded in common experiences and philosophies, which are typically adopted by professional organizations and provide a sense of professional identity (Feeney, 2010).

Knowledge of how to best educate children is of little use if neither parents nor teachers and bureaucrats would allow professionalism to take its course. A new agency model offers a framework to better understand the positioning of early childhood care and education practitioners in policy reform and reflect on the highly problematic and politicized construction of professionalism that results from the accountability model of education policy. Developing a code helps to understand professional responsibilities, find wise resolutions, and prioritize professional obligations within these ethical dilemmas (Feeney, 2010). Thus, core learning priorities have been developed in Argentina (UNESCO, 2006b) and Australia has adopted an early childhood code of ethics (Kennedy, 2009). Education professionals can strengthen the community of early childhood educators by paying attention to professional ethics and remembering to keep moral compasses pointed in the direction of achieving what is best for all young children and families (Feeney, 2010).

At the transition from the early childhood settings of preschool and daycare to the formal kindergarten classroom, play-based to academic-based learning can be measured by formal and informal assessments at the beginning of the kindergarten year (Chapman, 2010; New, 2003). Preschool experiences build knowledge that is proven to assist children through their first 4 formative educational years (H. Gardner, 2011; Hysell, 2013; New, 2003; Piaget, 1964; Vygotsky, 1978). Studies involving India's early childhood code of ethics have shown that children who receive a preschool education are more likely to continue and succeed in their elementary education compared to those who do not attend preschool (Ohara, 2013).

In 2005, Philippine President Gloria Macapagal-Arroyos asked Congress to add a year of education to extend into the preprimary age group. The Philippine national preschool education program aims to ensure that all 5-year-olds have access to quality preschool education programs (UNESCO, 2006a). The Bolsa Familia Program in Brazil ensures early access for lower income children. The program also makes kindergarten accessible to children from lower income families (Bullrich & Zinny, 2011).

The more countries expand their preprimary education programs, the more can be learned and the more is needed to be learned about how best to educate young children. More data become available every day, and researchers need to capitalize on this growth to answer important questions about when to put children into formal schooling. As a result, this will ensure that children have ample opportunities to realize and achieve justice, equality, and the utility of adequate education.

Mill (2001/1859) argued that government has a role to play in educating children when their parents would not. In a private market for education, wealthier families are enrolled in better networked private schools and receive better benefits. Where they exist, public preprimary schools increasingly serve the most disadvantaged populations of families and children. This affects the quality of education (Fiske & Ladd, 2000; Hsieh & Urquiola, 2006; UNESCO, 2015).

FUTURE STUDIES

Future studies should seek to narrow the gap between Eastern and Western ethics and epistemologies by investigating the extent to which each civilization ontologically combines individualism and communalism. Specifically, future studies should explore the role of individualism in the creation of new knowledge and the extent to which communalism inhabits individual initiative and creativity.

CONCLUSION

Ethically speaking, Kant was deontologically oriented. For him, duties and obligations were paramount. Because ethical behavior entails living up to one's duties and obligations, Kant believed that humans ought to first determine the obligations that nature allotted them. According to Kant's theory of category imperatives, certain behaviors are moral and ethical while others are not. It is imperative that humans perform those acts that are good (e.g., keeping a promise) and refrain from performing acts that are bad (e.g., lying.).

As the human race progresses through time and space in this one world, it is imperative that cultural differences cease to assign different interpretations for similar actions or activities, thereby ensuring confusion and disharmony. The harmony that is held so dear in Confucianism is in nowise ethically restricted to Eastern civilizations; harmony is also a Western ethical principle. Likewise, the speed with which Confucius heritage cultures have implemented science and technology exemplifies appreciation for Western-oriented rationality and epistemology. The incentive for a Kantian categorical imperative—a universal ethical epistemology across cultures and civilizations—outweighs any national interest when considering all of humanity. Technology, as exemplified by the Internet, verifies the Kant was right in his assertion that good and bad do not change with geographic, political, cultural, and national orientations. Computers installed and operational on one continent can be accessed and operated by people on other continents. Although rationality may vary according to cultures and civilizations, the facts that education reveals are invariable. Ontological truth should therefore form the basis of the Kantian categorical imperative across all cultures and civilizations worldwide.

REFERENCES

Ananiadou, K., & Claro, M. (2009). *21st century skills and competences for new millennium learners in OECD countries.* OECD Education Working Papers, No. 41. Paris, France: OECD. Retrieved from 10.1787/218525261154

Barnett, W. (1995). Long-term effects of early childhood programs on cognitive and school outcomes. *The Future of Children*, *5*(3), 25–50. doi:10.2307/1602366

Bath, C. (2013). Conceptualising listening to young children as an ethic of care in early childhood education and care. *Children & Society*, *27*(5), 361–371. doi:10.1111/j.1099-0860.2011.00407.x

Berk, L. E., Mann, T. D., & Ogan, A. T. (2006). Make-believe play: Wellspring for development of self-regulation. In D. G. Singer, R. M. Golinkoff, & K. A. Hirsh-Pasek (Eds.), *Play= learning: How play motivates and enhances children's cognitive and social-emotional growth* (pp. 74–100). New York, NY: Oxford University Press. doi:10.1093/acprof:oso/9780195304381.003.0005

Bleakley, A., Brice, J., & Bligh, J. (2008). Thinking the post-colonial in medical education. *Medical Education*, *42*(3), 266–270. doi:10.1111/j.1365-2923.2007.02991.x PMID:18275413

Bodrova, E. (2008). Make-believe play versus academic skills: A Vygotskian approach to today's dilemma of early childhood education. *European Early Childhood Research Journal*, *16*(3), 357–369. doi:10.1080/13502930802291777

Bodrova, E., & Leong, D. J. (2006). Vygotskian perspectives on teaching and learning early literacy. In S. B. Neuman & D. K. Dickinson (Eds.), *Handbook of early literacy research* (Vol. 2, pp. 243–256). New York, NY: Guilford.

Bremberg, S. (2009). A perfect 10: Why Sweden comes out on top in early child development programming. *Pediatrics & Child Health*, *14*(10), 677–680. Retrieved from https://www.ncbi.nlm.nih.gov/pmc/articles/PMC2807813/pdf/pch14677.pdf

Briggs, K., Workman, J. P., & York, A. S. (2013). Collaborating to cheat: A game theoretic exploration of academic dishonesty in teams. *Academy of Management Learning & Education*, *12*(1), 4–17. doi:10.5465/amle.2011.0140

Brooks, J. (1995). *Training and development competence: A practical guide*. London: Kogan Page.

Bullrich, E., & Zinny, G. S. (2011). Argentina's new national goal. *Council of the Americas Quarterly*, *5*(4), 34.

Burns, R. (1995). *The adult learner at work*. Sydney, Australia: Business and Professional.

Chapman, A. M. (2010). *Examining the effects of pre-kindergarten enrollment on kindergarten reading readiness* (Doctoral dissertation). Tennessee State University, Nashville, TN.

Collins, W. A., Madsen, S. D., & Susman-Stillman, A. (2002). Parenting during middle childhood. In M. H. Bornstein (Ed.), *Children and parenting*: Handbook of parenting. Mahwah, NJ: Erlbaum.

Creswell, J. W. (2009). *Research design: Qualitative, quantitative, and mixed methods approaches*. Thousand Oaks, CA: Sage.

Dahlberg, G., & Moss, P. (2005). *Ethics and politics in early childhood education.* New York, NY: Routledge. doi:10.4324/9780203463529

Darling-Hammond, L. (2006). Constructing 21st-century teacher education. *Journal of Teacher Education, 57*(3), 300–314. doi:10.1177/0022487105285962

De Grauwe, A. (2007). Transforming school supervision into a tool for quality improvement. *International Review of Education, 53*(5/6), 709–714. doi:10.1007/s11159-007-9057-9

Dewey, J. (2011). *The child and the curriculum.* University of Chicago Press. (Original work published 1902)

Dickinson, D. K., & Sprague, K. E. (2003). *From low-income families. In Handbook of early literacy research.* New York, NY: Guilford.

Eisenberg, N., Gershoff, E. T., Fabes, R. A., Shepard, S. A., Cumberland, A. J., Losoya, S. H., & Murphy, B. C. et al. (2001). Mothers' emotional expressivity and children's behavior problems and social competence: Mediation through children's regulation. *Developmental Psychology, 37*(4), 475–490. doi:10.1037/0012-1649.37.4.475 PMID:11444484

Elliott, J., & Grigorenko, E. L. (2007). Editorial: Are Western educational theories and practices truly universal? *Comparative Education, 43*(1), 1–4. doi:10.1080/03050060601160929

Feeney, S. (2010). Ethics today in early care and education: Review, reflection, and the future. *Young Children, 65*(2), 72–77. Retrieved from ERIC database. (EJ898695)

Fink, L. D. (2013). *Creating significant learning experiences: An integrated approach to designing college courses.* San Francisco, CA: Wiley.

Fiske, E. B., & Ladd, H. F. (2000). *When schools compete: A cautionary tale.* Washington, DC: Brookings. 10.1080/02680930110041410

García, O. (2011). *Bilingual education in the 21st century: A global perspective.* West Sussex, UK: Wiley. doi:10.1080/08878730009555246

Gardner, D. P. (1983). *A nation at risk.* Washington, DC: The National Commission on Excellence in Education, U.S. Department of Education. Retrieved from http://files.eric.ed.gov/fulltext/ED226006.pdf

Gardner, H. (2011). *Frames of mind: The theory of multiple intelligences.* New York, NY: Basic.

Gaskins, I. W., & Labbo, L. D. (2007). Diverse perspectives on helping young children build important foundational language and print skills. *Reading Research Quarterly, 42*(3), 438–451. doi:10.1598/RRQ.42.3.10

Gay, G., & Howard, T. C. (2000). Multicultural teacher education for the 21st century. *Teacher Educator, 36*(1), 1–16. doi:10.1080/08878730009555246

Genc, B., & Bada, E. (2005). Culture in language learning and teaching. *The Reading Matrix, 5*(1). Retrieved from http://www.readingmatrix.com/articles/genc_bada/article.pdf

Ginsburg, H., & Opper, S. (1979). *Piaget's theory of intellectual development* (2nd ed.). Englewood Cliffs, NJ: Prentice Hall.

Hatch, J. A. (2002). Accountability shovedown: Resisting the standards movement in early childhood education. *Phi Delta Kappan, 83*(6), 457–462. doi:10.1177/003172170208300611

Hatch, J. A., & Grieshaber, S. (2002). Child observation and accountability in early childhood education: Perspective from Australia and the United states. *Early Childhood Education Journal, 29*(4), 227–231. doi:10.1023/A:1015177406713

Hsieh, C., & Urquiola, M. (2006). The effects of generalized school choice on achievement and stratification: Evidence from Chile's voucher program. *Journal of Public Economics, 90*(8-9), 1477–1503. doi:10.1016/j.jpubeco.2005.11.002

Hysell, J. C. (2013). *What do they know when they get there? The relationship of Head Start, More at Four/NC pre-K, private preschool programs and no preschool experiences to kindergarteners' reading/literacy readiness* (Doctoral dissertation). Available from ProQuest Dissertations and Theses database. (UMI No. 3592597)

Ishikida, M. Y. (2005). *Japanese education in the 21st century*. Tokyo, Japan: Center for U.S.-Japan Comparative Social Studies.

Janus, M., & Duku, E. (2007). The school entry gap: Socioeconomic, family, and health factors associated with children's school readiness to learn. *Early Education and Development, 18*(3), 375–403. doi:10.1080/10409280701610796a

Joy, S., & Kolb, D. A. (2009). Are there cultural differences in learning style? *International Journal of Intercultural Relations, 33*(1), 69–85. .11.00210.1016/j.ijintrel.2008

Kennedy, A. (2009). Ethics: A part of everyday practice in child care. *Putting Children First, 29*, 9–11. Retrieved from http://ncac.acecqa.gov.au/educator-resources/pcf-articles/Ethics_a_part%20_of_everyday_practice_Mar09.pdf

Knowles, M. S. (1990). *The adult learner: A neglected species* (4th ed.). Houston, TX: Gulf.

Knowles, M. S. (1995). Designs for adult learning: Practical resources, exercises, and course outlines from the father of adult learning. Alexandria, VA: American Society for Training and Development (ASTD).

Knowles, M. S., Holton, E. F. III, & Swanson, R. A. (2014). *The adult learner: The definitive classic in adult education and human resource development.* London: Routledge.

Lapointe, V. R., Ford, L., & Zumbo, B. D. (2007). Examining the relationship between neighborhood environment and school readiness for kindergarten children. *Early Education and Development, 18*(3), 473–495. doi:10.1080/10409280701610846

Lee, C.-Y. (1998). English for nursing purposes: A needs assessment for professional-oriented curriculum design. *Academic Journal of Kang-Ning, 1*(1), 55–72. Retrieved from http://daa.ukn.edu.tw/ezfiles/6/1006/img/210/4.pdf

Leon Siantz, M. L. D., & Meleis, A. I. (2007). Integrating cultural competence into nursing education and practice: 21st century action steps. *Journal of Transcultural Nursing, 18*(Suppl. 1), 86S–90S. doi:10.1177/1043659606296465 PMID:17357259

Levin, H., Belfield, C., Muennig, P., & Rouse, C. (2007). *The costs and benefits of an excellent education for all of America's children* (Vol. 9). New York, NY: Teachers College.

McKay, S. L. (2003). Toward an appropriate EIL pedagogy: Re-examining common ELT assumptions. *International Journal of Applied Linguistics, 13*(1), 1–22. doi:10.1111/1473-4192.00035

McMullen, M., Elicker, J., Wang, J., Erdiller, A., Lee, S., Lin, C., & Sun, P. (2005). Comparing beliefs about appropriate practice among early childhood education and care professionals from U.S., China, Taiwan, Korea and Turkey. *Early Childhood Quarterly, 20*(4), 451–464. doi:10.1016/j.ecresq.2005.10.005

McMullen, M. B. (1998). The beliefs and practices of early childhood educators in the U.S.: Does specialized preparation make a difference in adoptive of best practices? *International Journal of Early Childhood Education, 3*, 3–29. Retrieved from http://210.101.116.28/W_files/kiss5/29200214_pv.pdf

McMullen, M. B. (2001). Distinct in beliefs/united in concerns: Listening to strongly DAP and strongly traditional k-primary teachers. *Journal of Early Childhood Teacher Education, 22*(3), 123–133. doi:10.1080/1090102010220301

Mezirow, J. (1981). A critical theory of adult learning and education. *Adult Education*, *32*(1), 3–24. doi:10.1177/074171368103200101

Mill, J. S. (1861). *Utilitarianism* (R. Crisp, Ed.). Oxford, UK: Oxford University Press.

Mill, J. S. (2001). *On liberty*. Kitchener, Canada: Batoche. Retrieved from http://socserv.mcmaster.ca/econ/ugcm/3ll3/mill/liberty.pdf (Original work published 1859)

Nambissan, G. B. (2012). Private schools for the poor: Business as usual? *Economic and Political Weekly*, *47*(41), 51–58. Retrieved from http://www.epw.in/journal/2012/41/special-articles/private-schools-poor.html

New, R. (2003). Handbook of early literacy research. In S. B. Neuman & D. K. Dickinson (Eds.), *Early literacy and developmentally appropriate practice: Rethinking the paradigm* (Vol. 1, pp. 245–262). New York, NY: Guilford.

Nguyen, P. M., Terlouw, C., & Pilot, A. (2006). Culturally appropriate pedagogy: The case of group learning in a Confucian Heritage culture context. *Intercultural Education*, *17*(1), 1–19. doi:10.1080/14675980500502172

Nisbett, R. E., Peng, K., Choi, I., & Norenzayan, A. (2001). Culture and systems of thought-holistic versus analytic cognition. *Psychological Review*, *108*(2), 291–310. doi:10.1037/0033-295X.108.2.291 PMID:11381831

O'Neill, H. M., & Pfeiffer, C. A. (2012). The impact of honour codes and perceptions of cheating on academic cheating behaviours, especially for MBA bound undergraduates. *Accounting Education*, *21*(3), 231–245. doi:10.1080/09639284.2011.590012

Ohara, Y. (2013). *Early childhood care and education in India: ECED around the world*. Tokyo, Japan: Waseda University.

Osgood, J. (2006). Deconstructing professionalism in early childhood education: Resisting the regulatory gaze. *Contemporary Issues in Early Childhood*, *7*(1), 5–14. doi:10.2304/ciec.2006.7.1.5

Paton, H. J. (1971). *The categorical imperative: A study in Kant's moral philosophy* (Vol. 1023). Philadelphia: University of Pennsylvania Press.

Pew Center on the States. (2005). *Pre-K now*. Washington, DC: Author.

Piaget, J. (1964). Part I: Cognitive development in children: Piaget development and learning. *Journal of Research in Science Teaching, 2*, 176–186. Retrieved from 10.1002/tea.3360020306

Piaget, J. (1972). *The principles of genetic epistemology* (W. Mays, Trans.). New York, NY: Basic. (Original work published 1970)

Piaget, J. (1988). *Structuralism* (C. Maschler, Trans.). New York, NY: Harper & Row. (Original work published 1970)

Postman, N. (1995). *The end of education*. New York, NY: Vintage.

Rawls, J. (1999). *A theory of justice*. Cambridge, MA: Harvard University Press.

Schulz, R. A. (1991). Second language acquisition theories and teaching practice: How do they fit? *Modern Language Journal*, *75*(1), 17–26. doi:10.1111/j.1540-4781.1991.tb01078.x

Scovel, T. (1978). The effect of affect on foreign language learning: A review of the anxiety research. *Language Learning*, *28*(1), 129–142. doi:10.1111/j.1467-1770.1978.tb00309.x

Skinner, B. F. (1950). Are theories of learning necessary? *Psychological Review*, *57*(4), 193–216. doi:10.1037/h0054367 PMID:15440996

Stigler, J. W., & Stevenson, H. W. (1992). The learning gap: Why our schools are failing and what we can learn from Japanese and Chinese education. New York, NY: Summit.

Tompkins, G., Campbell, R., Green, D., & Smith, C. (2014). *Literacy for the 21st century: A balanced approach*. Melbourne, Australia: Pearson.

Tweed, R. G., & Lehman, D. R. (2002). Learning considered within a cultural context: Confucian and Socratic approaches. *The American Psychologist*, *57*(2), 89–99. doi:10.1037/0003-066X.57.2.89 PMID:11899565

U.K. Department of Education. (2014). *Statutory framework for the early years foundation stage: Setting the standards for learning, development and care for children from birth to five*. London: Author.

United Nations Educational, Scientific and Cultural Organization (UNESCO). (2006a). *EFA global monitoring report 2006: Literacy for life*. Paris, France: Author.

United Nations Educational, Scientific and Cultural Organization (UNESCO). (2006b). *Strong foundations: Early childhood care and education: Argentina: Early childhood care and education (EECE) programmes. Education for All Global Monitoring Report 2007*. Geneva, Switzerland: Author.

United Nations Educational, Scientific and Cultural Organization (UNESCO). (2015). *EFA global monitoring report 2015: Education for all 2000–2015: Achievements and challenges*. Paris, France: Author.

United Nations Educational, Scientific and Cultural Organization (UNESCO). (2016). *Institute for Statistics.* Retrieved from http://data.uis.uesco.org

van de Rijt, B., Godfrey, R., Augrey, C., Van Luit, J. E., Hasemann, K., Tancig, S., & Tzouriadou, M. et al. (2003). The development of early numeracy in Europe. *Journal of Early Childhood Research, 1*(2), 155–180. doi:10.1177/1476718X030012002

Vygotsky, L. S. (1978). *Mind in society: The development of the higher psychological processes.* Cambridge, MA: Harvard University Press.

Wang, Q., Pomerantz, E. M., & Chen, H. (2007). The role of parents' control in early adolescents' psychological functioning: A longitudinal investigation in the United States and China. *Child Development, 78*(5), 1592–1610. doi:10.1111/j.1467-8624.2007.01085.x PMID:17883450

Williams, B. (1973). A critique of utilitarianism. In G. Sher (Ed.), *Ethics-Essential readings in moral theory* (pp. 253–261). Cambridge, UK: Routledge.

Zaporozhets, A. (1986). *Izbrannye psychologicheskie trudy* [Selected works]. Moscow, Russia: Pedagogika.

Zigler, E. F., & Bishop-Josef, S. J. (2006). The cognitive child versus the whole child: Lessons from forty years of head start. In D. G. Singer, R. M. Golinkoff, & K. A. Hirsh-Pasek (Eds.), *Play = learning: How play motivates and enhances cognitive and social-emotional growth* (pp. 15–35). New York, NY: Oxford University Press. doi:10.1093/acprof:oso/9780195304381.003.0002

Zill, N., & Resnick, G. (2006). Handbook of early literacy research. In S. B. Neuman & D. K. Dickinson (Eds.), *Emergent literacy of low-income children in head start: Relationships with child and family characteristics, program factors, and classroom quality* (Vol. 2, pp. 243–256). New York, NY: Guilford.

KEY TERMS AND DEFINITIONS

Civilization: An advanced stage of human social development and organization that encompasses a society, culture, and a way of life in a particular area or region.

Confucian Cultures: Cultures of East Asian countries that have adopted the teachings of Chinese philosopher Confucius (551–479 B.C.E.). Confucian cultures are impregnated with philosophical, social, and religious principles of Confucius known as *Confucianism.*

Culture: Collectively regarded manifestations of human intelligent attainment that include the beliefs, language, customs, and arts of a particular society, group of people, or time period.

Curriculum (plural Curricula): Often used to describe guidelines that apply to goals, objectives, or plans of methods, materials, and assessments that are essential for effective learning. The four basic components of curriculum are goals (the expectations/benchmarks for teaching and learning involving a sequence of skills), methods (specific instructional methods to be used by the teacher), materials (tools and media used for teaching and learning), and assessment (the reasons and methods of measuring student progress). These guidelines generally apply to general education, in which the design of the components meets the students' educational needs across differing classrooms within a school system.

Ethical Dilemma: Confusion regarding the right course of action or approach to take in solving a problem or implementing a given course of action that calls into question several conflicting moral and ethical principles.

Rawlsian: Pertaining to a theory of political philosophy and ethics developed by John Rawls that states that social institutions should function on the basis of justice that ensures the wellbeing of all peoples. Rawlsism attempts to solve problems by advocating egalitarian principles that ensure equal rights and liberties.

Utilitarianism: An ethical philosophy that states that happiness that accrues to the greatest number of people is considered the greatest utility. This philosophy portends that an action is morally right if its consequences lead to happiness, pleasure, or fulfillment and wrong if it leads to unhappiness or pain.

Weaponize: To effectuate a concept and make it practical.

Related References

To continue our tradition of advancing academic research, we have compiled a list of recommended IGI Global readings. These references will provide additional information and guidance to further enrich your knowledge and assist you with your own research and future publications.

Adeyemo, O. (2013). The nationwide health information network: A biometric approach to prevent medical identity theft. In *User-driven healthcare: Concepts, methodologies, tools, and applications* (pp. 1636–1649). Hershey, PA: IGI Global. doi:10.4018/978-1-4666-2770-3.ch081

Adler, M., & Henman, P. (2009). Justice beyond the courts: The implications of computerisation for procedural justice in social security. In A. Martínez & P. Abat (Eds.), *E-justice: Using information communication technologies in the court system* (pp. 65–86). Hershey, PA: IGI Global. doi:10.4018/978-1-59904-998-4.ch005

Aflalo, E., & Gabay, E. (2013). An information system for coping with student dropout. In L. Tomei (Ed.), *Learning tools and teaching approaches through ICT advancements* (pp. 176–187). Hershey, PA: IGI Global. doi:10.4018/978-1-4666-2017-9.ch016

Ahmed, M. A., Janssen, M., & van den Hoven, J. (2012). Value sensitive transfer (VST) of systems among countries: Towards a framework. *International Journal of Electronic Government Research*, 8(1), 26–42. doi:10.4018/jegr.2012010102

Aikins, S. K. (2008). Issues and trends in internet-based citizen participation. In G. Garson & M. Khosrow-Pour (Eds.), *Handbook of research on public information technology* (pp. 31–40). Hershey, PA: IGI Global. doi:10.4018/978-1-59904-857-4.ch004

Aikins, S. K. (2009). A comparative study of municipal adoption of internet-based citizen participation. In C. Reddick (Ed.), *Handbook of research on strategies for local e-government adoption and implementation: Comparative studies* (pp. 206–230). Hershey, PA: IGI Global. doi:10.4018/978-1-60566-282-4.ch011

Aikins, S. K. (2012). Improving e-government project management: Best practices and critical success factors. In *Digital democracy: Concepts, methodologies, tools, and applications* (pp. 1314–1332). Hershey, PA: IGI Global. doi:10.4018/978-1-4666-1740-7.ch065

Akabawi, M. S. (2011). Ghabbour group ERP deployment: Learning from past technology failures. In E. Business Research and Case Center (Ed.), Cases on business and management in the MENA region: New trends and opportunities (pp. 177-203). Hershey, PA: IGI Global. doi:10.4018/978-1-60960-583-4.ch012

Akabawi, M. S. (2013). Ghabbour group ERP deployment: Learning from past technology failures. In *Industrial engineering: Concepts, methodologies, tools, and applications* (pp. 933–958). Hershey, PA: IGI Global. doi:10.4018/978-1-4666-1945-6.ch051

Akbulut, A. Y., & Motwani, J. (2008). Integration and information sharing in e-government. In G. Putnik & M. Cruz-Cunha (Eds.), *Encyclopedia of networked and virtual organizations* (pp. 729–734). Hershey, PA: IGI Global. doi:10.4018/978-1-59904-885-7.ch096

Akers, E. J. (2008). Technology diffusion in public administration. In G. Garson & M. Khosrow-Pour (Eds.), *Handbook of research on public information technology* (pp. 339–348). Hershey, PA: IGI Global. doi:10.4018/978-1-59904-857-4.ch033

Al-Shafi, S. (2008). Free wireless internet park services: An investigation of technology adoption in Qatar from a citizens' perspective. *Journal of Cases on Information Technology*, *10*(3), 21–34. doi:10.4018/jcit.2008070103

Al-Shafi, S., & Weerakkody, V. (2009). Implementing free wi-fi in public parks: An empirical study in Qatar. *International Journal of Electronic Government Research*, *5*(3), 21–35. doi:10.4018/jegr.2009070102

Aladwani, A. M. (2002). Organizational actions, computer attitudes and end-user satisfaction in public organizations: An empirical study. In C. Snodgrass & E. Szewczak (Eds.), *Human factors in information systems* (pp. 153–168). Hershey, PA: IGI Global. doi:10.4018/978-1-931777-10-0.ch012

Aladwani, A. M. (2002). Organizational actions, computer attitudes, and end-user satisfaction in public organizations: An empirical study. *Journal of Organizational and End User Computing, 14*(1), 42–49. doi:10.4018/joeuc.2002010104

Allen, B., Juillet, L., Paquet, G., & Roy, J. (2005). E-government and private-public partnerships: Relational challenges and strategic directions. In M. Khosrow-Pour (Ed.), *Practicing e-government: A global perspective* (pp. 364–382). Hershey, PA: IGI Global. doi:10.4018/978-1-59140-637-2.ch016

Alshawaf, A., & Knalil, O. E. (2008). IS success factors and IS organizational impact: Does ownership type matter in Kuwait? *International Journal of Enterprise Information Systems, 4*(2), 13–33. doi:10.4018/jeis.2008040102

Ambali, A. R. (2009). Digital divide and its implication on Malaysian e-government: Policy initiatives. In H. Rahman (Ed.), *Social and political implications of data mining: Knowledge management in e-government* (pp. 267–287). Hershey, PA: IGI Global. doi:10.4018/978-1-60566-230-5.ch016

Amoretti, F. (2007). Digital international governance. In A. Anttiroiko & M. Malkia (Eds.), *Encyclopedia of digital government* (pp. 365–370). Hershey, PA: IGI Global. doi:10.4018/978-1-59140-789-8.ch056

Amoretti, F. (2008). Digital international governance. In A. Anttiroiko (Ed.), *Electronic government: Concepts, methodologies, tools, and applications* (pp. 688–696). Hershey, PA: IGI Global. doi:10.4018/978-1-59904-947-2.ch058

Amoretti, F. (2008). E-government at supranational level in the European Union. In A. Anttiroiko (Ed.), *Electronic government: Concepts, methodologies, tools, and applications* (pp. 1047–1055). Hershey, PA: IGI Global. doi:10.4018/978-1-59904-947-2.ch079

Amoretti, F. (2008). E-government regimes. In A. Anttiroiko (Ed.), *Electronic government: Concepts, methodologies, tools, and applications* (pp. 3846–3856). Hershey, PA: IGI Global. doi:10.4018/978-1-59904-947-2.ch280

Amoretti, F. (2009). Electronic constitution: A Braudelian perspective. In F. Amoretti (Ed.), *Electronic constitution: Social, cultural, and political implications* (pp. 1–19). Hershey, PA: IGI Global. doi:10.4018/978-1-60566-254-1.ch001

Amoretti, F., & Musella, F. (2009). Institutional isomorphism and new technologies. In M. Khosrow-Pour (Ed.), *Encyclopedia of information science and technology* (2nd ed.; pp. 2066–2071). Hershey, PA: IGI Global. doi:10.4018/978-1-60566-026-4.ch325

Andersen, K. V., & Henriksen, H. Z. (2007). E-government research: Capabilities, interaction, orientation, and values. In D. Norris (Ed.), *Current issues and trends in e-government research* (pp. 269–288). Hershey, PA: IGI Global. doi:10.4018/978-1-59904-283-1.ch013

Anderson, K. V., & Henriksen, H. Z. (2005). The first leg of e-government research: Domains and application areas 1998-2003. *International Journal of Electronic Government Research*, *1*(4), 26–44. doi:10.4018/jegr.2005100102

Anttiroiko, A. (2009). Democratic e-governance. In M. Khosrow-Pour (Ed.), *Encyclopedia of information science and technology* (2nd ed.; pp. 990–995). Hershey, PA: IGI Global. doi:10.4018/978-1-60566-026-4.ch158

Association, I. R. (2010). *Networking and telecommunications: Concepts, methodologies, tools and applications* (Vols. 1–3). Hershey, PA: IGI Global. doi:10.4018/978-1-60566-986-1

Association, I. R. (2010). *Web-based education: Concepts, methodologies, tools and applications* (Vols. 1–3). Hershey, PA: IGI Global. doi:10.4018/978-1-61520-963-7

Baker, P. M., Bell, A., & Moon, N. W. (2009). Accessibility issues in municipal wireless networks. In C. Reddick (Ed.), *Handbook of research on strategies for local e-government adoption and implementation: Comparative studies* (pp. 569–588). Hershey, PA: IGI Global. doi:10.4018/978-1-60566-282-4.ch030

Becker, S. A., Keimer, R., & Muth, T. (2010). A case on university and community collaboration: The sci-tech entrepreneurial training services (ETS) program. In S. Becker & R. Niebuhr (Eds.), *Cases on technology innovation: Entrepreneurial successes and pitfalls* (pp. 68–90). Hershey, PA: IGI Global. doi:10.4018/978-1-61520-609-4.ch003

Becker, S. A., Keimer, R., & Muth, T. (2012). A case on university and community collaboration: The sci-tech entrepreneurial training services (ETS) program. In Regional development: Concepts, methodologies, tools, and applications (pp. 947-969). Hershey, PA: IGI Global. doi:10.4018/978-1-4666-0882-5.ch507

Bernardi, R. (2012). Information technology and resistance to public sector reforms: A case study in Kenya. In T. Papadopoulos & P. Kanellis (Eds.), *Public sector reform using information technologies: Transforming policy into practice* (pp. 59–78). Hershey, PA: IGI Global. doi:10.4018/978-1-60960-839-2.ch004

Bernardi, R. (2013). Information technology and resistance to public sector reforms: A case study in Kenya. In *User-driven healthcare: Concepts, methodologies, tools, and applications* (pp. 14–33). Hershey, PA: IGI Global. doi:10.4018/978-1-4666-2770-3.ch002

Bolívar, M. P., Pérez, M. D., & Hernández, A. M. (2012). Municipal e-government services in emerging economies: The Latin-American and Caribbean experiences. In Y. Chen & P. Chu (Eds.), *Electronic governance and cross-boundary collaboration: Innovations and advancing tools* (pp. 198–226). Hershey, PA: IGI Global. doi:10.4018/978-1-60960-753-1.ch011

Borycki, E. M., & Kushniruk, A. W. (2010). Use of clinical simulations to evaluate the impact of health information systems and ubiquitous computing devices upon health professional work. In S. Mohammed & J. Fiaidhi (Eds.), *Ubiquitous health and medical informatics: The ubiquity 2.0 trend and beyond* (pp. 552–573). Hershey, PA: IGI Global. doi:10.4018/978-1-61520-777-0.ch026

Borycki, E. M., & Kushniruk, A. W. (2011). Use of clinical simulations to evaluate the impact of health information systems and ubiquitous computing devices upon health professional work. In *Clinical technologies: Concepts, methodologies, tools and applications* (pp. 532–553). Hershey, PA: IGI Global. doi:10.4018/978-1-60960-561-2.ch220

Buchan, J. (2011). Developing a dynamic and responsive online learning environment: A case study of a large Australian university. In B. Czerkawski (Ed.), *Free and open source software for e-learning: Issues, successes and challenges* (pp. 92–109). Hershey, PA: IGI Global. doi:10.4018/978-1-61520-917-0.ch006

Buenger, A. W. (2008). Digital convergence and cybersecurity policy. In G. Garson & M. Khosrow-Pour (Eds.), *Handbook of research on public information technology* (pp. 395–405). Hershey, PA: IGI Global. doi:10.4018/978-1-59904-857-4.ch038

Burn, J. M., & Loch, K. D. (2002). The societal impact of world wide web - Key challenges for the 21st century. In A. Salehnia (Ed.), *Ethical issues of information systems* (pp. 88–106). Hershey, PA: IGI Global. doi:10.4018/978-1-931777-15-5.ch007

Burn, J. M., & Loch, K. D. (2003). The societal impact of the world wide web-Key challenges for the 21st century. In M. Khosrow-Pour (Ed.), *Advanced topics in information resources management* (Vol. 2, pp. 32–51). Hershey, PA: IGI Global. doi:10.4018/978-1-59140-062-2.ch002

Bwalya, K. J., Du Plessis, T., & Rensleigh, C. (2012). The "quicksilver initiatives" as a framework for e-government strategy design in developing economies. In K. Bwalya & S. Zulu (Eds.), *Handbook of research on e-government in emerging economies: Adoption, e-participation, and legal frameworks* (pp. 605–623). Hershey, PA: IGI Global. doi:10.4018/978-1-4666-0324-0.ch031

Cabotaje, C. E., & Alampay, E. A. (2013). Social media and citizen engagement: Two cases from the Philippines. In S. Saeed & C. Reddick (Eds.), *Human-centered system design for electronic governance* (pp. 225–238). Hershey, PA: IGI Global. doi:10.4018/978-1-4666-3640-8.ch013

Camillo, A., Di Pietro, L., Di Virgilio, F., & Franco, M. (2013). Work-groups conflict at PetroTech-Italy, S.R.L.: The influence of culture on conflict dynamics. In B. Christiansen, E. Turkina, & N. Williams (Eds.), *Cultural and technological influences on global business* (pp. 272–289). Hershey, PA: IGI Global. doi:10.4018/978-1-4666-3966-9.ch015

Capra, E., Francalanci, C., & Marinoni, C. (2008). Soft success factors for m-government. In A. Anttiroiko (Ed.), *Electronic government: Concepts, methodologies, tools, and applications* (pp. 1213–1233). Hershey, PA: IGI Global. doi:10.4018/978-1-59904-947-2.ch089

Cartelli, A. (2009). The implementation of practices with ICT as a new teaching-learning paradigm. In A. Cartelli & M. Palma (Eds.), *Encyclopedia of information communication technology* (pp. 413–417). Hershey, PA: IGI Global. doi:10.4018/978-1-59904-845-1.ch055

Charalabidis, Y., Lampathaki, F., & Askounis, D. (2010). Investigating the landscape in national interoperability frameworks. *International Journal of E-Services and Mobile Applications*, 2(4), 28–41. doi:10.4018/jesma.2010100103

Charalabidis, Y., Lampathaki, F., & Askounis, D. (2012). Investigating the landscape in national interoperability frameworks. In A. Scupola (Ed.), *Innovative mobile platform developments for electronic services design and delivery* (pp. 218–231). Hershey, PA: IGI Global. doi:10.4018/978-1-4666-1568-7.ch013

Chen, I. (2005). Distance education associations. In C. Howard, J. Boettcher, L. Justice, K. Schenk, P. Rogers, & G. Berg (Eds.), *Encyclopedia of distance learning* (pp. 599–612). Hershey, PA: IGI Global. doi:10.4018/978-1-59140-555-9.ch087

Chen, I. (2008). Distance education associations. In L. Tomei (Ed.), *Online and distance learning: Concepts, methodologies, tools, and applications* (pp. 562–579). Hershey, PA: IGI Global. doi:10.4018/978-1-59904-935-9.ch048

Chen, Y. (2008). Managing IT outsourcing for digital government. In A. Anttiroiko (Ed.), *Electronic government: Concepts, methodologies, tools, and applications* (pp. 3107–3114). Hershey, PA: IGI Global. doi:10.4018/978-1-59904-947-2.ch229

Chen, Y., & Dimitrova, D. V. (2006). Electronic government and online engagement: Citizen interaction with government via web portals. *International Journal of Electronic Government Research, 2*(1), 54–76. doi:10.4018/jegr.2006010104

Chen, Y., & Knepper, R. (2005). Digital government development strategies: Lessons for policy makers from a comparative perspective. In W. Huang, K. Siau, & K. Wei (Eds.), *Electronic government strategies and implementation* (pp. 394–420). Hershey, PA: IGI Global. doi:10.4018/978-1-59140-348-7.ch017

Chen, Y., & Knepper, R. (2008). Digital government development strategies: Lessons for policy makers from a comparative perspective. In H. Rahman (Ed.), *Developing successful ICT strategies: Competitive advantages in a global knowledge-driven society* (pp. 334–356). Hershey, PA: IGI Global. doi:10.4018/978-1-59904-654-9.ch017

Cherian, E. J., & Ryan, T. W. (2014). Incongruent needs: Why differences in the iron-triangle of priorities make health information technology adoption and use difficult. In C. El Morr (Ed.), *Research perspectives on the role of informatics in health policy and management* (pp. 209–221). Hershey, PA: IGI Global. doi:10.4018/978-1-4666-4321-5.ch012

Cho, H. J., & Hwang, S. (2010). Government 2.0 in Korea: Focusing on e-participation services. In C. Reddick (Ed.), *Politics, democracy and e-government: Participation and service delivery* (pp. 94–114). Hershey, PA: IGI Global. doi:10.4018/978-1-61520-933-0.ch006

Chorus, C., & Timmermans, H. (2010). Ubiquitous travel environments and travel control strategies: Prospects and challenges. In M. Wachowicz (Ed.), *Movement-aware applications for sustainable mobility: Technologies and approaches* (pp. 30–51). Hershey, PA: IGI Global. doi:10.4018/978-1-61520-769-5.ch003

Chuanshen, R. (2007). E-government construction and China's administrative litigation act. In A. Anttiroiko & M. Malkia (Eds.), *Encyclopedia of digital government* (pp. 507–510). Hershey, PA: IGI Global. doi:10.4018/978-1-59140-789-8.ch077

Ciaghi, A., & Villafiorita, A. (2012). Law modeling and BPR for public administration improvement. In K. Bwalya & S. Zulu (Eds.), *Handbook of research on e-government in emerging economies: Adoption, e-participation, and legal frameworks* (pp. 391–410). Hershey, PA: IGI Global. doi:10.4018/978-1-4666-0324-0.ch019

Ciaramitaro, B. L., & Skrocki, M. (2012). mHealth: Mobile healthcare. In B. Ciaramitaro (Ed.), Mobile technology consumption: Opportunities and challenges (pp. 99-109). Hershey, PA: IGI Global. doi:10.4018/978-1-61350-150-4.ch007

Comite, U. (2012). Innovative processes and managerial effectiveness of e-procurement in healthcare. In A. Manoharan & M. Holzer (Eds.), *Active citizen participation in e-government: A global perspective* (pp. 206–229). Hershey, PA: IGI Global. doi:10.4018/978-1-4666-0116-1.ch011

Cordella, A. (2013). E-government success: How to account for ICT, administrative rationalization, and institutional change. In J. Gil-Garcia (Ed.), *E-government success factors and measures: Theories, concepts, and methodologies* (pp. 40–51). Hershey, PA: IGI Global. doi:10.4018/978-1-4666-4058-0.ch003

Cropf, R. A. (2009). ICT and e-democracy. In M. Khosrow-Pour (Ed.), *Encyclopedia of information science and technology* (2nd ed.; pp. 1789–1793). Hershey, PA: IGI Global. doi:10.4018/978-1-60566-026-4.ch281

Cropf, R. A. (2009). The virtual public sphere. In M. Pagani (Ed.), *Encyclopedia of multimedia technology and networking* (2nd ed.; pp. 1525–1530). Hershey, PA: IGI Global. doi:10.4018/978-1-60566-014-1.ch206

D'Abundo, M. L. (2013). Electronic health record implementation in the United States healthcare industry: Making the process of change manageable. In V. Wang (Ed.), *Handbook of research on technologies for improving the 21st century workforce: Tools for lifelong learning* (pp. 272–286). Hershey, PA: IGI Global. doi:10.4018/978-1-4666-2181-7.ch018

Damurski, L. (2012). E-participation in urban planning: Online tools for citizen engagement in Poland and in Germany. *International Journal of E-Planning Research*, *1*(3), 40–67. doi:10.4018/ijepr.2012070103

de Almeida, M. O. (2007). E-government strategy in Brazil: Increasing transparency and efficiency through e-government procurement. In M. Gascó-Hernandez (Ed.), *Latin America online: Cases, successes and pitfalls* (pp. 34–82). Hershey, PA: IGI Global. doi:10.4018/978-1-59140-974-8.ch002

de Juana Espinosa, S. (2008). Empirical study of the municipalitites' motivations for adopting online presence. In A. Anttiroiko (Ed.), *Electronic government: Concepts, methodologies, tools, and applications* (pp. 3593–3608). Hershey, PA: IGI Global. doi:10.4018/978-1-59904-947-2.ch262

de Souza Dias, D. (2002). Motivation for using information technology. In C. Snodgrass & E. Szewczak (Eds.), *Human factors in information systems* (pp. 55–60). Hershey, PA: IGI Global. doi:10.4018/978-1-931777-10-0.ch005

Demediuk, P. (2006). Government procurement ICT's impact on the sustainability of SMEs and regional communities. In S. Marshall, W. Taylor, & X. Yu (Eds.), *Encyclopedia of developing regional communities with information and communication technology* (pp. 321–324). Hershey, PA: IGI Global. doi:10.4018/978-1-59140-575-7.ch056

Devonshire, E., Forsyth, H., Reid, S., & Simpson, J. M. (2013). The challenges and opportunities of online postgraduate coursework programs in a traditional university context. In B. Tynan, J. Willems, & R. James (Eds.), *Outlooks and opportunities in blended and distance learning* (pp. 353–368). Hershey, PA: IGI Global. doi:10.4018/978-1-4666-4205-8.ch026

Di Cerbo, F., Scotto, M., Sillitti, A., Succi, G., & Vernazza, T. (2007). Toward a GNU/Linux distribution for corporate environments. In S. Sowe, I. Stamelos, & I. Samoladas (Eds.), *Emerging free and open source software practices* (pp. 215–236). Hershey, PA: IGI Global. doi:10.4018/978-1-59904-210-7.ch010

Diesner, J., & Carley, K. M. (2005). Revealing social structure from texts: Meta-matrix text analysis as a novel method for network text analysis. In V. Narayanan & D. Armstrong (Eds.), *Causal mapping for research in information technology* (pp. 81–108). Hershey, PA: IGI Global. doi:10.4018/978-1-59140-396-8.ch004

Dologite, D. G., Mockler, R. J., Bai, Q., & Viszhanyo, P. F. (2006). IS change agents in practice in a US-Chinese joint venture. In M. Hunter & F. Tan (Eds.), *Advanced topics in global information management* (Vol. 5, pp. 331–352). Hershey, PA: IGI Global. doi:10.4018/978-1-59140-923-6.ch015

Drnevich, P., Brush, T. H., & Luckock, G. T. (2011). Process and structural implications for IT-enabled outsourcing. *International Journal of Strategic Information Technology and Applications*, 2(4), 30–43. doi:10.4018/jsita.2011100103

Dwivedi, A. N. (2009). *Handbook of research on information technology management and clinical data administration in healthcare* (Vols. 1–2). Hershey, PA: IGI Global. doi:10.4018/978-1-60566-356-2

Elbeltagi, I., McBride, N., & Hardaker, G. (2006). Evaluating the factors affecting DSS usage by senior managers in local authorities in Egypt. In M. Hunter & F. Tan (Eds.), *Advanced topics in global information management* (Vol. 5, pp. 283–307). Hershey, PA: IGI Global. doi:10.4018/978-1-59140-923-6.ch013

Eom, S., & Fountain, J. E. (2013). Enhancing information services through public-private partnerships: Information technology knowledge transfer underlying structures to develop shared services in the U.S. and Korea. In J. Gil-Garcia (Ed.), *E-government success around the world: Cases, empirical studies, and practical recommendations* (pp. 15–40). Hershey, PA: IGI Global. doi:10.4018/978-1-4666-4173-0.ch002

Esteves, T., Leuenberger, D., & Van Leuven, N. (2012). Reaching citizen 2.0: How government uses social media to send public messages during times of calm and times of crisis. In K. Kloby & M. D'Agostino (Eds.), *Citizen 2.0: Public and governmental interaction through web 2.0 technologies* (pp. 250–268). Hershey, PA: IGI Global. doi:10.4018/978-1-4666-0318-9.ch013

Estevez, E., Fillottrani, P., Janowski, T., & Ojo, A. (2012). Government information sharing: A framework for policy formulation. In Y. Chen & P. Chu (Eds.), *Electronic governance and cross-boundary collaboration: Innovations and advancing tools* (pp. 23–55). Hershey, PA: IGI Global. doi:10.4018/978-1-60960-753-1.ch002

Ezz, I. E. (2008). E-governement emerging trends: Organizational challenges. In A. Anttiroiko (Ed.), *Electronic government: Concepts, methodologies, tools, and applications* (pp. 3721–3737). Hershey, PA: IGI Global. doi:10.4018/978-1-59904-947-2.ch269

Fabri, M. (2009). The Italian style of e-justice in a comparative perspective. In A. Martínez & P. Abat (Eds.), *E-justice: Using information communication technologies in the court system* (pp. 1–19). Hershey, PA: IGI Global. doi:10.4018/978-1-59904-998-4.ch001

Fagbe, T., & Adekola, O. D. (2010). Workplace safety and personnel well-being: The impact of information technology. *International Journal of Green Computing*, *1*(1), 28–33. doi:10.4018/jgc.2010010103

Fagbe, T., & Adekola, O. D. (2011). Workplace safety and personnel well-being: The impact of information technology. In *Global business: Concepts, methodologies, tools and applications* (pp. 1438–1444). Hershey, PA: IGI Global. doi:10.4018/978-1-60960-587-2.ch509

Farmer, L. (2008). Affective collaborative instruction with librarians. In S. Kelsey & K. St.Amant (Eds.), *Handbook of research on computer mediated communication* (pp. 15–24). Hershey, PA: IGI Global. doi:10.4018/978-1-59904-863-5.ch002

Favier, L., & Mekhantar, J. (2007). Use of OSS by local e-administration: The French situation. In K. St.Amant & B. Still (Eds.), *Handbook of research on open source software: Technological, economic, and social perspectives* (pp. 428–444). Hershey, PA: IGI Global. doi:10.4018/978-1-59140-999-1.ch033

Fernando, S. (2009). Issues of e-learning in third world countries. In M. Khosrow-Pour (Ed.), *Encyclopedia of information science and technology* (2nd ed.; pp. 2273–2277). Hershey, PA: IGI Global. doi:10.4018/978-1-60566-026-4.ch360

Filho, J. R., & dos Santos, J. R. Junior. (2009). Local e-government in Brazil: Poor interaction and local politics as usual. In C. Reddick (Ed.), *Handbook of research on strategies for local e-government adoption and implementation: Comparative studies* (pp. 863–878). Hershey, PA: IGI Global. doi:10.4018/978-1-60566-282-4.ch045

Fletcher, P. D. (2004). Portals and policy: Implications of electronic access to U.S. federal government information services. In A. Pavlichev & G. Garson (Eds.), *Digital government: Principles and best practices* (pp. 52–62). Hershey, PA: IGI Global. doi:10.4018/978-1-59140-122-3.ch004

Fletcher, P. D. (2008). Portals and policy: Implications of electronic access to U.S. federal government information services. In A. Anttiroiko (Ed.), *Electronic government: Concepts, methodologies, tools, and applications* (pp. 3970–3979). Hershey, PA: IGI Global. doi:10.4018/978-1-59904-947-2.ch289

Forlano, L. (2004). The emergence of digital government: International perspectives. In A. Pavlichev & G. Garson (Eds.), *Digital government: Principles and best practices* (pp. 34–51). Hershey, PA: IGI Global. doi:10.4018/978-1-59140-122-3.ch003

Franzel, J. M., & Coursey, D. H. (2004). Government web portals: Management issues and the approaches of five states. In A. Pavlichev & G. Garson (Eds.), *Digital government: Principles and best practices* (pp. 63–77). Hershey, PA: IGI Global. doi:10.4018/978-1-59140-122-3.ch005

Gaivéo, J. M. (2013). Security of ICTs supporting healthcare activities. In M. Cruz-Cunha, I. Miranda, & P. Gonçalves (Eds.), *Handbook of research on ICTs for human-centered healthcare and social care services* (pp. 208–228). Hershey, PA: IGI Global. doi:10.4018/978-1-4666-3986-7.ch011

Garson, G. D. (1999). *Information technology and computer applications in public administration: Issues and trends*. Hershey, PA: IGI Global. doi:10.4018/978-1-87828-952-0

Garson, G. D. (2003). Toward an information technology research agenda for public administration. In G. Garson (Ed.), *Public information technology: Policy and management issues* (pp. 331–357). Hershey, PA: IGI Global. doi:10.4018/978-1-59140-060-8.ch014

Garson, G. D. (2004). The promise of digital government. In A. Pavlichev & G. Garson (Eds.), *Digital government: Principles and best practices* (pp. 2–15). Hershey, PA: IGI Global. doi:10.4018/978-1-59140-122-3.ch001

Garson, G. D. (2007). An information technology research agenda for public administration. In G. Garson (Ed.), *Modern public information technology systems: Issues and challenges* (pp. 365–392). Hershey, PA: IGI Global. doi:10.4018/978-1-59904-051-6.ch018

Gasco, M. (2007). Civil servants' resistance towards e-government development. In A. Anttiroiko & M. Malkia (Eds.), *Encyclopedia of digital government* (pp. 190–195). Hershey, PA: IGI Global. doi:10.4018/978-1-59140-789-8.ch028

Gasco, M. (2008). Civil servants' resistance towards e-government development. In A. Anttiroiko (Ed.), *Electronic government: Concepts, methodologies, tools, and applications* (pp. 2580–2588). Hershey, PA: IGI Global. doi:10.4018/978-1-59904-947-2.ch190

Ghere, R. K. (2010). Accountability and information technology enactment: Implications for social empowerment. In E. Ferro, Y. Dwivedi, J. Gil-Garcia, & M. Williams (Eds.), *Handbook of research on overcoming digital divides: Constructing an equitable and competitive information society* (pp. 515–532). Hershey, PA: IGI Global. doi:10.4018/978-1-60566-699-0.ch028

Gibson, I. W. (2012). Simulation modeling of healthcare delivery. In A. Kolker & P. Story (Eds.), *Management engineering for effective healthcare delivery: Principles and applications* (pp. 69–89). Hershey, PA: IGI Global. doi:10.4018/978-1-60960-872-9.ch003

Gil-Garcia, J. R. (2007). Exploring e-government benefits and success factors. In A. Anttiroiko & M. Malkia (Eds.), *Encyclopedia of digital government* (pp. 803–811). Hershey, PA: IGI Global. doi:10.4018/978-1-59140-789-8.ch122

Gil-Garcia, J. R., & González Miranda, F. (2010). E-government and opportunities for participation: The case of the Mexican state web portals. In C. Reddick (Ed.), *Politics, democracy and e-government: Participation and service delivery* (pp. 56–74). Hershey, PA: IGI Global. doi:10.4018/978-1-61520-933-0.ch004

Goldfinch, S. (2012). Public trust in government, trust in e-government, and use of e-government. In Z. Yan (Ed.), *Encyclopedia of cyber behavior* (pp. 987–995). Hershey, PA: IGI Global. doi:10.4018/978-1-4666-0315-8.ch081

Goodyear, M. (2012). Organizational change contributions to e-government project transitions. In S. Aikins (Ed.), *Managing e-government projects: Concepts, issues, and best practices* (pp. 1–21). Hershey, PA: IGI Global. doi:10.4018/978-1-4666-0086-7.ch001

Gordon, S., & Mulligan, P. (2003). Strategic models for the delivery of personal financial services: The role of infocracy. In S. Gordon (Ed.), *Computing information technology: The human side* (pp. 220–232). Hershey, PA: IGI Global. doi:10.4018/978-1-93177-752-0.ch014

Gordon, T. F. (2007). Legal knowledge systems. In A. Anttiroiko & M. Malkia (Eds.), *Encyclopedia of digital government* (pp. 1161–1166). Hershey, PA: IGI Global. doi:10.4018/978-1-59140-789-8.ch175

Graham, J. E., & Semich, G. W. (2008). Integrating technology to transform pedagogy: Revisiting the progress of the three phase TUI model for faculty development. In L. Tomei (Ed.), *Adapting information and communication technologies for effective education* (pp. 1–12). Hershey, PA: IGI Global. doi:10.4018/978-1-59904-922-9.ch001

Grandinetti, L., & Pisacane, O. (2012). Web services for healthcare management. In D. Prakash Vidyarthi (Ed.), *Technologies and protocols for the future of internet design: Reinventing the web* (pp. 60–94). Hershey, PA: IGI Global. doi:10.4018/978-1-4666-0203-8.ch004

Groenewegen, P., & Wagenaar, F. P. (2008). VO as an alternative to hierarchy in the Dutch police sector. In G. Putnik & M. Cruz-Cunha (Eds.), *Encyclopedia of networked and virtual organizations* (pp. 1851–1857). Hershey, PA: IGI Global. doi:10.4018/978-1-59904-885-7.ch245

Gronlund, A. (2001). Building an infrastructure to manage electronic services. In S. Dasgupta (Ed.), *Managing internet and intranet technologies in organizations: Challenges and opportunities* (pp. 71–103). Hershey, PA: IGI Global. doi:10.4018/978-1-878289-95-7.ch006

Gronlund, A. (2002). Introduction to electronic government: Design, applications and management. In Å. Grönlund (Ed.), *Electronic government: Design, applications and management* (pp. 1–21). Hershey, PA: IGI Global. doi:10.4018/978-1-930708-19-8.ch001

Gupta, A., Woosley, R., Crk, I., & Sarnikar, S. (2009). An information technology architecture for drug effectiveness reporting and post-marketing surveillance. In J. Tan (Ed.), *Medical informatics: Concepts, methodologies, tools, and applications* (pp. 631–646). Hershey, PA: IGI Global. doi:10.4018/978-1-60566-050-9.ch047

Hallin, A., & Lundevall, K. (2007). mCity: User focused development of mobile services within the city of Stockholm. In I. Kushchu (Ed.), Mobile government: An emerging direction in e-government (pp. 12-29). Hershey, PA: IGI Global. doi:10.4018/978-1-59140-884-0.ch002

Hallin, A., & Lundevall, K. (2009). mCity: User focused development of mobile services within the city of Stockholm. In S. Clarke (Ed.), Evolutionary concepts in end user productivity and performance: Applications for organizational progress (pp. 268-280). Hershey, PA: IGI Global. doi:10.4018/978-1-60566-136-0.ch017

Hallin, A., & Lundevall, K. (2009). mCity: User focused development of mobile services within the city of Stockholm. In D. Taniar (Ed.), Mobile computing: Concepts, methodologies, tools, and applications (pp. 3455-3467). Hershey, PA: IGI Global. doi:10.4018/978-1-60566-054-7.ch253

Hanson, A. (2005). Overcoming barriers in the planning of a virtual library. In M. Khosrow-Pour (Ed.), *Encyclopedia of information science and technology* (pp. 2255–2259). Hershey, PA: IGI Global. doi:10.4018/978-1-59140-553-5.ch397

Haque, A. (2008). Information technology and surveillance: Implications for public administration in a new word order. In T. Loendorf & G. Garson (Eds.), *Patriotic information systems* (pp. 177–185). Hershey, PA: IGI Global. doi:10.4018/978-1-59904-594-8.ch008

Hauck, R. V., Thatcher, S. M., & Weisband, S. P. (2012). Temporal aspects of information technology use: Increasing shift work effectiveness. In J. Wang (Ed.), *Advancing the service sector with evolving technologies: Techniques and principles* (pp. 87–104). Hershey, PA: IGI Global. doi:10.4018/978-1-4666-0044-7.ch006

Hawk, S., & Witt, T. (2006). Telecommunications courses in information systems programs. *International Journal of Information and Communication Technology Education, 2*(1), 79–92. doi:10.4018/jicte.2006010107

Helms, M. M., Moore, R., & Ahmadi, M. (2009). Information technology (IT) and the healthcare industry: A SWOT analysis. In J. Tan (Ed.), *Medical informatics: Concepts, methodologies, tools, and applications* (pp. 134–152). Hershey, PA: IGI Global. doi:10.4018/978-1-60566-050-9.ch012

Hendrickson, S. M., & Young, M. E. (2014). Electronic records management at a federally funded research and development center. In J. Krueger (Ed.), *Cases on electronic records and resource management implementation in diverse environments* (pp. 334–350). Hershey, PA: IGI Global. doi:10.4018/978-1-4666-4466-3.ch020

Henman, P. (2010). Social policy and information communication technologies. In J. Martin & L. Hawkins (Eds.), *Information communication technologies for human services education and delivery: Concepts and cases* (pp. 215–229). Hershey, PA: IGI Global. doi:10.4018/978-1-60566-735-5.ch014

Hismanoglu, M. (2011). Important issues in online education: E-pedagogy and marketing. In U. Demiray & S. Sever (Eds.), *Marketing online education programs: Frameworks for promotion and communication* (pp. 184–209). Hershey, PA: IGI Global. doi:10.4018/978-1-60960-074-7.ch012

Ho, K. K. (2008). The e-government development, IT strategies, and portals of the Hong Kong SAR government. In A. Anttiroiko (Ed.), *Electronic government: Concepts, methodologies, tools, and applications* (pp. 715–733). Hershey, PA: IGI Global. doi:10.4018/978-1-59904-947-2.ch060

Holden, S. H. (2003). The evolution of information technology management at the federal level: Implications for public administration. In G. Garson (Ed.), *Public information technology: Policy and management issues* (pp. 53–73). Hershey, PA: IGI Global. doi:10.4018/978-1-59140-060-8.ch003

Holden, S. H. (2007). The evolution of federal information technology management literature: Does IT finally matter? In G. Garson (Ed.), *Modern public information technology systems: Issues and challenges* (pp. 17–34). Hershey, PA: IGI Global. doi:10.4018/978-1-59904-051-6.ch002

Holland, J. W. (2009). Automation of American criminal justice. In M. Khosrow-Pour (Ed.), *Encyclopedia of information science and technology* (2nd ed.; pp. 300–302). Hershey, PA: IGI Global. doi:10.4018/978-1-60566-026-4.ch051

Holloway, K. (2013). Fair use, copyright, and academic integrity in an online academic environment. In *Digital rights management: Concepts, methodologies, tools, and applications* (pp. 917–928). Hershey, PA: IGI Global. doi:10.4018/978-1-4666-2136-7.ch044

Horiuchi, C. (2005). E-government databases. In L. Rivero, J. Doorn, & V. Ferraggine (Eds.), *Encyclopedia of database technologies and applications* (pp. 206–210). Hershey, PA: IGI Global. doi:10.4018/978-1-59140-560-3.ch035

Horiuchi, C. (2006). Creating IS quality in government settings. In E. Duggan & J. Reichgelt (Eds.), *Measuring information systems delivery quality* (pp. 311–327). Hershey, PA: IGI Global. doi:10.4018/978-1-59140-857-4.ch014

Hsiao, N., Chu, P., & Lee, C. (2012). Impact of e-governance on businesses: Model development and case study. In *Digital democracy: Concepts, methodologies, tools, and applications* (pp. 1407–1425). Hershey, PA: IGI Global. doi:10.4018/978-1-4666-1740-7.ch070

Huang, T., & Lee, C. (2010). Evaluating the impact of e-government on citizens: Cost-benefit analysis. In C. Reddick (Ed.), *Citizens and e-government: Evaluating policy and management* (pp. 37–52). Hershey, PA: IGI Global. doi:10.4018/978-1-61520-931-6.ch003

Hunter, M. G., Diochon, M., Pugsley, D., & Wright, B. (2002). Unique challenges for small business adoption of information technology: The case of the Nova Scotia ten. In S. Burgess (Ed.), *Managing information technology in small business: Challenges and solutions* (pp. 98–117). Hershey, PA: IGI Global. doi:10.4018/978-1-930708-35-8.ch006

Hurskainen, J. (2003). Integration of business systems and applications in merger and alliance: Case metso automation. In T. Reponen (Ed.), *Information technology enabled global customer service* (pp. 207–225). Hershey, PA: IGI Global. doi:10.4018/978-1-59140-048-6.ch012

Iazzolino, G., & Pietrantonio, R. (2011). The soveria.it project: A best practice of e-government in southern Italy. In D. Piaggesi, K. Sund, & W. Castelnovo (Eds.), *Global strategy and practice of e-governance: Examples from around the world* (pp. 34–56). Hershey, PA: IGI Global. doi:10.4018/978-1-60960-489-9.ch003

Imran, A., & Gregor, S. (2012). A process model for successful e-government adoption in the least developed countries: A case of Bangladesh. In F. Tan (Ed.), *International comparisons of information communication technologies: Advancing applications* (pp. 321–350). Hershey, PA: IGI Global. doi:10.4018/978-1-61350-480-2.ch014

Inoue, Y., & Bell, S. T. (2005). Electronic/digital government innovation, and publishing trends with IT. In M. Khosrow-Pour (Ed.), *Encyclopedia of information science and technology* (pp. 1018–1023). Hershey, PA: IGI Global. doi:10.4018/978-1-59140-553-5.ch180

Islam, M. M., & Ehsan, M. (2013). Understanding e-governance: A theoretical approach. In M. Islam & M. Ehsan (Eds.), *From government to e-governance: Public administration in the digital age* (pp. 38–49). Hershey, PA: IGI Global. doi:10.4018/978-1-4666-1909-8.ch003

Jaeger, B. (2009). E-government and e-democracy in the making. In M. Khosrow-Pour (Ed.), *Encyclopedia of information science and technology* (2nd ed.; pp. 1318–1322). Hershey, PA: IGI Global. doi:10.4018/978-1-60566-026-4.ch208

Jain, R. B. (2007). Revamping the administrative structure and processes in India for online diplomacy. In A. Anttiroiko & M. Malkia (Eds.), *Encyclopedia of digital government* (pp. 1418–1423). Hershey, PA: IGI Global. doi:10.4018/978-1-59140-789-8.ch217

Jain, R. B. (2008). Revamping the administrative structure and processes in India for online diplomacy. In A. Anttiroiko (Ed.), *Electronic government: Concepts, methodologies, tools, and applications* (pp. 3142–3149). Hershey, PA: IGI Global. doi:10.4018/978-1-59904-947-2.ch233

Jauhiainen, J. S., & Inkinen, T. (2009). E-governance and the information society in periphery. In C. Reddick (Ed.), *Handbook of research on strategies for local e-government adoption and implementation: Comparative studies* (pp. 497–514). Hershey, PA: IGI Global. doi:10.4018/978-1-60566-282-4.ch026

Jensen, M. J. (2009). Electronic democracy and citizen influence in government. In C. Reddick (Ed.), *Handbook of research on strategies for local e-government adoption and implementation: Comparative studies* (pp. 288–305). Hershey, PA: IGI Global. doi:10.4018/978-1-60566-282-4.ch015

Jiao, Y., Hurson, A. R., Potok, T. E., & Beckerman, B. G. (2009). Integrating mobile-based systems with healthcare databases. In J. Erickson (Ed.), *Database technologies: Concepts, methodologies, tools, and applications* (pp. 484–504). Hershey, PA: IGI Global. doi:10.4018/978-1-60566-058-5.ch031

Joia, L. A. (2002). A systematic model to integrate information technology into metabusinesses: A case study in the engineering realms. In F. Tan (Ed.), *Advanced topics in global information management* (Vol. 1, pp. 250–267). Hershey, PA: IGI Global. doi:10.4018/978-1-930708-43-3.ch016

Jones, T. H., & Song, I. (2000). Binary equivalents of ternary relationships in entity-relationship modeling: A logical decomposition approach. *Journal of Database Management, 11*(2), 12–19. doi:10.4018/jdm.2000040102

Juana-Espinosa, S. D. (2007). Empirical study of the municipalitites' motivations for adopting online presence. In L. Al-Hakim (Ed.), *Global e-government: Theory, applications and benchmarking* (pp. 261–279). Hershey, PA: IGI Global. doi:10.4018/978-1-59904-027-1.ch015

Jun, K., & Weare, C. (2012). Bridging from e-government practice to e-government research: Past trends and future directions. In K. Bwalya & S. Zulu (Eds.), *Handbook of research on e-government in emerging economies: Adoption, e-participation, and legal frameworks* (pp. 263–289). Hershey, PA: IGI Global. doi:10.4018/978-1-4666-0324-0.ch013

Junqueira, A., Diniz, E. H., & Fernandez, M. (2010). Electronic government implementation projects with multiple agencies: Analysis of the electronic invoice project under PMBOK framework. In J. Cordoba-Pachon & A. Ochoa-Arias (Eds.), *Systems thinking and e-participation: ICT in the governance of society* (pp. 135–153). Hershey, PA: IGI Global. doi:10.4018/978-1-60566-860-4.ch009

Juntunen, A. (2009). Joint service development with the local authorities. In C. Reddick (Ed.), *Handbook of research on strategies for local e-government adoption and implementation: Comparative studies* (pp. 902–920). Hershey, PA: IGI Global. doi:10.4018/978-1-60566-282-4.ch047

Kamel, S. (2001). *Using DSS for crisis management.* Hershey, PA: IGI Global. doi:10.4018/978-1-87828-961-2.ch020

Kamel, S. (2006). DSS for strategic decision making. In M. Khosrow-Pour (Ed.), *Cases on information technology and organizational politics & culture* (pp. 230–246). Hershey, PA: IGI Global. doi:10.4018/978-1-59904-411-8.ch015

Kamel, S. (2009). The software industry in Egypt as a potential contributor to economic growth. In M. Khosrow-Pour (Ed.), *Encyclopedia of information science and technology* (2nd ed.; pp. 3531–3537). Hershey, PA: IGI Global. doi:10.4018/978-1-60566-026-4.ch562

Kamel, S., & Hussein, M. (2008). Xceed: Pioneering the contact center industry in Egypt. *Journal of Cases on Information Technology, 10*(1), 67–91. doi:10.4018/jcit.2008010105

Kamel, S., & Wahba, K. (2003). The use of a hybrid model in web-based education: "The Global campus project. In A. Aggarwal (Ed.), *Web-based education: Learning from experience* (pp. 331–346). Hershey, PA: IGI Global. doi:10.4018/978-1-59140-102-5.ch020

Kardaras, D. K., & Papathanassiou, E. A. (2008). An exploratory study of the e-government services in Greece. In G. Garson & M. Khosrow-Pour (Eds.), *Handbook of research on public information technology* (pp. 162–174). Hershey, PA: IGI Global. doi:10.4018/978-1-59904-857-4.ch016

Kassahun, A. E., Molla, A., & Sarkar, P. (2012). Government process reengineering: What we know and what we need to know. In *Digital democracy: Concepts, methodologies, tools, and applications* (pp. 1730–1752). Hershey, PA: IGI Global. doi:10.4018/978-1-4666-1740-7.ch086

Khan, B. (2005). Technological issues. In B. Khan (Ed.), *Managing e-learning strategies: Design, delivery, implementation and evaluation* (pp. 154–180). Hershey, PA: IGI Global. doi:10.4018/978-1-59140-634-1.ch004

Khasawneh, A., Bsoul, M., Obeidat, I., & Al Azzam, I. (2012). Technology fears: A study of e-commerce loyalty perception by Jordanian customers. In J. Wang (Ed.), *Advancing the service sector with evolving technologies: Techniques and principles* (pp. 158–165). Hershey, PA: IGI Global. doi:10.4018/978-1-4666-0044-7.ch010

Khatibi, V., & Montazer, G. A. (2012). E-research methodology. In A. Juan, T. Daradoumis, M. Roca, S. Grasman, & J. Faulin (Eds.), *Collaborative and distributed e-research: Innovations in technologies, strategies and applications* (pp. 62–81). Hershey, PA: IGI Global. doi:10.4018/978-1-4666-0125-3.ch003

Kidd, T. (2011). The dragon in the school's backyard: A review of literature on the uses of technology in urban schools. In L. Tomei (Ed.), *Online courses and ICT in education: Emerging practices and applications* (pp. 242–257). Hershey, PA: IGI Global. doi:10.4018/978-1-60960-150-8.ch019

Kidd, T. T. (2010). My experience tells the story: Exploring technology adoption from a qualitative perspective - A pilot study. In H. Song & T. Kidd (Eds.), *Handbook of research on human performance and instructional technology* (pp. 247–262). Hershey, PA: IGI Global. doi:10.4018/978-1-60566-782-9.ch015

Kieley, B., Lane, G., Paquet, G., & Roy, J. (2002). e-Government in Canada: Services online or public service renewal? In Å. Grönlund (Ed.), Electronic government: Design, applications and management (pp. 340-355). Hershey, PA: IGI Global. doi:10.4018/978-1-930708-19-8.ch016

Kim, P. (2012). "Stay out of the way! My kid is video blogging through a phone!": A lesson learned from math tutoring social media for children in underserved communities. In *Wireless technologies: Concepts, methodologies, tools and applications* (pp. 1415–1428). Hershey, PA: IGI Global. doi:10.4018/978-1-61350-101-6.ch517

Kirlidog, M. (2010). Financial aspects of national ICT strategies. In S. Kamel (Ed.), *E-strategies for technological diffusion and adoption: National ICT approaches for socioeconomic development* (pp. 277–292). Hershey, PA: IGI Global. doi:10.4018/978-1-60566-388-3.ch016

Kisielnicki, J. (2006). Transfer of information and knowledge in the project management. In E. Coakes & S. Clarke (Eds.), *Encyclopedia of communities of practice in information and knowledge management* (pp. 544–551). Hershey, PA: IGI Global. doi:10.4018/978-1-59140-556-6.ch091

Kittner, M., & Van Slyke, C. (2006). Reorganizing information technology services in an academic environment. In M. Khosrow-Pour (Ed.), *Cases on the human side of information technology* (pp. 49–66). Hershey, PA: IGI Global. doi:10.4018/978-1-59904-405-7.ch004

Knoell, H. D. (2008). Semi virtual workplaces in German financial service enterprises. In P. Zemliansky & K. St. Amant (Eds.), *Handbook of research on virtual workplaces and the new nature of business practices* (pp. 570–581). Hershey, PA: IGI Global. doi:10.4018/978-1-59904-893-2.ch041

Koh, S. L., & Maguire, S. (2009). Competing in the age of information technology in a developing economy: Experiences of an Indian bank. In S. Koh & S. Maguire (Eds.), *Information and communication technologies management in turbulent business environments* (pp. 326–350). Hershey, PA: IGI Global. doi:10.4018/978-1-60566-424-8.ch018

Kollmann, T., & Häsel, M. (2009). Competence of information technology professionals in internet-based ventures. In I. Lee (Ed.), *Electronic business: Concepts, methodologies, tools, and applications* (pp. 1905–1919). Hershey, PA: IGI Global. doi:10.4018/978-1-60566-056-1.ch118

Kollmann, T., & Häsel, M. (2009). Competence of information technology professionals in internet-based ventures. In A. Cater-Steel (Ed.), *Information technology governance and service management: Frameworks and adaptations* (pp. 239–253). Hershey, PA: IGI Global. doi:10.4018/978-1-60566-008-0.ch013

Kollmann, T., & Häsel, M. (2010). Competence of information technology professionals in internet-based ventures. In *Electronic services: Concepts, methodologies, tools and applications* (pp. 1551–1565). Hershey, PA: IGI Global. doi:10.4018/978-1-61520-967-5.ch094

Kraemer, K., & King, J. L. (2006). Information technology and administrative reform: Will e-government be different? *International Journal of Electronic Government Research*, 2(1), 1–20. doi:10.4018/jegr.2006010101

Kraemer, K., & King, J. L. (2008). Information technology and administrative reform: Will e-government be different? In D. Norris (Ed.), *E-government research: Policy and management* (pp. 1–20). Hershey, PA: IGI Global. doi:10.4018/978-1-59904-913-7.ch001

Lampathaki, F., Tsiakaliaris, C., Stasis, A., & Charalabidis, Y. (2011). National interoperability frameworks: The way forward. In Y. Charalabidis (Ed.), *Interoperability in digital public services and administration: Bridging e-government and e-business* (pp. 1–24). Hershey, PA: IGI Global. doi:10.4018/978-1-61520-887-6.ch001

Lan, Z., & Scott, C. R. (1996). The relative importance of computer-mediated information versus conventional non-computer-mediated information in public managerial decision making. *Information Resources Management Journal, 9*(1), 27–0. doi:10.4018/irmj.1996010103

Law, W. (2004). *Public sector data management in a developing economy.* Hershey, PA: IGI Global. doi:10.4018/978-1-59140-259-6.ch034

Law, W. K. (2005). Information resources development challenges in a cross-cultural environment. In M. Khosrow-Pour (Ed.), *Encyclopedia of information science and technology* (pp. 1476–1481). Hershey, PA: IGI Global. doi:10.4018/978-1-59140-553-5.ch259

Law, W. K. (2009). Cross-cultural challenges for information resources management. In M. Khosrow-Pour (Ed.), *Encyclopedia of information science and technology* (2nd ed.; pp. 840–846). Hershey, PA: IGI Global. doi:10.4018/978-1-60566-026-4.ch136

Law, W. K. (2011). Cross-cultural challenges for information resources management. In *Global business: Concepts, methodologies, tools and applications* (pp. 1924–1932). Hershey, PA: IGI Global. doi:10.4018/978-1-60960-587-2.ch704

Malkia, M., & Savolainen, R. (2004). eTransformation in government, politics and society: Conceptual framework and introduction. In M. Malkia, A. Anttiroiko, & R. Savolainen (Eds.), eTransformation in governance: New directions in government and politics (pp. 1-21). Hershey, PA: IGI Global. doi:10.4018/978-1-59140-130-8.ch001

Mandujano, S. (2011). Network manageability security. In D. Kar & M. Syed (Eds.), *Network security, administration and management: Advancing technology and practice* (pp. 158–181). Hershey, PA: IGI Global. doi:10.4018/978-1-60960-777-7.ch009

Marich, M. J., Schooley, B. L., & Horan, T. A. (2012). A normative enterprise architecture for guiding end-to-end emergency response decision support. In M. Jennex (Ed.), *Managing crises and disasters with emerging technologies: Advancements* (pp. 71–87). Hershey, PA: IGI Global. doi:10.4018/978-1-4666-0167-3.ch006

Markov, R., & Okujava, S. (2008). Costs, benefits, and risks of e-government portals. In G. Putnik & M. Cruz-Cunha (Eds.), *Encyclopedia of networked and virtual organizations* (pp. 354–363). Hershey, PA: IGI Global. doi:10.4018/978-1-59904-885-7.ch047

Martin, N., & Rice, J. (2013). Evaluating and designing electronic government for the future: Observations and insights from Australia. In V. Weerakkody (Ed.), *E-government services design, adoption, and evaluation* (pp. 238–258). Hershey, PA: IGI Global. doi:10.4018/978-1-4666-2458-0.ch014

i.   Martinez, A. C. (2008). Accessing administration's information via internet in Spain. In F. Tan (Ed.), *Global information technologies: Concepts, methodologies, tools, and applications* (pp. 2558–2573). Hershey, PA: IGI Global. doi:10.4018/978-1-59904-939-7.ch186

Mbarika, V. W., Meso, P. N., & Musa, P. F. (2006). A disconnect in stakeholders' perceptions from emerging realities of teledensity growth in Africa's least developed countries. In M. Hunter & F. Tan (Eds.), *Advanced topics in global information management* (Vol. 5, pp. 263–282). Hershey, PA: IGI Global. doi:10.4018/978-1-59140-923-6.ch012

Mbarika, V. W., Meso, P. N., & Musa, P. F. (2008). A disconnect in stakeholders' perceptions from emerging realities of teledensity growth in Africa's least developed countries. In F. Tan (Ed.), *Global information technologies: Concepts, methodologies, tools, and applications* (pp. 2948–2962). Hershey, PA: IGI Global. doi:10.4018/978-1-59904-939-7.ch209

Means, T., Olson, E., & Spooner, J. (2013). Discovering ways that don't work on the road to success: Strengths and weaknesses revealed by an active learning studio classroom project. In A. Benson, J. Moore, & S. Williams van Rooij (Eds.), *Cases on educational technology planning, design, and implementation: A project management perspective* (pp. 94–113). Hershey, PA: IGI Global. doi:10.4018/978-1-4666-4237-9.ch006

Melitski, J., Holzer, M., Kim, S., Kim, C., & Rho, S. (2008). Digital government worldwide: An e-government assessment of municipal web sites. In G. Garson & M. Khosrow-Pour (Eds.), *Handbook of research on public information technology* (pp. 790–804). Hershey, PA: IGI Global. doi:10.4018/978-1-59904-857-4.ch069

Memmola, M., Palumbo, G., & Rossini, M. (2009). Web & RFID technology: New frontiers in costing and process management for rehabilitation medicine. In L. Al-Hakim & M. Memmola (Eds.), *Business web strategy: Design, alignment, and application* (pp. 145–169). Hershey, PA: IGI Global. doi:10.4018/978-1-60566-024-0.ch008

Meng, Z., Fahong, Z., & Lei, L. (2008). Information technology and environment. In Y. Kurihara, S. Takaya, H. Harui, & H. Kamae (Eds.), *Information technology and economic development* (pp. 201–212). Hershey, PA: IGI Global. doi:10.4018/978-1-59904-579-5.ch014

Mentzingen de Moraes, A. J., Ferneda, E., Costa, I., & Spinola, M. D. (2011). Practical approach for implementation of governance process in IT: Information technology areas. In N. Shi & G. Silvius (Eds.), *Enterprise IT governance, business value and performance measurement* (pp. 19–40). Hershey, PA: IGI Global. doi:10.4018/978-1-60566-346-3.ch002

Merwin, G. A. Jr, McDonald, J. S., & Odera, L. C. (2008). Economic development: Government's cutting edge in IT. In M. Raisinghani (Ed.), *Handbook of research on global information technology management in the digital economy* (pp. 1–37). Hershey, PA: IGI Global. doi:10.4018/978-1-59904-875-8.ch001

Meso, P., & Duncan, N. (2002). Can national information infrastructures enhance social development in the least developed countries? An empirical investigation. In M. Dadashzadeh (Ed.), *Information technology management in developing countries* (pp. 23–51). Hershey, PA: IGI Global. doi:10.4018/978-1-931777-03-2.ch002

Meso, P. N., & Duncan, N. B. (2002). Can national information infrastructures enhance social development in the least developed countries? In F. Tan (Ed.), *Advanced topics in global information management* (Vol. 1, pp. 207–226). Hershey, PA: IGI Global. doi:10.4018/978-1-930708-43-3.ch014

Middleton, M. (2008). Evaluation of e-government web sites. In G. Garson & M. Khosrow-Pour (Eds.), *Handbook of research on public information technology* (pp. 699–710). Hershey, PA: IGI Global. doi:10.4018/978-1-59904-857-4.ch063

Mingers, J. (2010). Pluralism, realism, and truth: The keys to knowledge in information systems research. In D. Paradice (Ed.), *Emerging systems approaches in information technologies: Concepts, theories, and applications* (pp. 86–98). Hershey, PA: IGI Global. doi:10.4018/978-1-60566-976-2.ch006

Mital, K. M. (2012). ICT, unique identity and inclusive growth: An Indian perspective. In A. Manoharan & M. Holzer (Eds.), *E-governance and civic engagement: Factors and determinants of e-democracy* (pp. 584–612). Hershey, PA: IGI Global. doi:10.4018/978-1-61350-083-5.ch029

Mizell, A. P. (2008). Helping close the digital divide for financially disadvantaged seniors. In F. Tan (Ed.), *Global information technologies: Concepts, methodologies, tools, and applications* (pp. 2396–2402). Hershey, PA: IGI Global. doi:10.4018/978-1-59904-939-7.ch173

Molinari, F., Wills, C., Koumpis, A., & Moumtzi, V. (2011). A citizen-centric platform to support networking in the area of e-democracy. In H. Rahman (Ed.), *Cases on adoption, diffusion and evaluation of global e-governance systems: Impact at the grass roots* (pp. 282–302). Hershey, PA: IGI Global. doi:10.4018/978-1-61692-814-8.ch014

Molinari, F., Wills, C., Koumpis, A., & Moumtzi, V. (2013). A citizen-centric platform to support networking in the area of e-democracy. In H. Rahman (Ed.), *Cases on progressions and challenges in ICT utilization for citizen-centric governance* (pp. 265–297). Hershey, PA: IGI Global. doi:10.4018/978-1-4666-2071-1.ch013

Monteverde, F. (2010). The process of e-government public policy inclusion in the governmental agenda: A framework for assessment and case study. In J. Cordoba-Pachon & A. Ochoa-Arias (Eds.), *Systems thinking and e-participation: ICT in the governance of society* (pp. 233–245). Hershey, PA: IGI Global. doi:10.4018/978-1-60566-860-4.ch015

Moodley, S. (2008). Deconstructing the South African government's ICT for development discourse. In A. Anttiroiko (Ed.), *Electronic government: Concepts, methodologies, tools, and applications* (pp. 622–631). Hershey, PA: IGI Global. doi:10.4018/978-1-59904-947-2.ch053

Moodley, S. (2008). Deconstructing the South African government's ICT for development discourse. In C. Van Slyke (Ed.), *Information communication technologies: Concepts, methodologies, tools, and applications* (pp. 816–825). Hershey, PA: IGI Global. doi:10.4018/978-1-59904-949-6.ch052

Mora, M., Cervantes-Perez, F., Gelman-Muravchik, O., Forgionne, G. A., & Mejia-Olvera, M. (2003). DMSS implementation research: A conceptual analysis of the contributions and limitations of the factor-based and stage-based streams. In G. Forgionne, J. Gupta, & M. Mora (Eds.), *Decision-making support systems: Achievements and challenges for the new decade* (pp. 331–356). Hershey, PA: IGI Global. doi:10.4018/978-1-59140-045-5.ch020

Mörtberg, C., & Elovaara, P. (2010). Attaching people and technology: Between e and government. In S. Booth, S. Goodman, & G. Kirkup (Eds.), *Gender issues in learning and working with information technology: Social constructs and cultural contexts* (pp. 83–98). Hershey, PA: IGI Global. doi:10.4018/978-1-61520-813-5.ch005

Murphy, J., Harper, E., Devine, E. C., Burke, L. J., & Hook, M. L. (2011). Case study: Lessons learned when embedding evidence-based knowledge in a nurse care planning and documentation system. In A. Cashin & R. Cook (Eds.), *Evidence-based practice in nursing informatics: Concepts and applications* (pp. 174–190). Hershey, PA: IGI Global. doi:10.4018/978-1-60960-034-1.ch014

Mutula, S. M. (2013). E-government's role in poverty alleviation: Case study of South Africa. In H. Rahman (Ed.), *Cases on progressions and challenges in ICT utilization for citizen-centric governance* (pp. 44–68). Hershey, PA: IGI Global. doi:10.4018/978-1-4666-2071-1.ch003

Nath, R., & Angeles, R. (2005). Relationships between supply characteristics and buyer-supplier coupling in e-procurement: An empirical analysis. *International Journal of E-Business Research*, *1*(2), 40–55. doi:10.4018/jebr.2005040103

Nissen, M. E. (2006). Application cases in government. In M. Nissen (Ed.), *Harnessing knowledge dynamics: Principled organizational knowing & learning* (pp. 152–181). Hershey, PA: IGI Global. doi:10.4018/978-1-59140-773-7.ch008

Norris, D. F. (2003). Leading-edge information technologies and American local governments. In G. Garson (Ed.), *Public information technology: Policy and management issues* (pp. 139–169). Hershey, PA: IGI Global. doi:10.4018/978-1-59140-060-8.ch007

Norris, D. F. (2008). Information technology among U.S. local governments. In G. Garson & M. Khosrow-Pour (Eds.), *Handbook of research on public information technology* (pp. 132–144). Hershey, PA: IGI Global. doi:10.4018/978-1-59904-857-4.ch013

Northrop, A. (1999). The challenge of teaching information technology in public administration graduate programs. In G. Garson (Ed.), *Information technology and computer applications in public administration: Issues and trends* (pp. 1–22). Hershey, PA: IGI Global. doi:10.4018/978-1-87828-952-0.ch001

Northrop, A. (2003). Information technology and public administration: The view from the profession. In G. Garson (Ed.), *Public information technology: Policy and management issues* (pp. 1–19). Hershey, PA: IGI Global. doi:10.4018/978-1-59140-060-8.ch001

Northrop, A. (2007). Lip service? How PA journals and textbooks view information technology. In G. Garson (Ed.), *Modern public information technology systems: Issues and challenges* (pp. 1–16). Hershey, PA: IGI Global. doi:10.4018/978-1-59904-051-6.ch001

Null, E. (2013). Legal and political barriers to municipal networks in the United States. In A. Abdelaal (Ed.), *Social and economic effects of community wireless networks and infrastructures* (pp. 27–56). Hershey, PA: IGI Global. doi:10.4018/978-1-4666-2997-4.ch003

Okunoye, A., Frolick, M., & Crable, E. (2006). ERP implementation in higher education: An account of pre-implementation and implementation phases. *Journal of Cases on Information Technology*, *8*(2), 110–132. doi:10.4018/jcit.2006040106

Olasina, G. (2012). A review of egovernment services in Nigeria. In A. Tella & A. Issa (Eds.), *Library and information science in developing countries: Contemporary issues* (pp. 205–221). Hershey, PA: IGI Global. doi:10.4018/978-1-61350-335-5.ch015

Orgeron, C. P. (2008). A model for reengineering IT job classes in state government. In G. Garson & M. Khosrow-Pour (Eds.), *Handbook of research on public information technology* (pp. 735–746). Hershey, PA: IGI Global. doi:10.4018/978-1-59904-857-4.ch066

Owsinski, J. W., & Pielak, A. M. (2011). Local authority websites in rural areas: Measuring quality and functionality, and assessing the role. In Z. Andreopoulou, B. Manos, N. Polman, & D. Viaggi (Eds.), *Agricultural and environmental informatics, governance and management: Emerging research applications* (pp. 39–60). Hershey, PA: IGI Global. doi:10.4018/978-1-60960-621-3.ch003

Owsiński, J. W., Pielak, A. M., Sęp, K., & Stańczak, J. (2014). Local web-based networks in rural municipalities: Extension, density, and meaning. In Z. Andreopoulou, V. Samathrakis, S. Louca, & M. Vlachopoulou (Eds.), *E-innovation for sustainable development of rural resources during global economic crisis* (pp. 126–151). Hershey, PA: IGI Global. doi:10.4018/978-1-4666-4550-9.ch011

Pagani, M., & Pasinetti, C. (2008). Technical and functional quality in the development of t-government services. In A. Anttiroiko (Ed.), *Electronic government: Concepts, methodologies, tools, and applications* (pp. 2943–2965). Hershey, PA: IGI Global. doi:10.4018/978-1-59904-947-2.ch220

Pani, A. K., & Agrahari, A. (2005). On e-markets in emerging economy: An Indian experience. In M. Khosrow-Pour (Ed.), *Advanced topics in electronic commerce* (Vol. 1, pp. 287–299). Hershey, PA: IGI Global. doi:10.4018/978-1-59140-819-2.ch015

Papadopoulos, T., Angelopoulos, S., & Kitsios, F. (2011). A strategic approach to e-health interoperability using e-government frameworks. In A. Lazakidou, K. Siassiakos, & K. Ioannou (Eds.), *Wireless technologies for ambient assisted living and healthcare: Systems and applications* (pp. 213–229). Hershey, PA: IGI Global. doi:10.4018/978-1-61520-805-0.ch012

Papadopoulos, T., Angelopoulos, S., & Kitsios, F. (2013). A strategic approach to e-health interoperability using e-government frameworks. In *User-driven healthcare: Concepts, methodologies, tools, and applications* (pp. 791–807). Hershey, PA: IGI Global. doi:10.4018/978-1-4666-2770-3.ch039

Papaleo, G., Chiarella, D., Aiello, M., & Caviglione, L. (2012). Analysis, development and deployment of statistical anomaly detection techniques for real e-mail traffic. In T. Chou (Ed.), *Information assurance and security technologies for risk assessment and threat management: Advances* (pp. 47–71). Hershey, PA: IGI Global. doi:10.4018/978-1-61350-507-6.ch003

Papp, R. (2003). Information technology & FDA compliance in the pharmaceutical industry. In M. Khosrow-Pour (Ed.), *Annals of cases on information technology* (Vol. 5, pp. 262–273). Hershey, PA: IGI Global. doi:10.4018/978-1-59140-061-5.ch017

Parsons, T. W. (2007). Developing a knowledge management portal. In A. Tatnall (Ed.), *Encyclopedia of portal technologies and applications* (pp. 223–227). Hershey, PA: IGI Global. doi:10.4018/978-1-59140-989-2.ch039

Passaris, C. E. (2007). Immigration and digital government. In A. Anttiroiko & M. Malkia (Eds.), *Encyclopedia of digital government* (pp. 988–994). Hershey, PA: IGI Global. doi:10.4018/978-1-59140-789-8.ch148

Pavlichev, A. (2004). The e-government challenge for public administration. In A. Pavlichev & G. Garson (Eds.), *Digital government: Principles and best practices* (pp. 276–290). Hershey, PA: IGI Global. doi:10.4018/978-1-59140-122-3.ch018

Penrod, J. I., & Harbor, A. F. (2000). Designing and implementing a learning organization-oriented information technology planning and management process. In L. Petrides (Ed.), *Case studies on information technology in higher education: Implications for policy and practice* (pp. 7–19). Hershey, PA: IGI Global. doi:10.4018/978-1-878289-74-2.ch001

Planas-Silva, M. D., & Joseph, R. C. (2011). Perspectives on the adoption of electronic resources for use in clinical trials. In M. Guah (Ed.), *Healthcare delivery reform and new technologies: Organizational initiatives* (pp. 19–28). Hershey, PA: IGI Global. doi:10.4018/978-1-60960-183-6.ch002

Pomazalová, N., & Rejman, S. (2013). The rationale behind implementation of new electronic tools for electronic public procurement. In N. Pomazalová (Ed.), *Public sector transformation processes and internet public procurement: Decision support systems* (pp. 85–117). Hershey, PA: IGI Global. doi:10.4018/978-1-4666-2665-2.ch006

Postorino, M. N. (2012). City competitiveness and airport: Information science perspective. In M. Bulu (Ed.), *City competitiveness and improving urban subsystems: Technologies and applications* (pp. 61–83). Hershey, PA: IGI Global. doi:10.4018/978-1-61350-174-0.ch004

Poupa, C. (2002). Electronic government in Switzerland: Priorities for 2001-2005 - Electronic voting and federal portal. In Å. Grönlund (Ed.), *Electronic government: Design, applications and management* (pp. 356–369). Hershey, PA: IGI Global. doi:10.4018/978-1-930708-19-8.ch017

Powell, S. R. (2010). Interdisciplinarity in telecommunications and networking. In *Networking and telecommunications: Concepts, methodologies, tools and applications* (pp. 33–40). Hershey, PA: IGI Global. doi:10.4018/978-1-60566-986-1.ch004

Priya, P. S., & Mathiyalagan, N. (2011). A study of the implementation status of two e-governance projects in land revenue administration in India. In M. Shareef, V. Kumar, U. Kumar, & Y. Dwivedi (Eds.), *Stakeholder adoption of e-government services: Driving and resisting factors* (pp. 214–230). Hershey, PA: IGI Global. doi:10.4018/978-1-60960-601-5.ch011

Prysby, C., & Prysby, N. (2000). Electronic mail, employee privacy and the workplace. In L. Janczewski (Ed.), *Internet and intranet security management: Risks and solutions* (pp. 251–270). Hershey, PA: IGI Global. doi:10.4018/978-1-878289-71-1.ch009

Prysby, C. L., & Prysby, N. D. (2003). Electronic mail in the public workplace: Issues of privacy and public disclosure. In G. Garson (Ed.), *Public information technology: Policy and management issues* (pp. 271–298). Hershey, PA: IGI Global. doi:10.4018/978-1-59140-060-8.ch012

Prysby, C. L., & Prysby, N. D. (2007). You have mail, but who is reading it? Issues of e-mail in the public workplace. In G. Garson (Ed.), *Modern public information technology systems: Issues and challenges* (pp. 312–336). Hershey, PA: IGI Global. doi:10.4018/978-1-59904-051-6.ch016

Radl, A., & Chen, Y. (2005). Computer security in electronic government: A state-local education information system. *International Journal of Electronic Government Research*, *1*(1), 79–99. doi:10.4018/jegr.2005010105

Rahman, H. (2008). Information dynamics in developing countries. In C. Van Slyke (Ed.), *Information communication technologies: Concepts, methodologies, tools, and applications* (pp. 104–114). Hershey, PA: IGI Global. doi:10.4018/978-1-59904-949-6.ch008

Ramanathan, J. (2009). Adaptive IT architecture as a catalyst for network capability in government. In P. Saha (Ed.), *Advances in government enterprise architecture* (pp. 149–172). Hershey, PA: IGI Global. doi:10.4018/978-1-60566-068-4.ch007

Ramos, I., & Berry, D. M. (2006). Social construction of information technology supporting work. In M. Khosrow-Pour (Ed.), *Cases on information technology: Lessons learned* (Vol. 7, pp. 36–52). Hershey, PA: IGI Global. doi:10.4018/978-1-59140-673-0.ch003

Ray, D., Gulla, U., Gupta, M. P., & Dash, S. S. (2009). Interoperability and constituents of interoperable systems in public sector. In V. Weerakkody, M. Janssen, & Y. Dwivedi (Eds.), *Handbook of research on ICT-enabled transformational government: A global perspective* (pp. 175–195). Hershey, PA: IGI Global. doi:10.4018/978-1-60566-390-6.ch010

Reddick, C. G. (2007). E-government and creating a citizen-centric government: A study of federal government CIOs. In G. Garson (Ed.), *Modern public information technology systems: Issues and challenges* (pp. 143–165). Hershey, PA: IGI Global. doi:10.4018/978-1-59904-051-6.ch008

Reddick, C. G. (2010). Citizen-centric e-government. In C. Reddick (Ed.), *Homeland security preparedness and information systems: Strategies for managing public policy* (pp. 45–75). Hershey, PA: IGI Global. doi:10.4018/978-1-60566-834-5.ch002

Reddick, C. G. (2010). E-government and creating a citizen-centric government: A study of federal government CIOs. In C. Reddick (Ed.), *Homeland security preparedness and information systems: Strategies for managing public policy* (pp. 230–250). Hershey, PA: IGI Global. doi:10.4018/978-1-60566-834-5.ch012

Reddick, C. G. (2010). Perceived effectiveness of e-government and its usage in city governments: Survey evidence from information technology directors. In C. Reddick (Ed.), *Homeland security preparedness and information systems: Strategies for managing public policy* (pp. 213–229). Hershey, PA: IGI Global. doi:10.4018/978-1-60566-834-5.ch011

Reddick, C. G. (2012). Customer relationship management adoption in local governments in the United States. In S. Chhabra & M. Kumar (Eds.), *Strategic enterprise resource planning models for e-government: Applications and methodologies* (pp. 111–124). Hershey, PA: IGI Global. doi:10.4018/978-1-60960-863-7.ch008

Reeder, F. S., & Pandy, S. M. (2008). Identifying effective funding models for e-government. In A. Anttiroiko (Ed.), *Electronic government: Concepts, methodologies, tools, and applications* (pp. 1108–1138). Hershey, PA: IGI Global. doi:10.4018/978-1-59904-947-2.ch083

Riesco, D., Acosta, E., & Montejano, G. (2003). An extension to a UML activity graph from workflow. In L. Favre (Ed.), *UML and the unified process* (pp. 294–314). Hershey, PA: IGI Global. doi:10.4018/978-1-93177-744-5.ch015

Ritzhaupt, A. D., & Gill, T. G. (2008). A hybrid and novel approach to teaching computer programming in MIS curriculum. In S. Negash, M. Whitman, A. Woszczynski, K. Hoganson, & H. Mattord (Eds.), *Handbook of distance learning for real-time and asynchronous information technology education* (pp. 259–281). Hershey, PA: IGI Global. doi:10.4018/978-1-59904-964-9.ch014

Roche, E. M. (1993). International computing and the international regime. *Journal of Global Information Management, 1*(2), 33–44. doi:10.4018/jgim.1993040103

Rocheleau, B. (2007). Politics, accountability, and information management. In G. Garson (Ed.), *Modern public information technology systems: Issues and challenges* (pp. 35–71). Hershey, PA: IGI Global. doi:10.4018/978-1-59904-051-6.ch003

Rodrigues Filho, J. (2010). E-government in Brazil: Reinforcing dominant institutions or reducing citizenship? In C. Reddick (Ed.), *Politics, democracy and e-government: Participation and service delivery* (pp. 347–362). Hershey, PA: IGI Global. doi:10.4018/978-1-61520-933-0.ch021

Rodriguez, S. R., & Thorp, D. A. (2013). eLearning for industry: A case study of the project management process. In A. Benson, J. Moore, & S. Williams van Rooij (Eds.), Cases on educational technology planning, design, and implementation: A project management perspective (pp. 319-342). Hershey, PA: IGI Global. doi:10.4018/978-1-4666-4237-9.ch017

Roman, A. V. (2013). Delineating three dimensions of e-government success: Security, functionality, and transformation. In J. Gil-Garcia (Ed.), *E-government success factors and measures: Theories, concepts, and methodologies* (pp. 171–192). Hershey, PA: IGI Global. doi:10.4018/978-1-4666-4058-0.ch010

Ross, S. C., Tyran, C. K., & Auer, D. J. (2008). Up in smoke: Rebuilding after an IT disaster. In H. Nemati (Ed.), *Information security and ethics: Concepts, methodologies, tools, and applications* (pp. 3659–3675). Hershey, PA: IGI Global. doi:10.4018/978-1-59904-937-3.ch248

Ross, S. C., Tyran, C. K., Auer, D. J., Junell, J. M., & Williams, T. G. (2005). Up in smoke: Rebuilding after an IT disaster. *Journal of Cases on Information Technology*, *7*(2), 31–49. doi:10.4018/jcit.2005040103

Roy, J. (2008). Security, sovereignty, and continental interoperability: Canada's elusive balance. In T. Loendorf & G. Garson (Eds.), *Patriotic information systems* (pp. 153–176). Hershey, PA: IGI Global. doi:10.4018/978-1-59904-594-8.ch007

Rubeck, R. F., & Miller, G. A. (2009). vGOV: Remote video access to government services. In A. Scupola (Ed.), Cases on managing e-services (pp. 253-268). Hershey, PA: IGI Global. doi:10.4018/978-1-60566-064-6.ch017

Saekow, A., & Boonmee, C. (2011). The challenges of implementing e-government interoperability in Thailand: Case of official electronic correspondence letters exchange across government departments. In Y. Charalabidis (Ed.), *Interoperability in digital public services and administration: Bridging e-government and e-business* (pp. 40–61). Hershey, PA: IGI Global. doi:10.4018/978-1-61520-887-6.ch003

Saekow, A., & Boonmee, C. (2012). The challenges of implementing e-government interoperability in Thailand: Case of official electronic correspondence letters exchange across government departments. In *Digital democracy: Concepts, methodologies, tools, and applications* (pp. 1883–1905). Hershey, PA: IGI Global. doi:10.4018/978-1-4666-1740-7.ch094

Sagsan, M., & Medeni, T. (2012). Understanding "knowledge management (KM) paradigms" from social media perspective: An empirical study on discussion group for KM at professional networking site. In M. Cruz-Cunha, P. Gonçalves, N. Lopes, E. Miranda, & G. Putnik (Eds.), *Handbook of research on business social networking: Organizational, managerial, and technological dimensions* (pp. 738–755). Hershey, PA: IGI Global. doi:10.4018/978-1-61350-168-9.ch039

Sahi, G., & Madan, S. (2013). Information security threats in ERP enabled e-governance: Challenges and solutions. In *Enterprise resource planning: Concepts, methodologies, tools, and applications* (pp. 825–837). Hershey, PA: IGI Global. doi:10.4018/978-1-4666-4153-2.ch048

Sanford, C., & Bhattacherjee, A. (2008). IT implementation in a developing country municipality: A sociocognitive analysis. *International Journal of Technology and Human Interaction*, *4*(3), 68–93. doi:10.4018/jthi.2008070104

Schelin, S. H. (2003). E-government: An overview. In G. Garson (Ed.), *Public information technology: Policy and management issues* (pp. 120–138). Hershey, PA: IGI Global. doi:10.4018/978-1-59140-060-8.ch006

Schelin, S. H. (2004). Training for digital government. In A. Pavlichev & G. Garson (Eds.), *Digital government: Principles and best practices* (pp. 263–275). Hershey, PA: IGI Global. doi:10.4018/978-1-59140-122-3.ch017

Schelin, S. H. (2007). E-government: An overview. In G. Garson (Ed.), *Modern public information technology systems: Issues and challenges* (pp. 110–126). Hershey, PA: IGI Global. doi:10.4018/978-1-59904-051-6.ch006

Schelin, S. H., & Garson, G. (2004). Theoretical justification of critical success factors. In G. Garson & S. Schelin (Eds.), *IT solutions series: Humanizing information technology: Advice from experts* (pp. 4–15). Hershey, PA: IGI Global. doi:10.4018/978-1-59140-245-9.ch002

Scime, A. (2002). Information systems and computer science model curricula: A comparative look. In M. Dadashzadeh, A. Saber, & S. Saber (Eds.), *Information technology education in the new millennium* (pp. 146–158). Hershey, PA: IGI Global. doi:10.4018/978-1-931777-05-6.ch018

Scime, A. (2009). Computing curriculum analysis and development. In M. Khosrow-Pour (Ed.), *Encyclopedia of information science and technology* (2nd ed.; pp. 667–671). Hershey, PA: IGI Global. doi:10.4018/978-1-60566-026-4.ch108

Scime, A., & Wania, C. (2008). Computing curricula: A comparison of models. In C. Van Slyke (Ed.), *Information communication technologies: Concepts, methodologies, tools, and applications* (pp. 1270–1283). Hershey, PA: IGI Global. doi:10.4018/978-1-59904-949-6.ch088

Seidman, S. B. (2009). An international perspective on professional software engineering credentials. In H. Ellis, S. Demurjian, & J. Naveda (Eds.), *Software engineering: Effective teaching and learning approaches and practices* (pp. 351–361). Hershey, PA: IGI Global. doi:10.4018/978-1-60566-102-5.ch018

Seifert, J. W. (2007). E-government act of 2002 in the United States. In A. Anttiroiko & M. Malkia (Eds.), *Encyclopedia of digital government* (pp. 476–481). Hershey, PA: IGI Global. doi:10.4018/978-1-59140-789-8.ch072

Seifert, J. W., & Relyea, H. C. (2008). E-government act of 2002 in the United States. In A. Anttiroiko (Ed.), *Electronic government: Concepts, methodologies, tools, and applications* (pp. 154–161). Hershey, PA: IGI Global. doi:10.4018/978-1-59904-947-2.ch013

Seufert, S. (2002). E-learning business models: Framework and best practice examples. In M. Raisinghani (Ed.), *Cases on worldwide e-commerce: Theory in action* (pp. 70–94). Hershey, PA: IGI Global. doi:10.4018/978-1-930708-27-3.ch004

Shareef, M. A., & Archer, N. (2012). E-government service development. In M. Shareef, N. Archer, & S. Dutta (Eds.), *E-government service maturity and development: Cultural, organizational and technological perspectives* (pp. 1–14). Hershey, PA: IGI Global. doi:10.4018/978-1-60960-848-4.ch001

Shareef, M. A., & Archer, N. (2012). E-government initiatives: Review studies on different countries. In M. Shareef, N. Archer, & S. Dutta (Eds.), *E-government service maturity and development: Cultural, organizational and technological perspectives* (pp. 40–76). Hershey, PA: IGI Global. doi:10.4018/978-1-60960-848-4.ch003

Shareef, M. A., Kumar, U., & Kumar, V. (2011). E-government development: Performance evaluation parameters. In M. Shareef, V. Kumar, U. Kumar, & Y. Dwivedi (Eds.), *Stakeholder adoption of e-government services: Driving and resisting factors* (pp. 197–213). Hershey, PA: IGI Global. doi:10.4018/978-1-60960-601-5.ch010

Shareef, M. A., Kumar, U., Kumar, V., & Niktash, M. (2012). Electronic-government vision: Case studies for objectives, strategies, and initiatives. In M. Shareef, N. Archer, & S. Dutta (Eds.), *E-government service maturity and development: Cultural, organizational and technological perspectives* (pp. 15–39). Hershey, PA: IGI Global. doi:10.4018/978-1-60960-848-4.ch002

Shukla, P., Kumar, A., & Anu Kumar, P. B. (2013). Impact of national culture on business continuity management system implementation. *International Journal of Risk and Contingency Management*, 2(3), 23–36. doi:10.4018/ijrcm.2013070102

Shulman, S. W. (2007). The federal docket management system and the prospect for digital democracy in U S rulemaking. In G. Garson (Ed.), *Modern public information technology systems: Issues and challenges* (pp. 166–184). Hershey, PA: IGI Global. doi:10.4018/978-1-59904-051-6.ch009

Simonovic, S. (2007). Problems of offline government in e-Serbia. In A. Anttiroiko & M. Malkia (Eds.), *Encyclopedia of digital government* (pp. 1342–1351). Hershey, PA: IGI Global. doi:10.4018/978-1-59140-789-8.ch205

Simonovic, S. (2008). Problems of offline government in e-Serbia. In A. Anttiroiko (Ed.), *Electronic government: Concepts, methodologies, tools, and applications* (pp. 2929–2942). Hershey, PA: IGI Global. doi:10.4018/978-1-59904-947-2.ch219

Singh, A. M. (2005). Information systems and technology in South Africa. In M. Khosrow-Pour (Ed.), *Encyclopedia of information science and technology* (pp. 1497–1502). Hershey, PA: IGI Global. doi:10.4018/978-1-59140-553-5.ch263

Singh, S., & Naidoo, G. (2005). Towards an e-government solution: A South African perspective. In W. Huang, K. Siau, & K. Wei (Eds.), *Electronic government strategies and implementation* (pp. 325–353). Hershey, PA: IGI Global. doi:10.4018/978-1-59140-348-7.ch014

Snoke, R., & Underwood, A. (2002). Generic attributes of IS graduates: An analysis of Australian views. In F. Tan (Ed.), *Advanced topics in global information management* (Vol. 1, pp. 370–384). Hershey, PA: IGI Global. doi:10.4018/978-1-930708-43-3.ch023

Sommer, L. (2006). Revealing unseen organizations in higher education: A study framework and application example. In A. Metcalfe (Ed.), *Knowledge management and higher education: A critical analysis* (pp. 115–146). Hershey, PA: IGI Global. doi:10.4018/978-1-59140-509-2.ch007

Song, H., Kidd, T., & Owens, E. (2011). Examining technological disparities and instructional practices in English language arts classroom: Implications for school leadership and teacher training. In L. Tomei (Ed.), *Online courses and ICT in education: Emerging practices and applications* (pp. 258–274). Hershey, PA: IGI Global. doi:10.4018/978-1-60960-150-8.ch020

Speaker, P. J., & Kleist, V. F. (2003). Using information technology to meet electronic commerce and MIS education demands. In A. Aggarwal (Ed.), *Web-based education: Learning from experience* (pp. 280–291). Hershey, PA: IGI Global. doi:10.4018/978-1-59140-102-5.ch017

Spitler, V. K. (2007). Learning to use IT in the workplace: Mechanisms and masters. In M. Mahmood (Ed.), *Contemporary issues in end user computing* (pp. 292–323). Hershey, PA: IGI Global. doi:10.4018/978-1-59140-926-7.ch013

Stellefson, M. (2011). Considerations for marketing distance education courses in health education: Five important questions to examine before development. In U. Demiray & S. Sever (Eds.), *Marketing online education programs: Frameworks for promotion and communication* (pp. 222–234). Hershey, PA: IGI Global. doi:10.4018/978-1-60960-074-7.ch014

Straub, D. W., & Loch, K. D. (2006). Creating and developing a program of global research. *Journal of Global Information Management, 14*(2), 1–28. doi:10.4018/jgim.2006040101

Straub, D. W., Loch, K. D., & Hill, C. E. (2002). Transfer of information technology to the Arab world: A test of cultural influence modeling. In M. Dadashzadeh (Ed.), *Information technology management in developing countries* (pp. 92–134). Hershey, PA: IGI Global. doi:10.4018/978-1-931777-03-2.ch005

Straub, D. W., Loch, K. D., & Hill, C. E. (2003). Transfer of information technology to the Arab world: A test of cultural influence modeling. In F. Tan (Ed.), *Advanced topics in global information management* (Vol. 2, pp. 141–172). Hershey, PA: IGI Global. doi:10.4018/978-1-59140-064-6.ch009

Suki, N. M., Ramayah, T., Ming, M. K., & Suki, N. M. (2013). Factors enhancing employed job seekers intentions to use social networking sites as a job search tool. In A. Mesquita (Ed.), *User perception and influencing factors of technology in everyday life* (pp. 265–281). Hershey, PA: IGI Global. doi:10.4018/978-1-4666-1954-8.ch018

Suomi, R. (2006). Introducing electronic patient records to hospitals: Innovation adoption paths. In T. Spil & R. Schuring (Eds.), *E-health systems diffusion and use: The innovation, the user and the use IT model* (pp. 128–146). Hershey, PA: IGI Global. doi:10.4018/978-1-59140-423-1.ch008

Swim, J., & Barker, L. (2012). Pathways into a gendered occupation: Brazilian women in IT. *International Journal of Social and Organizational Dynamics in IT*, 2(4), 34–51. doi:10.4018/ijsodit.2012100103

Tarafdar, M., & Vaidya, S. D. (2006). Adoption and implementation of IT in developing nations: Experiences from two public sector enterprises in India. In M. Khosrow-Pour (Ed.), *Cases on information technology planning, design and implementation* (pp. 208–233). Hershey, PA: IGI Global. doi:10.4018/978-1-59904-408-8.ch013

Tarafdar, M., & Vaidya, S. D. (2008). Adoption and implementation of IT in developing nations: Experiences from two public sector enterprises in India. In G. Garson & M. Khosrow-Pour (Eds.), *Handbook of research on public information technology* (pp. 905–924). Hershey, PA: IGI Global. doi:10.4018/978-1-59904-857-4.ch076

Thesing, Z. (2007). Zarina thesing, pumpkin patch. In M. Hunter (Ed.), *Contemporary chief information officers: Management experiences* (pp. 83–94). Hershey, PA: IGI Global. doi:10.4018/978-1-59904-078-3.ch007

Thomas, J. C. (2004). Public involvement in public administration in the information age: Speculations on the effects of technology. In M. Malkia, A. Anttiroiko, & R. Savolainen (Eds.), *eTransformation in governance: New directions in government and politics* (pp. 67–84). Hershey, PA: IGI Global. doi:10.4018/978-1-59140-130-8.ch004

Treiblmaier, H., & Chong, S. (2013). Trust and perceived risk of personal information as antecedents of online information disclosure: Results from three countries. In F. Tan (Ed.), *Global diffusion and adoption of technologies for knowledge and information sharing* (pp. 341–361). Hershey, PA: IGI Global. doi:10.4018/978-1-4666-2142-8.ch015 van Grembergen, W., & de Haes, S. (2008). IT governance in practice: Six case studies. In W. van Grembergen & S. De Haes (Eds.), *Implementing information technology governance: Models, practices and cases* (pp. 125–237). Hershey, PA: IGI Global. doi:10.4018/978-1-59904-924-3.ch004

van Os, G., Homburg, V., & Bekkers, V. (2013). Contingencies and convergence in European social security: ICT coordination in the back office of the welfare state. In M. Cruz-Cunha, I. Miranda, & P. Gonçalves (Eds.), *Handbook of research on ICTs and management systems for improving efficiency in healthcare and social care* (pp. 268–287). Hershey, PA: IGI Global. doi:10.4018/978-1-4666-3990-4.ch013

Velloso, A. B., Gassenferth, W., & Machado, M. A. (2012). Evaluating IBMEC-RJ's intranet usability using fuzzy logic. In M. Cruz-Cunha, P. Gonçalves, N. Lopes, E. Miranda, & G. Putnik (Eds.), *Handbook of research on business social networking: Organizational, managerial, and technological dimensions* (pp. 185–205). Hershey, PA: IGI Global. doi:10.4018/978-1-61350-168-9.ch010

Villablanca, A. C., Baxi, H., & Anderson, K. (2009). Novel data interface for evaluating cardiovascular outcomes in women. In A. Dwivedi (Ed.), *Handbook of research on information technology management and clinical data administration in healthcare* (pp. 34–53). Hershey, PA: IGI Global. doi:10.4018/978-1-60566-356-2.ch003

Villablanca, A. C., Baxi, H., & Anderson, K. (2011). Novel data interface for evaluating cardiovascular outcomes in women. In *Clinical technologies: Concepts, methodologies, tools and applications* (pp. 2094–2113). Hershey, PA: IGI Global. doi:10.4018/978-1-60960-561-2.ch806

Virkar, S. (2011). Information and communication technologies in administrative reform for development: Exploring the case of property tax systems in Karnataka, India. In J. Steyn, J. Van Belle, & E. Mansilla (Eds.), *ICTs for global development and sustainability: Practice and applications* (pp. 127–149). Hershey, PA: IGI Global. doi:10.4018/978-1-61520-997-2.ch006

Virkar, S. (2013). Designing and implementing e-government projects: Actors, influences, and fields of play. In S. Saeed & C. Reddick (Eds.), *Human-centered system design for electronic governance* (pp. 88–110). Hershey, PA: IGI Global. doi:10.4018/978-1-4666-3640-8.ch007

Wallace, A. (2009). E-justice: An Australian perspective. In A. Martínez & P. Abat (Eds.), *E-justice: Using information communication technologies in the court system* (pp. 204–228). Hershey, PA: IGI Global. doi:10.4018/978-1-59904-998-4.ch014

Wang, G. (2012). E-democratic administration and bureaucratic responsiveness: A primary study of bureaucrats' perceptions of the civil service e-mail box in Taiwan. In K. Kloby & M. D'Agostino (Eds.), *Citizen 2.0: Public and governmental interaction through web 2.0 technologies* (pp. 146–173). Hershey, PA: IGI Global. doi:10.4018/978-1-4666-0318-9.ch009

Wangpipatwong, S., Chutimaskul, W., & Papasratorn, B. (2011). Quality enhancing the continued use of e-government web sites: Evidence from e-citizens of Thailand. In V. Weerakkody (Ed.), *Applied technology integration in governmental organizations: New e-government research* (pp. 20–36). Hershey, PA: IGI Global. doi:10.4018/978-1-60960-162-1.ch002

Wedemeijer, L. (2006). Long-term evolution of a conceptual schema at a life insurance company. In M. Khosrow-Pour (Ed.), *Cases on database technologies and applications* (pp. 202–226). Hershey, PA: IGI Global. doi:10.4018/978-1-59904-399-9.ch012

Whybrow, E. (2008). Digital access, ICT fluency, and the economically disadvantages: Approaches to minimize the digital divide. In F. Tan (Ed.), *Global information technologies: Concepts, methodologies, tools, and applications* (pp. 1409–1422). Hershey, PA: IGI Global. doi:10.4018/978-1-59904-939-7.ch102

Whybrow, E. (2008). Digital access, ICT fluency, and the economically disadvantages: Approaches to minimize the digital divide. In C. Van Slyke (Ed.), *Information communication technologies: Concepts, methodologies, tools, and applications* (pp. 764–777). Hershey, PA: IGI Global. doi:10.4018/978-1-59904-949-6.ch049

Wickramasinghe, N., & Geisler, E. (2010). Key considerations for the adoption and implementation of knowledge management in healthcare operations. In M. Saito, N. Wickramasinghe, M. Fuji, & E. Geisler (Eds.), *Redesigning innovative healthcare operation and the role of knowledge management* (pp. 125–142). Hershey, PA: IGI Global. doi:10.4018/978-1-60566-284-8.ch009

Wickramasinghe, N., & Geisler, E. (2012). Key considerations for the adoption and implementation of knowledge management in healthcare operations. In *Organizational learning and knowledge: Concepts, methodologies, tools and applications* (pp. 1316–1328). Hershey, PA: IGI Global. doi:10.4018/978-1-60960-783-8.ch405

Wickramasinghe, N., & Goldberg, S. (2007). A framework for delivering m-health excellence. In L. Al-Hakim (Ed.), *Web mobile-based applications for healthcare management* (pp. 36–61). Hershey, PA: IGI Global. doi:10.4018/978-1-59140-658-7.ch002

Wickramasinghe, N., & Goldberg, S. (2008). Critical success factors for delivering m-health excellence. In N. Wickramasinghe & E. Geisler (Eds.), *Encyclopedia of healthcare information systems* (pp. 339–351). Hershey, PA: IGI Global. doi:10.4018/978-1-59904-889-5.ch045

Wyld, D. (2009). Radio frequency identification (RFID) technology. In J. Symonds, J. Ayoade, & D. Parry (Eds.), *Auto-identification and ubiquitous computing applications* (pp. 279–293). Hershey, PA: IGI Global. doi:10.4018/978-1-60566-298-5.ch017

Yaghmaei, F. (2010). Understanding computerised information systems usage in community health. In J. Rodrigues (Ed.), *Health information systems: Concepts, methodologies, tools, and applications* (pp. 1388–1399). Hershey, PA: IGI Global. doi:10.4018/978-1-60566-988-5.ch088

Yee, G., El-Khatib, K., Korba, L., Patrick, A. S., Song, R., & Xu, Y. (2005). Privacy and trust in e-government. In W. Huang, K. Siau, & K. Wei (Eds.), *Electronic government strategies and implementation* (pp. 145–190). Hershey, PA: IGI Global. doi:10.4018/978-1-59140-348-7.ch007

Yeh, S., & Chu, P. (2010). Evaluation of e-government services: A citizen-centric approach to citizen e-complaint services. In C. Reddick (Ed.), *Citizens and e-government: Evaluating policy and management* (pp. 400–417). Hershey, PA: IGI Global. doi:10.4018/978-1-61520-931-6.ch022

Young-Jin, S., & Seang-tae, K. (2008). E-government concepts, measures, and best practices. In A. Anttiroiko (Ed.), *Electronic government: Concepts, methodologies, tools, and applications* (pp. 32–57). Hershey, PA: IGI Global. doi:10.4018/978-1-59904-947-2.ch004

Yun, H. J., & Opheim, C. (2012). New technology communication in American state governments: The impact on citizen participation. In K. Bwalya & S. Zulu (Eds.), *Handbook of research on e-government in emerging economies: Adoption, e-participation, and legal frameworks* (pp. 573–590). Hershey, PA: IGI Global. doi:10.4018/978-1-4666-0324-0.ch029

Zhang, N., Guo, X., Chen, G., & Chau, P. Y. (2011). User evaluation of e-government systems: A Chinese cultural perspective. In F. Tan (Ed.), *International enterprises and global information technologies: Advancing management practices* (pp. 63–84). Hershey, PA: IGI Global. doi:10.4018/978-1-60960-605-3.ch004

Zuo, Y., & Hu, W. (2011). Trust-based information risk management in a supply chain network. In J. Wang (Ed.), *Supply chain optimization, management and integration: Emerging applications* (pp. 181–196). Hershey, PA: IGI Global. doi:10.4018/978-1-60960-135-5.ch013

Compilation of References

Adams, G., & Mullen, E. (2013). Increased voting for candidates who compensate victims rather than punish offenders. *Social Justice Research*, *26*(2), 168–192. doi:10.1007/s11211-013-0179-x

Adams, V. H., Snyder, C. R., Rand, K. L., Kings, E. A., Sigmon, D. R., & Pulvers, K. M. (2003). Hope in the workplace. In R. A. Giacalone & C. L. Jurkiewicz (Eds.), *Handbook of workplace spirituality and organizational performance* (pp. 367–377). New York, NY: Sharpe.

Aguinis, H., & Glavas, A. (2012). What we know and don't know about corporate social responsibility: A review and research agenda. *Journal of Management*, *38*(4), 932–968. doi:10.1177/0149206311436079

Ahmad, N., & Ramayah, T. (2012). Does the notion of 'doing well by doing good' prevail among entrepreneurial ventures in a developing nation? *Journal of Business Ethics*, *106*(4), 479–490. doi:10.1007/s10551-011-1012-9

Ahmed, J., & Shaikh, B. T. (2009). The many faces of supplier induced demand in health care. *Iranian Journal of Public Health*, *38*(2), 139–141. Retrieved from https://www.researchgate.net/publication/233864600_The_Many_Faces_of_Supplier_Induced_Demand_in_Health_Care

Akabayashi, A., & Slingsby, B. (2003). Biomedical ethics in Japan: The second stage. *Cambridge Quarterly of Healthcare Ethics*, *12*(3), 261–264. doi:10.1017/S0963180103123079 PMID:12889330

Alas, R. (2006). Ethics in countries with different cultural dimensions. *Journal of Business Ethics*, *69*(3), 237–247. doi:10.1007/s10551-006-9088-3

Aletras, V. (2012). *Health, healthcare and healthcare business.* Retrieved from Hellenic Open University DMY60 Economic and Financial Management of Health Care Services: https://study.eap.gr/login/index.php

Allan, G. (2003). A critique of using grounded theory as a research method. *Electronic Journal of Business Research Methods*, *2*(1), 1–10. Retrieved from http://citeseerx.ist.psu.edu/viewdoc/download?doi=10.1.1.464.1384&rep=rep1&type=pdf

Alphabet Investor Relations. (2017, August 7). *Google code of conduct.* Retrieved September 22, 2017, from https://abc.xyz/investor/other/google-code-of-conduct.html

Ambler, W. H. (1985). Aristotle's understanding of the naturalness of the city. *The Review of Politics*, *47*(2), 163–185. doi:10.1017/S0034670500036688

American Medical Association & New York Academy of Medicine. (1848). *Code of medical ethics* (A. H. Byfield, Ed.). Retrieved from https://play.google.com/books/reader?id=chY6AQ AAMAAJ&printsec=frontcover&output=reader&hl=en&pg=GBS.PP1

Anagnostopoulos, F., & Papadatou, D. (1992). Factor composition and internal consistency of the questionnaire for recording burnout in a sample of nurses. *Psihologijske Teme*, *5*(3), 183–202. doi:10.5281/zenodo.44229

Ananiadou, K., & Claro, M. (2009). *21st century skills and competences for new millennium learners in OECD countries*. OECD Education Working Papers, No. 41. Paris, France: OECD. Retrieved from 10.1787/218525261154

Andersen, P. A., & Andersen, J. F. (2005). Measurements of perceived nonverbal immediacy. In V. Manusov (Ed.), *The sourcebook of nonverbal measures: Going beyond words* (pp. 113–126). Mahwah, NJ: Erlbaum.

Anderson, C., Ames, D. R., & Gosling, S. D. (2008). Punishing hubris: The perils of overestimating one's status in a group. *Personality and Social Psychology Bulletin*, *34*(1), 90–101. doi:10.1177/0146167207307489 PMID:18162658

Anderson, M. S., & Steneck, N. H. (Eds.). (2011). *International research collaborations: Much to be gained, many ways to get in trouble*. Routledge.

Andreoli, N., & Lefkowitz, J. (2009). Individual and organizational antecedents of misconduct in organizations. *Journal of Business Ethics*, *85*(3), 309–332. doi:10.1007/s10551-008-9772-6

Arbib, M. A. (2005). From monkey-like action recognition to human language: An evolutionary framework for neurolinguistics. *Behavioral and Brain Sciences*, *28*(2), 105–167. doi:10.1017/S0140525X05000038 PMID:16201457

Ardichvili, A., Jondle, D., & Kowske, B. (2010). Dimensions of ethical business cultures: Comparing data from 13 countries of Europe, Asia, and the Americas. *Human Resource Development International*, *13*(3), 299–315. doi:10.1080/13678868.2010.483818

Aristotle, . (2000). *Nicomachean ethics* (R. Crisp, Trans.). Cambridge, UK: Cambridge University Press. doi:10.1017/CBO9780511802058

Arnhart, L. (1990). Aristotle, chimpanzees and other political animals. *Social Sciences Information. Information Sur les Sciences Sociales*, *29*(3), 477–557. doi:10.1177/053901890029003003

Arnhart, L. (1994). The Darwinian biology of Aristotle's political animals. *American Journal of Political Science*, *38*(2), 464–485. doi:10.2307/2111413

Arnhart, L. (1995). The new Darwinian naturalism in political theory. *The American Political Science Review*, *89*(2), 389–400. doi:10.2307/2082432

Arrow, K. J. (1963). Uncertainty and the welfare economics of medical care. *The American Economic Review, 53*(5), 941–973. Retrieved from http://www.jstor.org/stable/1812044

Arvidsson, A., & Peitersen, N. (2013). *The ethical economy: Rebuilding value after the crisis.* New York, NY: Columbia University Press.

Asai, A., Kadooka, Y., & Aizawa, K. (2012). Arguments against promoting organ transplants from brain-dead donors, and views of contemporary Japanese on life and death. *Bioethics, 26*(4), 215–223. doi:10.1111/j.1467-8519.2010.01839.x PMID:20731646

Asgary, N., & Mitschow, M. C. (2002). Toward a model for international business ethics. *Journal of Business Ethics, 36*(3), 239–246. doi:10.1023/A:1014057122480

Ashcraft, D. (2011). *Personality theories workbook* (5th ed.). Belmont, CA: Cengage.

Ashforth, B. E., Gioia, D. A., Robinson, S. L., & Treviño, L. K. (2008). Re-viewing organizational corruption. *Academy of Management Review, 33*(3), 670–684. doi:http://dx.org/10.5465/AMR.2008.32465714

Ashkanasy, N. M., Falkus, S., & Callan, V. J. (2000). Predictors of ethical code use and ethical tolerance in the public sector. *Journal of Business Ethics, 25*(3), 237–253. doi:10.1023/A:1006001722137

Ashley, B. M., DeBlois, J., & O'Rourke, K. D. (2006). *Health care ethics: A Catholic theological analysis.* Washington, DC: Georgetown University Press.

Assmann, J. (2008). *Of God and gods: Egypt, Israel, and the rise of monotheism.* Madison, WI: University of Wisconsin Press.

Aune, B. (2014). *Kant's theory of morals.* Princeton, NJ: Princeton University Press.

Axinn, C., Blair, M., Heorhiadi, A., & Thach, S. (2004). Comparing ethical ideologies across cultures. *Journal of Business Ethics, 54*(2), 103–119. doi:10.1007/s10551-004-0663-1

Bacha, E., & Walker, S. (2013). The relationship between transformational leadership and followers' perceptions of fairness. *Journal of Business Ethics, 116*(3), 667–680. doi:10.1007/s10551-012-1507-z

Bagheri, A. (2009). Japan organ transplantation law: Past, present and future. *Asian Bioethics Review, 1*(4), 452–456. Available from https://muse.jhu.edu/article/416370/pdf

Bailey, C. (2011). Does the Defining Issues Test measure ethical judgment ability or political position? *The Journal of Social Psychology, 151*(3), 314–330. doi:10.1080/00224545.2010.481690 PMID:21675184

Baker, E. (Ed.). (2013). *Social contract: Essays by Locke, Hume and Rousseau.* London: Oxford University Press.

Banks, A., & Valentino, N. (2012). Emotional substrates of white racial attitudes. *American Journal of Political Science*, *56*(2), 286–297. doi:10.1111/j.1540-5907.2011.00561.x

Bannon, D. (2003). Voting, non-voting and consumer buying behaviour: Non-voter segmentation (NVS) and the underlining causes of electoral inactivity. *Journal of Public Affairs*, *3*(2), 138–151. doi:10.1002/pa.142

Barnett, W. (1995). Long-term effects of early childhood programs on cognitive and school outcomes. *The Future of Children*, *5*(3), 25–50. doi:10.2307/1602366

Bass, B. M., & Steidlmeier, P. (1999). Ethics, character, and authentic transformational leadership behavior. *The Leadership Quarterly*, *10*(2), 181–217. doi:(99)00016-810.1016/S1048-9843

Bass, B. M. (1985). *Leadership and performance beyond expectations*. New York, NY: The Free Press.

Bass, B. M. (1990). *Handbook of leadership, theory, research, and managerial applications*. New York, NY: The Free Press.

Bate, P. (Director). (2003). *Congo: White king, red rubber, black death* [Documentary series episode]. British Broadcasting Corporation. Retrieved September 22, 2017, from https://topdocumentaryfilms.com/congo-white-king-red-rubber-black-death/

Bath, C. (2013). Conceptualising listening to young children as an ethic of care in early childhood education and care. *Children & Society*, *27*(5), 361–371. doi:10.1111/j.1099-0860.2011.00407.x

Baumeister, R. F. (2005). *The cultural animal: Human nature, meaning, and social life*. New York, NY: Oxford University Press. doi:10.1093/acprof:oso/9780195167030.001.0001

Bays, D. H. (2003, June). Chinese Protestant Christianity today. *The China Quarterly*, *174*, 488–504. doi:10.1017/S0009443903000299

Beauchamp, T., & Childress, J. (2012). *Principles of biomedical ethics* (7th ed.). New York, NY: Oxford University Press.

Bechtereva, N., & Kambarova, D. (1985). Neurophysiology of emotions and some general brain mechanisms. In B. D. Kirdcaldy (Ed.), *Individual differences in movement* (pp. 169–192). Springer Netherlands; doi:10.1007/978-94-009-4912-6_8

Beekun, R., & Westerman, J. (2012). Spirituality and national culture as antecedents to ethical decision-making: A comparison between the United States and Norway. *Journal of Business Ethics*, *110*(1), 33–44. doi:10.1007/s10551-011-1145-x

Benos, A. (1996). Competition or solidarity: The proposal of primary health care. In G. Kyriopoulos & T. Filalithis (Eds.), *Health policy in Greece: The crossroads of choices* (pp. 43–53). Athens: Themelio.

Bentham, J. (2000). *An introduction to the principles of morals and legislation*. Retrieved from http://socserv.mcmaster.ca/econ/ugcm/3ll3/bentham/morals.pdf (Original work published 1781)

Berebitsky, J. (2000). *Like our very own: Adoption and the changing culture of motherhood, 1851-1950*. University Press of Kansas.

Berger, J. (2009). Replicating Milgram: Would people still obey today? *The American Psychologist, 64*(1), 1–11. doi:10.1037/a0010932 PMID:19209958

Bergstrand, F., & Landgren, J. (2011, August). Visual reporting in time-critical work: Exploring video use in emergency response. In *Proceedings of the 13th International Conference on Human Computer Interaction With Mobile Devices and Services* (pp. 415–424). Academic Press.

Berk, L. E., Mann, T. D., & Ogan, A. T. (2006). Make-believe play: Wellspring for development of self-regulation. In D. G. Singer, R. M. Golinkoff, & K. A. Hirsh-Pasek (Eds.), *Play= learning: How play motivates and enhances children's cognitive and social-emotional growth* (pp. 74–100). New York, NY: Oxford University Press. doi:10.1093/acprof:oso/9780195304381.003.0005

Berrone, P., Surroca, J., & Tribó, J. A. (2007). Corporate ethical identity as a determinant of firm performance: A test of the mediating role of stakeholder satisfaction. *Journal of Business Ethics, 76*(1), 35–53. doi:10.1007/s10551-006-9276-1

Beversluis, E. H. (1987). Is there "no such thing as business ethics"? *Journal of Business Ethics, 6*(2), 81–88. doi:10.1007/BF00382021

Bian, Y. (1997). Bringing strong ties back in: Indirect ties, network bridges, and job searches in China. *American Sociological Review, 62*(3), 366–385. doi:10.2307/2657311

Billioud, S., & Thoraval, J. (2009). 'Lijiao': The return of ceremonies honoring Confucius in mainland China. *China Perspectives, 80*, 82–100. Available from http://search.informit. com.au/documentSummary;dn=371300199876172;res=IELHSS

Bird, S. J. (1996). The role of science professionals in teaching responsible research conduct. *Bioscience, 46*(10), 783–786. doi:10.2307/1312856

Bird, S. J. (2003). Ethics as a core competency in science and engineering. *Science and Engineering Ethics, 9*(4), 443–444. doi:10.1007/s11948-003-0042-9 PMID:14652897

Bird, S. J., & Sieber, J. E. (2005). Teaching ethics in science and engineering: Effective online education. *Science and Engineering Ethics, 11*(3), 323–328. doi:10.1007/s11948-005-0001-8 PMID:16190273

Biron, M. (2010). Negative reciprocity and the association between perceived organizational ethical values and organizational deviance. *Human Relations, 63*(6), 875–897. doi:10.1177/0018726709347159

Bischoff, I., Neuhaus, C., Trautner, P., & Weber, B. (2013). The neuroeconomics of voting: Neural evidence of different sources of utility in voting. *Journal of Neuroscience, Psychology, and Economics, 6*(4), 215–235. doi:10.1037/npe0000016

Black, M. (1976). Are there any philosophically interesting questions in technology? *PSA: Proceedings of the Biennial Meeting of the Philosophy of Science Association, 1976*(2), 185–193. Available from http://www.journals.uchicago.edu/doi/pdfplus/10.1086/psaprocbienmeetp.1976.2.192381

Black, C. E. (1943). *The establishment of constitutional government in Bulgaria*. Princeton, NJ: Princeton University Press.

Bleakley, A., Brice, J., & Bligh, J. (2008). Thinking the post-colonial in medical education. *Medical Education, 42*(3), 266–270. doi:10.1111/j.1365-2923.2007.02991.x PMID:18275413

Blodgett, J., Bakir, A., & Rose, G. (2008). A test of the validity of Hofstede's cultural framework. *Journal of Consumer Marketing, 25*(6), 339–349. doi:10.1108/07363760810902477

Blumstein, A., Fabelo Martin, T., Horn, J., Lehman, D., Tacha, R., & Petersili, J. (2005). *Commentaries on: Sentencing and corrections in the 21st Century: Setting the stage for the future*. Retrieved from https://www.ncjrs.gov/pdffiles1/nij/189106-2a.pdf

Bodrova, E. (2008). Make-believe play versus academic skills: A Vygotskian approach to today's dilemma of early childhood education. *European Early Childhood Research Journal, 16*(3), 357–369. doi:10.1080/13502930802291777

Bodrova, E., & Leong, D. J. (2006). Vygotskian perspectives on teaching and learning early literacy. In S. B. Neuman & D. K. Dickinson (Eds.), *Handbook of early literacy research* (Vol. 2, pp. 243–256). New York, NY: Guilford.

Boer-Jacobs, D., & Fischer, R. (2013). How and when do personal values guide our attitudes and sociality? Explaining cross-cultural variability in attitude-value linkages. *Psychological Bulletin, 139*(5), 1113–1147. doi:10.1037/a0031347 PMID:23339521

Boester, F. (1957). *Summary report of initial organization, ISS delegation: Korea. International Social Service – American Branch (Folder: ISS 1957, box 4). Social Welfare History Archives, Elmer L*. Minneapolis, MN: Anderson Library, University of Minnesota.

Bookman, M. Z., & Bookman, K. R. (2007). *Medical tourism in developing countries*. New York, NY: Palgrave. doi:10.1057/9780230605657

Boulouta, I., & Pitelis, C. N. (2014). Who needs CSR? The impact of corporate social responsibility on national competitiveness. *Journal of Business Ethics, 119*(3), 349–364. doi:10.1007/s10551-013-1633-2

Bowles, M., DeHart, D., & Webb, J. R. (2012). Family influences on female offenders' substance use: The role of adverse childhood events among incarcerated women. *Journal of Family Violence, 27*(7), 681–686. doi:10.1007/s10896-012-9450-4

Brammer, S., Jackson, G., & Matten, D. (2012). Corporate social responsibility and institutional theory: New perspectives on private governance. *Socio-economic Review, 10*(1), 3–28. doi:10.1093/ser/mwr030

Brandt, R. B. (1959). *Ethical theory: The problems of normative and critical ethics.* Retrieved from https://babel.hathitrust.org/cgi/pt?id=uc1.b3423294;view=1up;seq=7

Bremberg, S. (2009). A perfect 10: Why Sweden comes out on top in early child development programming. *Pediatrics & Child Health, 14*(10), 677–680. Retrieved from https://www.ncbi. nlm.nih.gov/pmc/articles/PMC2807813/pdf/pch14677.pdf

Bremer, J. (2008). How global is the global compact? *Business Ethics (Oxford, England), 17*(3), 227–244. doi:10.1111/j.1467-8608.2008.00533.x

Brennan, W. H. (1973). *The Russian foreign ministry and the alliance with Germany, 1878-1884.* Ann Arbor, MI: University of Michigan Press.

Bretzke, J. T. (1996). Cultural particularity and the globalisation of ethics in the light of inculturation. *Pacifica, 9*(1), 69–86. doi:10.1177/1030570X9600900106

Brief, A. P., Burke, M. J., George, J. M., Robinson, B. S., & Webster, J. (1988). Should negative affectivity remain an unmeasured variable in the study of job stress? *The Journal of Applied Psychology, 73*(2), 193–198. doi:10.1037/0021-9010.73.2.193 PMID:3384771

Briggs, K., Workman, J. P., & York, A. S. (2013). Collaborating to cheat: A game theoretic exploration of academic dishonesty in teams. *Academy of Management Learning & Education, 12*(1), 4–17. doi:10.5465/amle.2011.0140

Brooks, J. (1995). *Training and development competence: A practical guide.* London: Kogan Page.

Brown, M. E., & Mitchell, M. S. (2015). Ethical and unethical leadership: Exploring new avenues for future research. *Business Ethics Quarterly, 20*(4), 583–616.

Brown, M. E., & Treviño, L. K. (2006). Ethical leadership: A review and future directions. *The Leadership Quarterly, 17*(6), 595–616. doi:10.1016/j.leaqua.2006.10.004

Brown, M. E., & Treviño, L. K. (2014). Do role models matter? An investigation of role modeling as an antecedent of perceived ethical leadership. *Journal of Business Ethics, 122*(4), 587–598. doi:10.1007/s10551-013-1769-0

Brown, M. E., Treviño, L. K., & Harrison, D. A. (2005). Ethical leadership: A social learning perspective for construct development and testing. *Organizational Behavior and Human Decision Processes, 97*(2), 117–134. doi:10.1016/j.obhdp.2005.03.002

Buciuniene, I., & Kazlauskaite, R. (2012). The linkage between HRM, CSR and performance outcomes. *Baltic Journal of Management, 7*(1), 5–24. doi:10.1108/17465261211195856

Buck, P. S. (n.d.). *The waiting children.* International Social Service – American Branch (Folder 34: Associations: Welcome House, 1955-, box 23). Social Welfare History Archives, Elmer L. Anderson Library, University of Minnesota, Minneapolis, MN.

Bullock, M., & Panicker, S. (2003). Ethics for all: Differences across scientific society codes. *Science and Engineering Ethics, 9*(2), 159–170. doi:10.1007/s11948-003-0003-3 PMID:12774648

Bullrich, E., & Zinny, G. S. (2011). Argentina's new national goal. *Council of the Americas Quarterly, 5*(4), 34.

Bureau of Labor Statistics. (2010). *Labor force statistics from the current population survey.* Retrieved from http://www.bls.gov/cps/

Bureau of Labor Statistics. (2012). *Labor force statistics from the current population survey.* Retrieved from http://www.bls.gov/cps/cpsaat11.htm

Burnside, J. M. (1956). *International Social Service – American Branch (Folder: ISS-Branches, 1-1956-Dec. 1956, Korea "RRA-5," Box 35). Social Welfare History Archives, Elmer L.* Minneapolis, MN: Anderson Library, University of Minnesota. [Letter]

Burns, R. (1995). *The adult learner at work.* Sydney, Australia: Business and Professional.

Buttigieg, S. C., Rathert, C., D'Aunno, T. A., & Savage, G. T. (2015). International research in health care management: Its need in the 21st century, methodological challenges, ethical issues, pitfalls, and practicalities. *Advances in Health Care Management, 17*, 3–22. doi:10.1108/S1474-823120140000017001 PMID:25985505

Byrne, D. (1997). An overview (and underview) of research and theory within the attraction paradigm. *Journal of Social and Personal Relationships, 14*(3), 417–431. doi:10.1177/0265407597143008

Cacioppo, J. T., & Petty, R. E. (1982). The need for cognition. *Journal of Personality and Social Psychology, 42*(1), 116–131. doi:10.1037/0022-3514.42.1.116

Cacioppo, J. T., Petty, R. E., Feinstein, J., & Jarvis, W. (1996). Dispositional differences in cognitive motivation: The life and times of individuals varying in need for cognition. *Psychological Bulletin, 119*(2), 197–253. doi:10.1037/0033-2909.119.2.197

Cai, Y., Jo, H., & Pan, C. (2012). Doing well while doing bad? CSR in controversial industry sectors. *Journal of Business Ethics, 108*(4), 467–480. doi:10.1007/s10551-011-1103-7

Caldwell, J. C. (1957). *Children of calamity.* The John Day Company.

Callahan, D., & Jennings, B. (2002). Ethics and public health: Forging a strong relationship. *American Journal of Public Health, 92*(2), 169–176. doi:10.2105/AJPH.92.2.169 PMID:11818284

Carasco, E. F., & Singh, J. B. (2003). The content and focus of the codes of ethics of the world's largest transnational corporations. *Business and Society Review, 108*(1), 71–94. doi:10.1111/1467-8594.00007

Cardy, R., & Servarajan, T. (2006). Assessing ethical behaviour: The impact of outcomes on judgment bias. *Journal of Managerial Psychology, 21*(1), 52–72. doi:10.1108/02683940610643215

Carpenter, S. R. (1978). Developments in the philosophy of technology in America. *Technology and Culture, 19*(1), 93–99. doi:10.2307/3103310

Carr, A. (1968). Is business bluffing ethical? *Harvard Business Review, 46*, 143–153. Retrieved from https://hbr.org/1968/01/is-business-bluffing-ethical

Carroll, A. B., & Buchholtz, A. K. (2014). *Business and society: Ethics, sustainability, and stakeholder management*. Stamford, CT: Nelson Education.

Carroll, A. B., & Shabana, K. M. (2010). The business case for corporate social responsibility: A review of concepts, research and practice. *International Journal of Management Reviews, 12*(1), 85–105. doi:10.1111/j.1468-2370.2009.00275.x

Carroll, A., & Buchholtz, A. (2008). *Business and society: Ethics and stakeholder management* (7th ed.). Mason, OH: South-western.

Cartwright, J. (2016). *Evolution and human behaviour: Darwinian perspectives on the human condition*. London: Palgrave Macmillan.

Celosse, K. (2015). *Interactions between personality traits of law enforcement and corrections officers, and attitudes toward felony drug offenders* (Unpublished doctoral dissertation). Chicago School of Professional Psychology, Los Angeles, CA.

Chamberlin, L. (1956). *Letter to Susan Pettiss dated February 2, 1956. International Social Service–American Branch (Folder: ISS-Branches, Korea, "RRA-5" 1-1956-December 1956, box 35). Social Welfare History Archives, Elmer L.* Minneapolis, MN: Anderson Library, University of Minnesota.

Champion, D. (2001). Criminal courts: Structure, process, and issues (3rd ed.). Upper Saddle River, NJ: Academic Press.

Chang, K. C. (1983). *Art, myth, and ritual: The path to political authority in ancient China*. Cambridge, MA: Harvard University Press.

Chang, K. C. (1994). Ritual and power. In R. E. Murowchick (Ed.), *Cradles of civilization: China: Ancient culture, modern land*. Norman, OK: University of Oklahoma Press.

Chapman, A. M. (2010). *Examining the effects of pre-kindergarten enrollment on kindergarten reading readiness* (Doctoral dissertation). Tennessee State University, Nashville, TN.

Cheng, M. M. (2003). House church movements and religious freedom in China. *China. International Journal (Toronto, Ont.), 1*(01), 16–45. doi:10.1142/S0219747203000049

Chiang, S.-C., Chan, H.-Y., Chen, C.-H., Sun, H.-J., Chang, H.-J., Chen, W. J., & Chen, C.-K. (2006). Recidivism among male subjects incarcerated for illicit drug use in Taiwan. *Psychiatry and Clinical Neurosciences, 60*(4), 444–451. doi:10.1111/j.1440-1819.2006.01530.x PMID:16884446

Child Placement Service. (ca. 1954-1955). Rules of procedure for adoption of Korean child by American adoptive parent. International Social Service–American Branch (Folder: ISS-Branches, Korea, "RRA-5" Refugee Relief Program, 1954-Dec. 1955, box 35). Social Welfare History Archives, Elmer L. Anderson Library, University of Minnesota, Minneapolis, MN.

Chin, W. W., Salisbury, W. D., Pearson, A. W., & Stollak, M. J. (1999). Perceived cohesion in small groups: Adapting and testing the Perceived Cohesion Scale in a small group setting. *Small Group Research, 30*(6), 751–766. doi:10.1177/104649649903000605

Chirani, E., Taleghani, M., & Moghadam, N. E. (2012). Brand performance and brand equity. *Interdisciplinary Journal of Contemporary Research in Business*, *3*, 1033–1036. Retrieved from http://www.journal-archieves14.webs.com/jan12.pdf

Cho, G. M. (2008). *Haunting the Korean diaspora: Shame, secrecy, and the forgotten war.* Minneapolis, MN: University of Minnesota Press.

Choi, H., & Moon, D. (2016). Perceptions of corporate social responsibility in the capital market. *Journal of Applied Business Research*, *32*(5), 1507–1518. doi:10.19030/jabr.v32i5.9777

Choy, C. C. (2007). Institutionalizing international adoption: The historical origins of Korean adoption in the United States. In K. J. S. Bergquist, M. E. Vonk, D. S. Kim, & M. D. Feit (Eds.), International Korean adoption: A fifty-year history of policy and practice (25-42). Haworth Press, Inc.

Choy, C. C. (2013). *Global families: A history of Asian international adoption in America.* New York University Press. doi:10.18574/nyu/9780814717226.001.0001

Christodoulides, G., & Chernatony, L. D. (2010). Consumer-based brand equity conceptualisation and measurement: A literature review. *International Journal of Market Research*, *52*(1), 43–66. doi:10.2501/S1470785310201053

Chun, E., & Evans, A. (2016). Rethinking cultural competence in higher education: An ecological framework for student development. *ASHE Higher Education Report*, *42*(4), 7–162. doi:10.1002/aehe.20102

Chung, K. Y., Eichenseher, J. W., & Taniguchi, T. (2008). Ethical perceptions of business students: Differences between East Asia and the USA and among "Confucian" cultures. *Journal of Business Ethics*, *79*(1), 121–132. doi:10.1007/s10551-007-9391-7

Chun, J., Shin, Y., Choi, J., & Kim, M. (2013). How does corporate ethics contribute to firm financial performance? The mediating role of collective organizational commitment and organizational citizenship behavior. *Journal of Management*, *39*(4), 853–877. doi:10.1177/0149206311419662

Clark, M. J. (2012). Cross-cultural research: Challenge and competence. *International Journal of Nursing Practice*, *18*(s2), 28–37. doi:10.1111/j.1440-172X.2012.02026.x PMID:22776530

Clayton, A., O'Connell, M. J., Bellamy, C., Benedict, P., & Rowe, M. (2013). The Citizenship Project part II: Impact of a citizenship intervention on clinical and community outcomes for persons with mental illness and criminal justice involvement. *American Journal of Community Psychology*, *51*(1-2), 114–122. doi:10.1007/s10464-012-9549-z PMID:22869206

Cohrs, J. C., Moschner, B., Maes, J., & Kielmann, S. (2005). The motivational bases of right-wing authoritarianism and social dominance orientation: Relations to values and attitudes in the aftermath of September 11, 2001. *Personality and Social Psychology Bulletin*, *31*(10), 1425–1434. doi:10.1177/0146167205275614 PMID:16143673

Coleman, J. S. (1988). Social capital in the creation of human capital. *American Journal of Sociology*, *94*, S95–S120. doi:10.1086/228943

Collins, W. A., Madsen, S. D., & Susman-Stillman, A. (2002). Parenting during middle childhood. In M. H. Bornstein (Ed.), *Children and parenting*: Handbook of parenting. Mahwah, NJ: Erlbaum.

Colquitt, J. A. (2012). Organizational justice. In S. W. J. Kozlowski (Ed.), *The Oxford handbook of organizational psychology* (Vol. 1, pp. 526–547). New York, NY: Oxford University Press.

Cooper, C. S. (2007). Drug courts - just the beginning: Getting other areas of public policy in sync. *Substance Use & Misuse, 42*(2-3), 243–256. doi:10.1080/10826080601141982 PMID:17558929

Cooper, R., & David, R. (1986). The biological concept of race and its application to public health and epidemiology. *Journal of Health Politics, Policy and Law, 11*(1), 97–116. doi:10.1215/03616878-11-1-97 PMID:3722786

Corti, E. C. (1934). *The downfall of three dynasties*. London, UK: Methuen.

Corti, E. C. (1954). *Alexander von Battenberg*. London, UK: Cassell.

Cortina, L. M., Magley, V. J., Williams, J. H., & Langhout, R. D. (2001). Incivility in the workplace: Incidence and impact. *Journal of Occupational Health Psychology, 6*(1), 64–80. doi:10.1037/1076-8998.6.1.64 PMID:11199258

Cosmo, V. A., Jr. (2017). Accounting plan plagiarism: Is it time to strengthen the CPA Code of Professional Conduct? *Pennsylvania CPA Journal, 88*(1), 14–16. Retrieved from https://www.picpa.org/articles/

Crampton, R. J. (1983). Bulgaria 1878-1918. Boulder, CO: East European Monographs.

Crampton, R. J. (2007). *Bulgaria*. Oxford, UK: Oxford University Press.

Crawford, J. T., Brady, J. L., Pilanski, J. M., & Erny, H. (2013). Differential effects of Right-Wing Authoritarianism and Social Dominance Orientation on political candidate support: The moderating role of message framing. *Journal of Social and Political Psychology, 1*(1), 5–28. doi:10.5964/jspp.v1i1.170

Creel, T. (2012). How corporate social responsibility influences brand equity. *Management Accounting Quarterly, 13*(4), 20–24. Retrieved from https://www.imanet.org/insights-and-trends/management-accounting-quarterly/maq-index/2012/summer-2012?ssopc=1

Creswell, J. W. (2009). *Research design: Qualitative, quantitative, and mixed methods approaches*. Thousand Oaks, CA: Sage.

Crooks, V. A., Kingsbury, P., Snyder, J., & Johnston, R. (2010). What is known about the patient's experience of medical tourism? A scoping review. *BMC Health Services Research, 10*(1), 1–12. doi:10.1186/1472-6963-10-266 PMID:20825667

Crowson, H. M. (2009). Are all conservatives alike? A study of the psychological correlates of cultural and economic conservatism. *The Journal of Psychology, 143*(5), 449–463. doi:10.3200/JRL.143.5.449-463 PMID:19943397

Cua, A. S. (2003). The ethical significance of shame: Insights of Aristotle and Xunzi. *Philosophy East & West, 53*(2), 147–202. doi:10.1353/pew.2003.0013

Cumings, B. (2010). *The Korean War: A history.* New York, NY: The Random House Publishing Group.

Curran, L. (2005). Social work's revised maternalism: Mothers, workers, and welfare in early Cold War America, 1946-1963. *Journal of Women's History, 17*(1), 112–136. doi:10.1353/jowh.2005.0005

Dadhich, A., & Bhal, K. T. (2008). Ethical leader behaviour and leader-member exchange as predictors of subordinate behaviors. *Vikalpa: The Journal for Decision Makers, 33*(4), 15–25. doi:http:/dx.org/10.1177/0256090920080402

Daft, R. (2007). *The leadership experience* (4th ed.). Mason, OH: Thomson.

Dahlberg, G., & Moss, P. (2005). *Ethics and politics in early childhood education.* New York, NY: Routledge. doi:10.4324/9780203463529

Dancy, J. (2006). *Ethics without principles.* Oxford, UK: Oxford University Press.

Darling-Hammond, L. (2006). Constructing 21st-century teacher education. *Journal of Teacher Education, 57*(3), 300–314. doi:10.1177/0022487105285962

Dautenhahn, K. (2001). The narrative intelligence hypothesis: In search of the transactional format of narratives in humans and other social animals. In M. Beynon, C. L. Nehaniv, & K. Dautenhah (Eds.), *Cognitive technology: Instruments of mind* (pp. 248–266)., doi:10.1007/3-540-44617-6_25

Davaki, K., & Mossialos, E. (2005). Plusça change: Health sector reforms in Greece. *Journal of Health Politics, Policy and Law, 30*(1-2), 143–168. doi:10.1215/03616878-30-1-2-143 PMID:15943391

Davcik, N. S., Vinhas da Silva, R., & Hair, J. F. (2015). Towards a unified theory of brand equity: Conceptualizations, taxonomy and avenues for future research. *Journal of Product and Brand Management, 24*(1), 3–17. doi:10.1108/JPBM-06-2014-0639

Davis, J., Bernardi, R., & Bosco, S. (2013). Examining the use of Hofstede's uncertainty avoidance construct in a major role in ethics research. *International Business Research, 6*(1), 63–75. doi:10.5539/ibr.v6n1p63

Davis, K. (1973). The case for and against business assumption of social responsibilities. *Academy of Management Journal, 16*(2), 312–322. doi:10.2307/255331

Davis, M. (1996). *The politics of philosophy: A commentary on Aristotle's politics.* Savage, MD: Rowman & Littlefield.

De Bary, W. T. (1988). *The trouble with Confucianism. The Tanner lectures on human values.* Retrieved from http://tannerlectures.utah.edu/_documents/a-to-z/d/debary89.pdf

De Grauwe, A. (2007). Transforming school supervision into a tool for quality improvement. *International Review of Education, 53*(5/6), 709–714. doi:10.1007/s11159-007-9057-9

De Vries, R., Rott, L. M., & Paruchuri, Y. (2010). Normative environment in international science. In M. S. Anderson & N. H. Stencek (Eds.), *International research collaborations: Much to be gained, many ways to get in trouble* (pp. 105–120). New York, NY: Routledge.

de Waal, F. B. (2003). *Morality and the social instincts: Continuity with the other primates.* Retrieved from http://courses.washington.edu/evpsych/de%20Waal%20on%20morality %20 2005.pdf

De Wree, E., De Ruyver, B., & Pauwels, L. (2009). Criminal justice responses to drug offences: Recidivism following the application of alternative sanctions in Belgium. *Drugs Education Prevention & Policy, 16*(6), 550–560. doi:10.3109/09687630802133632

Dellaportas, S. (2006). Making a difference with a discrete course on accounting ethics. *Journal of Business Ethics, 65*(4), 391–404. doi:10.1007/s10551-006-0020-7

Demirtas, O., & Akdogan, A. A. (2015). The effect of ethical leadership behavior on ethical climate, turnover intention, and affective commitment. *Journal of Business Ethics, 130*(1), 59–67. doi:10.1007/s10551-014-2196-6

Deonna, J., & Teroni, F. (2011). Is shame a social emotion? In A. K. Ziv, K. Lehrer, & H. B. Schmid (Eds.), *Self-evaluation: Affective and social grounds of intentionality* (pp. 193–212)., doi:10.1007/978-94-007-1266-9_11

Deshpande, S. P., Joseph, J., & Prasad, R. (2006). Factors impacting ethical behavior in hospitals. *Journal of Business Ethics, 69*(2), 207–216. doi:10.1007/s10551-006-9086-5

Deus Ex Machina: The influence of polling place on voting behavior. (n.d.). *Political Psychology, 31*(2), 209–225. doi:*3*(2).10.1111/j.1467-9221.2009.00749.x

Dewey, J. (2011). *The child and the curriculum.* University of Chicago Press. (Original work published 1902)

Diallo, D. A., Doumbo, O. K., Plowe, C. V., Wellems, T. E., Emanuel, E. J., & Hurst, S. A. (2005). Community permission for medical research in developing countries. *Clinical Infectious Diseases, 41*(2), 255–259. doi:10.1086/430707 PMID:15983925

Diamantopoulos, D. (2002). *Modern dictionary of the basic concept of the material-technical, spiritual and ethical civilization.* Athens: Patakis.

Dickinson, D. K., & Sprague, K. E. (2003). *From low-income families. In Handbook of early literacy research.* New York, NY: Guilford.

Dickson, M. A., & Chang, R. K. (2015). Apparel manufacturers and the business case for social sustainability: World class CSR and business model innovation. *Journal of Corporate Citizenship, 2015*(57), 55–72. doi:10.9774/GLEAF.4700.2015.ma.00006

Dill, D. D. (1982). The structure of the academic profession: Toward a definition of ethical issues. *The Journal of Higher Education, 53*(3), 255–267. doi:10.2307/ 1981746

Diniz, D., & Velez, A. C. (2001). Feminist bioethics: the emergence of the oppressed. In R. Tong (Ed.), *Globalizing feminist ethics* (pp. 62–72). Boulder, CO: Westview.

Diop, C. A. (1974). *The African origin of civilization: Myth or reality.* Chicago, IL: Lawrence Hill.

Dodds, D. (1961). *Fundamental principles in intercountry adoption. International Social Service – American Branch (Folder 34: Children: Intercountry Adoption General, 1954-1962, box 10) Social Welfare History Archives, Elmer L.* Minneapolis, MN: Anderson Library, University of Minnesota.

Doh, J., Husted, B., Matten, D., & Santoro, M. (2010). Ahoy there! Toward greater congruence and synergy between international business and business ethics theory and research. *Business Ethics Quarterly, 20*(3), 481–502. doi:10.5840/beq201020331

Donnelly, J. (2013). *Universal human rights in theory and practice.* Ithaca, NY: Cornell University Press.

Dracopolou, S. (Ed.). (2006). *Ethics and values in healthcare management.* New York, NY: Routledge.

Dranove, D. (1988). Demand inducement and the physician/patient relationship. *Economic Enquiry, 26*(2), 281–298. doi:10.1111/j.1465-7295.1988.tb01494.x PMID:10287407

Drucker, E. (1999). Drug prohibition and public health: 25 years of evidence. *Public Health Reports, 114*(1), 1–17. doi:10.1093/phr/114.1.14 PMID:9925168

Dunfee, T. W., Smith, N. C., & Ross, W. T. Jr. (1999). Social contracts and marketing ethics. *Journal of Marketing, 63*(3), 14–32. doi:10.2307/1251773

Durbin, P. T. (2008). Engineering professional ethics in a broader dimension. *Interdisciplinary Science Reviews, 33*(3), 226–233. doi:10.1179/174327908X366914

Du, S., Bhattacharya, C. B., & Sen, S. (2007). Reaping relational rewards from corporate social responsibility: The role of competitive positioning. *International Journal of Research in Marketing, 24*(3), 224–241. doi:10.1016/j.ijresmar.2007.01.001

Du, S., & Vieira, E. T. (2012). Striving for legitimacy through corporate social responsibility: Insights from oil companies. *Journal of Business Ethics, 11*(4), 413–427. doi:10.1007/s10551-012-1490-4

Dyck, B., & Neubert, M. (2008). *Management: Current practices and new directions.* Boston, MA: Houghton Mifflin Harcourt.

Eberle, D., Berens, G., & Li, T. (2013). The impact of interactive corporate social responsibility communication on corporate reputation. *Journal of Business Ethics, 118*(4), 731–746. doi:10.1007/s10551-013-1957-y

Ebrey, P. B. (2014). *Confucianism and family rituals in Imperial China: A social history of writing about rites*. Princeton, NJ: Princeton University Press.

Egels-Zandén, N., & Merk, J. (2014). Private regulation and trade union rights: Why codes of conduct have limited impact on trade union rights. *Journal of Business Ethics*, *123*(3), 461–473. doi:10.1007/s10551-013-1840-x

Ehrnrooth, J. C. G. (1886). K Noveishei istorii bolgarii. *Russkaiā Starina*, *LII*, 475–483.

Eisenberg, N., Gershoff, E. T., Fabes, R. A., Shepard, S. A., Cumberland, A. J., Losoya, S. H., & Murphy, B. C. et al. (2001). Mothers' emotional expressivity and children's behavior problems and social competence: Mediation through children's regulation. *Developmental Psychology*, *37*(4), 475–490. doi:10.1037/0012-1649.37.4.475 PMID:11444484

El-Astal, M. (2005). Culture influence on educational public relations officers' ethical judgments: A cross-national study. *Public Relations Review*, *31*(3), 362–375. doi:10.1016/j.pubrev.2005.05.019

Elff, M., & Rossteutscher, S. (2011). Stability or decline? Class, religion and the vote in Germany. *German Politics*, *20*(1), 107–127. doi:10.1080/09644008.2011.554109

Elliott, J., & Grigorenko, E. L. (2007). Editorial: Are Western educational theories and practices truly universal? *Comparative Education*, *43*(1), 1–4. doi:10.1080/03050060601160929

Elving, W., Golob, U., Podnar, K., Ellerup-Nielsen, A., & Thomson, C. (2015). The bad, the ugly and the good: New challenges for CSR communication. *Corporate Communications*, *20*(2), 118–127. doi:10.1108/CCIJ-02-2015-0006

Eng, I., & Lin, Y. M. (2002). Religious festivities, communal rivalry, and restructuring of authority relations in rural Chaozhou, Southeast China. *The Journal of Asian Studies*, *61*(4), 1259–1285. doi:10.2307/3096442

Escobar Pérez, B., & Mar Miras Rodríguez, M. (2013). Spanish savings banks' social commitment: Just pretty words? *Social Responsibility Journal*, *9*(3), 427–440. doi:10.1108/SRJ-09-2011-0084

Euwema, M., Kop, N., & Bakker, A. (2004). The behaviour of police officers in conflict situations: How burnout and reduced dominance contribute to better outcomes. *Work and Stress*, *18*(1), 23–38. doi:10.1080/0267837042000209767

Everhart, S., Vazquez, J. M., & McNab, R. M. (2009). Corruption, governance, investment and growth in emerging markets. *Applied Economics*, *41*(13), 1579–1594. doi:10.1080/00036840701439363

Falk, A., & Szech, N. (2013). Morals and markets. *Science*, *340*(6133), 707–711. doi:10.1126/science.1231566 PMID:23661753

Falkenström, E., Ohlsson, J., & Höglund, A. T. (2016). Developing ethical competence in healthcare management. *Journal of Workplace Learning*, *28*(1), 17–32. doi:10.1108/JWL-04-2015-0033

Feeney, S. (2010). Ethics today in early care and education: Review, reflection, and the future. *Young Children*, *65*(2), 72–77. Retrieved from ERIC database. (EJ898695)

Felce, D., & Perry, J. (1995). Quality of life: It's definition and measurement. *Research in Developmental Disabilities, 1*(4), 51–74. doi:10.1016/0891-4222(94)00028-8 PMID:7701092

Felder, R. M., & Brent, R. (2003). Designing and teaching courses to satisfy the ABET engineering criteria. *Journal of Engineering Education, 92*(1), 7–25. doi:10.1002/j.2168-9830.2003.tb00734.x

Feldman, D. C., & Alnold, H. J. (1983). *Managing individual and group behavior in organizations.* New York, NY: McGraw Hill.

Fellner, J. (2009). Race, drugs, and law enforcement in the United States. *Stanford Law & Policy Review, 20*(2), 257–291. Available from http://heinonline.org/HOL/LandingPage?handle=hein.journals/stanlp20&div=20&id=&page=

Ferrell, O., Fraedrich, J., & Ferrell, L. (2008). *Business ethics: Ethical decision making and cases.* Boston, MA: Houghton Mifflin.

Feuchtwang, S. (2000). Religion as resistance. In E. J. Perry & M. Selden (Eds.), *Chinese Society: Change, conflict and resistance* (pp. 161–177). London: Routledge.

Fink, L. D. (2013). *Creating significant learning experiences: An integrated approach to designing college courses.* San Francisco, CA: Wiley.

Finley, G. E. (1999). Children of adoptive families. In W. K. Silverman & T. H. Ollendick (Eds.), Developmental issues in the clinical treatment of children (pp. 358-370). Boston: Allyn & Bacon.

Fisher, C. B. (2003). Developing a code of ethics for academics. *Science and Engineering Ethics, 9*(2), 171–179. doi:10.1007/s11948-003-0004-2 PMID:12774649

Fisher, C. B. (2008). *Decoding the ethics code: A practical guide for psychologists* (2nd ed.). Thousand Oaks, CA: Sage.

Fisher, C. M., & Lovell, A. (2009). *Business ethics and values: Individual, corporate and international perspectives.* Harlow, UK: Pearson.

Fiske, E. B., & Ladd, H. F. (2000). *When schools compete: A cautionary tale.* Washington, DC: Brookings. 10.1080/02680930110041410

Flad, R. (2008). Divination and power. *Current Anthropology, 49*(3), 403–437. doi:10.1086/588495

Flanagan, O. (1991). *Varieties of moral personality: Ethics and psychological realism.* Cambridge, MA: Harvard University Press.

Flannery, K., & Marcus, J. (2012). *The creation of inequality: How our prehistoric ancestors set the stage for monarchy, slavery, and empire.* Cambridge, MA: Harvard University Press. doi:10.4159/harvard.9780674064973

Folland, S., Goodman, A. C., & Stano, M. (2016). *The economics of health and health care: Pearson international edition.* Routledge.

Folland, S., Goodman, A., & Stano, M. (2012). *The economics of health and health care* (7th ed., pp. 305–308). Boston, MA: Pearson.

Foura, G. (2012). *Profitable unnecessary industry of caesarean sections*. Retrieved from http://news.kathimerini.gr/4dcgi/_w_articles_ell_1_15/01/2012_469283

Franke, G., & Nadler, S. (2008). Culture, economic development, and national ethical attitudes. *Journal of Business Research, 61*(3), 254–264. doi:10.1016/j.jbusres.2007.06.005

Freeman, R. E., Harrison, J. S., Wicks, A. C., Parmar, B. L., & De Colle, S. (2010). *Stakeholder theory: The state of the art*. Cambridge, MA: Cambridge University Press. doi:10.1017/CBO9780511815768

French, P. A. (1995). *Corporate ethics*. New York: Harcourt.

Friedman, M. (1962). *Capitalism and freedom*. Chicago, IL: University of Chicago Press.

Friedman, M. (2007). The social responsibility of business is to increase its profits. In R. F. Chadwick & D. Schroeder (Eds.), *Corporate ethics and corporate governance* (pp. 173–178). Berlin: Springer; doi:10.1007/978-3-540-70818-6_14

Friend, C. (2004). Social contract theory. In *Internet encyclopedia of philosophy*. Retrieved from http://www.iep.utm.edu/soc-cont/

Frisch, C., & Huppenbauer, M. (2014). New insights into ethical leadership: A qualitative investigation of the experiences of executive ethical leaders. *Journal of Business Ethics, 123*(1), 23–43. http:/dx.org/10.1007/s10551-013-1797-9

Frith, C. D., & Frith, U. (2007). Social cognition in humans. *Current Biology, 17*(16), R724–R732. doi:10.1016/j.cub.2007.05.068 PMID:17714666

Fukuyama, F. (1995). Trust: The social virtues and the creation of prosperity. New York, NY: The Free Press (A Division of Simon & Schuster, Inc.).

Fung, C. (2000). The drinks are on us: Ritual, social status, and practice in Dawenkou burials, North China. *Journal of East Asian Archaeology, 2*(1), 67–92. doi:10.1163/156852300509808

Gandolfi, F. (2012). A conceptual discussion of transformational leadership and intercultural competence. *Review of International Comparative Management, 13*(4), 522–534.

García, O. (2011). *Bilingual education in the 21st century: A global perspective*. West Sussex, UK: Wiley. doi:10.1080/08878730009555246

Gardner, D. P. (1983). *A nation at risk*. Washington, DC: The National Commission on Excellence in Education, U.S. Department of Education. Retrieved from http://files.eric.ed.gov/fulltext/ED226006.pdf

Gardner, H. (2011). *Frames of mind: The theory of multiple intelligences*. New York, NY: Basic.

Gaskins, I. W., & Labbo, L. D. (2007). Diverse perspectives on helping young children build important foundational language and print skills. *Reading Research Quarterly*, *42*(3), 438–451. doi:10.1598/RRQ.42.3.10

Gatto, J., Kerbrat, C., & Oliveira, P. D. E. (2010). Prejudice in the police: On the processes underlying the effects of selection. *European Journal of Social Psychology*, *269*, 252–269. doi:10.1002/ejsp

Gatto, J., & Dambrun, M. (2012). Authoritarianism, social dominance, and prejudice among junior police officers. *Social Psychology*, *43*(2), 61–66. doi:10.1027/1864-9335/a000081

Genc, B., & Bada, E. (2005). Culture in language learning and teaching. *The Reading Matrix*, *5*(1). Retrieved from http://www.readingmatrix.com/articles/genc_bada/article.pdf

Germain, M. L. (2012). Traits and skills theories as the nexus between leadership and expertise: Reality or fallacy? *Performance Improvement*, *51*(5), 32–39. doi:10.1002/pfi.21265

Germain, M. L., & Tejeda, M. J. (2009). *Development and preliminary validation of a psychometric measure of expertise*. New Orleans, LA: Society for Industrial and Organizational Psychology. doi:10.1037/e518422013-695

Gert, B., & Gert, J. (2016, Spring). The definition of morality. In E. N. Zalta (Ed.), *The Stanford encyclopedia of philosophy*. Retrieved from https://plato.stanford.edu/archives/spr2016/entries/morality-definition/

Gherghina, S. C., & Simionescu, L. N. (2015). Does entrepreneurship and corporate social responsibility act as catalyst towards firm performance and brand value? *International Journal of Economics and Finance*, *7*(4), 23–34. doi:10.5539/ijef.v7n4p23

Gholipour. T., Nayeri, H., & Mehdi. (2012). Academic journal investigation of attitudes about corporate social responsibility: Business students in Iran. *African Journal of Business Management*, *6*(14), 5105-5113. doi: 10.5897/AJBM11.2699

Ghosh, D., Ghosh, P., & Das, B. (2013). Brand personality from corporate social responsibility: A critical review of the brand image through CSR. *Parikalpana: KIIT Journal of Management*, *9*, 22-33. Retrieved from http://connection.ebscohost.com/c/ articles/93980833

Giannouli, V. (2014a). The moral values for social welfare: The importance of moral values for companies in the health sector. *European Business Ethics Network*, 1-26. Retrieved from http://www.eben.gr/wp-content/uploads/2014/12/hthikes_axies_sto_xwro_tis_ygeias_vaitsa_giannouli.pdf

Giannouli, V. (2014b). *Emotional leadership in health care units: Relationships of leaders-subordinates* (Unpublished master's thesis). Hellenic Open University, Patras, Greece.

Giannouli, V., Mistraletti, G., & Umbrello, M. (2017). ICU experience for patients' relatives: Is information all that matters? *Intensive Care Medicine*, *43*(5), 722–723. doi:10.1007/s00134-017-4723-2 PMID:28236257

Giberson, T. R., Resick, C. J., & Dickson, M. W. (2005). Embedding leader characteristics: An examination of homogeneity of personality and values in organizations. *The Journal of Applied Psychology, 90*(5), 1002–1010. doi:10.1037/0021-9010.90.5.1002 PMID:16162072

Giessner, S., & Quaquebeke, N. (2011). Using a relational models perspective to understand normatively appropriate conduct in ethical leadership. *Journal of Business Ethics, 95*(S1), 43–55. doi:10.1007/s10551-011-0790-4

Gift, M., Gift, P., & Zheng, Q. (2013). Cross-cultural perceptions of business ethics: Evidence from the United States and China. *Journal of Business Ethics, 114*(4), 633–642. doi:10.1007/s10551-013-1709-z

Gill, S. (2009). Is gender inclusivity an answer to ethical issues in business? An Indian stance. *Gender in Management, 25*(1), 37–63. doi:10.1108/17542411011019922

Gilmartin, M. J., & Freeman, R. E. (2002). Business ethics and health care: A stakeholder perspective. *Health Care Management Review, 27*(2), 52–65. doi:10.1097/00004010-200204000-00006 PMID:11985291

Ginsburg, H., & Opper, S. (1979). *Piaget's theory of intellectual development* (2nd ed.). Englewood Cliffs, NJ: Prentice Hall.

Gladney, D. C. (2009). Islam in China: State policing and identity politics. In Y. Ashiwa & D. Wank (Eds.), *Making religion, making the state: The politics of religion in modern China* (pp. 151–178). Palo Alto, CA: Stanford University Press.

Godos-Díez, J., Fernández-Gago, R., & Martínez-Campillo, A. (2011). How important are CEOs to CSR practices? An analysis of the mediating effect of the perceived role of ethics and social responsibility. *Journal of Business Ethics, 98*(4), 531–548. doi:10.1007/s10551-010-0609-8

Goldman, A., & Tabak, N. (2010). Perception of ethical climate and its relationship to nurses' demographic characteristics and job satisfaction. *Nursing Ethics, 17*(2), 233–246. http://dx.doi.org/10.1177/0969733009352048

Goldstein, R. B., Bigelow, C., McCusker, J., Lewis, B. F., & Mundt, K. a, & Powers, S. I. (2001). Antisocial behavioral syndromes and return to drug use following residential relapse prevention/health education treatment. *The American Journal of Drug and Alcohol Abuse, 27*(3), 453–82. Retrieved from http://www.ncbi.nlm.nih.gov/pubmed/11506262

Goodrich, B. *The Calvinist work ethic and consumerism* [Lecture]. Retrieved from http://carbon.ucdenver.edu/~bgoodric/The%20Calvinist%20Work%20Ethic%20an%20 Consumerism.htm

Goossaert, V., & Palmer, D. A. (2011). *The religious question in modern China*. University of Chicago Press. doi:10.7208/chicago/9780226304182.001.0001

Gordenker, A. (2014, July 18). Organ donation. *The Japan Times*. Retrieved from http://www.japantimes.co.jp/news/2014/07/18/reference/organ-donation/#.WWATFNOGPGI

Gounaris, A. (2008). Business and moral responsibility. *CRS Review,* 3. Retrieved from http://www.academia.edu/456272/Business_and_Moral_Responsibility

Gounaris, A. (2012). From business ethics to the compulsory 'fair play'. *Corporate Social Responsibility,* 16-17. Retrieved from http://www.academia.edu/456270/From_Business_Ethics_to_Forced_Fair_Play_

Government Gazette of the Hellenic Republic. (2011). *N. 3918* (ΦΕΚ Α' 31/2-3-2011 τεχ. Α'). Retrieved from http://www.eopyy.gov.gr/Home/StartPage?a_HomePage=Index

Graen, G. B., & Cashman, J. (1975). A role-making model of leadership in formal organizations: A developmental approach. In J. G. Hunt & L. L. Larson (Eds.), *Leadership frontiers* (pp. 143–165). Kent, OH: Kent State University Press.

Graham, J., Nosek, B., & Haidt, J. (2012). The moral stereotypes of liberals and conservatives: Exaggeration of differences across the political spectrum. *PLoS One, 7*(12), e50092. doi:10.1371/journal.pone.0050092 PMID:23251357

Grant, A. M. (2012). Leading with meaning: Beneficiary contact, prosocial impact, and the performance effects of transformational leadership. *Academy of Management Journal, 55*(2), 458–476. doi:10.5465/amj.2010.0588

Gratier, M. (2003). Expressive timing and interactional synchrony between mothers and infants: Cultural similarities, cultural differences, and the immigration experience. *Cognitive Development, 18*(4), 533–554. doi:10.1016/j.cogdev.2003.09.009

Green, E. G. T., Thomsen, L., Sidanius, J., Staerklé, C., & Potanina, P. (2009). Reactions to crime as a hierarchy regulating strategy: The moderating role of social dominance orientation. *Social Justice Research, 22*(4), 416–436. doi:10.1007/s11211-009-0106-3

Greenspan, S. (2014). *Eleven most popular sports in the world.* Retrieved from http://www.11points.com/Sports/11_Most_Popular_Sports_in_the_World

Greenspan, S. I., & Shanker, S. (2009). The first idea: How symbols, language, and intelligence evolved from our primate ancestors to modern humans. Cambridge, MA: Da Capo.

Griffiths, J. G. (1991). *The divine verdict: A study of divine judgement in the ancient religions.* Brill.

Grootaert, C., & van Bastelaer, T. (2002). Introduction and overview. In C. Grootaert & T. Bastelaer (Eds.), The role of social capital in development: An empirical assessment (p. 4). New York, NY: Cambridge University Press. doi:10.1017/CBO9780511492600.002

Haley, H., & Sidanius, J. (2005). Person organization congruence and the maintenance of group-based social hierarchy: A Social Dominance perspective. *Group Processes & Intergroup Relations, 8*(2), 187–203. doi:10.1177/1368430205051067

Hall, R. C. (2011). Bulgaria in the First World War. *Historian, 73*(2), 300–315. doi:10.1111/j.1540-6563.2011.00293.x

Hamilton, K., & Langhorne, R. (2011). *The practice of diplomacy: Its evolution, theory, and administration* (2nd ed.). New York, NY: Routledge.

Hampton, J. (1988). *Hobbes and the social contract tradition.* New York, NY: Cambridge University Press.

Hancey, J. O. (1976). John Locke and the law of nature. *Political Theory, 4*(4), 439–454. doi:10.1177/009059177600400404

Hansson, S. O. (2011). Do we need a special ethics for research? *Science and Engineering Ethics, 17*(1), 21–29. doi:10.1007/s11948-009-9186-6 PMID:19941087

Harman, G. (2000). Moral relativism defended. In G. Harman (Ed.), *Explaining value and other essays in moral philosophy* (pp. 3–19). Oxford, UK: Clarendon. doi:10.1093/0198238045.003.0001

Harris, J. (2007). Do firms do 'worse' by doing 'bad'? Financial misrepresentation and subsequent firm performance. *Academy of Management Proceedings*, 1-6. doi: 10.5465/AMBPP.2007.26508370

Harris, C. E., Pritchard, M. S., & Rabins, M. J. (2000). *Engineering ethics: Concepts and cases* (2nd ed.). Belmont, CA: Wadsworth/Thomson.

Harris, J. R. (1990). Ethical values of individuals at different levels in the organizational hierarchy of a single firm. *Journal of Business Ethics, 9*(9), 741–750. doi:10.1007/BF00386357

Hartman, L. P., DesJardins, J. R., & MacDonald, C. (2014). *Business ethics: Decision making for personal integrity and social responsibility.* New York, NY: McGraw-Hill.

Haslam, S. A., & Reicher, S. D. (2012). Contesting the "nature" of conformity: What Milgram and Zimbardo's studies really show. *PLoS Biology, 10*(11), e1001426. doi:10.1371/journal.pbio.1001426 PMID:23185132

Hatch, J. A. (2002). Accountability shovedown: Resisting the standards movement in early childhood education. *Phi Delta Kappan, 83*(6), 457–462. doi:10.1177/003172170208300611

Hatch, J. A., & Grieshaber, S. (2002). Child observation and accountability in early childhood education: Perspective from Australia and the United states. *Early Childhood Education Journal, 29*(4), 227–231. doi:10.1023/A:1015177406713

Hatemi, P. K., & McDermott, R. (Eds.). (2011). *Man is by nature a political animal: Evolution, biology, and politics.* University of Chicago Press. doi:10.7208/chicago/9780226319117.001.0001

Healy, L. M. (2012). The history and development of social work. In L. M. Healy & R. J. Link (Eds.), Handbook of international social work: Human rights, development, and the global profession (55-62). Oxford University Press.

Hearn, N. (2010). Theory of desistance. *International Journal of Criminology*, 1–48. Retrieved from http://www.search.org/files/pdf/Hearn_Theory_of_Desistance_IJC_Nov_2010.pdf

Hellriegel, D., Slocum, J. W., & Jackson, S. E. (2002). *Management: A competency-based approach* (9th ed.). Cincinnati, OH: South-Western.

Helmig, B., Spraul, K., & Ingenhoff, D. (2016). Under positive pressure: How stakeholder pressure affects corporate social responsibility implementation. *Business & Society*, *55*(2), 151–187. doi:10.1177/0007650313477841

Herkert, J. R. (2002). Continuing and emerging issues in engineering ethics education. *Bridge*, *32*(3), 8–13. Retrieved from https://www.nae.edu/File.aspx?id=7378&v=f37740e0

Herman, B. (2013). Morality and everyday life. In The American Philosophical Association centennial series (pp. 655–670). Academic Press. doi:10.5840/apapa201396

Herman, E. (2008). *Kinship by design*. Chicago: The University of Chicago. doi:10.7208/chicago/9780226328072.001.0001

Hildebrand, D., Sen, S., & Bhattacharya, C. B. (2011). Corporate social responsibility: A corporate marketing perspective. *European Journal of Marketing*, *45*(9/10), 1353–1364. doi:10.1108/03090561111151790

Hindriks, F. (2014). How autonomous are collective agents? Corporate rights and normative individualism. *Erkenntnis*, *79*(S9), 1565–1585. doi:10.1007/s10670-014-9629-6

HM Inspectorate of Prisons and HM Inspectorate of Constabulatory. (2012). *Expectations for Police Custody: Criteria for assessing the treatment of and conditions of detainees in police custody* (version 2, 2012). Retrieved from https://www.justiceinspectorates.gov.uk/hmicfrs/media/police-custody-expectations-full-document-20120118.pdf

HM Inspectorate of Prisons and HM Inspectorate of Constabulatory. (2014). *Criteria for assessing the treatment of prisoners and conditions in prisons*. Retrieved from https://www.justiceinspectorates.gov.uk/hmiprisons/

Hobbes, T. (1660). *The leviathan*. Retrieved from http://coral.ufsm.br/gpforma/2senafe/PDF/b36.pdf

Hobbes, T. (1651). *Leviathan or the matter, forme, and power of a commonwealth ecclesiasticall and civill* (R. Hay, Ed.). London, England: Andrew Crooke. Retrieved from http://socserv2.socsci.mcmaster.ca/econ/ugcm/3ll3/hobbes/Leviathan.pdf

Hobbes, T. (1994). Leviathan. In E. Curley (Ed.), *Leviathan, with selected variants from the Latin edition of 1668*. Indianapolis, IN: Hackett. (Original work published 1651)

Hochfield, E. (1963). Across national boundaries: Problems in the handling of international adoptions, dependency and custody cases. *Juvenile Court Judges Journal*, *14*(3), 3–7. doi:10.1111/j.1755-6988.1963.tb00251.x

Hofstede, G. (1984). *Culture's consequences*. Thousand Oaks, CA: Sage.

Hofstede, G. (2001). *Culture's consequences: Comparing values, behaviors, institutions, and organizations across nations* (2nd ed.). Thousand Oaks, CA: Sage.

Hofstede, G. (2011). Dimensionalizing cultures-The Hofstede model in context. *Online Readings in Psychology and Culture, 2*(1). doi:10.9707/2307-0919.1014

Holland, D., & Albrecht, C. (2013). The worldwide academic field of business ethics: Scholars' perceptions of the most important issues. *Journal of Business Ethics, 117*(4), 777–788. doi:10.1007/s10551-013-1718-y

Holzer, A. (2012, August 31). Stanford officials face civil charges. *Wall Street Journal, 259*(52), C3.

How we care for Googlers. (2017). Retrieved September 23, 2017, from https://careers.google.com/how-we-care-for-googlers/

Howell, S. (Ed.). (2005). *The ethnography of moralities*. London: Routledge.

Hsieh, C., & Urquiola, M. (2006). The effects of generalized school choice on achievement and stratification: Evidence from Chile's voucher program. *Journal of Public Economics, 90*(8-9), 1477–1503. doi:10.1016/j.jpubeco.2005.11.002

Hsu, K. (2012). The advertising effects of corporate social responsibility on corporate reputation and brand equity: Evidence from the life insurance industry in Taiwan. *Journal of Business Ethics, 109*(2), 189–201. doi:10.1007/s10551-011-1118-0

Huang, K. (2014). Dyadic nexus fighting two-front battles: A study of the microlevel process of the official-religion-state relationship in china. *Journal for the Scientific Study of Religion, 53*(4), 706–721. doi:10.1111/jssr.12149

Hübinette, T. (2006). From orphan trains to babylifts: Colonial trafficking, empire building, and social engineering. In J. J. Trenka, J. C. Oparah, & S. Y. Shin (Eds.), Outsiders within: Writing on transracial adoption (pp. 139-149). South End Press.

Hurdis, R. (2007). Lifting the shroud of silence: A Korean adoptee's search for truth, legitimacy, and justice. In K. J. S. Bergquist, M. E. Vonk, D. S. Kim, & M. D. Feit (Eds.), International Korean adoption: A fifty-year history of policy and practice (pp. 171-185). Haworth Press, Inc.

Hwang, A., & Francesco, A. M. (2010). The Influence of individualism-Collectivism and power distance on use of feedback channels and consequences for learning. *Academy of Management Learning & Education, 9*(2), 243–257. doi:10.5465/AMLE.2010.51428546

Hwang, K. K. (2001). The deep structure of Confucianism: A social psychological approach. *Asian Philosophy, 11*(3), 179–204. doi:10.1080/09552360120116928

Hyde, L., & Hyde, V. P. (1958). A study of proxy adoptions. International Social Service – American Branch (Folder 14: Child Welfare League or America & International Social Service (American Branch), box 11). Social Welfare History Archives, Elmer L. Anderson Library, University of Minnesota, Minneapolis, MN.

Hysell, J. C. (2013). *What do they know when they get there? The relationship of Head Start, More at Four/NC pre-K, private preschool programs and no preschool experiences to kindergarteners' reading/literacy readiness* (Doctoral dissertation). Available from ProQuest Dissertations and Theses database. (UMI No. 3592597)

Ibrahim, N., Howard, D., & Angelidis, J. P. (2008). The relationship between religiousness and corporate social responsibility orientation: Are there differences between business managers and students? *Journal of Business Ethics*, 78(1-2), 165–174. doi:10.1007/s10551-006-9321-0

IGI Global Dictionary. (2017). *What is ethical value*. Retrieved from https://www.igi-global.com/dictionary/ethical-value/10274

Ingram, P., & Clay, K. (2000). The choice-within-constraints new institutionalism and implications for sociology. *Annual Review of Sociology*, 26(1), 525–546. retrieved from http://www.columbia.edu/~pi17/525.pdf. doi:10.1146/annurev.soc.26.1.525

International Social Service – American Branch. (1957a). *Home study material for intercountry adoption applications. International Social Service – American Branch (Folder 3: Miscell. Forms for Adoption Proceedings, box 11)*. Social Welfare History Archives, Elmer L. Minneapolis, MN: Anderson Library, University of Minnesota.

International Social Service – American Branch. (1957b). *Report on September 27th, 1957 workshop on intercountry adoptions*. International Social Service – American Branch (Folder 36: Children: Intercountry Adoption Conferences and Workshops, box 10). Social Welfare History Archives, Elmer L. Anderson Library, University of Minnesota, Minneapolis, MN.

International Social Service – American Branch. (1962). *A report to child welfare agencies on the placement of children from Korea into the United States. International Social Service – American Branch (Folder 25: Korea Adoptions Questions, box 34). Social Welfare History Archives, Elmer L.* Minneapolis, MN: Anderson Library, University of Minnesota.

International Social Service – American Branch. (n.d.). *Guideline for supervisory reports*. International Social Service – American Branch (Folder 3: Miscell. Forms for Adoption Proceedings, box 11). Social Welfare History Archives, Elmer L. Anderson Library, University of Minnesota, Minneapolis, MN.

International Social Service Korea Project (n.d.). [document summarizing ISS-Korea project]. International Social Service – American Branch (Folder 25: Korea Adoptions Questions, box 34). Social Welfare History Archives, Elmer L. Anderson Library, University of Minnesota, Minneapolis, MN.

International Social Service, Inc. (1957). *In a world they never made: The story of International Social Service. International Social Service – American Branch (Folder 3: Miscellaneous Folder, box 47). Social Welfare History Archives, Elmer L.* Minneapolis, MN: Anderson Library, University of Minnesota.

International Social Service, Inc. (1967). *Results of leadership, demonstrations, and training in South Korea by International Social Service 1954-1966. International Social Service – American Branch (Folder: To Korea, Reports & Visits, box 35). Social Welfare History Archives, Elmer L.* Minneapolis, MN: Anderson Library, University of Minnesota.

International Social Service, Inc. (2015). *Vision and mission*. Retrieved from http://www.iss-ssi.org/index.php/en/home/mission

International Social Service, Inc. (n.d.). *International Social Service, a history, 1921-1955.* International Social Service – American Branch (Folder 23, box 3). Social Welfare History Archives, Elmer L. Anderson Library, University of Minnesota, Minneapolis, MN.

Internet Live Stats. (n.d.). *Internet users*. Retrieved from www.internetlivestats.com

Irvin, B. C. (1955). *Letter to Mrs. Oak Soon Hong dated June 21, 1955. International Social Service – American Branch (Folder: ISS-Branches, Korea, "RRA-5," Refugee Relief Program, 1954-December 1955, box 35). Social Welfare History Archives, Elmer L.* Minneapolis, MN: Anderson Library, University of Minnesota.

Ishikida, M. Y. (2005). *Japanese education in the 21st century*. Tokyo, Japan: Center for U.S.-Japan Comparative Social Studies.

Iyioke, I. V. (2016). *Re-conceptualizing responsibility in clinical trials: An insight with the African notion of self* (Unpublished doctoral dissertation). Michigan State University, East Lansing, MI.

Jacobs, K. (2011). *Assessing the relationship between servant leadership and effective teaching in a private university setting* (Doctoral dissertation). Northcentral University. Retrieved from http://library.ncu.edu/ncu_diss/default.aspx

Jacobs, M. D. (2009). *White mother to a dark race: Settler colonialism, maternalism, and the removal of indigenous children in the American West and Australia, 1880-1940*. University of Nebraska Press.

Janus, M., & Duku, E. (2007). The school entry gap: Socioeconomic, family, and health factors associated with children's school readiness to learn. *Early Education and Development, 18*(3), 375–403. doi:10.1080/10409280701610796a

Japan Times. (2007, February 18). *Scandal over Ehime doc's transplants grows wider*. Retrieved from http://www.japantimes.co.jp/news/2007/02/18/national/scandal-over-ehime-docs-transplants-grows-wider/#.WV6z09OGPGI

Jelavich, C. (1958). *Tsarist Russia and Balkan nationalism: Russian influence in the internal affairs of Bulgaria and Serbia, 1879-1886*. Berkeley, CA: University of California Press.

Jin, K. K., Drozdenko, R., & DeLoughy, S. (2013). The role of corporate value clusters in ethics, social responsibility, and performance: A study of financial professionals and implications for the financial meltdown. *Journal of Business Ethics, 112*(1), 15–24. doi:10.1007/s10551-012-1227-4

Johnsen, B., Granheim, P. K., & Helgesen, J. (2011). Exceptional prison conditions and the quality of prison life: Prison size and prison culture in Norwegian closed prisons. *European Journal of Criminology, 8*(6), 515–529. doi:10.1177/1477370811413819

Jones, J. M. (2011, December 12). Record 64% rate honesty, ethics of members of congress low. *Politics*. Retrieved from http://www.gallup.com/poll/151460/Record-Rate-Honesty-Ethics-Members-Congress-Low.aspx

Jones, H. B. Jr, Furnham, A., & Deile, A. J. (2010). Religious orientation and the Protestant Work Ethic. *Mental Health, Religion & Culture, 13*(7-8), 697–706. doi:10.1080/13674670802111862

Jose, A., & Thibodeaux, M. S. (1999). Institutionalization of ethics: The perspective of managers. *Journal of Business Ethics, 22*(2), 133–143. doi:10.1023/A:1006027423495

Joy, S., & Kolb, D. A. (2009). Are there cultural differences in learning style? *International Journal of Intercultural Relations, 33*(1), 69–85. .11.00210.1016/j.ijintrel.2008

Joyce, K. (2013). *The child catchers: Rescue, trafficking, and the new gospel of adoption*. Public Affairs.

Juergensmeyer, M., Kitts, M., & Jerryson, M. (Eds.). (2013). *The Oxford handbook of religion and violence*. Oxford, UK: Oxford University Press.

Kalb, M. (2015). *Imperial Gamble: Putin, Ukraine, and the New Cold War*. Washington, DC: Brookings Institution.

Kalshoven, K., Den Hartog, D. N., & De Hoogh, A. H. B. (2011). Ethical leadership at work questionnaire (ELW): Development and validation of a multidimensional measure. *The Leadership Quarterly, 22*(1), 51–69. doi:10.1016/j.leaqua.2010.12.007

Kant, I. (2007). *Fundamental principles of the metaphysic of morals* (N. Y. New York, Trans.). Dover: T. K. Abbott. (Original work published 1879)

Kanungo, R. N. (2001). Ethical values of transactional and transformational leaders. *Canadian Journal of Administrative Sciences/Revue Canadienne des Sciences de l'Administration, 18*(4), 257-265. doi: 10.1111/j.1936-4490.2001.tb00261.x

Karimi, S., Khorasani, E., Keyvanara, M., & Afshari, S. (2015). Factors affecting physicians' behaviors in induced demand for health services. *International Journal of Educational and Psychological Researches, 1*(1), 43–51. doi:10.4103/2395-2296.147469

Kateb, G. (1992). *The inner ocean: Individualism and democratic culture*. Ithaca, NY: Cornell University Press.

Kavali, S., Tzokas, N., & Saren, M. (2001). Corporate ethics: An exploration of contemporary Greece. *Journal of Business Ethics, 30*(1), 87–104. doi:10.1023/A:1006215311621

Keightley, D. (2012). *Working for his majesty*. Berkeley, CA: University of California Institute of East Asian Studies.

Kelbessa, W. (2005). *The utility of ethical dialogue for marginalized voices in Africa*. Retrieved from http://pubs.iied.org/pdfs/13508IIED.pdf?

Keller, K. L., & Lehmann, D. R. (2006). Brands and branding: Research findings and future priorities. *Marketing Science, 25*(6), 740–759. doi:10.1287/mksc.1050.0153

Kennan, G. F. (1979). *The decline of Bismarck's European order: Franco-Russian relations, 1875-1890*. Princeton, NJ: Princeton University Press.

Kennedy, A. (2009). Ethics: A part of everyday practice in child care. *Putting Children First, 29*, 9–11. Retrieved from http://ncac.acecqa.gov.au/educator-resources/pcf-articles/Ethics_a_part%20_of_everyday_practice_Mar09.pdf

Kentikelenis, A., Karanikolos, M., Reeves, A., McKee, M., & Stuckler, D. (2014). Greece's health crisis: From austerity to denialism. *Lancet, 383*(9918), 748–753. doi:10.1016/S0140-6736(13)62291-6 PMID:24560058

Keung, E. K. (2011). *What factors of cultural intelligence predict transformational leadership: A study of international school leaders* (Doctoral dissertation). Liberty University, Lynchburg, VA.

Khan, A. A., & Manwani, D. T. (2013). Sustainability & corporate brand equity through corporate social responsibility initiatives. *Asia Pacific Journal of Management & Entrepreneurship Research, 2*, 267-279. Retrieved from https://www.questia.com/library/ journal/1P3-2974214771

Khera, I. (2010). Ethics perceptions of the U.S. and its large developing-country trading partners. *Global Management Journal, 2*(1), 33–41. Retrieved from http://globalmj.eu/wp-content/uploads/2012/02/GMJ_No1_2010.pdf#page=33

Khinduka, S. K. (1971). Social work in the Third World. *The Social Service Review, 45*(1), 62–73. doi:10.1086/642647

Khorasani, E., Keyvanara, M., Karimi, S., & Jazi, M. J. (2014). Views of health system experts on macro factors of induced demand. *International Journal of Preventive Medicine, 5*(10), 1286–1298. PMID:25400888

Kil, A., & Houlberg, K. (2014). How does copayment for health care services affect demand, health and redistribution? A systematic review of the empirical evidence from 1990 to 2011. *The European Journal of Health Economics, 15*(8), 813–828. doi:10.1007/s10198-013-0526-8 PMID:23989938

Kim, E. (2007). Remembering loss: The Koreanness of overseas adopted Koreans. In K. J. S. Bergquist, M. E. Vonk, D. S. Kim, & M. D. Feit (Eds.), International Korean adoption: A fifty-year history of policy and practice (pp. 115-129). Haworth Press, Inc.

Kim, J. R. (2006). Scattered seeds: The Christian influence on Korean adoption. In J. J. Trenka, J. C. Oparah, & S. Y. Shin (Eds.), Outsiders within: Writing on transracial adoption (pp. 151-162). South End Press.

Kim, E. J. (2010). *Adopted territory: Transnational Korean adoptees and the politics of belonging.* Durham, NC: Duke University Press. doi:10.1215/9780822392668

Kindopp, J. (2004). Fragmented yet defiant: Protestant resilience under Chinese Communist Party rule. In, J. Kindopp & C. L. Hamrin (Eds.), God and Caesar in China: Policy implications of church-state tensions (pp. 122–148). Washington, DC: Brookings.

Kinner, S. A., & Milloy, M.-J. (2011). Collateral consequences of an ever-expanding prison system. *CMAJ: Canadian Medical Association Journal = Journal de l'Association Medicale Canadienne, 183*(5), 632. doi:10.1503/cmaj.101848

Kirkpatrick, S. A., & Locke, E. A. (1996). Direct and indirect effects of three charismatic leadership components on performance and attitudes. *The Journal of Applied Psychology, 81*(1), 36–51. doi:10.1037/0021-9010.81.1.36

Kitchin, T. (2003). Corporate social responsibility: A brand explanation. *Journal of Brand Management, 10*(4), 312–326. doi:10.1057/palgrave.bm.2540127

Klein, C. (2003). *Cold War orientalism: Asia in the middlebrow imagination, 1945-1961.* Berkeley, CA: University of California Press.

Kleinig, J., & Murtagh, K. (2005). Disenfranchising Felons. *Journal of Applied Philosophy, 22*(3), 217–239. doi:10.1111/j.1468-5930.2005.00307.x

Knight, C. (2015). Trauma-informed social work practice: Practice considerations and challenges. *Clinical Social Work Journal, 43*(1), 25–37. doi:10.1007/s10615-014-0481-6

Knowles, M. S. (1995). Designs for adult learning: Practical resources, exercises, and course outlines from the father of adult learning. Alexandria, VA: American Society for Training and Development (ASTD).

Knowles, E. D., Lowery, B. S., Shulman, E. P., & Schaumberg, R. L. (2013). Race, ideology, and the Tea Party: A longitudinal study. *PLoS One, 8*(6), e67110. doi:10.1371/journal.pone.0067110 PMID:23825630

Knowles, M. S. (1990). *The adult learner: A neglected species* (4th ed.). Houston, TX: Gulf.

Knowles, M. S., Holton, E. F. III, & Swanson, R. A. (2014). *The adult learner: The definitive classic in adult education and human resource development.* London: Routledge.

Koch, A. (1887). *Prince Alexander of Battenberg; Reminiscences of his reign in Bulgaria, from authentic sources.* London, UK: Whitaker.

Kohlberg. (1984). *The psychology of moral development: The nature and validity of moral stages.* San Francisco, CA: Harper and Row.

Kohlberg, L. (1969). Stage and sequence: The cognitive-developmental approach to socialization. In D. Goslin (Ed.), *Handbook of socialization theory and research* (pp. 347–480). Retrieved from https://books.google.com/

Koocher, G. P., & Keith-Speigel, P. (2008). *Ethics in psychology and the mental health professions: Standards and cases* (3rd ed.). Oxford, UK: Oxford University Press.

Korean Institute of Military History. (2001). *The Korean War*. Lincoln, NE: University of Nebraska Press.

Koven, S., & Michel, S. (Eds.). (1993). *Mothers of a new world: Maternalist politics and the origins of welfare states*. Routledge.

Kraten, M. (2013). Why Libor manipulation matters. *The CPA Journal, 83*(9), 6–10.

Krichefsky, G. D. (1958). Immigrant orphans. I & N Reporter [Article]. International Social Service – American Branch (Folder: Immigration: Re: Admission of Foreign Orphans to US (proposed by INS), box 13). Social Welfare History Archives, Elmer L. Anderson Library, University of Minnesota, Minneapolis, MN.

Kroll, K. (2012). Keeping the company safe: Preventing and detecting fraud. *Financial Executive, 28*(7), 20–23.

Krutch, J. W. (1959). *Human nature and the human condition: Texte imprimé*. New York, NY: Random House.

Kukla, R. (2014). Living with pirates: Common morality and embodied practice. *Cambridge Quarterly of Healthcare Ethics, 23*(1), 75–85. doi:10.1017/S0963180113000480 PMID:24256603

Kulkarni, S., & Ramamoorthy, N. (2011). Leader–member exchange, subordinate stewardship, and hierarchical governance. *International Journal of Human Resource Management, 22*(13), 2770–2793. doi:10.1080/09585192.2011.599954

Kumagai, A. K., & Lypson, M. L. (2009). Beyond cultural competence: Critical consciousness, social justice, and multicultural education. *Academic Medicine, 84*(6), 782–787. doi:10.1097/ACM.0b013e3181a42398 PMID:19474560

Kumar, N., & Lee, C. C. (2014). Regulatory focus and workplace behavior. *Journal of General Management, 39*(4), 27–53. doi:10.1177/030630701403900403

Kuper, S. (2010). *Soccer against the enemy: How the world's most popular sport starts and fuels revolutions and keeps dictators in power*. New York, NY: Nation.

Kuper, S. (2011). *Soccer men: Profiles of the rogues, geniuses, and neurotics who dominate the world's most popular sport*. New York, NY: Nation.

Kutsarov, P. (2003). *Vossoedinenie Bolgarii v 1885 Godu i Rossiĭskaia Imperiia* (Unpublished doctoral dissertation). Rossiĭskaia Akademiia Nauk, Institut Slavianovedeniia, Moscow.

L'vov, E. (1886). *Rumeliĭskiĭ perevorot*. Moscow.

LaBelle, R., Stoddart, G., & Rice, T. (1994). A re-examination of the meaning and importance of supplier-induced demand. *Journal of Health Economics, 13*(3), 347–368. doi:10.1016/0167-6296(94)90036-1 PMID:10138860

Ladd-Taylor, M. (1994). *Mother-work: Women, child welfare, and the state, 1890-1930* (Vol. 88). Urbana, IL: University of Illinois Press.

Lai, C., Chiu, C., Yang, C., & Pai, D. (2010). The effects of corporate social responsibility on brand performance: The mediating effect of industrial brand equity and corporate reputation. *Journal of Business Ethics*, *95*(3), 457–469. doi:10.1007/s10551-010-0433-1

Lalande, A. (1955). *Dictionary of philosophy*. Athens: Papyrus.

Laliberté, A. (2011). Buddhist revival under state watch. *Journal of Current Chinese Affairs*, *40*(2), 107–134. Retrieved from https://journals.sub.uni-hamburg.de/giga/jcca/article/view/419/417

Landau, R., & Osmo, R. (2003). Professional and personal hierarchies of ethical principles. *International Journal of Social Welfare*, *12*(1), 42–49. doi:10.1111/1468-2397.00007

Langeliers, A. L. A. I., Amin, S., & Toole, S. K. O. (2010). Correctional officers and attitudes toward mental illness. American Psychological Association 2010 Convention Presentation.

Lapointe, V. R., Ford, L., & Zumbo, B. D. (2007). Examining the relationship between neighborhood environment and school readiness for kindergarten children. *Early Education and Development*, *18*(3), 473–495. doi:10.1080/10409280701610846

Larrick, R. P., Nisbett, R. E., & Morgan, J. N. (1993). Who uses the cost-benefit rules of choice? Implications for the normative status of microeconomic theory. *Organizational Behavior and Human Decision Processes*, *56*(3), 331–347. doi:10.1006/obhd.1993.1058

Larsson, M., Bjorklund, F., & Backstrom, M. (2012). Right-wing authoritarianism is a risk factor for torture-like abuse, but so is social dominance orientation. *Personality and Individual Differences*, *53*(7), 927–929. doi:10.1016/j.paid.2012.06.015

Lattimore, P. K., Barrick, K., Dawes, D., Steffey, D., & Visher, C. A. (2012). *Prisoner reentry services: What worked for SVORI evaluation participants? Final Report*. Retrieved from https://www.nij.gov/topics/corrections/reentry/pages/evaluation-svori.aspx

LaVeist, T. A. (1994). Beyond dummy variables and sample selection: What health services researchers ought to know about race as a variable. *Health Services Research*, *29*(1), 1. PMID:8163376

Lee, C.-Y. (1998). English for nursing purposes: A needs assessment for professional-oriented curriculum design. *Academic Journal of Kang-Ning*, *1*(1), 55–72. Retrieved from http://daa.ukn.edu.tw/ezfiles/6/1006/img/210/4.pdf

Leon Siantz, M. L. D., & Meleis, A. I. (2007). Integrating cultural competence into nursing education and practice: 21st century action steps. *Journal of Transcultural Nursing*, *18*(Suppl. 1), 86S–90S. doi:10.1177/1043659606296465 PMID:17357259

Leroy, H., Palanski, M. E., & Simons, T. (2012). Authentic leadership and behavioral integrity as drivers of follower commitment and performance. *Journal of Business Ethics*, *107*(3), 255–264. doi:10.1007/s10551-011-1036-1

Levin, H., Belfield, C., Muennig, P., & Rouse, C. (2007). *The costs and benefits of an excellent education for all of America's children* (Vol. 9). New York, NY: Teachers College.

Liakos, A., & Giannitsi, S. (1984). The reliability and validity of the amended Greek Spielberger anxiety scale. *Encephalos, 21*, 71–76.

Lian, H., Ferris, D. L., & Brown, D. J. (2012). Does power distance exacerbate or mitigate the effects of abusive supervision? It depends on the outcome. *The Journal of Applied Psychology, 97*(1), 107–123. doi:10.1037/a0024610 PMID:21766996

Lian, L. K., & Tui, L. G. (2012). Leadership styles and organizational citizenship behavior: The mediating effect of subordinates' competence and downward influence tactics. *The Journal of Applied Business and Economics, 13*(2), 59–96.

Liaropoulos, L. (1998). Ethics and the management of health care in Greece. In S. Dracopoulou (Ed.), *Ethics and values in health care management* (pp. 148–171). London, UK: Routledge.

Libby, T., & Thorne, L. (2007). The development of a measure of auditors' virtue. *Journal of Business Ethics, 71*(1), 89–99. doi:10.1007/s10551-006-9127-0

Li, N., & Murphy, W. (2012). A three-country study of unethical sales behaviors. *Journal of Business Ethics, 111*(2), 219–235. doi:10.1007/s10551-012-1203-z

Lipman, M. (1991). *Thinking in education*. Cambridge, UK: Cambridge University Press.

Liu, L. (1996). Mortuary ritual and social hierarchy in the Longshan culture. *Early China, 21*, 1–46. Retrieved from http://www.jstor.org/stable/23351730

Liu, C. M., & Lin, C. P. (2016). Corporate ethical values and turnover intention. *Journal of Leadership & Organizational Studies, 23*(4), 397–409. doi:10.1177/1548051816632358

Liu, L. (2000). Ancestor worship: An archaeological investigation of ritual activities in Neolithic North China. *Journal of East Asian Archaeology, 2*(1/2), 129–164. doi:10.1163/156852300509826

Liu, M., Wong, I., Shi, G., Chu, R., & Brock, J. (2014). The impact of corporate social responsibility (CSR) performance and perceived brand quality on customer-based brand preference. *Journal of Services Marketing, 28*, 181–194. doi:10.1108/JSM-09-2012-0171

Lo, B. (2015). *Russia and the New World Disorder*. London, UK: Brookings Institution.

Locke, J. (2002). *Essays on the law of nature: The Latin text with a translation, introduction and notes, together with transcripts of Locke's shorthand in his journal for 1676* (W. von Leyden, Trans. & Ed.). Oxford, UK: Oxford University Press.

Loeb, S. E. (1978). *Ethics in the accounting profession*. New York, NY: Wiley.

Lok, P., & Crawford, J. (2004). The effect of organizational culture and leadership style on job satisfaction and organizational commitment: A cross-national comparison. *Journal of Management Development, 23*(4), 321–338. doi:10.1108/02621710410529785

Lopatta, K., Buchholz, F., & Kaspereit, T. (2015). Asymmetric information and corporate social responsibility. *Business & Society*, *55*(3), 458–488. doi:10.1177/0007650315575488

Loui, M. C. (2005). Ethics and the development of professional identities of engineering students. *Journal of Engineering Education*, *94*(4), 383–390. doi:10.1002/j.2168-9830.2005.tb00866.x

Luo, X., & Bhattacharya, C. (2006). Corporate social responsibility, customer satisfaction, and market value. *Journal of Marketing*, *70*(4), 1–18. doi:10.1509/jmkg.70.4.1

Luu, T. T. (2012). Behind brand performance. *Asia-Pacific Journal of Business Administration*, *4*(1), 42–57. doi:10.1108/17574321211207962

Lynch, W. T. (1997). Teaching engineering ethics in the United States. *IEEE Technology and Society Magazine*, *16*(4), 27–36. doi:10.1109/44.642561

Lyons, K. H., Hokenstad, T., Pawar, M., Huegler, N., & Hall, N. (Eds.). (2012). *The Sage handbook of international social work*. Sage.

MacBeth, A., & Gumley, A. (2012). Exploring compassion: A meta-analysis of the association between self-compassion and psychopathology. *Clinical Psychology Review*, *32*(6), 545-552. 10.1016/j.cpr.2012.06.003

MacGahan, J. A. (1876, August 22). The Turkish atrocities in Bulgaria: Horrible scenes at Batak. *The Daily News*, pp. 5–6. Retrieved from http://www.attackingthedevil.co.uk/related/macgahan.php

MacNab, B., Brislin, R., Worthley, R., Galperin, B. L., Jenner, S., Lituchy, T. R., & Bess, D. et al. (2007). Culture and ethics management: Whistle-blowing and internal reporting within a NAFTA country context. *International Journal of Cross Cultural Management*, *7*(1), 5–28. doi:10.1177/1470595807075167

Madsen, R. (2007). *Democracy's dharma: Religious renaissance and political development in Taiwan*. Berkeley, CA: University of California Press. doi:10.1525/california/9780520252271.001.0001

Magnani, L. (2011). *Understanding violence: The intertwining of morality, religion and violence: A philosophical stance* (Vol. 1). 10.1007/978-3-642-21972-6

Mahbubani, K. (2014, December 4). Why Asia is on the brink of a golden era. *Bangladesh – Audacity of Hope*. Retrieved from https://mygoldenbengal.wordpress.com/2014/12/04/why-asia-is-on-the-brink-of-a-golden-era/

Mahbubani, K. (2008). The case against the West: America and Europe in the Asian century. *Foreign Affairs*, *87*(3), 111–124. Retrieved from http://www.jstor.org/stable/20032654

Mahbubani, K. (2011). Can Asia re-legitimize global governance? *Review of International Political Economy*, *18*(1), 131–139. doi:10.1080/09692290.2011.545217

Maier, D. S. (2012). *What's so good about biodiversity?* New York, NY: Springer. doi:10.1007/978-94-007-3991-8

Maignan, I., Ferrell, O. C., & Ferrell, L. (2005). A stakeholder model for implementing social responsibility in marketing. *European Journal of Marketing*, *39*(9/10), 956–977. doi:10.1108/03090560510610662

Malka, A., & Lelkes, Y. (2010). More than ideology: Conservative–Liberal identity and receptivity to political cues. *Social Justice Research*, *23*, 156–188. doi:10.1007/s11211-010-0114-3

Malka, A., Lelkes, Y., Srivastava, S., Cohen, A. B., & Miller, D. T. (2012). The association of religiosity and political conservatism: The role of political engagement. *Political Psychology*, *33*(2), 275–299. doi:10.1111/j.1467-9221.2012.00875.x

Malpas, J. (2012). In *The Stanford Encyclopedia of Philosophy*. Retrieved from http://plato.stanford.edu/archives/win2012/entries/davidson/

Margolin, G. (1982). Ethical and legal considerations in marital and family therapy. *The American Psychologist*, *37*(7), 788–801. doi:10.1037/0003-066X.37.7.788 PMID:7137697

Marre, D., & Briggs, L. (Eds.). (2009). *International adoption: Global inequalities and the circulation of children*. NYU Press. doi:10.18574/nyu/9780814791011.001.0001

Marsh, C. (2013). Business executives' perceptions of ethical leadership and its development. *Journal of Business Ethics*, *114*(3), 565–582. doi:10.1007/s10551-012-1366-7

Marta, J., Heiss, C. M., & De Lurgio, S. A. (2008). An exploratory comparison of ethical perceptions of Mexican and US marketers. *Journal of Business Ethics*, *82*(3), 539–555. doi:10.1007/s10551-007-9575-1

Martin, M. W., & Schinzinger, R. (2005). *Ethics in engineering* (4th ed.). New York, NY: McGraw-Hill.

Masters, R. D. (1989a). Gradualism and discontinuous change in evolutionary theory and political philosophy. *Journal of Social and Biological Structures*, *12*(2/3), 281–301. doi:10.1016/0140-1750(89)90051-1

Masters, R. D. (1989b). *The nature of politics*. New Haven, CT: Yale University Press.

Matsaganis, M. (1999). Public intervention in the health sector. In V. Aletras, M. Matsaganis, & D. Niakas (Eds.), *Economic and financial management of healthcare services* (Vol. A, pp. 15–39). Patras: Hellenic Open University Publishing.

Mattera, M., & Baena, V. (2015). The key to carving out a high corporate reputation based on innovation: Corporate social responsibility. *Social Responsibility Journal*, *11*(2), 221–241. doi:10.1108/SRJ-03-2013-0035

Maxwell-Smith, M. A., Seligman, C., Conway, P., & Cheung, I. (2015). Individual differences in commitment to value-based beliefs and the amplification of perceived belief dissimilarity effects. *Journal of Personality*, *83*(2), 127–141. doi:10.1111/jopy.12089 PMID:24444458

May, E. T. (1995). *Barren in the promised land: Childless Americans and the pursuit of happiness.* Basic Books.

May, E. T. (2008). *Homeward bound: American families in the Cold War Era.* New York, NY: Basic Books.

Mayer, D. M., Aquino, K., Greenbaum, R. L., & Kuenzi, M. (2012). Who displays ethical leadership, and why does it matter? An examination of antecedents and consequences of ethical leadership. *Academy of Management Journal, 55*(1), 151–171. doi:10.5465/amj.2008.0276

Mbiti, J. S. (1970). *African Religions and Philosophy.* London, UK: Longman.

Mccabe, A. C., Ingram, R., & Data-On, M. C. (2006). The business of ethics and gender. *Journal of Business Ethics, 64*(2), 101–116. doi:10.1007/s10551-005-3327-x

Mccarty, M., Aussenberg, R. A., Falk, G., & Carpenter, D. H. (2013). Drug testing and crime-related restrictions in TANF, SNAP, and housing assistance. Washington, DC: Academic Press.

McCrae, R. R., & Costa, P. T. Jr. (1997). Personality trait structure as a human universal. *The American Psychologist, 52*(5), 509–516. doi:10.1037/0003-066X.52.5.509 PMID:9145021

McCuddy, M. K. (2012). The pursuit of profits in different industries: What is the impact of practice of business ethics? *Journal of the Academy of Business & Economics, 12*(5), 67–78.

McGuire, J. B., Sundgren, A., & Schneeweis, T. (1988). Corporate social responsibility and firm financial performance. *Academy of Management Journal, 31*(4), 854–872. doi:10.2307/256342

McKay, S. L. (2003). Toward an appropriate EIL pedagogy: Re-examining common ELT assumptions. *International Journal of Applied Linguistics, 13*(1), 1–22. doi:10.1111/1473-4192.00035

McLean, G. F. (1993). Integrating ethics and design. *Technology and Society Magazine, IEEE, 12*(3), 19–30. doi:10.1109/MTAS.1993.232282

McMullen, M. B. (1998). The beliefs and practices of early childhood educators in the U.S.: Does specialized preparation make a difference in adoptive of best practices? *International Journal of Early Childhood Education, 3*, 3–29. Retrieved from http://210.101.116.28/W_files/kiss5/29200214_pv.pdf

McMullen, M. B. (2001). Distinct in beliefs/united in concerns: Listening to strongly DAP and strongly traditional k-primary teachers. *Journal of Early Childhood Teacher Education, 22*(3), 123–133. doi:10.1080/1090102010220301

McMullen, M., Elicker, J., Wang, J., Erdiller, A., Lee, S., Lin, C., & Sun, P. (2005). Comparing beliefs about appropriate practice among early childhood education and care professionals from U.S., China, Taiwan, Korea and Turkey. *Early Childhood Quarterly, 20*(4), 451–464. doi:10.1016/j.ecresq.2005.10.005

Meara, N., Schmidt, L., & Day, J. (1996). Principles and virtues: A foundation for ethical decisions. *The Counseling Psychologist, 24*(1), 4–77. doi:10.1177/0011000096241002

Melo, T., & Garrido-Morgado, A. (2012). Corporate reputation: A combination of social responsibility and industry. *Corporate Social Responsibility and Environmental Management, 19*(1), 11–31. doi:10.1002/csr.260

Menkiti, I. (1984). Person and community in African traditional thought. In R. Wright (Ed.), *African Philosophy* (pp. 171–181). New York, NY: University Press of America.

Metz, T. (2010). Recent work in African ethics. *Journal of Moral Education, 39*(3), 381–391. doi:10.1080/03057240.2010.497618

Mezirow, J. (1981). A critical theory of adult learning and education. *Adult Education, 32*(1), 3–24. doi:10.1177/074171368103200101

Midgley, J. (1990). International social work: Learning from the Third World. *Social Work, 35*(4), 295–301.

Mikołajek-Gocejna, M. (2016). The relationship between corporate social responsibility and corporate financial performance – Evidence from empirical studies. *Comparative Economic Research, 19*(4), 67–83. doi:10.1515/cer-2016-0030

Milesi, P., & Alberici, A. I. (2016). Pluralistic morality and collective action: The role of moral foundations. *Group Processes & Intergroup Relations*. doi:10.1177/1368430216675707

Milgram, S. (1974). *Obedience to authority: An experimental view*. New York, NY: Harper & Row.

Miliutin, D. A. (1947). Dnevnik D.A. Miliutin. Moscow: Gosudarstvennaia biblioteka SSSR imeni V.I. Lenina, Otdel rukopiseĭ.

Miller, E. J. (2009). Drugs, courts, and the new penology. *Stanford Law & Policy Review, 20*(2), 417–461. Retrieved from https://ssrn.com/abstract=1464353

Mill, J. S. (1861). *Utilitarianism* (R. Crisp, Ed.). Oxford, UK: Oxford University Press.

Mill, J. S. (2001). *On liberty*. Kitchener, Canada: Batoche. Retrieved from http://socserv.mcmaster.ca/econ/ugcm/3ll3/mill/liberty.pdf (Original work published 1859)

Ministry of Social Affairs. (ca. 1956). *Social welfare in Korea*. [Document]. International Social Service – American Branch (Folder: ISS-Branches, 1-1956-Dec 1956, Korea "RRA-5," Box 35). Social Welfare History Archives, Elmer L. Anderson Library, University of Minnesota, Minneapolis, MN.

Mink, G. (1995). *The wages of motherhood: Inequality in the welfare state, 1917-1942*. Cornell University Press.

Minogiannis, P. (2016). Tomorrow's public hospital in Greece: Managing health care in the post crisis era. *Social Cohesion and Development, 7*(1), 69-80. Retrieved from http://ejournals.epublishing.ekt.gr/index.php/SCAD/article/viewFile/8990/9184

Mitcham, C. (2009). A historico-ethical perspective on engineering education: From use and convenience to policy engagement. *Engineering Studies, 1*(1), 35–53. doi:10.1080/19378620902725166

Mondak, J. J., & Canache, D. (2013). Personality and political culture in the American States. *Political Research Quarterly*. doi: 10.1177/1065912913495112

Moon, K. H. S. (1997). *Sex among allies: Military prostitution in U.S.–Korea relations.* New York, NY: Columbia University Press.

Moraitis, E. (1996). A realistic proposal for the creation of a modern primary health care system in Greece. In G. Kyriopoulos & T. Filalithis (Eds.), *Primary health care in Greece* (pp. 180–185). Athens: Themelio.

Morris, C. W. (Ed.). (2000). *The social contract theorists: Critical essays on Hobbes, Locke, and Rousseau.* Toronto: Rowman & Littlefield.

Mossialos, E., Allin, S., & Davaki, K. (2005). Analysing the Greek health system: A tale of fragmentation and inertia. *Health Economics, 14*(1), S151–S168. doi:10.1002/hec.1033 PMID:16161195

Moyo, M., Goodyear-Smith, F. A., Weller, J., Robb, G., & Shulruf, B. (2016). Healthcare practitioners' personal and professional values. *Advances in Health Sciences Education: Theory and Practice, 21*(2), 257–286. doi:10.1007/s10459-015-9626-9 PMID:26215664

Mulgan, R. G. (1974). Aristotle's doctrine that man is a political animal. *Hermes, 102*(3), 438–445. Retrieved from http://www.jstor.org/stable/4475868

Murphy, P. E., Laczniak, G. R., & Wood, G. (2007). An ethical basis for relationship marketing: A virtue ethics perspective. *European Journal of Marketing, 41*(1/2), 37–57. doi:10.1108/03090560710718102

Nahavandi, A. (2003). *The art and science of leadership* (3rd ed.). Upper Saddle River, NJ: Prentice Hall.

Nakamura, K., Shimai, S., Kikuchi, S., Takahashi, H., Tanaka, M., Nakano, S., & Yamamoto, M. et al. (1998). Increases in body mass index and waist circumference as outcomes of working overtime. *Occupational Medicine, 48*(3), 169–173. doi:10.1093/occmed/48.3.169 PMID:9659726

Nakanishi, N., Yoshida, H., Nagano, K., Kawashimo, H., Nakamura, K., & Tatara, K. (2001). Long working hours and risk for hypertension in Japanese male white collar workers. *Journal of Epidemiology and Community Health, 55*(5), 316–322. doi:10.1136/jech.55.5.316 PMID:11297649

Nambissan, G. B. (2012). Private schools for the poor: Business as usual? *Economic and Political Weekly, 47*(41), 51–58. Retrieved from http://www.epw.in/journal/2012/41/special-articles/private-schools-poor.html

Nam, H. H., Jost, J. T., & Van Bavel, J. J. (2013). "Not for all the tea in China!" political ideology and the avoidance of dissonance-arousing situations. *PLoS One, 8*(4), e59837. doi:10.1371/journal.pone.0059837 PMID:23620724

Narochnitskiĭ, A. L. (1978). *Rossiiā ĭ natsĭonal'no-osvoboditel'naiā bor'ba na Balkanakh, 1875-1878: Sbornik dokumentov*. Moscow: Nauka.

Natarajan, N. et al.. (2008). *Substance abuse treatment and public safety*. Washington, DC: Justice Policy Institute.

Neff, K. D. (2011). Self-compassion, self-esteem, and well-being. *Social and Personality Psychology Compass, 5*(1), 1–12. doi:10.1111/j.1751-9004.2010.00330.x

Neff, K. D., & Germer, C. K. (2013). A pilot study and randomized controlled trial of the mindful self-compassion program. *Journal of Clinical Psychology, 69*(1), 28–44. doi:10.1002/jclp.21923 PMID:23070875

Neff, K. D., Kirkpatrick, K. L., & Rude, S. S. (2007). Self-compassion and adaptive psychological functioning. *Journal of Research in Personality, 41*(1), 139–154. doi:10.1016/j.jrp.2006.03.004

Neubert, M. J., Wu, C., & Roberts, J. A. (2013). The influence of ethical leadership and regulatory focus on employee outcomes. *Business Ethics Quarterly, 23*(2), 269–296. doi:10.5840/beq201323217

Neumann, Y., & Reichel, A. (1987). *The development of attitudes toward business ethics questionnaire (ATBEQ): Concepts, dimensions, and relations to work values*. Working Paper, Department of Industrial Engineering and Management, Ben Gurion University of the Negev, Israel.

New, R. (2003). Handbook of early literacy research. In S. B. Neuman & D. K. Dickinson (Eds.), *Early literacy and developmentally appropriate practice: Rethinking the paradigm* (Vol. 1, pp. 245–262). New York, NY: Guilford.

Nguyen, P. M., Terlouw, C., & Pilot, A. (2006). Culturally appropriate pedagogy: The case of group learning in a Confucian Heritage culture context. *Intercultural Education, 17*(1), 1–19. doi:10.1080/14675980500502172

Niakas, D. (1999). Methods of compensation and financing of suppliers. In V. Aletras, M. Matsaganis, & D. Niakas (Eds.), *Economic and financial management of healthcare services* (Vol. A, pp. 87–98). Patras: Hellenic Open University Publishing.

Nicholson, T., Duncan, D. F., White, J., & Watkins, C. (2012). Focusing on abuse, not use: A proposed new direction for US drug policy. *Drugs Education Prevention & Policy, 19*(4), 303–308. doi:10.3109/09687637.2012.682231

Nielsen, R. P. (2010). High-leverage finance capitalism, the economic crisis, structurally related ethics issues, and potential reforms. *Business Ethics Quarterly, 20*(2), 299–330. doi:10.5840/beq201020222

Nisbett, R. E., Peng, K., Choi, I., & Norenzayan, A. (2001). Culture and systems of thought: Holistic versus analytic cognition. *Psychological Review, 108*(2), 291–310. doi:10.1037/0033-295X.108.2.291 PMID:11381831

Norris, S. P., & Ennis, R. H. (1989). *Evaluating critical thinking*. Pacific Grove, CA: Midwest.

Northcott, F., Rosicky, J. G., Elvin, A., Ayoub, J., & Lambert, C. (2012). International Social Service: Addressing the need for intercountry casework. In L. M. Healy & R. J. Link (Eds.), Handbook of international social work: Human rights, development, and the global profession (pp. 95-101). Oxford University Press.

Nussbaum, M. C. (1999). Virtue ethics: A misleading category? *The Journal of Ethics, 3*(3), 163–201. doi:10.1023/A:1009877217694

O'Neill, H. M., & Pfeiffer, C. A. (2012). The impact of honour codes and perceptions of cheating on academic cheating behaviours, especially for MBA bound undergraduates. *Accounting Education, 21*(3), 231–245. doi:10.1080/09639284.2011.590012

Object. (n.d.). In *Stanford Encyclopedia of Philosophy online*. Retrieved from http://plato.stanford.edu/entries/object/

Oh, A. H. (2005). A new kind of missionary work: Christians, Christian Americans, and the adoption of Korean GI babies, 1955-1961. *Women's Studies Quarterly, 33*(3/4), 161–188.

Oh, A. H. (2015). *To save the children of Korea: The Cold War origins of international adoption*. Stanford University Press.

Ohara, Y. (2013). *Early childhood care and education in India: ECED around the world*. Tokyo, Japan: Waseda University.

Oikonomou, N., & Tountas, Y. (2011). The Greek economic crisis: A primary health-care perspective. *Lancet, 377*(9759), 28–29. doi:10.1016/S0140-6736(10)62336-7 PMID:21195247

Okere, T. (2005). *Philosophy, culture, and society in Africa*. Afro-Orbis.

Olsen, H. (1961). *Memo to district direct service supervisors from Hilmer Olsen, Chief of Direct Services, Wisconsin State Department of Public Welfare, Division for Children and Youth. International Social Service – American Branch (Folder: ISS-Branches, Korea, "RRA-5" 1-1956 – December 1956, box 35). Social Welfare History Archives, Elmer L.* Minneapolis, MN: Anderson Library, University of Minnesota.

Olsen, M. E. (1991). *Societal dynamics: Exploring macrosociology*. Englewood Cliffs, NJ: Prentice-Hall.

Onyewuenyi, I. (2005). *The African origin of Greek philosophy: An exercise in Afrocentrism*. University of Nigeria Press.

Onywuenyi, I. (1991). Is there an African philosophy? In T. Serequeberhan (Ed.), *African Philosophy: The essential readings* (pp. 29–46). Minneapolis, MN: Paragon.

Orszag, P. R. (2008). *The effects of recent turmoil in the financial markets on retirement security*. Retrieved from http://democrats-edworkforce.house.gov/imo/media/doc/2008-10-07-PeterOrszag.pdf

Osei, E. T. (2015). *The relationships between corporate supervisors' ethics-related actions and organizational success* (Doctoral dissertation). Available from ProQuest Dissertations and Theses database. (UMI No. 3684883)

Osgood, J. (2006). Deconstructing professionalism in early childhood education: Resisting the regulatory gaze. *Contemporary Issues in Early Childhood*, *7*(1), 5–14. doi:10.2304/ciec.2006.7.1.5

Our genes, our choices (n.d.). *Science sidebars*. Retrieved from http://www.pbs.org/inthebalance/archives/ourgenes/science_sidebars.html

Packer, G. (2014, December 1). The Quiet German. *The New Yorker*. Retrieved from http://www.newyorker.com/magazine/2014/12/01/quiet-german

Panagopoulos, C. (2013). Positive social pressure and prosocial motivation: Evidence from a large-scale field experiment on voter mobilization. *Political Psychology*, *34*(2), 265–275. doi:10.1111/pops.12007

Parboteeah, K. P., & Cullen, J. B. (2003). Social institutions and work centrality: Explorations beyond national culture. *Organization Science*, *14*(2), 137–148. doi:10.1287/orsc.14.2.137.14989

Parensov, P. D. (1900). V Bolgarii: vospominaniye ofitsera general'nago shtaba. Russkaīa Starina, 101, 107-127, 359-381, 593-602.

Parensov, P. D. (1906). V Bolgarii: vospominaniye ofitsera general'nago shtaba. *Russkaīa Starina*, *125*, 62-74, 272-287, 509-527.

Parensov, P. D. (1908b). V Bolgarii: vospominaniye ofitsera general'nago shtaba. *Russkaīa Starina, 134*, 17-47, 257-282.

Parensov, P. D. (1908a). V Bolgarii: Vospominaniye ofitsera general'nago shtaba. *Russkaīa Starina, 132*, 257–270.

Park Nelson, K. (2006). Shopping for children in the international marketplace. In J. J. Trenka, J. C. Oparah, & S. Y. Shin (Eds.), Outsiders within: Writing on transracial adoption (pp. 89-104). South End Press.

Pate, S. (2014). *From orphan to adoptee: U.S. empire and genealogies of Korean adoption*. Minneapolis, MN: University of Minnesota Press. doi:10.5749/minnesota/9780816683055.001.0001

Paton, H. J. (1971). *The categorical imperative: A study in Kant's moral philosophy* (Vol. 1023). Philadelphia: University of Pennsylvania Press.

Pearce, C. L., Manz, C. C., & Sims, H. P. Jr. (2008). The roles of vertical and shared leadership in the enactment of executive corruption: Implications for research and practice. *The Leadership Quarterly*, *19*(3), 353–359. doi:10.1016/j.leaqua.2008.03.007

Peperzak, A. (Ed.). (2013). *Ethics as first philosophy: The significance of Emmanuel Levinas for philosophy, literature and religion*. New York, NY: Routledge.

Peppas, S. C., & Peppas, G. J. (2000). Business ethics in the European Union: A study of Greek attitudes. *Management Decision*, *38*(6), 369–376. doi:10.1108/00251740010373070

Perkins, D. N. (1995). *Outsmarting IQ: The emerging science of learnable intelligence*. New York, NY: Free Press.

Peterson, M., & Søndergaard, M. (2011). Traditions and transitions in quantitative societal culture research in organization studies. *Organization Studies*, *32*(11), 1539–1558. doi:10.1177/0170840611421255

Peterson, R. A., Albaum, G., Merunka, D., Munuera, T. L., & Smith, S. M. (2010). Effects of nationality, gender and religiosity on business related ethics. *Journal of Business Ethics*, *96*(4), 573–587. doi:10.1007/s10551-010-0485-2

Petryna, A. (2009). *When experiments travel: Clinical trials and the global search for human subjects*. Princeton, NJ: Princeton University Press. doi:10.1515/9781400830824

Pettiss, S. T. (1956). *Special aspects of casework with families separated by national boundaries* [Paper presented at the 1956 National Conference of Social Work]. International Social Service – American Branch (Folder: Associations: National Conference on Social Welfare (formerly on Social Work) 1954-1959, box 22. Social Welfare History Archives, Elmer L. Anderson Library, University of Minnesota, Minneapolis, MN.

Pettiss, S. T. (1955a). *Letter to Ellen Trigg Visser dated June 2, 1955. International Social Service – American Branch (Folder: ISS-Branches, Korea, "RRA-5" Refugee Relief Program 1954-December 1955, box 35). Social Welfare History Archives, Elmer L.* Minneapolis, MN: Anderson Library, University of Minnesota.

Pettiss, S. T. (1955b). *Letter to Mrs. Oak Soon Hong dated February 3, 1955. International Social Service – American Branch (Folder: ISS-Branches, Korea, "RRA-5" Refugee Relief Program 1954-December 1955, box 35). Social Welfare History Archives, Elmer L.* Minneapolis, MN: Anderson Library, University of Minnesota.

Pettiss, S. T. (1955c). *Letter to Ellen Trigg Visser received January 15, 1955. International Social Service – American Branch (Folder: ISS-Branches, Korea, "RRA-5" Refugee Relief Program 1954-December 1955, box 35). Social Welfare History Archives, Elmer L.* Minneapolis, MN: Anderson Library, University of Minnesota.

Pettiss, S. T. (1958). *Effect of adoptions from foreign children on U.S. adoption standards and practices, Child Welfare, July 1958. International Social Service – American Branch (Folder 9: Adoption Manual and Other Printed Material, box 11). Social Welfare History Archives, Elmer L.* Minneapolis, MN: Anderson Library, University of Minnesota.

Pew Center on the States. (2005). *Pre-K now.* Washington, DC: Author.

Philosophical and Sociological Dictionary. (1995). Athens: Kapopoulos.

Piaget, J. (1964). Part I: Cognitive development in children: Piaget development and learning. *Journal of Research in Science Teaching, 2,* 176–186. Retrieved from 10.1002/tea.3360020306

Piaget, J. (1965). *The moral judgment of the child* (M. Gabain, Trans.). New York, NY: Free Press. (Original work published 1932)

Piaget, J. (1972). *The principles of genetic epistemology* (W. Mays, Trans.). New York, NY: Basic. (Original work published 1970)

Piaget, J. (1988). *Structuralism* (C. Maschler, Trans.). New York, NY: Harper & Row. (Original work published 1970)

Pillai, P. (2012). Cultural directions and origins of everyday decisions. *Integrative Psychological & Behavioral Science, 46*(2), 235–242. doi:10.1007/s12124-012-9196-9 PMID:22403021

Piot, C. (1999). *Remotely global: Village modernity in West Africa.* Chicago, IL: The University of Chicago Press.

Plant, R. J. (2010). Mom: The transformation of motherhood in modern. University of Chicago Press.

Pletz, J. (1999). *Being ethical.* New York, NY: Nova.

Podsakoff, N. P., Whiting, S. W., Podsakoff, P. M., & Blume, B. D. (2009). Individual- and organizational-level consequences of organizational citizenship behaviors: A meta-analysis. *The Journal of Applied Psychology, 94*(1), 122–141. doi:10.1037/a0013079 PMID:19186900

Ponnu, C. H., & Tennakoon, G. (2009). The association between ethical leadership and employee outcomes – the Malaysian case. *Electronic Journal of Business Ethics and Organization Studies, 14*(1), 21-32. Retrieved from http://urn.fi/URN:NBN:fi:jyu-201010052947

Postman, N. (1995). *The end of education.* New York, NY: Vintage.

Pratto, F., Sidanius, J., & Levin, S. (2006). Social dominance theory and the dynamics of intergroup relations: Taking stock and looking forward. *European Review of Social Psychology, 17*(1), 271–320. doi:10.1080/10463280601055772

Prochaska, J. O. (1991). Assessing how people change. *Cancer, 67*(S3), 805–807. doi:10.1002/1097-0142(19910201)67:3+<805::AID-CNCR2820671409>3.0.CO;2-4 PMID:1986849

Prochaska, J. O., DiClemente, C. C., & Norcross, J. C. (1992). In search of how people change: Applications to addictive behaviors. *The American Psychologist, 47*(9), 1102–1114. doi:10.1037/0003-066X.47.9.1102 PMID:1329589

Project Management Institute. (2010). *Code of ethics and professional conduct*. Retrieved from https://www.pmi.org/about/ethics/code

Pučėtaitė, R., & Lämsä, A. M. (2008). Developing organizational trust through advancement of employees' work ethic in a post-socialist context. *Journal of Business Ethics, 82*(2), 325–337. doi:10.1007/s10551-008-9922-x

Queen Victoria of Great Britain. (1926). *The letters of Queen Victoria: A selection from Her Majesty's correspondence and journal between the years 1862 and 1878*. London: J. Murray.

Radev, S. (1911). *Stroitelite na săvremenna Bălgarija*. Sofia, Bulgaria: P. Glushkov.

Ragsdale, H., & Ponomarev, V. N. (1993). *Imperial Russian foreign policy*. Washington, DC: Woodrow Wilson Center.

Raible, J. (2006). Lifelong impact, enduring need. In J. J. Trenka, J. C. Oparah, & S. Y. Shin (Eds.), Outsiders within: Writing on transracial adoption (pp. 179-188). South End Press.

Rakas, S. (2011). Global business ethics - Utopia or reality. *Megatrend Review, 8*(2), 385-406. Available from http://connection.ebscohost.com/c/articles/70970531/global-business-ethics-utopia-reality

Ramírez, L., Levy, S. R., & Hughes, J. M. (2010). Considering the roles of culture and social status: The Protestant Work Ethic and egalitarianism. *Revista latinoamericano de piscologica, 42*(3), 381-390. doi:.10.14349/rlp.v42i3.580

Rattinger, H., & Steinbrecher, M. (2011). Economic voting in times of economic crisis. *German Politics, 20*(1), 128–145. doi:10.1080/09644008.2011.554111

Rawls, J. (1999). *A theory of justice*. Cambridge, MA: Harvard University Press.

Raz, J. (1986). *The morality of freedom*. Oxford University Press.

Redfield, P. (2013). *Life in crisis: The ethical journey of doctors without borders*. Berkeley, CA: University of California Press. Retrieved from http://www.jstor.org/stable/10.1525/j.ctt24hsw6

Redmond, B. (2009). Lesson 8 commentary: Intergroup theories: How do the people around me influence me? In *Work Attitudes and Motivation*. The Pennsylvania State University World Campus.

Rehnquist, J. (2001). *The globalization of clinical trials: A growing challenge in protecting human subjects*. Washington, DC: Department of Health and Human Services. Retrieved from https://oig.hhs.gov/oei/reports/oei-01-00-00190.pdf

Reinarman, C. (2000). The Dutch example shows that liberal drug laws can be beneficial. In S. Barbour (Ed.), *Drug legalization: Current controversies* (pp. 102–108). San Diego, CA: Greenhaven.

Reinhart, K. (2015a). Religion, violence, and emotion: Modes of religiosity in the neolithic and bronze age of Northern China. *Journal of World Prehistory*, *28*(2), 113–177. doi:10.1007/s10963-015-9086-4

Reinhart, K. (2015b). Ritual feasting and empowerment at Yanshi Shangcheng. *Journal of Anthropological Archaeology*, *39*, 76–109. doi:10.1016/j.jaa.2015.01.001

Rendtorff, J. D. (2002). Basic ethical principles in European bioethics and biolaw: Autonomy, dignity, integrity and vulnerability – Towards a foundation of bioethics and biolaw. *Medicine, Health Care, and Philosophy*, *5*(5), 235–244. doi:10.1023/A:1021132602330 PMID:12517031

Resick, C., Hanges, P., Dickson, M., & Mitchelson, J. (2006). A cross-cultural examination of the endorsement of ethical leadership. *Journal of Business Ethics*, *63*(4), 345–359. doi:10.1007/s10551-005-3242-1

Reuber, A., & Fischer, E. (2010). Organizations behaving badly: When are discreditable actions likely to damage organizational reputation? *Journal of Business Ethics*, *93*(1), 39–50. doi:10.1007/s10551-009-0180-3

Richardson, J. (1981). The inducement hypothesis: That doctors generate demand for their own services. In J. Van der Gaag & M. Perlmand (Eds.), *Health, economics and health economics* (pp. 189–214). Amsterdam: North-Holland.

Richardson, J., & Peacock, S. (2006). Supplier-induced demand: Reconsidering the theories and new Australian evidence. *Applied Health Economics and Health Policy*, *5*(2), 87–98. doi:10.2165/00148365-200605020-00003 PMID:16872250

Riggio, R. E. (2009). Are you a transformational leader? *Psychology Today*. Retrieved from https://www.psychologytoday.com/blog/cutting-edge-leadership/200903/are-you-transformational-leader

Rizzolatti, G., & Arbib, M. A. (1998). Language within our grasp. *Trends in Neurosciences*, *21*(5), 188–194. doi:10.1016/S0166-2236(98)01260-0 PMID:9610880

Robbins, J. (2004). *Becoming sinners: Christianity and moral torment in a Papua New Guinea society* (Vol. 4). Berkeley, CA: University of California Press.

Robertson, C., Olson, B., Gilley, K., & Bao, Y. (2008). A cross-cultural comparison of ethical orientations and willingness to sacrifice ethical standards: China versus Peru. *Journal of Business Ethics*, *81*(2), 413–425. doi:10.1007/s10551-007-9504-3

Rosenthal, L., Levy, S., & Moyer, A. (2011). Protestant work ethic's relation to intergroup and policy attitudes: A meta-analytic review. *European Journal of Social Psychology*, *41*(7), 874–885. doi:10.1002/ejsp.832

Rousseau, J. J. (2002). *The social contract and the first and second discourses* (D. Dunn, Ed.). New Haven, CT: Yale University Press. (Original work published 1755)

Rule, N. O., Freeman, J. B., Moran, J. M., Gabrieli, J. D., Adams, R. B. Jr, & Ambady, N. (2009). Voting behavior is reflected in amygdala response across cultures. *Social Cognitive and Affective Neuroscience*, 5(2-3), 349–355. doi:10.1093/scan/nsp046 PMID:19966327

Rushton, C. H. (2016). Creating a culture of ethical practice in health care delivery systems. *The Hastings Center Report*, 46(S1), 28–31. doi:10.1002/hast.628 PMID:27649916

Russell, N. (2014). Stanley Milgram's obedience to authority "relationship" condition: Some methodological and theoretical implications. *Social Sciences*, 3(3), 194–214. doi:10.3390/socsci3020194

Ryan, M. A. (2004). Beyond a Western bioethics? *Theological Studies*, 65(1), 158–177. doi:10.1177/004056390406500105 PMID:15515232

Rydstrøm, H. (2003). *Embodying morality: Growing up in rural North Vietnam*. Honolulu, HI: University of Hawaii Press.

Sacks, S., Sacks, J. Y., McKendrick, K., Banks, S., & Stommel, J. (2004). Modified TC for MICA offenders: Crime outcomes. *Behavioral Sciences & the Law*, 22(4), 477–501. doi:10.1002/bsl.599 PMID:15282836

Saeidi, S. P., Sofian, S., Saeidi, P., Saeidi, S. P., & Saaeidi, S. A. (2015). How does corporate social responsibility contribute to firm financial performance? The mediating role of competitive advantage, reputation, and customer satisfaction. *Journal of Business Research*, 68(2), 341–350. doi:10.1016/j.jbusres.2014.06.024

Santa Clara County v. Southern Pacific R. Co., 118 U.S. 394. (1886). Retrieved August 29, 2015, from https://supreme.justia.com/cases/federal/us/118/394/case.html

Satcher, D. (1996). *1994: Ten leading causes of death in the United States*. Atlanta, GA: Centers for Disease Control, National Center for Injury Prevention Control. Retrieved from http://www.cdc.gov/injury/wisqars/leadingcauses.html

Saurage-Altenloh, S. M. (2017). *The measured influence of supplier CSR on brand performance expectations in B2B relationships*. Retrieved from ProQuest Dissertations. (Order No. 10262262)

Saxonhouse, A. (1992). *The fear of diversity*. Chicago University Press.

Scarr, S. (1993). Biological and cultural diversity: The legacy of Darwin for development. *Child Development*, 64(5), 1333–1353. doi:10.2307/1131538 PMID:8222876

Schaubroeck, J. M., Hannah, S. T., Avolio, B. J., Kozlowski, S. W., Lord, R. G., Treviño, L. K., & Peng, A. C. et al. (2012). Embedding ethical leadership within and across organization levels. *Academy of Management Journal*, 55(5), 1053–1078. doi:10.5465/amj.2011.0064

Schepers, D. (2006). Three proposed perspectives of attitude toward business' ethical responsibilities and their implications for cultural comparison. *Business and Society Review*, 111(1), 15–36. doi:10.1111/j.1467-8594.2006.00259.x

Schoen, H. (2011). Merely a Referendum on Chancellor Merkel? Parties, Issues and Candidates in the 2009 German Federal Election. *German Politics*, *20*(1), 92–106. doi:10.1080/09644008.2011.554107

Scholtens, B., & Dam, L. (2007). Cultural values and international differences in business ethics. *Journal of Business Ethics*, *75*(3), 273–284. doi:10.1007/s10551-006-9252-9

Scholtens, B., & Kang, F. (2013). Corporate social responsibility and earnings management: Evidence from Asian economies. *Corporate Social Responsibility and Environmental Management*, *20*(2), 95–112. doi:10.1002/csr.1286

Schooler, C. (1996). Cultural and social-structural explanations of cross-national psychological differences. *Annual Review of Sociology*, *22*(1), 323–349. doi:10.1146/annurev.soc.22.1.323

Schrempf-Stirling, J., Palazzo, G., & Phillips, R. (2015). Historic corporate social responsibility. *Academy of Management Review*. doi:10.5465/amr.2014.0137

Schuh, S., Zhang, X., & Tian, P. (2013). For the good or the bad? Interactive effects of transformational moral and authoritarian leadership behaviors. *Journal of Business Ethics*, *116*(3), 629–640. doi:10.1007/s10551-012-1486-0

Schulz, R. A. (1991). Second language acquisition theories and teaching practice: How do they fit? *Modern Language Journal*, *75*(1), 17–26. doi:10.1111/j.1540-4781.1991.tb01078.x

Schumacher, E., & Wasieleski, D. (2013). Institutionalizing ethical innovation in organizations: An integrated causal model of moral innovation decision processes. *Journal of Business Ethics*, *113*(1), 15–37. doi:10.1007/s10551-012-1277-7

Schwartz, S. H. (1999). A theory of cultural values and some implications for work. *Applied Psychology*, *48*(1), 23–47. doi:10.1111/j.1464-0597.1999.tb00047.x

Schwartz, S. H., & Bardi, A. (2001). Value hierarchies across cultures taking a similarities perspective. *Journal of Cross-Cultural Psychology*, *32*(3), 268–290. doi:10.1177/0022022101032003002

Scott, W. R. (1995). *Institutions and organizations*. Thousand Oaks, CA: Sage.

Scovel, T. (1978). The effect of affect on foreign language learning: A review of the anxiety research. *Language Learning*, *28*(1), 129–142. doi:10.1111/j.1467-1770.1978.tb00309.x

Segon, M., & Booth, C. (2013). Values based approach to ethical culture: A case study. In M. Schwartz, H. Harris, & S. Cohen (Eds.), *Ethics, values and civil societies, Research in ethical issues in organizations* (Vol. 9, pp. 93–118). Bingley, UK: Emerald. doi:10.1108/S1529-2096(2013)0000009011

Settle, J. E., Dawes, C. T., & Fowler, J. H. (2009). The heritability of partisan attachment. *Political Research Quarterly*, *62*(3), 601–613. doi:10.1177/1065912908327607

Shafer, W. E., Fukukawa, K., & Lee, G. M. (2007). Values and the perceived importance of ethics and social responsibility: The US versus China. *Journal of Business Ethics, 70*(3), 265–284. http://hdl.handle.net/10.1007/s10551-006-9110-9. doi:10.1007/s10551-006-9110-9

Sharif, M. M., & Scandura, T. S. (2014). Do perceptions of ethical conduct matter during organizational change? Ethical leadership and employee involvement. *Journal of Business Ethics, 124*(2), 185–196. doi:10.1007/s10551-013-1869-x

Sharp, F. (1898). An objective study of some moral judgments. *The American Journal of Psychology, 9*(2), 198–234. doi:10.2307/1411759

Sheng, C., & Sheng, Q. (2004). *A defense of utilitarianism*. Lanham, MD: University.

Sherman, J. G. (2006). Prenuptial agreements: A new reason to revive an old rule. *Cleveland State Law Review, 53*, 359. Retrieved from http://scholarship.kentlaw.iit.edu/cgi/viewcontent.cgi?article=1561&context=fac_schol

Shim, K., & Yang, S.-U. (2016). The effect of bad reputation: The occurrence of crisis, corporate social responsibility, and perceptions of hypocrisy and attitudes toward a company. *Public Relations Review, 42*(1), 68–78. doi:10.1016/j.pubrev.2015.11.009

Shweta, J., & Srirang, J. (2013). Leader-member exchange: A critique of theory & practice. *Journal of Management & Public Policy, 4*(2), 42–53.

Sidanius, J., & Liu, J. (2001). The Gulf War and the Rodney King beating: Implications of the general conservatism and social dominance perspectives. *The Journal of Social Psychology, 132*(6), 685–700. doi:10.1080/00224545.1992.9712099

Sidanius, J., Liu, J., Shaw, J., & Pratto, F. (1994). Social dominance orientation hierarchy attenuators and hierarchy enhancers: Social dominance theory and the criminal justice system. *Journal of Applied Social Psychology, 24*(4), 338–366. doi:10.1111/j.1559-1816.1994.tb00586.x

Siegel, M., & Lotenberg, L. (2007). *Marketing public health: Strategies to promote social change*. Sudbury, MA: Jones and Bartlett.

Sigma-Muga, C., Daly, B. A., Oukal, D., & Kavut, L. (2005). The influence of nationality and gender on ethical sensitivity: An application of the issue-contingent model. *Journal of Business Ethics, 57*(2), 139–159. doi:10.1007/s10551-004-4601-z

Silverman, H. J. (2000, September). Organizational ethics in healthcare organizations: Proactively managing the ethical climate to ensure organizational integrity. HEC Forum, 2(3), 202-215. doi:10.1023/A:1008985411047

Silverstone, P. (2013a). A Novel approach to training police officers to interact with individuals who may have a psychiatric disorder. *The Journal of the American Academy of Psychiatry and the Law, 41*(3), 344–355. PMID:24051586

Silverstone, P. (2013b). Police training mental illness.pdf. *The Journal of the American Academy of Psychiatry and the Law, 41*(3), 344–355. PMID:24051586

Silverstone, P. H., Krameddine, Y. I., DeMarco, D., & Hassel, R. (2013). A novel approach to training police officers to interact with individuals who may have a psychiatric disorder. *The Journal of the American Academy of Psychiatry and the Law, 41*(3), 344–355. PMID:24051586

Simha, A., & Cullen, J. (2012). Ethical climates and their effects on organizational outcomes: Implications from the past and prophecies for the future. *The Academy of Management Perspectives, 26*(4), 20–34. doi:10.5465/amp.2011.0156

Simou, E., & Koutsogeorgou, E. (2014). Effects of the economic crisis on health and healthcare in Greece in the literature from 2009 to 2013: A systematic review. *Health Policy (Amsterdam), 115*(2), 111–119. doi:10.1016/j.healthpol.2014.02.002 PMID:24589039

Singhapakdi, A., Vitell, S., Rallapalli, K., & Kraft, K. (1996). The perceived role of ethics and social responsibility: A scale development. *Journal of Business Ethics, 15*(11), 1131–1140. doi:10.1007/BF00412812

Singh, N. (2004). From cultural models to cultural categories: A framework for cultural analysis. *The Journal of American Academy of Business, Cambridge*, 92–101. Retrieved from http://www.jaabc.com/journal.htm

Skazkin, S. D. (1928). *Konetsˇavstro-russko-germanskogo soiǔza*. Moscow: Ranion.

Skinner, B. F. (1950). Are theories of learning necessary? *Psychological Review, 57*(4), 193–216. doi:10.1037/h0054367 PMID:15440996

Skocpol, T. (1995). *Social policy in the United States: Future possibilities in historical perspective*. Princeton University Press.

Skyrms, B. (2014). *Evolution of the social contract*. Cambridge, UK: Cambridge University Press. doi:10.1017/CBO9781139924825

Slaughter, M. M. (1995). The legal construction of "Mother." In M. A. Fineman & I. Karpin (Eds.), Mothers in law: Feminist theory and the legal regulation of motherhood (pp. 73-100). Columbia University Press.

Sledge, S. (2015). An examination of corporate social responsibility practices and firm performance in U.S. corporations. *Academy of Strategic Management Journal, 14*(2), 171-184. Retrieved from https://www.questia.com/library/journal/1P3-3934076471

Sloth, K. H. (2006). Researching adoption: Whose perspective and what issues? In J. J. Trenka, J. C. Oparah, & S. Y. Shin (Eds.), Outsiders within: Writing on transracial adoption (pp. 253-258). South End Press.

Smith, A., & Hume, E. C. (2005). Linking culture and ethics: A comparison of accountants' ethical belief systems in the individualism/collectivism and power distance contexts. *Journal of Business Ethics, 62*(3), 209–220. doi:10.1007/s10551-005-4773-1

Smith, K. B., Oxley, D., Hibbing, M. V., Alford, J. R., & Hibbing, J. R. (2011). Disgust sensitivity and the neurophysiology of left-right political orientations. *PLoS One, 6*(10), e25552. doi:10.1371/journal.pone.0025552 PMID:22039415

Smith, L. T. (2012). *Decolonizing methodologies: Research and indigenous peoples* (2nd ed.). Zed Books.

Smith, P. B., & Schwartz, S. H. (1997). Values. In J. W. Berry, M. H. Segall, & C. Kagitcibasi (Eds.), Handbook of cross-cultural psychology. Boston, MA: Allyn & Bacon.

Sobolev, L. N. (1886). K noveishei istorii bolgarii. *Russkaiā Starina, LI,* 703–752.

Solving for sustainability. (2017) Retrieved September 22, 2017, from https://environment.google/approach/

Spielberger, C. D. (1983). *State-trait anxiety inventory: A comprehensive bibliography.* Palo Alto, CA: Consultant Psychologists.

Spurgeon, A., Harrington, J. M., & Cooper, C. L. (1997). Health and safety problems associated with long working hours: A review of the current position. *Occupational and Environmental Medicine, 54*(6), 367–375. doi:10.1136/oem.54.6.367 PMID:9245942

Srinivasan, V., Park, C. S., & Chang, D. R. (2005). An approach to the measurement, analysis, and prediction of brand equity and its sources. *Management Science, 51*(9), 1433–1448. doi:10.1287/mnsc.1050.0405

Stahl, G. K., & Sully de Luque, M. (2014). Antecedents of responsible leader behavior: A research synthesis, conceptual framework and agenda for future research. *Academy of Management Perspectives, 28*(3), 235–254. doi:doi:10.5465/amp.2013.0126

Stanaland, A. J. S., Lewin, M. O., & Murphy, P. E. (2011). Consumer perceptions of the antecedents and consequences of corporate social responsibility. *Journal of Business Ethics, 102*(1), 47–55. doi:10.1007/s10551-011-0904-z

Stanovich, K. E., & West, R. F. (1997). Reasoning independently of prior belief and individual differences in actively open-minded thinking. *Journal of Educational Psychology, 89*(2), 342–357. doi:10.1037/0022-0663.89.2.342

Stanovich, K. E., & West, R. F. (2000). Individual differences in reasoning: Implications for the rationality debate? *Behavioral and Brain Sciences, 23*(5), 645–665. doi:10.1017/S0140525X00003435 PMID:11301544

Staudt, S., Shao, C. Y., Dubinsky, A. J., & Wilson, P. H. (2014). Corporate social responsibility, perceived customer value, and customer-based brand equity: A cross-national comparison. *Journal of Strategic Innovation and Sustainability, 10*(1), 65–87. Retrieved from www.na-businesspress.com/JSIS/ADubinskyWeb10-1.pdf

Stedham, Y., & Beekun, R. (2013). Ethical judgment in business: Culture and differential perceptions of justice among Italians and Germans. *Business Ethics (Oxford, England)*, *22*(2), 189–201. doi:10.1111/beer.12018

Steinbauer, R., Renn, R., Taylor, R., & Njoroge, P. (2014). Ethical leadership and followers' moral judgment: The role of followers' perceived accountability and self-leadership. *Journal of Business Ethics*, *120*(3), 381–392. doi:10.1007/s10551-013-1662-x

Steinkraus, W. (1980). Socrates, Confucius, and the rectification of names. *Philosophy East & West*, *30*(2), 261–264. doi:10.2307/1398850

Stephens, G., & Greer, C. (1995). Doing business in Mexico: Understanding cultural differences: New field research clarifies how cultural differences play a role in U.S.-Mexican business alliances. *Organizational Dynamics*. Retrieved from http://www.journals.elsevier.com/organizational-dynamics/

Stevens, B. (1999). Communicating ethical values: A study of employee perceptions. *Journal of Business Ethics*, *20*(2), 113–120. doi:10.1023/A:1005869431079

Stigler, J. W., & Stevenson, H. W. (1992). The learning gap: Why our schools are failing and what we can learn from Japanese and Chinese education. New York, NY: Summit.

Stoilov, K. (1879). [Diary]. (Fond 600k, Opis 3, Delo 1), TSentralen d"rzhaven arkhiv Sofia, Bulgaria.

Stoilov, K. (1880). [Diary]. (Fond 600k, Opis 3, Delo 2), TSentralen d"rzhaven arkhiv Sofia, Bulgaria.

Stoilov, K. (1881). [Diary]. (Fond 600k, Opis 3, Delo 2), TSentralen d"rzhaven arkhiv Sofia, Bulgaria.

Stoilov, K. (1883). [Diary]. (Fond 600k, Opis 3, Delo 4), TSentralen d"rzhaven arkhiv Sofia, Bulgaria.

Stoilov, K. (1883). [Memorandum to Alexander von Battenberg]. (Fond 600k, Opis 3, Delo 383), TSentralen d"rzhaven arkhiv Sofia, Bulgaria.

Story, J., & Neves, P. (2014). When corporate social responsibility (CSR) increases performance: Exploring the role of intrinsic and extrinsic CSR attribution. *Business Ethics (Oxford, England)*, *24*(2), 111–124. doi:10.1111/beer.12084

Strubler, D., Park, S., Agarwal, A., & Cayo, K. (2012). Development of a macro-model of cross cultural ethics. *Journal of Legal, Ethical & Regulatory Issues*, *15*(2), 25-34. Available from http://law-journals-books.vlex.com/vid/development-macro-model-cross-cultural-ethics-370762482

Suen, H. K., & Yu, L. (2006). Chronic consequences of high-stakes testing? Lessons from the Chinese civil service exam. *Comparative Education Review*, *50*(1), 46–65. doi:10.1086/498328

Su, S. (2006). Cultural differences in determining the ethical perception and decision-making of future accounting professionals: A comparison between accounting students from Taiwan and the United States. *The Journal of American Academy of Business, Cambridge, 9*(1), 147. Retrieved from http://www.jaabc.com/journal.htm

Taghian, M., D'Souza, C., & Polonsky, M. (2015). A stakeholder approach to corporate social responsibility, reputation and business performance. *Social Responsibility Journal, 11*(2), 340–363. doi:10.1108/SRJ-06-2012-0068

Takei, H. (2011). Strategic frameworks of ethic management in MNEs: Theoretical discussions and model development. *Journal of Management Research, 3*(2), 1–15. doi:10.5296/jmr.v3i2.560

Tanner, C., Brugger, A., Van Schie, S., & Lebherz, C. (2010). Actions speak louder than words: The benefits of ethical behaviors of leaders. *The Journal of Psychology, 218*(4), 225–233.

Tanveer, M. A., Gill, H., & Ahmed, I. (2012). Why business students cheat? A study from Pakistan. *American Journal of Scientific Research, 78*, 24–32. Retrieved from http://search.proquest.com/openview/67e22ad71eac4b7ea0d8075e9d1e91df/1?pq-origsite=gscholar

Taylor, S. G. (2010). *Cold looks and hot tempers: Individual-level effects on incivility in the workplace* (Doctoral dissertation). Louisiana State University and Agricultural and Mechanical College, Baton Rouge, LA.

Thorne, D. M., Ferrell, O. C., & Ferrell, L. (2011). *Business and society: A strategic approach to social responsibility and ethics*. South-Western Cengage.

Thornton, L. F. (2013). *7 Lenses: Learning the principles and practices of ethical leadership*. Richmond, VA: Leading in Context, LLC.

Timmermann, J. (Ed.). (2009). *Kant's groundwork of the metaphysics of morals: A critical guide*. Cambridge, UK: Cambridge University Press. doi:10.1017/CBO9780511770760

Timms, N., & Timms, R. (1982). *Dictionary of social welfare*. London, UK: Routledge.

Tompkins, G., Campbell, R., Green, D., & Smith, C. (2014). *Literacy for the 21st century: A balanced approach*. Melbourne, Australia: Pearson.

Toor, S. R., & Ofori, G. (2009). Ethical leadership: Examining the relationships with full range leadership model, employee outcomes, and organizational culture. *Journal of Business Ethics, 90*(4), 533–547. doi:10.1007/s10551-009-0059-3

Topalli, V., Brezina, T., & Bernhardt, M. (2012). With God on my side: The paradoxical relationship between religious belief and criminality among hardcore street offenders. *Theoretical Criminology, 17*(1), 49–69. doi:10.1177/1362480612463114

Topor, F. S. (2014). A sentence repetition placement test for ESL/EFL learners in Japan. In V. Wang (Ed.), *Handbook of research on education and technology in a changing society* (pp. 971–988)., doi:10.4018/978-1-4666-6046-5.ch073

Torellia, C., & Kaikati, A. (2009). Values as predictors of judgments and behaviors: The role of abstract and concrete mindsets. *Journal of Personality and Social Psychology, 96*(1), 231–247. doi:10.1037/a0013836 PMID:19210077

Torluccio, G. (2012). *Economics, social responsibility and consumers. The ethical perception.* Bologna, Italy: Silvano Pagani.

Torres, A., Bijmolt, T. H. A., Tribó, J. A., & Verhoef, P. (2012). Generating global brand equity through corporate social responsibility to key stakeholders. *International Journal of Research in Marketing, 29*(1), 13–24. doi:10.1016/j.ijresmar.2011.10.002

Tountas, Y. (2007). *Induced demand and excessive use of health services.* Retrieved from http://panacea.med.uoa.gr/topic.aspx?id=813

Tountas, Y., Karnaki, P., & Pavi, E. (2002). Reforming the reform: The Greek National Health System in transition. *Health Policy (Amsterdam), 62*(1), 15–29. doi:10.1016/S0168-8510(01)00217-2 PMID:12151132

Tountas, Y., Karnaki, P., Pavi, E., & Souliotis, K. (2005). The "unexpected" growth of the private health sector in Greece. *Health Policy (Amsterdam), 74*(2), 167–180. doi:10.1016/j.healthpol.2005.01.013 PMID:16153477

Trattner, W. I. (1999). *From poor law to welfare state: A history of social welfare in America.* The Free Press.

Trenka, J. J., Oparah, J. C., & Shin, S. Y. (Eds.). (2006). *Outsiders within: Writing on transracial adoption.* South End Press.

Tsai, L. L. (2002). Cadres, temple and lineage institutions, and governance in rural China. *China Journal (Canberra, A.C.T.), 48*, 1–27. doi:10.2307/3182439

Tsui, A. S., & Farh, J. L. L. (1997). Where guanxi matters: Relational demography and guanxi in the Chinese context. *Work and Occupations, 24*(1), 56–79. doi:10.1177/0730888497024001005

Turner, J. H. (1997). *The institutional order.* New York, NY: Addison-Wesley.

Tweed, R. G., & Lehman, D. R. (2002). Learning considered within a cultural context: Confucian and Socratic approaches. *The American Psychologist, 57*(2), 89–99. doi:10.1037/0003-066X.57.2.89 PMID:11899565

Tzavaras, G. (2005). *The depreciation of values.* Athens: Indiktos.

U.K. Department of Education. (2014). *Statutory framework for the early years foundation stage: Setting the standards for learning, development and care for children from birth to five.* London: Author.

U.S. Census Bureau. (n.d.). *Foreign Trade.* Retrieved from https://www.census.gov/foreign-trade/balance/c2010.html

U.S.-Chile Free Trade Agreement. (2009). *United States Department of Agriculture Foreign Agricultural Service website*. Available from https://www.fas.usda.gov/data/free-trade-agreements-and-us-agriculture

Uehata, T. (1991). Long working hours and occupational stress-related cardiovascular attacks among middle-aged workers in Japan. *Journal of Human Ergology, 20*(2), 147–153. doi:10.11183/jhe1972.20.147 PMID:1842961

Underhill, A. (2002). *Craft production and social change in Northern China*. New York, NY: Kluwer; doi:10.1007/978-1-4615-0641-6

Unitarian Service Committee, Inc. (1956). *International Social Service – American Branch (Folder, 13: Unitarian Universalist Service Committee, Inc., box 23). Social Welfare History Archives, Elmer L.* Minneapolis, MN: Anderson Library, University of Minnesota. [Document introducing three Korean social workers on fellowship at the University of Minnesota School of Social Work]

United Nations Educational, Scientific and Cultural Organization (UNESCO). (2006a). *EFA global monitoring report 2006: Literacy for life*. Paris, France: Author.

United Nations Educational, Scientific and Cultural Organization (UNESCO). (2006b). *Strong foundations: Early childhood care and education: Argentina: Early childhood care and education (EECE) programmes. Education for All Global Monitoring Report 2007*. Geneva, Switzerland: Author.

United Nations Educational, Scientific and Cultural Organization (UNESCO). (2015). *EFA global monitoring report 2015: Education for all 2000–2015: Achievements and challenges*. Paris, France: Author.

United Nations Educational, Scientific and Cultural Organization (UNESCO). (2016). *Institute for Statistics*. Retrieved from http://data.uis.uesco.org

United Nations Educational, Scientific and Cultural Organization. (2005). Universal draft declaration on bioethics and human rights. SHS/EST/05/CONF.204/3REV. Paris, France: Author.

United Nations. (1999). U*niversal declaration of human rights. First adopted and proclaimed in 1948*. New York, NY: Author. Available at: http://www.un.org/Overview/rights.html

Ünsar, A., & Karalar, S. (2013). The effect of personality traits on leadership behavior: A research of students of business administration. *Economic Review: Journal of Economics & Business, 11*(2), 45–56.

Vaaland, T. I., Heide, M., & Grønhaug, K. (2008). Corporate social responsibility: Investigating theory and research in the marketing context. *European Journal of Marketing, 42*(9/10), 927–953. doi:10.1108/03090560810891082

Valentine, S., & Barnett, T. (2003). Ethics code awareness, perceived ethical values, and organizational commitment. *Journal of Personal Selling & Sales Management, 23*, 359–367. Retrieved from http://www.jstor.org/stable/40471934

Valentine, S., & Page, K. (2006). Nine to five: Skepticism of women's employment and ethical reasoning. *Journal of Business Ethics*, *63*(1), 53–61. doi:10.1007/s10551-005-7714-0

Valenzuela, L. M., Mulki, J. P., & Jaramillo, J. F. (2010). Impact of customer orientation, inducements and ethics on loyalty to the firm: Customers' Perspective. *Journal of Business Ethics*, *93*(2), 277–291. doi:10.1007/s10551-009-0220-z

Valk, M. A. (1956). *American Branch ISS: Adoption program – Korea, descriptive report by M. A. V., visit to Korea, November 21ˢᵗ–30ᵗʰ, 1956.* International Social Service – American Branch (Folder: Reports & Visits to Korea, 1956, box 35). Social Welfare History Archives, Elmer L. Anderson Library, University of Minnesota, Minneapolis, MN.

Vallaster, C., Lindgreen, A., & Maon, F. (2012). Strategically leveraging corporate social responsibility: A corporate branding perspective. *California Management Review*, *54*(3), 34–60. doi:10.1525/cmr.2012.54.3.34

Van Auken, S. (2016). Assessing the role of business faculty values and background in the recognition of an ethical dilemma. *Journal of Education for Business*, *91*(4), 211–218. doi:10.1080/08832323.2016.1160021

Van Beurden, P., & Gössling, T. (2008). The worth of values – A literature review on the relation between corporate social and financial performance. *Journal of Business Ethics*, *82*(2), 407–424. doi:10.1007/s10551-008-9894-x

van de Rijt, B., Godfrey, R., Augrey, C., Van Luit, J. E., Hasemann, K., Tancig, S., & Tzouriadou, M. et al. (2003). The development of early numeracy in Europe. *Journal of Early Childhood Research*, *1*(2), 155–180. doi:10.1177/1476718X030012002

Van Lange, A., Bekkers, R., Chirumbolo, A., & Leone, L. (2012). *Are conservatives less likely to be prosocial than liberals? From games to ideology, political preferences and voting.* Academic Press. doi:10.1002/per

Vanderburg, W. H. (1995). Preventive engineering: Strategy for dealing with negative social and environmental implications of technology. *Journal of Professional Issues in Engineering Education and Practice*, *121*(3), 155–160. doi:10.1061/(ASCE)1052-3928(1995)121:3(155)

VanSandt, C. V., & Neck, C. P. (2003). Bridging ethics and self-leadership: Overcoming ethical discrepancies between employee and organizational standards. *Journal of Business Ethics*, *43*(4), 363–38. doi:10.1023/A:1023009728390

Van-Tienen, M., Scheepers, P., Reitsma, J., & Schilderman, H. (2011). The role of religiosity for formal and informal volunteering in the Netherlands. *Voluntas*, *22*(3), 365–389. doi:10.1007/s11266-010-9160-6

Vitell, S., & Paolillo, J. (2004). A cross-cultural study of the antecedents of the perceived role of ethics and social responsibility. *Business Ethics (Oxford, England)*, *13*(2-3), 185–199. doi:10.1111/j.1467-8608.2004.00362.x

Vitell, S., Paolillo, J., & Thomas, J. (2003). The perceived role of ethics and social responsibility: A study of marketing professionals. *Business Ethics Quarterly*, *13*(1), 63–86. doi:10.5840/beq20031315

Vygotsky, L. S. (1978). *Mind in society: The development of the higher psychological processes.* Cambridge, MA: Harvard University Press.

Wade, C., & Tavris, C. (1993). *Critical and creative thinking.* New York, NY: Harper Collins.

Wagner .(1956). *Report of Meeting with Dr. Pierce of World Vision.* International Social Service – American Branch (Folder 29: Children: Independent Adoption Schemes – World Vision 1955–1960, Box 10). Social Welfare History Archives, Elmer L. Anderson Library, University of Minnesota, Minneapolis, MN.

Waldman, A., & Galvin, M. (2008). Alternative perspectives of responsible leadership. *Organizational Dynamics*, *37*(4), 327–341. doi:10.1016/j.orgdyn.2008.07.001

Walumbwa, F. O., Mayer, D. M., Wang, P., Wang, H., Workman, K., & Christensen, A. L. (2011). Linking ethical leadership to employee performance: The roles of leader–member exchange, self-efficacy, and organizational identification. *Organizational Behavior and Human Decision Processes*, *115*(2), 204–213. doi:10.1016/j.obhdp.2010.11.002

Wang, D. H., Chen, P., Yu, T. H., & Hsiao, C. (2015). The effects of corporate social responsibility on brand equity and firm performance. *Journal of Business Research*, *68*(11), 2232–2236. doi:10.1016/j.jbusres.2015.06.003

Wang, H., & Qian, C. (2011). Corporate philanthropy and corporate financial performance: The roles of stakeholder response and political access. *Academy of Management Journal*, *54*(6), 1159–1181. doi:10.5465/amj.2009.0548

Wang, L., & Juslin, H. (2009). The impact of Chinese culture on corporate social responsibility: The harmony approach. *Journal of Business Ethics*, *88*(S3), 433–451. doi:10.1007/s10551-009-0306-7

Wang, Q., Pomerantz, E. M., & Chen, H. (2007). The role of parents' control in early adolescents' psychological functioning: A longitudinal investigation in the United States and China. *Child Development*, *78*(5), 1592–1610. doi:10.1111/j.1467-8624.2007.01085.x PMID:17883450

Wang, Y., Hsu, L., & Chang, K. (2012). The relationship between corporate social responsibility and firm performance: An application of quantile regression. *Frontiers of Business Research in China*, *6*, 218–244. doi:10.3868/s070-001-012-0011-3

Warfield, G. P. (1958). *Letter from Gaither P. Warfield dated April 4, 1958. International Social Service – American Branch (Folder: Associations: Methodist Committee for Overseas Relief 1955-", box 22).* Social Welfare History Archives, Elmer L. Minneapolis, MN: Anderson Library, University of Minnesota.

Wartenberg, J. (2011). Human well-being at the heart of economics. *The Global Women's Project-Advancing human well-being and ecological sustainability.* Retrieved from https://www.coc.org/files/Briefing-Paper-5-Human-Wellbeing(1).pdf

Washington, M., & Ventresca, M. J. (2004). How organizations change: The role of institutional support mechanisms in the incorporation of higher education visibility strategies, 1874–1995. *Organization Science, 15*(1), 82–97. doi:10.1287/orsc.1030.0057

Weber Shandwick. (2016). *The company behind the brand II: In goodness we trust.* Retrieved from http://www.webershandwick.com/uploads/news/files/company-behind-the-brand-in-goodness-we-trust.pdf

Weber, E. (1959). The practice of intercountry casework. International Social Work, April 1959, 44-49. International Social Service – American Branch (Folder 3: Miscellaneous Folder, box 47). Social Welfare History Archives, Elmer L. Anderson Library, University of Minnesota, Minneapolis, MN.

Weber, M. (1951). *The religion of China: Confucianism and Taoism* (H. H. Gerth, Ed. & Trans.). Retrieved from https://books.google.com/

Weber, E. T. (2008). Religion, public reason, and humanism: Paul Kurtz on fallibilism and ethics. *Contemporary Pragmatism, 5*(2), 131–147. doi:10.1163/18758185-90000095

Weber, L. J., Wayland, M. T., & Holton, B. (2001). Health care professionals and industry: Reducing conflicts of interest and established best practices. *Archives of Physical Medicine and Rehabilitation, 82*(12), S20–S24. doi:10.1016/S0003-9993(01)65648-X PMID:11805916

Webley, S., & Werner, A. (2008). Corporate codes of ethics: Necessary but not sufficient. *Business Ethics (Oxford, England), 17*(4), 405–415. doi:10.1111/j.1467-8608.2008.00543.x

Wennberg, J., Barnes, B., & Zubkoff, M. (1982). Professional uncertainty and the problem of supplier-induced demand. *Social Science & Medicine, 16*(7), 811–824. doi:10.1016/0277-9536(82)90234-9 PMID:7100999

Westerman, J., Beekun, R., Stedham, Y., & Yamamura, J. (2007). Peers versus national culture: An analysis of antecedents to ethical decision-making. *Journal of Business Ethics, 75*(3), 239–252. doi:10.1007/s10551-006-9250-y

Whitaker, B., & Godwin, L. (2013). The antecedents of moral imagination in the workplace: A social cognitive theory perspective. *Journal of Business Ethics, 114*(1), 61–73. doi:10.1007/s10551-012-1327-1

Whitbeck, C. (1998). *Ethics in engineering practice and research.* New York, NY: Cambridge University Press. doi:10.1017/CBO9780511806193

White, B. J., & Montgomery, B. R. (1980). Corporate codes of conduct. *California Management Review, 23*(2), 80–87. doi:10.2307/41164921

White, H. (2005). The limits to optimism: Australia and the rise of China. *Australian Journal of International Affairs, 59*(4), 469–480. doi:10.1080/10357710500367273

White, H. (2011). Power shift: Rethinking Australia's place in the Asian century. *Australian Journal of International Affairs, 65*(1), 81–93. doi:10.1080/10357718.2011.535603

White, J. (2005). *Contemporary moral problems*. Belmont, CA: Cengage.

Wickeri, P. (1989). *Seeking the common ground: Protestant Christianity, the three-self movement, and China's United Front*. New York, NY: Orbis.

Wieland, J. (2010). Ethics and economic success: A contradiction in terms? Zeitschrift für Psychologie. *The Journal of Psychology, 218*(4), 243–245. doi:10.1027/0044-3409/a000034

Williams, B. (1973). A critique of utilitarianism. In G. Sher (Ed.), *Ethics-Essential readings in moral theory* (pp. 253–261). Cambridge, UK: Routledge.

Williams, R., & Elliott, L. (2010). *Crisis and recovery: Ethics, economics and justice*. Hampshire, UK: Palgrave Macmillan. doi:10.1057/9780230294912

Wilmoth, W., & O'Brien, W. (2011). White-collar crime with your company as the victim: Conducting a fraud investigation. *Energy & Mineral Law Institute, 32*(1), 4–31.

Wilson, D. B., Bouffard, L. A., & MacKenzie, D. L. (2005). A quantitative review of structured, group-oriented, cognitive-behavioral programs for offenders. *Criminal Justice and Behavior, 32*(2), 172–204. doi:10.1177/0093854804272889

Wilson, J. Q. (1993). *The moral sense*. New York, NY: Free Press.

Wilson, M. S., & Sibley, C. G. (2013). Social dominance orientation and right-wing authoritarianism: Additive and interactive effects on political conservatism. *Political Psychology, 34*(2), 277–284. doi:10.1111/j.1467-9221.2012.00929.x

Wong, D. B. (1984). *Moral relativity*. Berkeley, CA: University of California Press.

Wong, D. B. (2009). Comparative philosophy: Chinese and Western. In E. N. Zalta (Ed.), *The Stanford encyclopedia of philosophy* (Fall 2011 ed.). Retrieved from http://plato.stanford.edu/archives/fall2011/entries/comparphil-chiwes/

Wood, R. (2010). *Top 10 list of the world's most popular sports*. Retrieved from http://www.topendsports.com/world/lists/popular-sport/fans.htm

Woodbine, G. (2006). Gender issues impact the role of the moral agent in a rapidly developing economic zone of the People's Republic of China. *Journal of Asia-Pacific Business, 7*(3), 79–103. doi:10.1300/J098v07n03_05

World Health Organization. (2014). *Guidance framework for testing of genetically modified mosquitoes*. Retrieved from http://www.who.int/tdr/publications/year/2014/Guidance_framework_mosquitoes.pdf

Worthington, I., Ram, M., Boyal, H., & Shah, M. (2007). Researching the drivers of socially responsible purchasing: A cross-national study of supplier diversity initiatives. *Journal of Business Ethics, 79*(3), 319–331. doi:10.1007/s10551-007-9400-x

Yack, B. (1985). Community and conflict in Aristotle's political philosophy. *The Review of Politics, 47*(1), 92–112. doi:10.1017/S0034670500037761

Yang, C. (2014). Does ethical leadership lead to happy workers? A study on the impact of ethical leadership, subjective well-being, and life happiness in the Chinese culture. *Journal of Business Ethics, 123*(3), 513–525. doi:10.1007/s10551-013-1852-6

Yang, F. (2011). *Religion in China: Survival and revival under communist rule.* New York, NY: Oxford University Press. doi:10.1093/acprof:oso/9780199735655.001.0001

Young, H. (1958). *Letter to Susan Pettiss dated September 15, 1958. International Social Service – American Branch (Folder 14, box 10). Social Welfare History Archives, Elmer L.* Minneapolis, MN: Anderson Library, University of Minnesota.

Yueru, M., Weibo, C., Ribbens, B. A., & Juanmel, Z. (2013). Linking ethical leadership to employee creativity: Knowledge sharing and self-efficacy as mediators. *Social Behavior and Personality, 41*(9), 1409–1420. doi:10.2224/sbp.2013.41.9.1409

Yukl, G. A. (2013). *Leadership in organizations* (8th ed.). Albany, NY: Pearson.

Zabihollah, R. (2003). Causes, consequences, and deterrence of financial statement fraud. *Critical Perspectives on Accounting, 16*(3), 227–298. doi:10.1016/S1045-2354(03)00072-8

Zaccaro, S. J. (2007). Trait-based perspectives of leadership. *The American Psychologist, 62*(1), 6–16. doi:10.1037/0003-066X.62.1.6 PMID:17209675

Zaporozhets, A. (1986). *Izbrannye psychologicheskie trudy* [Selected works]. Moscow, Russia: Pedagogika.

Zechmeister, E. B., & Johnson, J. E. (1992). *Critical thinking: A functional approach.* Pacific Grove, CA: Thomson Brooks/Cole.

Zhang, J., & He, Y. (2014). Key dimensions of brand value co-creation and its impacts upon customer perception and brand performance: An empirical research in the context of industrial service. *Nankai Business Review International, 5*(1), 43–69. doi:10.1108/NBRI-09-2013-0033

Zhang, Y., LePine, J. A., Buckman, B. R., & Wei, F. (2014). It's not fair . . . or is it? The role of justice and leadership in explaining work stressor–job performance relationships. *Academy of Management Journal, 57*(3), 675–697. doi:10.5465/amj.2011.1110

Zheng, Q., Luo, Y., & Wang, S. (2014). Moral degradation, business ethics, and corporate social responsibility in a transitional economy. *Journal of Business Ethics, 120*(3), 405–421. doi:10.1007/s10551-013-1668-4

Zhu, Y., Sun, L., & Leung, A. S. M. (2014). Corporate social responsibility, firm reputation, and firm performance: The role of ethical leadership. *Asia Pacific Journal of Management, 31*(4), 925–947. doi:10.1007/s10490-013-9369-1

Zigler, E. F., & Bishop-Josef, S. J. (2006). The cognitive child versus the whole child: Lessons from forty years of head start. In D. G. Singer, R. M. Golinkoff, & K. A. Hirsh-Pasek (Eds.), *Play = learning: How play motivates and enhances cognitive and social-emotional growth* (pp. 15–35). New York, NY: Oxford University Press. doi:10.1093/acprof:oso/9780195304381.003.0002

Zill, N., & Resnick, G. (2006). Handbook of early literacy research. In S. B. Neuman & D. K. Dickinson (Eds.), *Emergent literacy of low-income children in head start: Relationships with child and family characteristics, program factors, and classroom quality* (Vol. 2, pp. 243–256). New York, NY: Guilford.

Zimbardo, P. (1971). The Stanford Prison Experiment: A simulation study of the psychology of imprisonment conducted August 1971 at Stanford University [Slideshow]. Manuscripts and archives, Stanford University, Stanford, CA.

Zimbardo, P. (2007). The Lucifer Effect: Understanding how good people turn evil. *Journal of the American Medical Association, 298*(11), 1338–1340. Available from http://go.galegroup.com/ps/anonymous?id=GALE%7CA179132813&sid=googleScholar&v=2.1&it=r&linkaccess=fulltext&issn=01200534&p=AONE&sw=w&authCount=1&isAnonymousEntry=true

Zimbardo, P. G. (1972). *The psychology of imprisonment: Privation, power and pathology*. Palo Alto, CA: Stanford University Press.

Zuo, J. (1991). Political religion: The case of the cultural revolution in China. *SA. Sociological Analysis, 52*(1), 99–110. doi:10.2307/3710718

Zylan, Y. (2000). Maternalism redefined: Gender, the state, and the politics of day care, 1945-1962. *Gender & Society, 14*(5), 608–629. doi:10.1177/089124300014005002

About the Contributors

F. Topor is a Scholar-Practitioner and President of International & Intercultural Communications, Francis Sigmund Topor conducts research and lecturers at a number of universities including Keio, Meiji Gakuin, and Seikei Universities in Tokyo, Japan. His expertise includes Japanese Sociolinguistics and psycholinguistics. Dr. Topor also currently provides intercultural communicative competency to Japanese multinational corporations in Tokyo; haven provided educational services to the Tokyo Metropolitan Board of Education for over six years. He has an extensive portfolio of writings including A Sentence Repetition Placement Test For EFL/ESL Learners In Japan and The Empowerment of Japanese Women: What Will the Social Impact Be?

* * *

Mark Anderson is an Assistant Professor of Business at Snow College in Ephraim, Utah, where he teaches a variety of business courses. Dr. Anderson has also taught at Frostburg State University, part of the university System of Maryland, where he taught upper division and MBA courses in Strategic Human Resource Management, Applied Change Management, Business Ethics & Social Responsibility, New Business Ventures, Business Plans and Compensation Management. He taught previously at Eastern Arizona College and coordinated the EAC Entrepreneurship curriculum. He has been the EAC Business Division Chair and Director of the Small Business Development Center. Dr. Anderson earned his PhD in Management, completing his dissertation on international ethical attitudes among business managers. He has also earned a BA in History from Lewis and Clark College in Portland, Oregon, and a Master of Business Administration degree in Finance and Accounting from Brigham Young University.

Karin Celosse has extensive experience teaching in online courses and programs, as well as in traditional on-ground colleges for the past six years, and also works at a U.S. State Prison as a Clinical Psychologist for California Department of Corrections and Rehabilitation. Previous experience consists of working with juvenile offenders at a County Probation Central Youth Reporting Center. Dr. Celosse also worked as a pre-doctoral mental health provider at Skid Row in Los Angeles and as an Intake Therapist at a drug and alcohol rehabilitation center. Prior to her work in the field of mental health, Dr. Celosse worked as an EMT and field training officer in the emergency medical services field for over a decade, and taught special education in the K-12 public school system. Dr. Celosse additionally has extensive training in community and forensic mental health, including: UCLA Integrated Substance Abuse Programs/OCHCA, Motivational Interviewing & Brief Interventions 9th Annual Community First Conference, Post-Traumatic Stress & First Responders Orange County Sheriffs Regional Training Academy, Coming together to reduce domestic violence (symposium), OCHCA –Behavioral Health Services Training: to include Psychopharmacology; 5150/5585 Designation; LGBT Transitional Aged Youth MH; Using play therapy to help children heal from trauma; Workplace violence/active shooter training. Dr. Celosse was a co-presenter at the 2017 Western American Correctional Health Services Association Symposium "Modern Challenges in Jails and Prisons", presenting on the topic of "Clinical vs Interpersonal Concerns in Managing Inmate Mental Health Complaints". Dr. Celosse has written several grant applications, including: NIJ Graduate Research Fellowship Program in the Social and Behavioral Sciences: NIJ–2015–3975; State of California Trauma Recovery Services Center funding opportunity for Centro De Bienestar De Familiar; and her Dissertation was focused on whether or not personality factors in law enforcement and corrections officers have an effect on perceptions around supportive community programs for formerly incarcerated persons with history of non-violent felony drug offense(s). Dr. Celosse's research interests include the psychopathology of power, especially as it relates to prejudice and discrimination. This includes exploring whether there are features of the self (e.g., self-presentation, self-compassion, self-identity, gender identity), social context (e.g., socioeconomic disadvantage, poverty, psychosocial stress) and experiences of social interaction (e.g., expectancy confirmation, attribution, persuasion, social exclusion) that protect, reinforce, disrupt, or undermine the basic behavioral and psychological mechanisms that support adaptive behavior.

Vaitsa Giannouli received her PhD in Neuroscience from the School of Medicine, Aristotle University of Thessaloniki. She is a cognitive psychologist and neuropsychologist. She is currently a research fellow at Aristotle University of Thessaloniki (AUTh), Greece. She has received numerous accolades and scholarships for her work as an undergraduate and graduate student. She is working as a research assistant and is involved in several cross-cultural research projects focusing on issues of cognition, emotion and lifespan development.

June C. Hysell is an adjunct professor for Rowan Cabarrus Community College specializing in Early Childhood Education courses. She has been a special education teacher for local public schools working with preschool, elementary and middle school grades as well as a teacher in the Head Start program. Dr. Hysell earned her Ph.D. in Professional Studies in Education from Capella University, a Master's degree in Elementary Education from Catawba College, a BSED from Cleveland State University in Special Education and two AAS degrees from Cuyahoga Community College in Early Childhood Education. Dr. Hysell lives with her husband, cats, dogs, chickens, and other pets in North Carolina. Dr. Hysell has 4 grown children who serve in military service in the U.S. Air Force.

Ike V. Iyioke has multidisciplinary backgrounds in philosophy, international relations, journalism and teaching. His career started as a lecturer at the College of Ecumenical Education, Enugu, Nigeria, where he taught social studies, general studies, and philosophy of education classes. Iyioke has also worked as a journalist with The Guardian Newspapers Ltd., Lagos. A recipient of MacArthur Foundation/SSRC fellowship, Iyioke relocated to Michigan State University and later obtained additional graduate degree in environmental journalism following which he has held a variety of editorial and administrative positions in that university. Iyioke's doctorate degree is in philosophy (bioethics). He likes to explore questions pertaining to moral philosophy, particularly bioethics. He is also interested in African philosophy, environmental ethics, environmental science public policy, and the role these play in moral thinking. His research interests include issues about research subject/participant selection; human experimentation; biomedical research partnerships between Africa & the West; environmental ethics; environmental justice/racism; eugenics; science of life extension; morality in primitive cultures; and, consumer right to know. Iyioke currently doubles as a researcher at Michigan State University and an adjunct professor at University of Michigan Flint's Department of Public Health and Health Sciences.

Shawyn Lee is an Assistant Professor in the Department of Social Work at the University of Minnesota, Duluth campus. Using historical research methodologies, Dr. Lee's research examines the maternalist ideologies that influenced the profession of social work and its involvement in early child-placing practices of Korean children displaced by the Korean War.

Enoch T Osei is an assistant professor of accounting at Bowie State University.

Phillip M. Randall, PhD, is currently the Managing Partner, The Thorndyke Group, a human capital consultancy specializing in individual and organizational effectiveness, Atlanta, GA; Faculty member, School of Business, Capella University, Minneapolis, MN; and Board member, Learnlong Institute for Education and Learning Research, Chicago, IL. He received his BA from the Youngstown State University, Youngstown, Ohio; MS from the University of Michigan, Ann Arbor, MI; and a PhD from The University of Akron, Akron, OH. He earned a Specialist in Aging certification from the Institute of Gerontology, University of Michigan and Wayne State University, Ann Arbor, MI.

Mikhail Sergeyevich Rekun is a historian of late Imperial Russia with research and teaching interests that include international relations, the role of the Balkans in 19th century politics, and the development of diplomatic practice. His current research looks at the way diplomacy was actually practiced by Russia in the late 19th century, and how on-the-ground realities influenced international relations. His book, 'Empire Unguided: How Russia lost Bulgaria, 1878-1886' (working title) is slated to be published by Lexington Books in 2018. Rekun received his Ph.D. from Northeastern University in 2016, his M.A. from Tufts University in 2011, and his B.A. from the University of Massachusetts at Amherst in 2009. He has also worked with the American Research Center in Sofia, Bulgaria.

Susan Saurage-Altenloh, PhD, is currently Chief Insights Officer and Founder of Saurage Research, Inc., a global research organization. Her firm specializes in innovative, hybrid research strategies that produce insights for a client list that includes numerous Fortune 500 companies. She received her BBA from HBU, Houston, Texas; an MBA from The University of Texas at Austin; and a PhD from Capella University.

Index

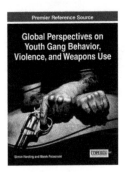

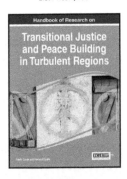
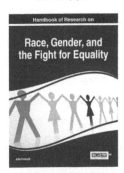

Stay Current on the Latest Emerging Research Developments

Become an IGI Global Reviewer for Authored Book Projects

Premier Reference Source

Emerging GIS Applications for Emergency and Disaster Management

Premier Reference Source

Managerial Strategies and Green Solutions for Project Sustainability

Premier Reference Source

Comparative Approaches to Using R and Python for Statistical Data Analysis

Premier Reference Source

Solutions for High-Touch Communications in a High-Tech World

The overall success of an authored book project is dependent on quality and timely reviews.

In this competitive age of scholarly publishing, constructive and timely feedback significantly decreases the turnaround time of manuscripts from submission to acceptance, allowing the publication and discovery of progressive research at a much more expeditious rate. Several IGI Global authored book projects are currently seeking highly qualified experts in the field to fill vacancies on their respective editorial review boards:

Applications may be sent to:
development@igi-global.com

Applicants must have a doctorate (or an equivalent degree) as well as publishing and reviewing experience. Reviewers are asked to write reviews in a timely, collegial, and constructive manner. All reviewers will begin their role on an ad-hoc basis for a period of one year, and upon successful completion of this term can be considered for full editorial review board status, with the potential for a subsequent promotion to Associate Editor.

If you have a colleague that may be interested in this opportunity, we encourage you to share this information with them.

Information Resources Management Association

Advancing the Concepts & Practices of Information Resources Management in Modern Organizations

Become an IRMA Member

Members of the **Information Resources Management Association (IRMA)** understand the importance of community within their field of study. The Information Resources Management Association is an ideal venue through which professionals, students, and academicians can convene and share the latest industry innovations and scholarly research that is changing the field of information science and technology. Become a member today and enjoy the benefits of membership as well as the opportunity to collaborate and network with fellow experts in the field.

IRMA Membership Benefits:

- **One FREE Journal Subscription**

- **30% Off Additional Journal Subscriptions**

- **20% Off Book Purchases**

- Updates on the latest events and research on Information Resources Management through the IRMA-L listserv.

- Updates on new open access and downloadable content added to Research IRM.

- A copy of the Information Technology Management Newsletter twice a year.

- A certificate of membership.

IRMA Membership $195

Scan code or visit **irma-international.org** and begin by selecting your free journal subscription.

Membership is good for one full year.

 InfoSci-OnDemand

Continuously updated with new material on a weekly basis, InfoSci®-OnDemand offers the ability to search through thousands of quality full-text research papers. Users can narrow each search by identifying key topic areas of interest, then display a complete listing of relevant papers, and purchase materials specific to their research needs.

Comprehensive Service

- Over 81,600+ journal articles, book chapters, and case studies.
- All content is downloadable in PDF format and can be stored locally for future use.

No Subscription Fees

- One time fee of $37.50 per PDF download.

Instant Access

- Receive a download link immediately after order completion!

Database Platform Features:

- Comprehensive Pay-Per-View Service
- Written by Prominent International Experts/Scholars
- Precise Search and Retrieval
- Updated With New Material on a Weekly Basis
- Immediate Access to Full-Text PDFs
- No Subscription Needed
- Purchased Research Can Be Stored Locally for Future Use

"It really provides an excellent entry into the research literature of the field. It presents a manageable number of highly relevant sources on topics of interest to a wide range of researchers. The sources are scholarly, but also accessible to 'practitioners'."

– Lisa Stimatz, MLS, University of North Carolina at Chapel Hill, USA

"It is an excellent and well designed database which will facilitate research, publication and teaching. It is a very very useful tool to have."

– George Ditsa, PhD, University of Wollongong, Australia

"I have accessed the database and find it to be a valuable tool to the IT/IS community. I found valuable articles meeting my search criteria 95% of the time."

– Lynda Louis, Xavier University of Louisiana, USA

Lightning Source UK Ltd.
Milton Keynes UK
UKHW032222211218
334395UK00002B/15/P